OP
10⁰⁰

Bookseller
91-6

Nigeria in the
First World War

Ibadan History Series

General Editor: J. F. A. Ajayi, Ph.D.
Vice-Chancellor: University of Lagos

Christian Missions in Nigeria 1841–1891*
by J. F. A. Ajayi
The Zulu Aftermath*
by J. D. Omer-Cooper
The Missionary Impact on Modern Nigeria 1842–1914*
by E. A. Ayandele
The Sokoto Caliphate*
by Murray Last
Benin and the Europeans 1485–1897*
by A. F. C. Ryder
Niger Delta Rivalry*
by Obaro Ikimę
The International Boundaries of Nigeria
by J. C. Anene
Revolution and Power Politics in Yorubaland 1840–1893*
by S. A. Akintoye
Power and Diplomacy in Northern Nigeria 1804–1906*
by R. A. Adelęyę
The Segu Tukulor Empire*
by B. O. Ọlọruntimęhin
The Warrant Chiefs*
by A. E. Afigbo
The Evolution of the Nigerian State*
by T. N. Tamuno
The New Ọyọ Empire*
by J. A. Atanda
The Malagasy and the Europeans
by P. M. Mutibwa
Western Yorubaland under European Rule 1889–1945
by A. I. Asiwaju
The Judicial System in Southern Nigeria 1854–1954
by Omoniyi Adewọye
Press and Politics in Nigeria 1880–1937
by Fred I. A. Omu
The Growth of Islam Among the Yoruba 1841–1908
by T. G. O. Gbadamosi
Benin Under British Administration
by P. A. Igbafe

* available in paperback

Ibadan History Series

General Editor J. F. A. Ajayi, Ph.D.

Nigeria in the First World War

Akinjide Osuntokun, Ph.D.

1979

Humanities Press

First published
in the United States of America 1979
by Humanities Press
171 First Avenue,
Atlantic Highlands,
NJ 07716

Library of Congress Cataloging in Publication Data

Osuntokun, Akinjide.
  Nigeria in the First World War.
  (Ibadan history series)
  Bibliography: p.
  Includes index.
  1. European War, 1914–1918—Nigeria. 2. Nigeria—
History. I. Title. II. Series.
D547.N57O88 1979   940.3′669   78–13665
ISBN 0–391–00916–8

Contents

List of maps

Introduction

This book developed from my doctoral dissertation entitled 'Nigeria in the First World War', completed at Dalhousie University, Halifax, Nova Scotia, Canada towards the end of 1970. I should like to seize this opportunity to express my profound gratitude to Dalhousie University, which awarded me the Izaak Walton Killam Memorial Scholarship, enabling me to carry out the research for this book. I should like to thank also Professor John Flint, my supervisor, who was most kind to me and gave me generous encouragement when my spirit was low and when I felt like throwing in the towel like a well-beaten boxer. I want to record my appreciation and gratitude to Professors J. F. Ade Ajayi and R. J. Gavin, my teachers at the University of Ibadan, who in the first place brought out the best in me as a student and encouraged me to pursue historical research to this present level. I am also very grateful to Professor Michael Crowder for being kind enough to read thoroughly this manuscript and to offer useful advice about its improvement.

I am greatly indebted to the staffs of the London Public Record Office and those of the Rhodes House Library, Oxford. This same gratitude goes to staffs of the British Museum, the Colindale newspaper section in particular, the Institute of Historical Research, London and the librarians of various institutes and colleges of the University of London, most especially that of the School of Oriental and African Studies. I also hereby place on record my gratitude to the staffs in Paris of the Bibliothèque Nationale, the Archives Nationales, Section Outre-Mer, the Archive de Ministère des Affaires Étrangères, at the Quai d'Orsay. The same appreciation is here expressed to the staffs in Hamburg, West Germany, of the Staatsarchiv, Weltwirtschaftsarchiv, Archiv der Handelskammer, Staat-und-Universität Hamburg, and particularly to Dr Helmut Bley and Herr Dr Professor Fritz Fischer, whose knowledge of war-time politics in Kaiser Wilhelm's Germany is well known.

This book is not an attempt to rewrite the history of the military operations in the Cameroons and East Africa, in which Nigeria was actively involved, for this has been sufficiently covered by military and official historians of the belligerent powers. A list of such books, monographs and diaries will be found in the bibliography. In spite of this extensive literature, however, very little attention has been paid to the effect of the war on the economic and socio-political development of Nigeria. The little knowledge we possess on the war-time administration of Nigeria is derived from the cursory treatment of it in a chapter in Margery Perham's *Lugard: The Years of Authority, 1898–1945*. Other less well-known writers have made slight references to the period as if the war was not of much importance in Nigeria's history.

In general the subject of the First World War and Nigeria has been submerged in the literature on Nigerian history by the attention paid to critical analyses of the successes and failures of indirect rule. This literature, much of it excellent, nevertheless tends to relegate the war to footnotes, or to treat it in terms of its side effects on the 'main theme', the pros and cons of indirect rule in Nigeria. The fact that the contribution of Nigeria was in the minor theatres of military operations or in the 'side shows' of the global military drama also seems to have made consideration of the role of the war and its effect on Nigeria, together with its aftermath, of less interest to scholars, who illogically assumed that since the war contribution of Nigeria was in the minor theatres, Nigeria's war effort and the impact of the war on Nigeria must also be a minor historical theme. A thorough and careful examination of available sources, however, reveals the extent to which Nigeria's economy and administration were affected by the war. In fact the period of the First World War, as will be seen in this book, constitutes an important phase in the country's history, its events illuminating the past and foreshadowing the future.

On the declaration of war by Great Britain on Germany, some fifty million Africans, almost half of whom were Nigerians, were directly or indirectly involved in a war of which the vast majority understood nothing, against an enemy generally unknown to them. The few educated Nigerians on the coast and in the various pockets of the hinterland with experience of commercial dealings with the Germans had not only benefited economically from such contacts but had increasingly come to prefer German merchants, with their generous credit terms, to the British traders. There also existed much antipathy on the part of educated Nigerians who were deliberately excluded from participation in the government of their country because the indirect rule system – the policy of administration through native chiefs – allowed no place for them in government. To the British, the Christian mission-educated elite were almost foreigners in their native land.

Lugard and the educated Nigerians had different notions of the British presence in Nigeria. Lugard, it appears, was more interested in the theory and practice of administration whereas the educated Nigerians saw administration not as an end in itself, but a means to an end, which was general enlightenment along European lines. Since there was a clash of motives and a difference in goals, it is not surprising that Lugard should detest these opponents of his administration. The real problem for British rule in Nigeria during this period arose from the attempt by the Governor-General to apply a common administrative policy to a politically and culturally variegated country like Nigeria and not actually from the educated Nigerians, who were only a nuisance and not much of a security risk.

It was the illiterate Nigerians who actually posed the greatest threat to British rule in Nigeria during the First World War. The involvement of Nigeria and the demand for troops first in the Cameroons and later in German East Africa necessarily led to withdrawal of troops from their garrison duties for war service. The Nigerian Government was of course aware of the danger involved in this move, but it was rightly conjectured that the Fulani-backed oligarchy in the Islamic emirates of Northern Nigeria would not lead their people to rebel against the British in spite of the call to arms of all Muslims by the Ottoman Caliph. This, to a large extent, was borne out by the steadfast loyalty of the Fulani rulers to the British during the war. The loyalty of the rulers should not be confused with the unreserved and total loyalty of the Hausa–Fulani *talakawa*. There is, however, no doubt that indirect rule and other policies pursued by the government had created a community of interests between the British and the Muslim hierarchy in Northern Nigeria. What is not generally known is that below the British-supported ruling class were significant resistance movements sometimes occasioned by the war but not necessarily caused by it. In fact not all the members of the ruling *élite* were steadfast in their support for the British as traditionally accepted; on the contrary, the British on some occasions had to resort to deposing and exiling unco-operative emirs and chiefs.

In the southern part of Nigeria the problem which the administration had to contend with at this time was that of ethnic plurality and cultural diversity. This in itself undermined any attempt at administrative uniformity in the country, a fact which the Governor-General, Sir Frederick Lugard, failed, or did not want, to understand. Lugard's attempt to bring some order into the 'administrative chaos' in which he thought Southern Nigeria had been thrown by his more cautious predecessors led to widespread revolts in the area.

It is not suggested however that changes in administrative policy were the sole causes of the revolts; it is realised that many forces combined to upset the delicate internal peace which existed before the war. Chief among them were the general instability accompanying the war, the ineffectiveness of the British administrative hold on some areas or the total lack of supervision of subordinate African staff by their British superiors. There was also the visible weakening of British power, through the withdrawal of the British military and administrative presence in outlying provinces. In addition there was the economic slow-down created by the disruption of the normal flow of trade and the general slump in the market for Nigeria's primary products like palm kernels and groundnuts, most of which had found their way to Germany before the war. The Nigerian Government was also forced by the tight monetary situation of the time to suspend all capital projects, thus further causing unemployment, recession and the attendant restlessness.

The demands of the imperial government on Nigerian peoples as soldiers and the recruitment campaigns launched to meet this demand further unsettled an already unstable society undergoing considerable socio-political change at the same time. To make matters worse, the Governor-General, rather than give the people time to get used to the various administrative measures, tried to introduce unpopular schemes which he considered in tune with his system of indirect rule. This rigid and inflexible pursuit during the war of a policy arrived at in peace-time was to lead to unnecessary bloodshed in some parts of Southern Nigeria.

Many and various factors were responsible for much of the

commotion that erupted in different parts of Nigeria during the war. In the predominantly Igbo south-east, the revolts were not really a novelty. The area had not been effectively occupied before the war because of the rather intractable nature of the administrative problem posed by a highly segmentary society with no centralised political organisations or easily identifiable foci of power. The revolts here in a sense were initial resistance movements against British administrative control. In the predominantly Yoruba south-west the revolts were mostly directed against illegitimate rulers or unaccustomed powers granted them by the colonial government. In the north, where the revolts were less serious but much more widely distributed than in the south, they were caused by the resentments harboured against the British by princes who had failed to secure thrones because of their hostility to alien *Nasara* rule. These princes were joined by religious fanatics and adventurers as well as by many *talakawa* manifesting greater resentments against either heavy taxation or overbearing authority.

As in many parts of the British Empire during this difficult time, attempts were made to exploit the economic situation in Nigeria. Combines were formed by the British trading firms with the purpose of lowering producer prices; as a result there emerged large companies with sufficient capital to drive smaller firms out of the produce-buying business and vegetable oils were purchased at rock-bottom prices. Finding that immense profits were being made as a result of this practice, the imperial government did attempt some form of war-time control which some important politicians wanted to perpetuate into a curious form of imperial preference, but this was resisted by the Nigerian administration. The end of the war did not immediately usher in an era of prosperity, since the value of money went down in the world-wide inflation that marked the period of peace.

Nigeria's military involvement was greatest in the Cameroons because it was only from there that the Germans could have threatened the country's security, and with the surrender of the Cameroons, Nigerian officials like their counterparts in other parts of the world were involved in the scramble for annexation and for secure borders that came with victory. Imperial interests were pitched against colonial interests and Nigerian administrators' demands for territories were sacrificed in the interest of Britain's world-wide strategic calculations as well as for the purpose of maintaining tolerable relations with the French, who were at this time vociferously condemning Britain for territorial aggrandisement.

The war ended in Nigeria with a dissatisfied and impatient people who clamoured for change. In response to all their demands came the rather flexible and liberal reforms of the post-war administration.

My approach to the writing of this book has been thematic rather than chronological and this has created many problems, though fewer, I believe, than would a chronological approach, with a narrative emphasis. It has been found necessary to divide the book into two main parts, one dealing with the war and its effect on Nigeria's economic and socio-political development and the other with Nigeria's external activities during the war; a third part rounds off the book with a chapter on the aftermath of the war.

The book is based mainly on Colonial Office files on Nigeria (the C.O. '83' series) as well as the files of the West African Frontier Force (the C.O. '445' series). Other primary materials are drawn from Admiralty files (the ADM. '137' series), the War Office (W.O. '106' and '158'). I have used Cabinet papers listed in the bibliography. I have drawn occasionally from private papers such as those of the Anti-Slavery and Aborigines Protection Society and the *Lugard Papers* at Rhodes House Library, Oxford, as well as from newspapers published in Britain and Nigeria. I have consulted French and German archival materials to supplement the British sources where this seemed necessary for balance. Other sources are cited in the notes and listed in the bibliography.

Jide Osuntokun
Department of History
University of Lagos
26 April 1977

To the memory of my late brother,
Captain Abiodun Osuntokun, A.M.I.Mech.E.(Eng.),
of the Nigerian Army Engineers.

PART 1

1 Nigeria on the eve of the First World War

When the First World War broke out in August 1914 Nigeria had been in existence in its present form for only eight months. On 1 January 1914 the hitherto separate British Protectorates of Northern and Southern Nigeria were amalgamated to form the Colony and Protectorate of Nigeria. The new administrative structures had barely been established when Nigeria was directly involved in the war against the Germans with an expeditionary force being mounted against their Kamerun Colony from September 1914 to March 1916. Throughout the war large numbers of Nigerian soldiers were involved in fighting for their British over-lords in the African campaigns, while Nigeria became an important source of raw materials for the Allies. The administration of Nigeria suffered as British officials left for the war and finance for imported goods became increasingly in short supply. The exigencies of war put severe strains on all the colonies involved in it, but in Nigeria they were particularly severe because the newly established administration had barely found its feet.

To understand properly the disturbed state of Nigeria during the war, it is necessary to look at the way in which the Northern and Southern Protectorates were brought together under one government by Sir Frederick Lugard, who was specially appointed and arrived in Lagos on 3 October 1912 to amalgamate them. The particular administrative solution he found for the unification of these two protectorates, which had very different backgrounds, exacerbated rather than reduced the strains the war placed on the government and economy of the country.

Lugard, who was appointed simultaneously Governor of the British Colony and Protectorate of Southern Nigeria and Governor of the British Protectorate of Northern Nigeria, already knew the country. He was the *conquistador* of the Northern Protectorate and had been its High Commissioner for six years from its inception

3

in 1900 to June 1906. From Northern Nigeria he left for Hong Kong, where he served as Governor for six years. When he returned to Nigeria he brought to the task of amalgamation very considerable experience as an administrator of an African colony, but an experience that was idiosyncratic because Northern Nigeria, as we shall see, was very different in its traditions from any other British colony or protectorate in Africa. Yet Lugard, firmly believing that the policies he had initiated in the Northern Protectorate were the best that could be devised for the government of Africans, chose to impose them on the Southern Protectorate, which had a very different historical tradition from that of the north, particularly in its experience of British administration.

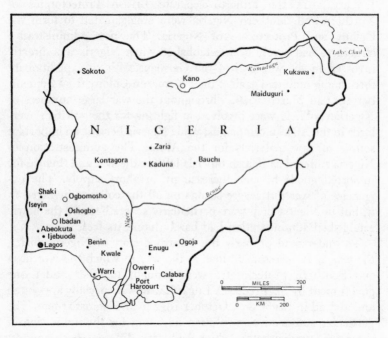

Nigeria, showing growing urban areas in 1914

Lugard was asked to amalgamate the two territories because the British Government felt that the maintenance of two separate but contiguous administrations was economically wasteful and administratively unwise. Furthermore, the British wanted to save themselves the trouble of aiding the Northern administration through an annual grant-in-aid of about £100,000 sterling while the Southern administration usually had more than a million pounds sterling surplus accruing to it from customs receipts.

The Northern Protectorate on amalgamation covered an area of 694,404·9 square kilometres. It comprised the greater part of the Sokoto Caliphate and Borno, together with a considerable area of land in which no states had been established. Lugard and his successors took the emirates of the Sokoto Caliphate as the basis for the establishment of a system of local government through existing indigenous authorities.[1] The emirs had a system of administration which with modification could usefully serve the British, who had not enough administrators available to rule the country directly because of their involvement in the Anglo-Boer War of 1899–1902 and because of the prohibitive expense employment of thousands of British administrators would have entailed. In the Fulani emirates under Lugard and his successors, there developed a particular type of indirect rule which was later to be imposed throughout Northern Nigeria, irrespective of whether the peoples outside the Caliphate had a tradition of strong centralised chieftaincy or not. It was this system that was later to be imposed on the Southern Protectorate and subsequently throughout most of British-controlled Africa.

The essential features of the system that distinguished it from other systems of indirect rule practised in the British Empire were:

(a) Direct taxation through native chiefs in their name and then the division of the taxes between the chiefs and the protectorate government, i.e. as a sort of tribute recognising the protectorate government's sovereignty. In the case of Kano or Sokoto, 70 per cent of total taxes was held by chiefs and 30 per cent by the protectorate government.

(b) The disbursement of the taxes retained by the chiefs as the basis of a budget and through a Native Treasury or *Beit et mal*. Muslim rulers became salaried officials, as did all their subordinates, and tribute or taxes had to be disbursed for approved projects etc.

(c) A third important feature of indirect rule as it operated in Northern Nigeria was the requirement that those in charge of the districts of an emirate or chieftaincy should reside in their district and not in the capital.

This system operated with relatively little difficulty in the

5

emirates of the dismembered Sokoto Caliphate and Borno where there was a sophisticated administration under a strong central authority with a long-standing tradition of taxation. It worked less well in chieftaincies like Bussa, where the chiefs never had the centralised power of the Fulani emirs and a tradition of taxation; it could hardly operate at all among an acephalous people like the Tiv.

When Lugard returned to Nigeria he saw that, by and large, the system of indirect rule in the Northern Protectorate had worked well, for the greater part of the protectorate was administered by strong chiefs. He did however have some reservations. By 1912 the northern emirates had been opened up by railways and this had vastly increased the available cash crops (especially groundnuts) for export, with the result that taxes had gone up and the revenue accruing to the native treasuries therefore rose considerably.[2] Lugard did not, however, like the idea of the semi-independent status of the emirates with its corollary of their financial independence from the protectorate government.

On the other hand Lugard was horrified by what he found in the Southern Protectorate. There were great varieties in the systems of local government operating throughout the protectorate, reflecting the piecemeal way in which it had been acquired by the British. Lagos island and its immediate neighbourhood constituted the colony of Lagos; it was administered as a typical crown colony with legislative and executive councils. The Egba kingdom maintained some form of quasi-independence. The other Yoruba states operated a loose form of indirect rule. The Benin kingdom in the absence of an Oba was under some form of direct administration. In the Niger Delta the 'House-rule system', by which the heads of small city states functioned as agents of the British Government, was inaugurated as a kind of indirect rule. In Igbo and Ibibio areas the Court rule system was in practice. This system, which was much abused by the so-called 'warrant chiefs', who were handpicked by the British and given warrants to rule over essentially 'chiefless' society, had become necessary because of what was considered the intractable problem of how to administer a seemingly uncontrollable people who did not have the external manifestations of ordered society found in the oba and emir among the Yoruba–Benin and Hausa–Fulani people.[3]

However great the variety in types of administration in the south, two things stood out clearly in contrast to the situation in the north. The first was that in none of these southern societies was there a tradition of taxation; the second was that in none of them was there to be found a ruler approximating in personal authority to that of a Fulani emir. Moreover, many societies in the south had for long been in contact with European trade and had been proselytised by Christian missions and were undergoing rapid social and economic change. The British administration and the company administration of George Goldie had introduced forces to the south which made for rapid material changes. Earlier governors in the south had tried to maintain law and order by balancing British penetration with peaceful co-existence with native rulers where they were easily identifiable. By maintaining peace, they provided the framework within which free enterprise and competition helped to promote the material development of Southern Nigeria and also to alter society itself. In this way they helped to make the society more mobile and created a situation where people had to sell their labour or produce, or both, to live and to buy the new luxuries brought into the country by European merchants.

Taxation in the south was indirect through customs duties on imports and because this did not need the co-operation of the local chiefs the administrators in the south, unlike their northern counterparts, had no reason for bolstering up the power of local chiefs. The emphasis in the south was on building of roads, railways and harbours and generally improving the infra-structure so as to create the necessary atmosphere for trade and material development. This suited the mercantile communities along the coast, since they were not particularly interested in the philosophy of the administration. The southern officials tended through daily contact with these mercantile communities to be influenced by their ideas to such an extent that the officials came to think too that like other tropical dependencies Nigeria existed for the benefit of the commerce of the 'mother country' and that the work of administration was to foster this spirit. These administrators were not doctrinaire in their attitude, as were some of their brethren in Northern Nigeria, rather they were pragmatists who saw that the system worked and were prepared to make it work better without disturbing the natural course of development. Southern Nigeria was open to so many external influences that a policy geared to maintaining the traditional order as in the north was doomed to failure.

The south also differed from the north in that it already had a substantial Western-educated elite of lawyers, doctors, journalists etc. who reacted strongly to Lugard. This group was concentrated mostly in Lagos, Ibadan, Abeokuta, Onitsha, Lokoja, Calabar, Zungeru and coastal towns such as Opobo, Forcados and Degema. The most vociferous of this group were the Lagosians, many of whom edited and published newspapers. Although the standard of Lagos journalism was not very high its effects on those who could read were considered by the administration damaging enough for attempts to be made to muzzle the press. What irked educated Nigerians most since the arrival of Lugard in Nigeria in 1912, was that he made it quite clear that the entire Southern Nigerian social and political situation must be made to conform to Northern Nigerian standards. His scheme of amalgamation consisted of administering the whole of Nigeria under himself as Governor-General, with subordinate governors in each of the two protectorates. The existing Southern Nigerian Legislative Council was effectively reduced in status to that of a town council with little more than the municipality of Lagos as its responsibility. Giving his reasons for abolishing the Southern Nigerian Legislative Council Lugard wrote:

> It is a cardinal principle of British Colonial policy that the interests of a large native population shall not be subject to the will either of a small European merchant class or of a small minority of educated and europeanised natives, who have little in common with them and whose interests are often opposed to theirs, thus in India the Governor-General legislates without reference to his council for 'scheduled' i.e., backward or primitive districts and for native states. In Natal the Governor had a commission as 'paramount chief' for the control of 'extra-colonial natives' and the legislative council cannot interfere with this jurisdiction. ... At the Cape the High Commissioner governed the Protectorates and legislated for them in a separate capacity from that which he occupied as Governor of Cape Colony.[4]

Lugard declared that to bring 'educated natives' and British commercial representatives into the legislative council would be a step in the wrong direction, and would lead to the exclusion of intelligent emirs and chiefs who could not speak English. He said 'a council in such circumstances is a veiled oligarchy of the worst description'.[5] Autocracy, he said, was preferable to such a legislative council.

8

The system of justice under the new dispensation provoked the angriest of debates. In the scheme of amalgamation the appellate jurisdiction of the Supreme Court, which formerly extended to the whole of Southern Nigeria, was to be limited strictly to the Colony proper and a few coastal or riverain towns outside the Colony.[6] 'Native Courts' and 'Native Councils' (presided over by the British district officers) had hitherto existed in the south; but in their place, provincial courts and 'Native Courts' were established in which Commissioners with no legal knowledge acted as judges in the former, while district officers were removed from the latter so that they became effective 'Native Courts' in their constitution. Lawyers were banned from these courts, which had capital powers. This caused much controversy between the Governor and his Chief Justice on the one hand and Nigerian lawyers,[7] and even one of Sir Frederick Lugard's judges, Mr Justice Stoker,[8] was opposed to the new practice. So also were Sir William Geary,[9] a British lawyer practising in Nigeria, and the usual humanitarian circles[10] in Britain as well as some local chiefs along the coast.[11] The Lugardian judicial system was geared to serve the administration and the idea of strengthened native courts was closely tied up with the indirect rule system; in other words, the judiciary became an arm of the administration.

Under the new system the Supreme Court had concurrent jurisdiction in civil and criminal cases whenever Europeans were concerned, but it had no original jurisdiction in the Protectorate in cases where Africans only were involved. The provincial courts had full civil and criminal jurisdiction over all Africans outside the jurisdiction of the Supreme Court. Both the Supreme Court and the provincial courts administered English law as modified by local ordinances and African customary laws. The judges of the provincial courts were Residents and other officers of the executive. No sentence of death or imprisonment over six months could be carried out unless sanctioned by the Chief Justice, but this was severely limited as far as the north was concerned. This power of review was just a ruse to fool those opposed to the power of inflicting capital punishment by a court where an accused was not legally represented. The fact that before hangings were carried out, cases were reviewed by the Chief Justice was no guarantee of fairness, since the Chief Justice could only review the evidence recorded. This did not ensure that the proper questions had been asked of the witnesses called and there was no assurance that the proper witnesses had been called, especially on behalf of the accused, and the Chief Justice's review was based on the assumption that the trial had been accurately reported.

In addition to the provincial courts Lugard set up four grades of 'Native Courts'. The highest grade had capital powers, but the proceedings there had to be sent to the Resident and confirmed by the Governor. But since neither Residents nor any other British official attended these courts, one is left with the feeling that no 'proceedings' were kept since the scribes in the north or the half literate clerks in the south could hardly have been expected to record what went on in these courts clearly. This novel judicial system aroused much anger and its introduction was delayed until it was forced through by proclamation in October 1914 when Nigeria and Great Britain were at war with Germany.

Mr Justice Stoker felt so strongly about the change in the judiciary that he resigned his appointment from the Nigerian bench in order to fight the issue in England, with no apparent success. Lugard's intention was to give the executive branch of government complete control over much of the judiciary, to strengthen 'Native Courts' in Southern Nigeria on the lines of the *Alkali*[12] courts in the north, and to exclude the 'horde' of native lawyers from all the courts except the Supreme Court. Lugard argued that the new system was administratively more feasible and convenient in that decisions could be reached on the spot rather than allowing appeals to the Supreme Court in Lagos to pile up until a full court could be convened to deal with them. Sir Willoughby Osborne, the Chief Justice of Southern Nigeria, however, was of the opinion that strengthening the judiciary by increasing the number of judges was perhaps a better course than limiting the appellate jurisdiction of the Supreme Court.[13] But the majority of the British officials in Nigeria were in favour of Lugard's *droit administratif* since it was designed to eliminate the influence of African lawyers in the south. Sir Edwin Speed, the former Chief Justice of the north who became the Chief Justice of the whole country because of his 'Lugardian' concept of law as an instrument of administrative policy, criticising the pre-Lugardian judiciary said: 'the staff was so small and its organisation so rudimentary that outside the trading centres and coast towns its criminal jurisdiction was only invoked for the purpose of adjudicating upon disputes on land boundaries fostered by native lawyers.'[14] Other officials in the south were of the opinion that the African lawyers were disrespectful to white men and were fostering the same attitude in their illiterate compatriots. The influence of these lawyers was so great, claimed an official, that 'it was impossible to ask the way of a native without being told, I must consult my lawyer first'.[15] In short, the weight of opinion within the administration was in favour of Lugard's judicial organisation, but in getting his way he struck a blow at the African lawyers' means of livelihood and incurred their hatred, which was unfortunate in view of the war that shortly broke out and the unco-operativeness of this class of men.

Even before the outbreak of the First World War educated Nigerians were so hostile to Lugard's indirect rule system that they saw nothing to redeem it. Lugard and the educated Nigerians had different notions about the British presence in Nigeria: Lugard seems to have placed much premium on administrative methods while educated Africans saw administration as a means to rapid economic and educational development along English lines. Since there was a clash of motives and a difference in goals, it is not surprising that Lugard should see these people in the worst possible light. He was full of contempt for the 'educated natives', whom he saw as agitators, people without roots, conspirators against the most reasonable form of government for subject races. In expressing his feelings to his wife about this class of men, he wrote: 'I am somewhat baffled as to how to get in touch with the educated native . . . to start with I am not in sympathy with him. His loud and arrogant conceit are distasteful to me and the lack of natural dignity and courtesy antagonise me'.[16] His contempt for the 'educated native' was not a unique personal foible found in Lugard alone; a good number of his officials shared his views. His brother was also bothered by 'these trousered negroes' who wanted to run Nigeria 'on would-be European lines'.[17]

Lugard was convinced that these educated Nigerians wanted to ruin his administration by fomenting trouble in the south. He claimed,

> 'they say that Lagos people will not be reduced to the "futile con-
> dition" of northern Nigeria without a protest . . . they had emissaries
> all over Ibadan, Oyo and all the Yoruba towns stirring up the
> people. I think it means some deep-seated plot. I am beginning to
> think they are hopeless and that any attempt to make any reform with
> their cooperation is impossible.'[18]

Lugard ought to have realised that whatever he called 'reform' meant 'reaction' to these people; and to expect them to co-operate with him showed how much he underrated the convictions of most of these people. Lugard however had the Colonial Office on his side in his effort to put these 'trousered negroes' in their place; when the question of local representation was broached in 1912 Charles Strachey minuted:

> the educated native barrister at Lagos is just as much a foreigner to the Efik or Ibo people . . . of the central and eastern provinces as the Englishman is . . . the problem is how to get the un-Europeanised native represented. He cannot be brought up to Lagos to sit at table with gentlemen in frock coats [educated Lagosians] and if he could, he would be too shy to talk. The solution is . . . rather to diminish than extend the powers of the Lagos Legislative Council and to continue governing the protectorate through chiefs and native councils.[19]

Sir John Anderson,[20] Permanent Under Secretary at the Colonial Office, put an end to any idea of educated Nigerians being brought into the Legislature when he minuted 'the Lagos lawyer is not a fit representative of the Protectorate native . . .'[21] Strachey at least conceded the fact that the 'gentlemen in frock coats' (a contemptuous euphemism for educated Nigerians) could speak for the south-western part of the country if not for the central and eastern provinces.

At the time Lugard embarked on his amalgamation scheme this polarisation of opinions, beliefs and views existed between the Africans, especially that vocal minority which could not be totally ignored, on one side and the colonial establishment on the other. Lugard, for good or evil, already had the reputation of being an uncompromising military man, acquired from his earlier services in Northern Nigeria where he had played the role of military proconsul and conqueror. This reputation was not one that would commend him to educated Nigerians, but it was of tremendous advantage to him in the north. The emirs there saw him as a firm person as well as somebody favourably disposed towards the maintenance of the status quo. Lugard's admirers in England saw his 'rough' background as particularly apposite for his appointment. Thus one editor commented, 'Lugard's military reputation will be no slight asset. Not that we apprehend a rising in the North, but our rule there rests on our ability to strike quickly and heavily, in no sense is it based on affection or even the loyalty of the people'.²² Lugard perhaps saw the world with military eyes – a world in which orders were given and obeyed without question, in which the superior was always right and in which force was supposed to be able to solve every human problem. His governorship was marred by innumerable 'punitive patrols'. It was this military background and his self-confessed egoism that led him to believe that he could carry out his scheme of amalgamation almost single handedly, listening to nobody but following his own intuition and dabbling in technicalities which by training he was unqualified to deal with.

Although Lugard had said the watchword of his administration would be decentralisation, he went on to concentrate all the vital powers in his own hands. He created a central secretariat, but nothing of any importance passed through the hands of the central secretary. Lugard's tenure of office marked a period of personal rule, and he preferred to rely on his 'rather defective memory' than allow files to pass through the secretariat. He also tried, unsuccessfully, to introduce a policy of 'continuous administration' of Nigeria by him no matter whether he was in England or in Nigeria.

Another innovation that Lugard proposed and was accepted by the Colonial Office, was for an annual meeting to be called the 'Nigerian Council', consisting of officials and non-officials from all over the protectorate and Lagos. They would sit and listen to the Governor dilating on the past, present and future of the country. They might talk and move resolutions which, however, would not be binding, for the council had no authority whatever. Lugard was borrowing a leaf from the practice in the Federated Malay States, where such a federal conference met last in 1903. This Malay Conference or Council consisted of the High Commissioner, the Resident-General, the Residents, the native rulers and principal chiefs and some leading Chinese.²³ Had Lugard looked at this institution closely he might have refrained from introducing an institution of no practical value to Nigeria. Although the Nigerian Council did no harm, it was a waste of time and the leading chiefs, who could not speak English, attended it only once or twice before its end. This council was thrown in as a sop to those who wanted a legislative council, in keeping with British Colonial government tradition. But if Lugard hoped to satisfy his critics by the creation of this ineffective 'talking shop' he was to be disappointed, for the result was further to alienate them since they were not allowed to participate in its deliberations.

In the amalgamation scheme the position of Lagos was very anomalous. It had an administrator and a legislative council but with practically no staff of its own; nearly all its revenue was turned into 'combined' revenue, and it had no voice in the protectorate's affairs, except that the administrator had a seat on the Executive Council and on the Nigerian Council.

The outcome of amalgamation was a jumbled confusion. All that could be said was that by 1 January 1914 a number of departments such as Customs, Railways, Marine and Public Works were amalgamated. The outcome of unification was so imperfect that it could hardly have been a permanent arrangement; 'with one man in practical control of the executive and legislative organs of all parts, the machine may work passably for sufficient time to enable the transition period to be left behind by which time the answer to the problem . . . will probably have become clear'.[24]

It was clear that important changes had to be made in the future, but it was the over-emphasis on the post of Governor-General and the idea of 'continuous administration' from England that was to cause chaos and military disaster on the Nigeria–Cameroons border during the immediate weeks after the outbreak of war, when Lugard was administering Nigeria from England.[25] Looking at amalgamation with the advantage of hindsight Sir Hugh Clifford commented in 1919:

amalgamation had no unifying effect, but in so far as an attempt at unification had been made, the efforts of the government appear to have been aimed at forcing the southern provinces to accept the peculiar systems and ideals of the North. This putting of 'old wine into new bottles' was followed by some of the explosive results that attribute to such experiments.[26]

At the same time as Lugard was effecting his bizarre amalgamation, rapid social and economic change was taking place in Nigeria on the eve of the war, particularly in the south. In spite of the still numerous 'punitive expeditions' and 'military patrols' involving the loss of the lives of several people, the country was settling down to a period of development everywhere. Thousands of men were gainfully employed in the building of the new port and railway terminus at Port Harcourt. The exploitation of the plateau tin mines was going on with much energy and infusion of more capital. Work was proceeding on the extension of Lagos harbour and wharves, the eastern railway was being built and a new source of coal supply at Udi near Enugu was being developed. Five thousand people were working on the Bukuru railway extension and double that number were employed on the eastern railway.[27] Recruitment was commenced in Zaria in 1913 for work on the Kakuri end of the eastern railway. Labour was in such demand on all capital projects that the merchants began to fear that the countryside might be denuded of agricultural workers, which would hurt the export trade of the country.

One of the great benefits of both the eastern railway and the Bukuru extension and the intensification of work on the Bauchi tin area, was that these projects were proceeding in predominantly 'unsettled' areas. The effect of the new development on the local people was profound and benefited the country. Wages, especially on the eastern railway, were paid in West African silver coins at the rate of one shilling a day. This currency was introduced in 1913[28] to replace United Kingdom coins, and was a welcome departure from the usual manillas or brassrods[29] which the merchants had selfishly clung to as a means of exchange instead of the legal currency. The involvement of a considerable number of Nigerians in the expanding economic life of the country was generally beneficial and led to a socially mobile population, which made recruitment easier when it became necessary during the war.

The rapid opening up of the country was not without its unsettling effect. The swift economic development and the opportunities consequently provided by this brought increasing numbers of foreigners into the country. These were mostly Europeans, other Africans and Arabs or Berbers. Present in the north, sometimes to the embarrassment of the government, especially in Kano and Katsina, were Arab merchants. Their numbers had gradually increased as peace and tranquillity were established in the country. These Arabs were mainly Tripolitanians who exported hides, skins and ostrich feathers with an annual turnover of £100,000 sterling.[30]

Many of the Tripolitanians did business with a Manchester firm named Raphael Hassan and Co. Ltd, in which the Niger Company had a controlling interest.[31] The presence of these Tripolitanians was in no way detrimental to British commercial interests, though during the war the matter assumed different proportions when the government was faced with a possible pan-Islamic threat. Fears as to the danger constituted by these Arabs were first expressed in 1912 by Temple, the Lieutenant-Governor of Northern Nigeria, when the Italians were finding it difficult to subdue the Senusi forces in Libya. Temple said the failure of the Italians in Tripolitania was a danger to Nigeria, and that if the Italians should be defeated as they had been by the Ethiopians at Adowa, 'a reaction amongst the Mohammedan population of Northern Nigeria very unfavourable to the government might occur'.[32] He foresaw a large number of emissaries circulating among the towns and villages in Northern Nigeria, explaining to the people that a Christian power had been success-fully kept at bay by a Muslim power for some time, and urging all Muslims to emulate the deeds of their co-religionists in the north. Temple commented: 'it is to be remembered that the inhabitants of Tripoli are intimately connected with the inhabitants of Kano and matters of even trivial importance occurring in Tripoli are known in Kano within three months and vice versa.'[33]

There were Turkish subjects scattered all over Nigeria, but not in large numbers; these were mostly Syrians and Lebanese traders. There were about sixty[34] of them before the war. In-dividually these Syrians did a relatively small business, but in aggregate their operations amounted to a fairly appreciable sum. They traded mostly in continental goods, such as scents, beads, cheap cutlery, jewellery, headwear and haberdashery. They lived among the people and had an influence disproportionate to their numbers. Economically they were of significance and a warning was sounded by the commercial intelligence officer for Southern Nigeria, who wrote: 'our own merchants should not ignore the Syrian competition which may become formidable as time goes on, in the same way that many of the Indian traders in East Africa have now become merchants, doing business on a large scale.'[35]

Other alien groups trading in Nigeria were the large numbers of Europeans, mostly British and Germans, concentrated in coastal towns and around the tin mines. They numbered more than one thousand in the south alone, with half that number in Lagos; they also formed a substantial group in the north. The government was responsible for the protection of the lives and property of these people, who were mostly representatives of firms based in Liver-pool, Manchester, Glasgow, London, Hamburg and Marseilles. They were constantly in contact with the Nigerians in the hinterland, hence their vulnerability in time of chaos and their influence for good or evil on the people with whom they traded.

Of all the firms in Nigeria, the position of the Niger Company was unique. It was deeply involved not just in the trade of Nigeria but also occasionally in political matters. The company was monopolistic in its attitude and managed to have its way because of its historical connection with the country.[36] The company sometimes tried to influence the economic policies[37] of the Nigerian Government, to the consternation of Lugard who deprecated the incessant meddling of the company. Other important companies were John Holt Ltd, the African Association, Miller Brothers Ltd, and the Compagnie Française de l'Afrique Occidentale (C.F.A.O.) which competed with powerful German firms in Southern Nigeria. The steamship company of Elder Dempster & Company Ltd was another that tried to exploit the imperial connection in its monopoly of the docking business in Nigeria.[38] In the carrying trade of Nigeria this company reached a *modus vivendi* with the German shipping company of Woermann Linie in 1895,[39] by which they shared the shipping business of Nigeria until the outbreak of the Great War.

When war actually broke out Nigeria, because of her economic dependence on German traders and the German market, the presence of 'enemy' subjects scattered all over the country, and the immensity and diversity of her population, had more than her normal share of problems. Coupled with this were the far-reaching and socially upsetting political and economic change which was taking place. Nigeria consequently found herself unprepared to cope with all the problems that arose at the onset of war.

Notes

1 See M. Crowder and O. Ikime (eds) *West African Chiefs*, University of Ife Press, 1970 (introduction).
2 C.O. 583/45/20906, J. A. Harding's minute, 8 April 1916; the amount disbursed by native treasuries in 1913 was put at £300,000.
3 See E. A. Afigbo, *The Warrant Chiefs*, Longman, London, 1972.
4 C.O. 583/10/9994, Lugard to Harcourt, 24 Feb. 1914.
5 C.O. 583/11/12729, Lugard to Colonial Office, 20 Feb. 1914.
6 *Ibid.* This included Onitsha on the Niger.

7 C.O. 583/15/23865, Lugard to Colonial Office, 29 June 1914. H. S. Pearce and Sapara Williams, Nigerian members of the Lagos Legislative Council both of whom were lawyers and in the good books of the government, joined Lagos and Calabar Bar Associations to condemn the new judicial system.

8 C.O. 583/14/19928. Stoker to Secretary of State, 24 April 1914. The British judge wrote: 'I cannot consent to hold courts otherwise than of the Supreme Court of Southern Nigeria.' A. J. Harding minuted on 30 April 1914: 'Mr. *Ultra Vires*, as I understand Mr. Stoker is called, should be told no useful purpose will be served by further discussion.'

9 In his book *Nigeria Under British Rule*, Methuen, London, 1927, p. 271, he commented: 'is not the government giving the native less than the British justice, they have a right to expect. When life is at stake surely there should be equal rights for the black as for the white man. In pioneer days a Khaki judge and a court martial may be necessary to preserve order: in a civilised state and in peace let the law run its usual course. If the life of the black man has to be taken, let it be according to the usual safeguards.'

10 C.O. 583/10/8606, Anti-Slavery and the Aborigines Protection Society to Colonial Office, 16 Dec. 1913: the secretary of this society protested: 'the bringing to the African of English justice is one of the most valuable assets to him'.

11 C.O. 583/11/12711, 27 April 1914, Eyo Honesty VIII (Obong of Creektown) Adam Ephraim Duke (Obong of Calabar) petitioned Lewis Harcourt. They asked for appeal to be allowed from provincial courts to the Supreme Court and for the deletion of the detestable punishment of flogging and whipping from the Provincial and Native Courts Ordinances. They argued that 'if it is contended that the principle of the provincial court is calculated to work for our ultimate good and is designed to speed up civilisation, it will be interesting to know why Lagos is exempted'.

12 *Alkali* Courts were 'Native Courts' in the north administering Muslim laws and presided over by the *Khadi* (judge). The highest of these Alkali courts was presided over by the grand-Khadi and appeals from there were made to the Emir's court.

13 C.O. 583/17360, memo by Sir Willoughby Osborne, 17 Dec. 1912. He also recommended the creation of a West African Supreme Court in order to make sure that properly constituted and 'full' courts heard cases.

14 Cmd. 468, 1919, xxxiv, 609, Lugard Report, p. 21.

15 C.O. 583/12/13499, March 1914. Ross, a puisne judge based in Calabar, said: 'these lawyers have no ... respect for the Powers that be ... on one occasion two or three lawyers demanded quarters from the district commissioner when attending assizes and threatened that if he refuse they would telegraph the Governor to make a report of him'.

16 Margery Perham, *Lugard: the Years of Authority 1898–1945*, Collins, London, 1960, pp. 389–90.

17 Major Edward Lugard, *Lugard Papers*, ii, p. 105. Major Lugard was his brother's well-paid political secretary.
18 Margery Perham, *op. cit.*, p. 391: Lugard to Flora, 2 Nov. 1912.
19 C.O. 554/10/13433, Charles Strachey's minute of 9 May 1912.
20 Sir John Anderson, G.C.M.G., K.C.B., 1858–1918. Entered Colonial Office 1879; secretary to the Colonial Conference 1902; Governor of the Straits Settlements and High Commissioner to the Federated Malay States, also High Commissioner to Labuan and its dependencies 1904–11; High Commissioner of Brunei and British agent for North Borneo, Sarawak, 1906; Under Secretary of State for the Colonies 1911–16; Governor of Ceylon 1916–18.
21 C.O. 554/10/13433, Sir John Anderson's minute, 10 May 1912.
22 *Lugard Papers*, i, p. 158. Quotation from *Equatorial and North Africa*, a journal published in October 1912.
23 C.O. 583/3/16460, A. J. Harding's minute, 16 June 1913.
24 *Ibid.*
25 C.O. 583/33/27195, Strachey's minute, 26 March 1917. Lugard, after denying knowledge of the whereabouts of 'Nigeria's Defence Scheme', finally discovered it in 'a brown paper parcel' in his home at Abinger. The Colonial Office clerks said this Defence Scheme ought to have been deposited at the Colonial Office, and that the unwarranted carrying about of files resulted in confusion both at the Colonial Office and in Nigeria.
26 C.O. 583/78/66560, Sir Hugh Clifford to Colonial Office, 28 Oct. 1919.
27 C.O. 583/7/327, Lugard to Colonial Office, 5 Jan. 1914.
28 Cd. 7791, xlv, 767, 1914–16. Report on the West African Currency Board.
29 C.O. 583/14/18826, Lugard to Colonial Office, 23 May 1914.
30 C.O. 583/16/28165, Lugard to Colonial Office, 14 July 1914.
31 *Ibid.* Hassan & Co. Ltd had a branch in Tripoli, which accounted for many Tripolitanians trading with the company.
32 C.O. 445/32/22309, C. L. Temple to Colonial Office, 24 June 1914.
33 *Ibid.*
34 *Ibid.*
35 C. A. Birtwistle to the Assistant Secretary, Commercial Department, Board of Trade, 24 Aug. 1912. Memo on British trade in Southern Nigeria (contained in report on British Trade in West Africa), published as Cd. 6771, 1913, p. 6.
36 The 1899 cession of the 'Niger territories' to the British Government involved the Imperial exchequer in paying the Royal Niger Company £865,000, while the Company still maintained rights to half the revenue derived from (a) royalty or percentage on gross value of minerals 'gotten or exported', (b) tax on profits, (c) fees from granting of licences to prospect or mine (this included leases). See C.O. 583/47/33583; also J. E. Flint, *Sir George Goldie and the Making of Nigeria*, pp. 308–11.
37 C.O. 583/13/16461, Lugard to Colonial Office, 13 May 1914. The Niger Company for instance several times provoked outcries from tin-mining companies by asking the government to raise the royalties,

half of which went to the company. The company at another time
prevented the government from lowering freight rates on railway
traffic because it claimed this would hurt the company's Niger river
transport service. See C.O. 583/4/29986, 1 Oct. 1913. An agreement
was signed with the government by the Niger Company concerning
railway rates to the effect that '. . . the published railway tariff . . .
shall not for the period of one year . . . be altered so as to undercut
the rates of the Niger route'. The Niger Company also delayed the
granting of a licence to the Woermann Linie or any other company to
establish a River transport service.

38 C.O. 583/10/8750, Lugard to Colonial Office, 28 Jan. 1914. Elder
Dempster and Co. prevented the Nigerian Government from agreeing
to Woermann line's decision to move its dock from Duala to Lagos
because Elder Dempster wanted to move theirs from Forcados to
Lagos and did not want competition.

39 A. G. Hopkins, 'Economic History of Lagos 1880–1914', London
University Ph.D. Thesis, 1962, pp. 323–4. By this agreement the two
firms undertook to charge the same freight and to offer a rebate to
those shippers who agreed not to make use of any other line.

2 Trade and war-time economy in Nigeria

The First World War upset the gradual economic development of Nigeria and caused a great deal of dislocation in the internal as well as the external flow of trade of the country. The fact that an event involving primarily European powers should reverberate with such effect on the economic life of Nigeria showed the extent to which Africa, especially West Africa, had become part of the Western European economic complex.

During the era of the 'scramble' the British had always dismissed any notion of monopoly by arguing that their colonial policy was based on healthy economic and commercial competition of citizens of all nations in their colonies, but they found to their chagrin that an 'open door' policy in Nigeria could not work in abnormal times such as war. Nigeria's economic well-being was by and large dependent on European demands and needs for vegetable oils, cotton, cocoa and tin.

The country's revenue was largely derived from two main sources which the war seriously affected. Two-thirds of the revenue came from railway receipts and customs duties.[1] The duties were almost entirely those levied on trade spirits (cheap gin), which were carried in German bottoms and came mainly from Holland.[2] The other sources of revenue were direct taxation, which was in force in Northern Nigeria, yielding about £300,000[3] in 1914, and court fees and fines collected mainly in the Southern courts where litigation was more rampant, and where the so-called 'Native Courts' had increasingly been used to raise revenue through the infliction of heavy fines. The war-time economic story of Nigeria was the cutting off of the connection between Nigeria and Germany and, later during the war, between Nigeria and Holland, and the attempt made to replace these two customers by finding other markets in foreign countries and expanding the market for Nigerian products in the Empire.

Nigeria had come to be heavily dependent on German capital

and enterprise because of the presence of very powerful German firms in the country. At the outbreak of the war there were nineteen German and Austro-Hungarian firms in Nigeria.[4] Five of these were important German trading houses and two were minor Austrian ones. The German firm of G. L. Gaiser dominated the Lagos export trade and to a certain extent the import trade as well. G. L. Gaiser was the successor of the German firm of William Oswald & Company, established in Lagos some years before the cession of the colony to Britain. At that time this German firm held a prominent position in Lagos. In 1865 the agent of G. O. Gaiser formed the 'Association of European Merchants of Lagos', which eventually transformed itself in 1897 into a Chamber of Commerce. In fact as from 1865 down to the outbreak of the war the Germans held the most prominent place in the commercial life of Lagos Colony and G. L. Gaiser had immense good-will and trade connections in the Colony and Yorubaland.[5]

The firm of Pagenstecher & Company was very strong in Warri and Benin divisions,[6] while the German Niger–Benue Transport Company was the only effective competitor with the Niger Company in the river transport business of Nigeria. This company was closely connected with the Woermann Linie, the most powerful shipping company on the West African coast. Then there was the old German firm of Witt & Busch, which since 1877 had been one of the most formidable rivals to English firms in Southern Nigeria.[7] The Germans were more popular in Nigeria than were the English, because of the generous credit facilities they gave to their African agents. In turn these agents carried German goods and good-will far into the interior, where means of communication and transport were still in the rudimentary stage.

The position of the Woermann Linie before the outbreak of the war was slightly different from those of other German firms because it did not compete 'unfairly' with British shipping companies. Before the war practically the whole of the produce shipments from British and German possessions in West Africa were carried by two groups of steamship companies, one British and one German. The British group was under the management of Elder Dempster & Company Ltd, and included the African Steamship Company, the British and African Steam Navigation Company Ltd, and the Elder Line Ltd.[8] The German group consisted of the Woermann Linie, the Hamburg–America line and

Hamburg–Bremen–Afrika Linie. Other lines had occasionally intervened in the carrying trade, but not to any great or lasting extent. An arrangement had been worked out between the two groups by which equal rates were charged on goods carried, this was done to make sure that each company maintained the same rate as the other in order to avoid unnecessary competition.

Goods were shipped by the steamers of both groups to Hamburg, Rotterdam and continental ports generally, but British ports were served exclusively by Elder Dempster ships, as part of the arrangement.[9] This British line sent regularly two cargo steamers a month from Hamburg to Lagos, calling *en route* at Rotterdam. The German line ran three cargo boats a month from Hamburg to Lagos, two of them picking up goods at Rotterdam on their way to Lagos, and there was a weekly service from Liverpool to Lagos; it can thus be seen that commercially Nigeria was better linked with the continent than with Britain.[10] The German vessels that plied the West African route were better built and specially adapted to West African trade.[11] It is therefore not surprising that Germany took a substantial amount of Nigeria's agricultural products, especially oil-producing nuts, before the war.

More than half of the total value of all produce exported in 1913 went to Germany, which included four-fifths of Nigeria's palm kernels.[12] Hamburg also took fifty per cent of Nigeria's untanned hides and skins, fifty-three per cent of her groundnuts, thirty-four per cent of her shea nuts, thirty per cent of Nigeria's timber and twelve and a half per cent of the country's palm oil.[13] Germany took produce from both the southern and northern parts of Nigeria and the geographical distribution of these agricultural products was significant in the sense that a general trade depression as a result of the withdrawal of German competition was bound to be felt all over the country.

The value of the imports from Germany was considerable and Germany's import market in Nigeria was expanding at an extraordinary pace before the war; it was surmised by the Commercial Intelligence Officer in Nigeria that if the upward trend had been maintained Germany and Holland combined would have reached parity with Britain in the import sector of Nigeria's trade by 1922.[14] If this had happened and the Germans had dominated both import and export trade of the country, it would have been a rebuttal to the Hobson–Leninist assertion of colonies being havens for capitalist exploitation by the ruling or occupying power.

German traders came to Nigeria primarily for palm kernels, for which they had a better market in Hamburg than British merchants possessed in Liverpool. When once established in Southern Nigeria, where for quite a considerable length of time trade by barter was the practice of commercial transaction, the German firms took up the sale of tobacco, trade spirits and also general manufactured goods. The great fidelity of large German firms in various parts of Nigeria to their country's trade interests contributed to the inroads being made into the import market as well as to the increase in the volume of German trade generally. As an illustration, Manchester goods consigned to German firms in Nigeria were usually sent to Hamburg in order that they might come out in German ships. The Germans also were faster in the delivery of goods to both English and German firms, so that even some of the British firms preferred their goods to come by German ships.[15]

The Germans specialised in bringing to Nigeria articles such as Fez caps of various kinds, most of which were made in the Austro-Hungarian Empire. They supplied practically the whole of the south-western part of Nigeria with gunpowder as well as 'dane guns',[16] most of which they themselves bought from Belgium. Other items carried by German traders were lager beers, coal, cordage and twine. Nigerians preferred German twine because it was more durable; it was widely used for making fishing nets on the coast. The Germans, because of their proximity to the Scandinavian countries, monopolised the rapidly increasing trade in stockfish which was valued at £111,000 in 1913.[17] The Germans were the only traders-importers who sold cutlasses or matchets in Nigeria. This item of trade was important not for its monetary value, but for its use and popularity throughout Nigeria for agricultural purposes such as the cutting down of trees and clearing of forests for cultivation of crops. These cutlasses were hafted by home industry in Germany, women and children being often thus employed in their own villages; the British could not compete in this line of import. The Germans also monopolised the trade in copper rods, because their rods were more easily worked by local blacksmiths into ornaments than those ordinarily obtainable in England.[18]

The Germans also intruded into a predominantly British sphere, that of textiles. The German speciality was in velvets and velveteens; some of the velvets were actually made in Lancashire, but sent to Germany for finishing. German dyers were cleverer than the British in making relatively low-quality cloth look when finished equal to one of higher value, and were thus able easily to undersell their English rivals. The German traders carried other items such as beads, most of which they bought from either Italy or Austria, as well as general household goods like cooking utensils and cutlery. The most important items of trade were trade spirits and 'rum'. The rum was produced from ordinary potato or grain, rather than molasses, and then flavoured and exported to Nigeria.

When war broke out on 14 August 1914 it was necessary to re-channel Nigeria's trade to avoid aiding the enemy, and with the prosecution of this policy the country suffered. The government was faced with the problem not only of finding markets for Nigeria's main staple, palm kernels, but also of finding alternative sources of revenue to the duties levied on trade spirits, as well as finding alternatives for German imports.

The Germans were suspended from trading on 21 September 1914 by A. G. Boyle, the Governor's Deputy, on his own initiative, but realising how vital the Germans were to the economic life of the country, the Colonial Office countermanded the order a week later.[19] The Germans recommenced trading but under certain restrictive conditions – they were made to report daily to police officers and to be in their houses before nine o'clock in the evening. They were not allowed to transfer money to Germany or, for security reasons, to get in touch with their headquarters in their homeland. These stringent measures were the prelude to the eventual cancellation of trade with Germany and Germans. On 7 November 1914 the Germans were interned as prisoners of war, following protests from London and Liverpool Chambers of Commerce, coupled with the allegation that the Germans were fomenting rebellions in the southern part of Nigeria.[20] The Comptroller of Customs, T. F. Burrowes, was subsequently appointed to supervise the disposal of goods and liquidation of the German firms, as well as paying British, Allied and neutral creditors of the German firms, in that order.

With the shut-down of German firms the Colonial Office was faced with the problem of finding markets for about four million pounds' worth of Nigerian produce which had hitherto been channelled to Germany by the German firms based in Nigeria. The most difficult was finding a market for the palm kernels (in particular), since Germany took practically the entire Nigerian crop worth over two million pounds and weighing 131,886 tons in 1913.[21] This was not an easy task since no country except Germany had enough crushing mills to deal with so large a quantity of palm kernels. The hardness of the kernel necessitated special machinery; when crushed, the kernel was placed in a special press and subjected to a very high temperature, and this made the oil flow out, and the resultant cake constituted a feeding stuff.[22]

Since setting up mills in England or converting some that already existed needed a lot of capital, the Colonial Office in conjunction with the Nigerian Government arranged a meeting with Sir William Lever of Lever Brothers Ltd, and the London and Liverpool Chambers of Commerce to find out what could be done to save Nigeria from economic disaster. At this time there were only three small crushing mills for palm kernels in England, and they were grossly incapable of handling the consignments of palm kernels which by now had become unmarketable.

The soap- and margarine-making companies told the Colonial Office that they would consider building new crushing mills, but that these would take at least six months to complete.[23] Despite this drawback, the industrialists saw a golden opportunity to seek government aid in monopolising the palm-kernel trade during and after the war. They asked the Colonial Office to give a firm undertaking that once the mills had been erected they would be protected against foreign competition, by the prohibition of the export of the oil-producing nuts to places outside the Empire. This of course ran completely counter to the still firmly held British policy of free trade with the colonies. The Colonial Office, while not in a position to refuse outright the offer of erection of new palm-kernel crushing mills on conditions favoured by Sir William Lever and his competitor, Joseph Crosfield of Crosfield & Sons Ltd, one of the biggest soap manufacturers in England, promised that further investigation into the matter would be ordered.[24]

While the home government was trying to grapple with the problem of markets for Nigeria's produce, the Nigerian Government too was faced with all kinds of problems connected with the country's internal flow of trade. There was the problem of shortage of credit, because the Bank of British West Africa, which had a monopoly of the banking business in Nigeria and other British possessions in West Africa, refused to grant the loans to trading firms that it used to do before the war because it saw no prospect of recovering them. This action led to shortage of silver coins, which were obtainable only from the bank, and this more than anything unsettled the commercial life of Nigeria, since merchants were not able to buy produce offered to them by Nigerian farmers.[25] The government for some time had to intervene, by accepting bills from commercial firms in exchange for cash because the bank refused to buy such bills. The mining companies, being the hardest hit, were loaned money by the government in order to ensure that they continued working so as to avoid laying off thousands of their employees. As government intervention increased, other firms connected with Nigeria's trade tried to shift their burden on the government, which could hardly bear its own.

Large companies like the Niger Company Ltd, John Holt Ltd, and Miller Brothers, asked the government to grant them one kind of relief or the other. The Niger Company Ltd, for instance, stated that the bulk of twelve months' purchases of produce which they had intended bringing to the coast during the flood season, i.e., June to September 1914, was now unmarketable because their principal market in Germany was closed; and no factories existed for their stock in England. The company therefore asked the government to give traders using the Niger River and railway for hauling their accumulated produce the option of payment of duties and railway charges by three months' acceptances, payable in London.[26] The government could certainly not agree to a proposal whereby large companies would be allowed to pay customs duty and rail charges some three months later than the date they were due; that would have amounted to giving large companies substantial loans, free of interest, while not extending the same facilities to the smaller ones. The Niger Company, with its large capital, should have been the last to ask for government assistance at a time when government revenue was decreasing at an alarming rate.

The Colonial Office advised the Nigerian administration that intervention should be undertaken only when the price of palm kernels fell so low that government had to step in to prevent permanent crippling of the industry. If such a situation were to arise the Nigerian Government could purchase from the exporting firms, so that they in turn could keep buying palm kernels offered by the middlemen and primary producers. The produce could then be stored in Britain, if possible by arrangement with manufacturers, and sold as opportunity offered, at a price sufficient to cover all expenses.[27] But even if this was possible, neither the home government nor the Nigerian administration had the necessary machinery for carrying out such a grandiose plan of state monopoly. Nothing on this line was done, and the trading houses were asked to look after their own interests.

The government of Nigeria was faced with a possible fall in customs receipts of up to £470,000 for 1915 and a drop of about £225,000 in railway receipts for the same year.[28] This was due to the decline in the purchasing capacity of British firms following increased cost of sea insurance and shipping, and to dislocation of the normal system of commercial credits and the non-payment of outstanding debts owed to them by German firms and tin-mining companies, which were out of business because of the close-down of the metal market towards the end of 1914.

The Colonial Office, anticipating all these difficulties, ordered the Nigerian Government to follow a policy of strict economy. The government was told to curtail the railway building programme, as well as other developmental activities that it had embarked upon before the war, but this had to be done in such a way as to cause a minimum of damage to work already begun. When the war broke out work was going ahead on the eastern railway that was to link Port Harcourt to the existing western line at Kaduna. By September 1914 more than three-quarters of a million pounds out of an estimated four million for the entire project had been spent. Besides the railway other projects such as the extension of Lagos harbour and wharves, the completion of the Lagos water supply and the building of a new capital at Kaduna, as well as the building of railway headquarters and workshops, were all under way with estimated costs totalling some millions of pounds.[29]

The projected total expenditure was well above the funds held by the Crown Agents in Nigeria's account,[30] and since the possibility of raising loans publicly was nil, the government had no choice but drastically to reduce its financial commitments. The Colonial Office ordered that work should stop on the Kaduna capital and the newly projected Yaba headquarters. Work was also suspended on the railway from Udi (Enugu) to Kaduna junction, although construction from both the Port Harcourt and Kaduna ends had started in 1913 and large quantities of material had been conveyed to each of these points, and in fact thirty miles from the Kaduna end had been completed before the out-break of war. The curtailment of these large capital projects caused serious loss and inconvenience to the Nigerian authorities in many different ways. Manufacturing firms in England protested against government cancellation of orders placed with them. Houses in Kaduna, for example, which were nearing completion could not be left uncompleted without considerable damage, and in this particular case Lugard refused to comply with the Secretary of State's order for a halt to all building programmes except where absolutely necessary.

Earlier on, the Governor-General had rather naïvely suggested that the time was very opportune for the introduction of direct taxation in the southern provinces; he was convinced that the institution of direct taxation all over the country would be necessary in order to raise much-needed revenue. This suggestion, coming after war broke out in Europe from a Governor supposedly administering Nigeria continuously even while on holiday, was described by Harcourt as a 'ludicrous suggestion in such a crisis as this . . .'.[31] He was warned by the Secretary of State, who as it turned out possessed remarkable foresight, that any action that might cause disaffection and agitation should not be taken during the war.

Other measures to raise internal revenue in the country received the administration's attention. Lugard resorted to the age-long expedient of indirect taxation through raising of the customs dues on tobacco and some foodstuffs such as rice and increasing the tax on corrugated or galvanised iron sheets and kerosene, as well as imposing a surtax of twenty-five per cent on all other dutiable articles.[32] Lugard argued that the increase of customs duty on tobacco was justified because he was of the opinion that the trade could stand the additional duty, despite the fact that the duty had been increased shortly before the war. With disarming honesty, he openly admitted that his intention was to tax people in the south. He said the increase would fall principally on people in the old Central and Eastern Provinces of Southern Nigeria, who had benefited greatly before the war from the great rise in the price of palm kernels.[33] He surmised that it was not unlikely that tobacco might, to some extent, take the place of trade spirits as a medium of exchange if there should be a deficiency of spirits. The wisdom of a policy which based war-time indirect taxation on pre-war prosperity is subject to question. So, also, was his argument that tobacco might become a substitute for trade spirits, for hardly can their importance in the life of the people be compared in terms of their use not only as a drink, but as something used for propitiating their gods and for other rituals.

Lugard, however, conceded the point that if trade in spirits was desired there was no reason why it could not continue, but that foreign liquor should be superseded by cheap spirits from Britain. Assuming that ocean trade routes remained open there appeared, he contended, no reason why the export of Holland's liquor should be interfered with by the war. But a problem that he did not foresee was to crop up later when it was discovered that raw materials for Dutch gin came from Germany. The surtax on all other dutiable articles affected textile manufactures, wearing apparel, salt, kolanuts, gunpowder, guns, soap, matches, hardware, earthenware and furniture. Raising the duty on cotton goods which came in before the war on an *ad valorem* basis was in order, since this increase would make it possible for the government to realise the same revenue as before on cotton goods, the price of which had fallen in England. The taxing of foodstuffs was regretted, but it was found necessary if only as a temporary war measure.

The Colonial Office continued to explore all possible ways of finding markets for the surplus Nigerian exports. The Foreign Office put pressure on the French Government and persuaded them to abolish the *surtax d'entrepôt* on palm kernels,[34] which had tended to keep out foreign palm kernels from the French market by taxing kernels coming from colonies other than those of France. Capitalists in Britain were persuaded to erect crushing mills for palm kernels, but there people feared risking a large amount of capital in erecting mills in England lest on cessation of hostilities, the continental firms with their ready market of oil cake should undersell them and so render their mills inoperative and involve them in the loss of capital invested. Even if the government was prepared to legislate to keep the trade in British hands during and after the war, there was still the problem of how the trade would be made profitable.

The interested industrialists contended that since the palm-kernel cake was not popular with British farmers, they were not sure that they could sell the palm-kernel oil as well as the cake profitably. It was made clear to the Colonial Office that the profit of the industry depended entirely on the sale of palm-kernel cake. The Germans had been able to make profits out of the industry because the cake was popular in Germany and Denmark among the farmers, but the British farmers would not touch it, and the possibility of making them use it for feeding pigs was in doubt. It was feared that British farmers were not likely to experiment with a new food offering no advantage in price over those they already knew, like cotton, linseed and other oil cakes at their disposal.

In spite of the propaganda campaign embarked upon in favour of palm-kernel cake by the Board of Agriculture and Fisheries,[35] the farmers complained that the carbohydrates in which palm-kernel cake was rich were fattening rather than milk-producing, and were much more readily and cheaply supplied by hay and linseed or cotton seed cake. Furthermore, the farmers and everybody concerned with the problem found it difficult to guess what the Germans mixed with the palm-kernel cake, or how they prepared it, to make it so successful. It was not known for example how the Germans counteracted the laxative effects of the palm-kernel cake, which were said to be the result of large amounts of woody fibre in the cake that had scouring and mechanically irritating effects on the intestines of cows, sheep and pigs.[36] As to getting the Dutch and Danes interested, the government felt that if unlimited quantities were exported to Holland and Denmark these might be passed to Germany by unscrupluous war-time profiteers in those two countries.

As a result attention was focused on the home and Empire markets. Efforts were directed at creating widespread interest in the subject throughout the United Kingdom: representations were made to millers, the margarine and soap manufacturers as well as farmers' organisations; lectures were organised by members of the Nigerian Government holidaying in Britain to stimulate the British public to accept the challenge posed by this particular problem.[37] It was pointed out that war-affected ports like Hull could take on the task of crushing palm kernels with much benefit to the town and to Nigeria. New factories were commended in Hull, London and Liverpool, so that by 1915 a substantial amount of Nigeria's palm kernels was being processed in these ports.[38]

What had happened was impressive. The industrialists and farmers had responded well to the enormous literature and propaganda that were put out to save the trade. The agricultural societies and clubs demonstrated that palm-kernel cake would, when used as feeding stuff, produce better milk or cheaper bacon than competing foods and by the end of 1915, partly as a result of the booming margarine trade and the increasing use of palm-kernel oil in making toilet soap as well as the investment of vast capital in the margarine trade and the protection of this particular trade from Dutch competition, the industry became firmly established in England.

In order to keep the trade in British hands after the war, in 1916 the government was induced to set up a Select Committee of the House of Commons under Arthur Steel-Maitland, Parliamentary Under-Secretary in the Colonial Office, to look into how the trade could be permanently retained by British manufacturers. The committee in its report recommended an export duty of £2 per ton[39] on any palm kernels exported outside the British Empire. This recommendation was accepted, but not without much debate in parliament and outside. West African merchants sought permission to export to neutral markets the surplus which glutted the British market. They argued that the mills in Britain and South Africa could not totally absorb all the palm kernels coming out of Nigeria and Sierra Leone, and in the dispute with the government, the West African merchants blamed the crushers, especially Sir William Lever, for unduly influencing the government in order to obtain a complete monopoly of the trade.[40] The imposition of the export duty was criticised in the Commons on the grounds that while thousands of West Africans were dying to preserve the Empire, the imperial government was imposing a monopoly on West African trade for the benefit of a few British traders, and Africans were made to sell their palm kernels at £2 below the actual market price.[41] The government was told that the existence of an export duty might create a tendency to combinations among merchants or among crushers in Britain, for the purpose of fixing the producer price at the lowest minimum. The committee agreed that this was a possibility, but they were of the opinion that 'pools have been known before the war, but have never lasted long and complaint has more generally been made of the insanity of the competition',[42] and said that the risk was worth taking, subject to the right of the colonial governments concerned to reduce the duty or abolish it altogether, if advantage was being taken of it to depress the prices paid to the primary producers.

This did not satisfy all those who cherished the idea of free trade. The *Manchester Guardian* maintained that taxing colonial produce constituted 'departures in Britain's colonial policy, departures undertaken without . . . any reference to the colonial territories concerned . . .', and went on: 'is Britain wise and indeed can she without violating the public international law of Europe arbitrarily impose an export duty of not less than £2 per ton upon vegetable oil and fat exports from the West African colonies?'[43] The paper maintained that the export tax on palm kernel was discriminatory since other oil-bearing nuts were left untaxed. It was further argued that the government seemed to have overlooked the position of the Niger and its affluents in international law. This was a reference to the freedom of trade in the Niger Basin, which was enshrined in the Berlin Act of 1884-5. The *Manchester Guardian* went on to say that the export duty would benefit only the monopoly which it would create, and not the British consumer. Furthermore, it would hit the Nigerian producer by depressing prices while the monopoly firms would be able to impose maximum prices on British consumers.

Debate on the imposition of the export duty continued until after the war, but it had hardly any effect on government policy in respect to the export duty question. As far as the government of Nigeria was concerned a solution, if only a temporary one, had been found to the problem of finding a market for palm kernels which on the outbreak of the war had seemed impossible.

Lugard again tried to use the financial crisis created by the war to force the Colonial Office to agree to his introducing direct taxation in 'advanced' areas like Oyo Province, Abeokuta and Benin Divisions in the southern provinces on similar lines to that operating in the northern part of Nigeria. This, apart from being connected with raising of revenue, was actually an administrative measure that Lugard had always felt was necessary in the 'unorganised' south. He said the year 1915 was 'exceptionally opportune' for the introduction of direct taxation, claiming that the innovation was acceptable to 'all native rulers concerned'.[44] He maintained that 'if the present opportunity is allowed to pass it will beyond doubt become more difficult as time passes' to introduce the measure; he continued that there would be some agitation among 'a particular class who had for some years been engaged in exploiting the native communities of Egba and Yorubaland to the increasing indignation of the chiefs and the people'.[45] The greatest value of his scheme, he claimed, was that it would ensure 'the selection of the most capable and most influential men as chiefs and advisers'. The chiefs would, according to Lugard, become more responsible when charged with the duty of assessment and collection of taxes. He was no doubt right when he said that his scheme would make the chiefs 'a part of the government of the country', what was not said was whether this itself was in the interest of the chiefs. He carried his argument to the logical conclusion when he wrote, 'the chiefs especially of the more advanced communities, must have an income out of which to live and support their position. Direct taxation with its corollary of a native treasury provides the means of giving to each person an adequate and measured salary.'[46]

Lugard was so sure of his system that he felt it must be a natural and self-evident thing. He claimed that even among 'unorganised' Ibo, Ibibio and 'Ijo' tribes where no tributes or means for collection existed, the family organisation would afford much assistance, as had been proved by the fact that large fines, which had from time to time been imposed for crimes committed by these people, had been successfully collected from the communities by the family heads. He said that in the north the Munshi (Tiv), who were similar to the Ibo and Ibibio, had been successfully assessed by district officers. He therefore saw no reason why the same could not be done in the south. In the Delta similar measures were needed, said the Governor, because of the decay of the 'House rule system' following the fall in the middleman's profits, one of the results of the opening up of the country by railways and roads. Lugard wanted to convert the 'heads of the Houses into territorial chiefs and profits made by members of their Houses into regularised tribute'.[47]

Before extending the scheme to the entire south he wished to experiment first with the 'advanced Yoruba, Egba and Benin states'. He was not the only one who thought the scheme would succeed, for some of his officers in these states were at one with him in recommending it to the Colonial Office. One of them said the scheme would be a huge success in Yorubaland because 'a large number of the people are Muslims and direct taxation is in accordance with their religion'.[48] This officer forgot that even if Yoruba people were Muslims, their type of Islam was based on different cultural and political foundations, unlike that in Hausaland, which provided the model of what was 'Islamic tradition' for the officials in Nigeria of the time.

Lugard thought all was set for the inauguration of his scheme but to his utter surprise the Colonial Office was not convinced. Sir George Fiddes[49] commented:

> I think it would be madness to allow it to proceed while the Cameroons Campaign is still in progress. Whatever the chiefs may think or say it is clear . . . that we may expect discontent and opposition in various quarters. It would only be prudent to wait till the troops return and we have their bayonets to support our philanthropy.[50]

His immediate superior Sir John Anderson said he did not see how imposition of taxation with the chiefs as principal collectors was going to make them 'capable and influential men' as Lugard suggested. He continued, 'after the trouble in Abeokuta, I am not disposed to underrate the capacity of the educated native from Lagos for giving trouble . . . with the present reports of punitive expeditions that we receive by every other mail and the whole of our striking forces tied up indefinitely in the Cameroons . . . it is difficult to find any justification for the Governor's haste'.[51]

Lugard was not prepared to accept that officials at home knew more about Nigeria than he did and he was not going to allow himself to be permanently silenced by the refusal to sanction his measure when the revenue of the country was falling daily, with no prospect of an early loan from the Imperial Treasury and with the surplus loan funds almost used up. Nigeria was also spending large amounts of money on the Cameroons campaign without knowing precisely what portion of it would be paid by the War Office. When the Governor tried to use the 'hard times' argument to bring the Native Treasuries in the northern provinces under direct government control, his action was disallowed by the Colonial Office on the grounds that such an attempt would defeat the aim of the Native Treasury organisation which was 'financial independence' from the colonial government.[52]

Checkmated on all fronts, Lugard decided to study further the financial situation of the country. He looked at the financial returns up to 1916[53] and saw how the war had seriously affected the country's main revenue sources – railways and customs duties. He knew that the situation of the railway was almost hopeless unless ships were made available to clear the ports of produce lying congested in wharves, railway wagons and sheds. Secondly, revenue on imports was going down as a result of over-taxation of imports. He arrived at his old conclusion that direct taxation should be the first step if the economy was to be saved. He told the Colonial Office that refusal to sanction this measure would be a 'moral victory for the educated coastal natives' who had threatened publicly to foment trouble if he introduced a 'northern policy' in the south. Furthermore, he suggested replacing import duty by export duty because of the declining inflow of imports into Nigeria. He said this was necessary because the expulsion of the large German trading community from Nigeria had proved from one point of view 'a calamity' by making possible the formation of a combine by the Liverpool firms to eliminate competition and fix prices. The merchants as a result were making huge profits on their export trade rather than on imports. He felt there was a complete reversal in the trade pattern of Nigeria, and urged that in the face of this exploitation by the Liverpool merchants, any export duty on major agricultural staples would fall on the 'combine' firms, since they had already reduced prices to the lowest possible limit.[54]

On direct taxation the Colonial Office felt less agitated. The Cameroons campaign was over by this time (1916) and with the return of the majority of government troops the administration was in a position to suppress any disturbances which might arise as a result of direct taxation. It was felt that the scheme could only be carried out by hard work and tact on the part of the commissioners and district officers of the provinces concerned, but owing to the war and the occupation of the Cameroons, the administrative staff was shorthanded. The proposal was sanctioned however, provided Lugard was ready to assume personal responsibility for the consequence.[55]

Concerning his proposal on export duty replacing customs duty, it was recalled that shortly after becoming High Commissioner for Northern Nigeria, Lugard suggested to the then High Commissioner of Southern Nigeria, Sir Ralph Moor, and the Governor of Lagos Colony, Sir William MacGregor, that import duties should be abandoned in favour of export duties (except for the retention of duty on spirits, guns, gunpowder, and salt).[56] The two southern administrators had flatly refused then. Lugard now decided to renew this proposal partly because the recommendation of the Committee on Edible and Oil-producing Nuts and Seeds had laid down a precedent, and also because of what Lugard called the 'unprecedented profits' that British merchants were making after the elimination of German competition.[57]

Plausible as some of Lugard's arguments were, there were obvious points against taxing exports. There was the possibility that the measure might not hit the merchants, but rather the tax might be passed on to producers, thus further depressing prices and discouraging peasant farmers from working because of lack of incentive. Export duty might be beneficial if the country imposing it had a monopoly of the produce on which it was imposed, but that was not so in the case of Nigeria. Even if it had been so, ships were not available to carry the produce offered, so while effective demand for palm produce in the United Kingdom was good, the demand for it in Nigeria was poor, and while the supply in Nigeria was ample, the supply in Liverpool was not, hence the high prices in Liverpool. There was also the possibility that if the price of palm-kernel oil went up, margarine-makers might shift to coconut oil, since the oils were interchangeable. Lugard nevertheless imposed export duties on palm kernel, palm oil and cocoa in August 1916.[58]

The economic situation in Nigeria was further complicated by the emergence of a combine created by the better established Liverpool firms. These firms entered into agreements with the double object of reducing to the minimum the price paid to Nigerian growers of oil-producing nuts and seeds and of ensuring that the trade remained in the hands of those firms entering the agreements.[59] The combine came into being after the German traders had been incarcerated in Nigeria and later sent out of the country as prisoners of war. The whole field being left wide open to them, these firms fixed prices to be paid and the places at which each firm might buy produce. The combine arranged the proportion of produce to be shipped by each party to the agreement. The agreement appears to have been limited mainly but not entirely to the southern trade, since the Niger Company, the main trading company in the north, was not a party to the agreement, but it nevertheless maintained close ties with the combine on the question of prices to be paid to sellers of produce.[60]

The combine firms used to purchase produce sufficient to fill the ships available, and since there were not many of these, they consequently deprived Nigerian traders and the 'non-combine' smaller British firms of any opportunity of shipping their purchases. The combine firms exploited the congested state of Lagos Harbour to draw the port and railway authorities into their ring. They made sure that they kept the wagons and railway sheds loaded with produce so that in order to release these for use by others, the authorities were forced to give shipping priority to the firms belonging to the ring of monopolists, thus helping to further the economic interests of the monopoly.

Elder Dempster, which enjoyed a monopoly of the shipping business, was forced into supporting the combine by their threat of a separate charter to compete in the shipping trade, an action which would have undermined Elder Dempster's monopoly. The problem really was getting the required number of ships to remove Nigerian products from the wharves promptly. Prize vessels (captured German ships) which might have afforded immediate relief of the congestion in Lagos were not being used when the situation first became critical. Elder Dempster did not really want the prize vessels, at least at the initial stages of the problem, since they would have been under direct government orders and might have competed with the shipping company.[61] When later the company wanted the Admiralty to grant it the use of the Woermann ships the Admiralty would only lend five vessels, four of which were quickly withdrawn. Furthermore, apart from losses at sea due to enemy action, sixteen of the company's ships were requisitioned for government work in 1915;[62] in order to offset these losses the company tried chartering more ships, but found the cost prohibitive. Even when they were ready to charter at a loss, some owners of vessels refused for climatic reasons to allow their vessels to go to the West Coast of Africa, while other markets of the world, especially Latin America, were so good and relatively safe from enemy action.[63] The sources of steamers were further depleted because French, Russian and Belgian ships were being sent to other parts of the world by their owners, apparently to avoid their being requisitioned by their own admiralties, with the effect that more British steamers were chartered on account of the Allied governments.

Unable to get the ships required, Elder Dempster could therefore not satisfy all parties in Nigeria, and in deciding to give preference to the combine firms was protecting its own interests. The new British firms and the Nigerians who made demands on the company could be comfortably ignored, for after all, the Nigerians used to patronise the German firms before the war and the new British firms' commercial operations were negligible.

The effect of this monopoly on Nigerian farmers was profound. The groundnut growers in the northern provinces, who had experienced a fifty per cent fall in prices, held back their stock of produce waiting for offers better than those of the 'combine' or the Niger Company, but they were fighting a losing battle since no other trader would offer prices higher than those already agreed to by the European firms. As a result of the depressed prices the Nigerian producer suffered severely at the hands of the merchants and he in turn was shy of growing and collecting produce since he could obtain so small a profit for it. As a consequence, the less remunerative produce was being abandoned. A case in point was the sheanut industry; cotton-growing was another and there was fear that the extremely promising trade in groundnuts in the north might become the third. Along the Lagos lagoon, the copra industry also was being crippled by the shortage of shipping.[64]

As a result of their monopoly of shipping space, the combine was attempting to crush out of existence their smaller competitors and thus they were able to control the markets in England by holding their stocks until higher prices were offered on the British market. Nigeria was at the mercy of the merchants and the shipping company.

While the government tried to ease the financial burden by reducing railway freight rates, in spite of the increased cost of coal and the impossibility of reducing expenditure in direct ratio with reductions in earnings, the shipping company for no justifiable reason again raised the already high freight rate towards the end of 1915.[65] The shipping rates before the war were already too high, and the removal of the German competition in shipping had the effect of giving the shipping company full cargoes outward and homeward, so that profit on the voyage of each ship was much greater than it ever was before, when ships often came out or went home half empty. The increased cost of running a ship was much more than covered by this extra profit and there were fewer vessels to maintain. By imposing a high rate the shipping company was co-operating with the combine in shutting out the Nigerian traders and the new competitors who had entered the produce trade. It was useless for the government to reduce railway rates if the shipping company was going to neutralise the action by raising shipping rates.[66]

Owing to the outcry of the Nigerian merchants and the 'non-combine' firms the Nigerian Government was forced to intervene. A committee was set up, comprising members of the same trading community that had formed the combine and a representative of the Niger Company, which was outside the combine but closely tied to it in regulating and lowering prices and in using their support and facilities to destroy the smaller firms. Other members of the committee were drawn from the Nigerian Railway and Marine departments.[67] This committee was charged with the duty of allotting space to shippers of produce. The railway was concerned because the large accumulation of exports in wagons at the railway terminal at Iddo threatened seriously to affect both the clearance of imports and the carriage of all traffic on the railway, including the river-borne trade which came through Baro on the Niger. In these very special circumstances it was found necessary to restrict the supply of wagons only to consignors who could guarantee their immediate discharge, either by direct shipment or into sheds at Lagos or elsewhere. The question of division of tonnage became a rather difficult one and the Liverpool Chamber of Commerce urged the necessity for a more definite basis of tonnage allotment between the lagoon and rail-borne trade of Lagos; and suggested that of the total tonnage available sixty per cent should be given to rail-borne trade and forty per cent to lagoon-borne trade, subject to certain seasonal adjustments. The combine was allotted sixty per cent of the rail-borne trade and the remaining forty went to the tin-mining companies, the British Cotton Growing Association and the Niger Company, and other non-combine firms.[68] Since the combine dominated both the Lagos and railway-borne trade, they managed to perpetuate their monopoly to the detriment of the smaller firms, which were forced to close down.

Lugard was sincerely concerned about the evil effect of monopoly, but since the government did not have the power or the experience to take over the shipping and produce-buying business he even suggested to the Colonial Office that the only solution was to publicise the potentialities of Nigeria in the United States with the aim of attracting powerful American capitalists to counterbalance the influence of the 'ring' firms in Nigeria. This suggestion was turned down. 'The American', wrote A. J. Harding, 'as a cure for combines is rather a speculation – he might be worse than the British combine, especially as combines are regarded as rather an American speciality which we can only imitate at a respectful distance.'[69]

When attempts were made to break the combine's hold on the Nigerian economy by permitting neutrals or even Allies to enter the Nigerian produce trade, the British firms were quick to appeal to patriotism and love of the Empire. They argued that it certainly could not be a wise policy to invite neutrals to Nigeria just for the purpose of controlling a ring of British merchants; and that the existence of this combine was no reason 'for giving away the fruits of the war to Neutrals who had not earned them'.[70] To the contention that the British had neither the capital nor the men to fill the void left by the Germans, the Association of West African Merchants claimed that they had invested about two million pounds – a rather spurious claim based on purchases of the liquidated German firms. They said their enemies claimed they had no men to carry out their trading operations effectively, but this was due to their encouraging their young men to join the colours. They argued that 'to suggest that their places should be filled by Neutrals is surely a strange message to send to those loyal men from the British government'.[71] The Association said that notwithstanding the shortage of men they had continued trading, with the help of their Nigerian assistants. To those who said that fresh energy was needed to develop Nigeria, they answered that were it not because of the 'enterprise and importunity of British merchants there would have been no colony or protectorate of Nigeria'. They maintained that contrary to the agitation against the combine, the conditions between 1914 and 1916 had necessitated close co-operation between all those who were interested in West African trade and that anything that had been done was justified, because since the outbreak of the war, fluctuations in market values had been very violent and frequent. The fluctuations in market prices yielded considerable speculative opportunities for loss as well as for profit. Profits, it was agreed, were made not only by West African merchants but also by dealers and crushers in England; but this hardly justifies their exploitation of the unstable economy.

Apart from price manipulations, there were several other clauses of variations in prices. On the outbreak of war, produce that was intended for the German market was diverted to England and had to be unloaded on to the English market, which naturally collapsed, so that British merchants trading in the interior of Nigeria where produce could be brought down by the Niger–Benue river system only during the rainy season found themselves in the position of having to market a whole season's produce bought on a pre-war competitive basis at an abnormal loss. Low prices for kernels prevailed for a time because the crushing capacity of Great Britain was inadequate to deal with the whole of the West African crop. Later on during the war, shortage of tonnage asserted itself and values for palm kernel and palm oil advanced to record prices.

The merchants claimed it was only when high prices were paid that those who in pre-war days had no interest in the produce trade began to agitate for shipping space. They argued that the low price paid on produce was because of the shift from import to export trade. Before the war produce was largely considered as a 'remittance', but because of the war it could no longer be so considered and had to bear a fair share of establishment expenses, and because of the various increases in the cost of labour, insurance and shipping, 'cost to market' of produce increased five-fold. They maintained that any departure from old methods was forced upon them by circumstances. Finally, the merchants claimed that even if they made huge profits, they were liable to an excess war profit tax of sixty per cent. The British merchants had a case and in war it is the strong and the lucky firms and industries who survive, and that was the case in Nigeria, where the smaller firms had to nurse their wounds until after the war when it was hoped that normal shipping facilities would be available to small and big firms.

The Nigerian or West African trade eventually began to interest bigger capitalists. Leading margarine and soap manufacturing companies such as Lever Bros Ltd, the Dutch firms of Anton Jurgens and Co. and Van den Bergh, which early in 1917 had established soap and margarine branch factories in England, began to take an interest in the West African trade. For Lever Bros Ltd it was not a new venture. They had in 1910 erected at Opobo in the Niger Delta and Apapa in Lagos palm-kernel crushing mills, but these mills had been closed down after a loss of £13,000 in 1913.[72] These mills were revived in 1916 in order to avoid paying the high rates levied on uncrushed kernels. But Levers did not foresee that there might be difficulty in shipping the oil to Britain and that produce would pile up at the mills for lack of ships to bring them to Europe. The mills were closed down again after the war because they were being run at a loss of £60,000 a year,[73] but they no doubt served their purpose during the war. Anton Jurgens and Co., the biggest margarine manufacturing firm in the world, in addition to their first trading premises acquired in Lagos in 1917, attempted to buy Miller

Bros Ltd so as to be able to secure adequate oil palm produce, but the Ministry of Food stood in the way of an agreement, arguing that 'the object to be kept in view is not merely to bring trade to U.K., it must be kept in British hands'.[74]

It was however realised that even if produce could be bought by branch firms in Nigeria, the key to the problem was the provision of adequate shipping space. It was believed that if this problem could be solved enormous profits would accrue from the trade. By 1916 Sir William Lever had made up his mind to go into the shipping business himself, though fearing reprisals from Elder Dempster – reprisals which could take the form of Elder Dempster setting up soap and margarine works – but since that would take some time, he took the risk and bought six ships belonging to Herbert Watson & Co. of Manchester at a price of £380,000 and with a capacity of 80,000 tons.[75]

Having bought the ships, Lever soon lost control of them in May 1917 when the government took control of the West African shipping trade (through a committee of the owners concerned) in order to ensure that private interest should not override national advantage in the allocation of tonnage. This measure did not result in any financial loss and according to Lever Bros Ltd the purchase of ships proved a huge success.[76] It was not Lever Bros Ltd alone that made huge profits on the West African trade during the war: the Niger Company, from moderate profits before the war, saw its earnings rise to produce an average profit of over a quarter of a million pounds a year by the end of the war.[77]

As from the end of 1916, the imperial government began to interfere with the West African trade more than it had done before. The taking over of Elder Dempster's line by the shipping controller was marked by a very substantial increase in freight.[78] Although loss of ships through intensified German submarine action in 1917 created some problems, the Ministry of Shipping was able to replace some of those lost. Government intervention resulted in faster movement of Nigeria's vegetable oils to Britain, in order to ensure an ample supply of glycerine, for which some of the oils were used, which was a very important item in the making of munitions. This meant greater demand for Nigerian exports, and by 1917 Nigeria's trade with the United States gradually replaced the former trade with Germany, with the result that the total value of exports in 1917 exceeded any previous records.[79]

Finding outlets for the country's exports, however, did not necessarily mean the creation of widespread prosperity among the people. The gains still went into the pockets of the large European firms engaged in the export business, and of the soap and margarine manufacturers in England as well as the imperial government. Low prices continued to be paid to primary producers in Nigeria until the end of the war. At this same time when agricultural products fetched very little on the Nigerian market, the price of textiles was so high that cotton-growing provinces like Zaria and Kano stopped exporting cotton and reserved them for their own looms. The price of most of the other articles in chief demand, such as salt, kerosene and textiles, increased by from one hundred and fifty to three hundred per cent. As an indication of the high price of imports, in 1917 for example the volume of commercial imports fell by more than 6,000 tons but their value increased by £634,000.[80] The shortage of silver coins further drove prices of imported goods up while depressing the prices paid to primary producers. The middlemen and merchants, especially outside Yorubaland and the coastal towns, resorted to the much preferred trade by barter, as it gave them an advantage over the ignorant peasants. But as the prices of imports increased out of proportion to what even the most gullible farmer believed to be excessive, Nigerian producers started demanding cash rather than exchange their produce for cloth or some other imported goods. When they managed to get cash they hoarded it, waiting for prices of imports to fall, thereby contributing to the scarcity of acceptable currency. The government was unable to get coins from the British Mint, which had been taken over by the Ministry of Munitions, and in 1917 had to issue currency notes which proved so unpopular that they had to be replaced by nickel-bronze coins later in the year.[81] The currency problem continued to plague the administration until after the war.

IMPERIAL GOVERNMENT CONTROL OF NIGERIA'S
VEGETABLE OILS

The big profits being made by merchants and crushers of palm kernels and other oil-producing nuts and seeds brought the British Government's attention to these products and there developed a movement for government control which was led by Alfred Bigland,[82] a member of the war-time administration. As has been pointed out earlier, before the war most of Nigeria's palm kernels went to Germany and her groundnuts to France, but by the end of 1916 oil-seed crushers had succeeded in adapting their plants for crushing palm kernels, and had even gone further and built new factories. Also at this time Britain had succeeded in absorbing the bulk of Nigerian and Gambian groundnuts. All this led to the conclusion that Britain needed these oils more than she had ever done before.

Early in 1917 Lord Davenport as Food Controller was contemplating the purchase at West African ports of palm kernels, but before he could conclude negotiations with West African traders, the control in England of oils and fats was handed over to the oils and fats department of the Ministry of Munitions with Alfred Bigland as Controller. At this time Bigland embarked on a programme for prohibiting, except under licence, the importation into England of all oils and fats and for making the Controller sole buyer of all imports into Britain.[83] The scheme provided for maintaining the existing machinery for collecting the produce in the colonies and for bringing it to Britain. The Controller was then to assume authority over it immediately on its arrival in England, taking it over at a fixed price, determining the uses to which it should be put and selling it to approved consumers. The actual machinery of purchase and sale was to be carried out on behalf of the Controller by a limited number of produce brokers, who for their services would be remunerated by commission. Before Bigland had a chance of failing or succeeding in this programme of 'state socialism', the scheme was abandoned in April 1917, the ostensible reason being that speculation had driven up prices so rapidly that it was essential to do something to stop the increase.[84] The most likely reason was the hostility of the Liverpool merchants, who were aware that the measure was aimed at them.

Since this complex scheme could not be adopted immediately Bigland introduced a scheme forbidding all wholesale purchases and sales of vegetable oils in the United Kingdom except under licence. This scheme came into force by an order of the Minister of Munitions on 1 May 1917. In spite of protest by the Colonial Office based on a technical point that the Munitions Ministry was dabbling in affairs that were outside its jurisdiction, the measure stood. Bigland fixed the maximum price of palm kernels at £26 a ton at Liverpool, £26 10s. a ton at Hull and that of palm oil at £44 net.[85] The Colonial Office agreed to these prices on the basis that they gave the merchant a price that would enable him to pay a fair, though not a high, price on the coast and yet have a margin above a bare profit, from which he could meet the steadily growing cost of his business, freight, casks, bags and insurance.

In July 1917 the oils and fats department was transferred back to the Ministry of Food and the Controller became director of the oils and fats section of the ministry, thus gaining more power and becoming just like any other head of a government department. Although Bigland was replaced as director, he was retained as a sort of adviser.

The whole situation changed at the end of August 1917 as a result of a visit to England by Monsieur Clementel, the French Minister of Commerce. A draft agreement for the establishment of a joint 'Anglo-French Oils and Fats Buying Executive'[86] was referred to an interdepartmental committee. The proposal was fraught with difficulties, since if France was to get a large supply of oil and fats, which of course was the French object of putting forward the proposal, Britain would apparently lose whatever France got, and large questions such as the possibility of the British Government's admitting the principle of equality of privations among the Allied nations, and French policies as regards shipping freights and prices to consumers, naturally came up, and these were bound to affect the West African colonies. The policy of the Ministry of Food was to endeavour to ensure that the necessary commodities should be sold to the consumer as cheaply as possible, and with this in mind they desired to obtain from the Ministry of Shipping 'Blue Book' rates of freight and to introduce a system of controlling produce from its source wherever they could do so, in order to limit to a reasonable figure the profits of each party through whom the produce passed and to reduce the number of those parties to the necessary minimum.

The view of the French Government on the other hand was not in accordance with the view of the Ministry of Food. The French Government appeared to have failed to control effectively their own ships and prices of oils and fats in France were very much higher than they were in Britain. Monsieur Clementel's argument was that it was a mistake (which Britain would regret after the war) to reduce freight rates below the ordinary market level by government chartering of ships at Blue-Book rates and through that and other means, such as controlling profits, to reduce or keep at low level the prices of commodities in Great Britain because the result would be that when peace came and war restrictions on freight and profits were relaxed there would be a sudden increase in freight and other charges and consequently a large increase in prices for consumers, which would be bad for Britain and cause discontent.[87]

Acting as if they were following the French example, the Ministry of Shipping in 1917 increased the rates from Lagos to Liverpool, for example, on groundnuts from £2 8s. per ton to £12 a ton, a five-fold increase.[88] Since the Ministry of Shipping paid Blue-Book rates to owners of requisitioned ships and themselves took the remainder, the ministry representing His Majesty's government was making a large profit. The ministry did this because merchants paid £2 10s. per ton for groundnuts in Lagos and sold them at £32 per ton in Liverpool.[89]

What really interested the Colonial Office was whether the Ministry of Shipping alone should benefit by the reduction through government action of the profits which the great difference between the prices in Nigeria and in England was giving to the merchants who had managed to ship their groundnuts. There was no reason why the profit should not have been shared between the government of the producing country and the government of the consuming country – either by the former imposing export duty and the Ministry of Shipping reducing the freight rates by an equivalent amount or by some arrangement for pooling and sharing the profits obtained on the freight rates.[90] The export duties imposed on palm kernels and palm oil in 1916 were bringing in useful revenue to Nigeria. The Colonial Office did not at that time impose duty on groundnuts because Lugard wanted to replace loss of import duties on spirits by export duties on produce from gin-drinking districts and not to tax the produce of northern provinces, where spirits were barred. The Colonial Office was also doubtful whether Nigerian groundnuts could stand an export duty, handicapped as they were by a long rail journey to the coast and being considerably farther from England and France than the groundnuts of Gambia and Senegal; the Colonial Office could not foresee the extraordinary rise in price of groundnuts, since in 1916 the price in Liverpool was £18 per ton compared with £32 a ton in 1917.[91]

If the Anglo-French Joint Executive proposal went through, there would still be a question of division of profits to be settled, for under the scheme of joint buying executive, as provisionally arranged, the joint executive would sell to other countries, Allied or neutral, such vegetable oils as were not needed by Britain and France. The idea was that this profit should be shared between the British and French Governments in proportion to the value of total purchase of oil-producing nuts and seeds from British and French possessions respectively.

Apparently the Ministry of Food as represented by Alfred Bigland was against any co-operation with the French. The Ministry's idea of reducing the prices of produce in England through the adoption of Blue-Book rates of freight and the systematic limitation of profits was designed to defeat the joint executive by presenting the French members with a *fait accompli*, which (they might urge) the British Government could not agree to disturb again by putting up prices.

As far as the Colonial Office was concerned Bigland's proposals raised some important questions affecting jurisdiction. The Colonial Office decided it would insist that the Ministry of Food must confine its functions of control to Britain and that if it was desired that prices in colonies or the countries to which produce might be shipped be regulated, that regulation would have to be done not by the Ministry of Food but by the Colonial Office. The Colonial Office also took the stand that any policy of the Ministry of Food that might appreciably affect either the producers – who in this case were practically all Africans – or the trade of any colony should be submitted to the Colonial Office before it was decided upon so that steps might be taken to safeguard colonial interests.

There were two methods of buying produce required in England: either through the government of the colony or through special agents in the colony who might act as sole buyer on behalf of the Ministry of Food; or the existing machinery of merchant firms might be utilised but their prices and profits controlled. The first arrangement was adopted in the case of the 1916–17 Egyptian cotton-seed crop, and a much smaller instance was the purchase through the Ceylon government of coconut oil for Britain.[92] The Ministry of Food entirely agreed with buying through a colonial government or other single agency in the colony and cutting out merchants.

This was really the point of the whole scheme. If it was possible to utilise the existing machinery of merchant firms, while controlling strictly their operations, there were considerable advantages from the colonial point of view, to say nothing of the interests of Britain, in doing so; if the merchant were cut out and left with only his trade in imports into the colony and the war continued for any considerable time the disorganisation of the ordinary machinery of trade in colonial produce might be serious for the colony when the war finally ended. The export business of West African merchants would have disappeared and not only would the machinery be disorganised and take time to reconstruct but there would be an unnecessarily free field for 'enemy' trade. In this sense the use and control of the existing merchants seemed to be in the national interest.

Alfred Bigland's idea was that, at any rate as far as West Africa was concerned, an association of merchants should be formed comprising as far as possible all merchants engaged in the trade, and that this association should provisionally settle between themselves the share of the trade to be carried out by each member. This provisional allocation would of course not be final until approved by the Ministry of Food. It seems clear that in such an association control would inevitably rest with the big, old-established firms whose relations with one another had been so close since the outbreak of war. It would be in the interests of these firms to do all they could to squeeze out their competitors and, having regard to their policy in the past, they would no doubt endeavour to do so. Since Alfred Bigland said the basis of allocation of trade among members of the association should be the amount of trade they did during a series of years, for example 1913 to 1916, the firms that had entered Nigeria after the expulsion of the Germans would be squeezed out. This plan also would rule out the 'native' firms who had no representatives in England and could hardly be expected to join an association formed in London.

The Colonial Office was not sure whether this complicated system of control would work, but nevertheless decided that the Governor-General of Nigeria should be consulted.[93] Walter Long asked for Lugard's views on the Ministry of Food's proposal for control through the colonial government, and the proposed Anglo-French buying executive. He went on to say that in view of the increase in freight rates on West African produce ordered by the Ministry of Shipping, he would like Lugard to find out exactly what a fair producer price would be, so that chiefs and government political officers in the interior of the country could be told what the fixed prices were. In order to ensure fair prices to

49

Nigerian producers, furthermore, the Secretary of State wanted the barter system suppressed.

With regard to fixed minimum price of produce for each centre, Lugard said this was impossible to determine, since producers hardly sold direct to European merchants. Purchases were for the most part made from middlemen and brokers; Lugard felt it would be impossible to create machinery to ensure that the producer received fixed prices. He was of the opinion that even if prices were fixed at each main centre the producer would still sell to the middlemen as he had done from time immemorial and the latter would pay less than the minimum price fixed at the capital, which was a good business practice if he was to make profit; Lugard was afraid that the middleman would tell the ignorant peasant farmers that the government had forbidden a higher price. This would be repeated from village to village and would create a bitter animus against the government. But assuming that centres where fixed prices operated were practicable, Lugard felt that such a system would restrict and hamper trade by confining the markets to those places for which prices could be fixed, and it would also involve supervision which could not be afforded during the war. The practice would no doubt divert trade from its natural channels and would greatly disorganise it.

With regard to sharing what one colonial official called the 'shipping plunder',[94] Lugard said that if any restrictions were placed on prices paid for produce, the only recipient should be the colonial government 'which is the direct trustee for merchants and natives alike'. He was opposed to the Anglo-French buying executive as well as to the Ministry of Food's proposal to use the colonial government as a buying agent. He said he had 'no desire to substitute a state monopoly in which government would be a partner'.[95]

Full control of the home market and indirectly the colonial market came into force on 1 July 1918 when the 'United Kingdom Oil Seed Products Association Ltd' was formed,[96] at the request and with the backing of the Ministry of Food. It was a 'combine' of vegetable, nut and seed crushers, and margarine and soap makers. The association was not welcome to the West African merchants but there was nothing they could do about it. The association was given the power:

(a) to control and regulate, or to assist in the control or regulation of the trade of seed crushers, oil extractors and oil refiners in

such a manner as may be deemed expedient by the Food Controller, or other competent authority in the National interests
and to this end to exercise all such powers and functions as may
from time to time be vested in the controller or other competent
authority.

(b) to purchase, acquire, sell, manufacture, distribute, realise and
dispose of and deal in or make, vary, put an end to, or release
arrangements made by members of the Association for the
purchase, acquisition, sale, manufacture, distribution, realisation,
disposal and dealing in all oils, oil seeds, nuts, kernels, their
resultant products and other articles in respect of which the
Food Controller . . . may make orders, or regulations under the
Defence of the Realm Act or otherwise, and for this purpose to
make, manage, vary, carry out and give effect to any arrangements with the Food Controller . . .[97]

The Association was to remain until the end of the war and would
disband when orders to that effect came from the government –
this did not happen until October 1919.[98]

The purchasing of vegetable oil nuts and seeds in West Africa
remained in the hands of the merchants, but they were hemmed
in by the condition that they could sell their purchases only
to the Food Ministry through the association at fixed prices.

This government control led to a slowing down in purchases
in Nigeria. Palm oil bought in the western provinces showed a
decrease of forty-two per cent, and in the central and eastern
provinces there was a decrease of twenty-two per cent in palm
oil and fourteen per cent in palm kernels in the 1917–18 buying
season. With the depreciation in money, the price being paid was
not only low but had very little purchasing power. The whole
operation – the maintenance of cheap prices in Britain, export
prohibitions in West Africa and high shipping freight rates – was
prejudicial to the oil-palm industry in Nigeria. But some officials
in Nigeria felt that the minimum prices paid for palm kernels
and palm oil should not be increased, fearing that if producers
got more for their labour they might stop harvesting since it was
wrongly conjectured that producers' wants were limited. The
same official argued that the producer price of groundnuts needed
to be increased to stimulate bigger plantation and export.[99] This
recommendation was based on the erroneous belief that not much
labour was expended in collecting palm fruits whereas groundnuts
required much more attention.

In many cases war tends to stimulate economic development,

51

especially in the realm of industrialisation and intelligent use of local resources when imports are difficult to get. This happened to a certain extent in Nigeria and led to substantial saving of money. The war and the scarcity of imported goods in general led Nigerian authorities to look carefully at local materials before clamouring for goods from Britain.[100] There was a certain absurdity, for example, in importing meat when large herds, estimated at about three million head of cattle and some six and a quarter million sheep and goats, roamed the savannah of Northern Nigeria. Thousands of pounds were saved on coal from 1917 onwards when the colliery at Udi became operational. The government erected sawmills to provide good timber for furniture instead of importing it. A carpentry workshop was established in Lagos to make furniture for all government houses. Limestone was discovered in several places in Nigeria, including a site eleven miles from the coal field, where it could be cheaply burnt and transported by rail. Limestone was also found at Itobi, twenty miles below Lokoja, and the government decided to make use of the various deposits to make cement because of the prohibitive prices charged by importing firms. Roofing tiles were produced to replace iron sheets, which were hardly obtainable during the war. All these saved the government thousands of pounds.[101]

The economy was sustained by an export duty on three staples – increased to six in 1918 – and by the twenty-five per cent surtax on all imports, and a surtax of thirty per cent on railway freights from 1917 onwards. There was increase also in the yield of direct taxation in the north and in Yorubaland (excluding Egbaland); the high prices of tin resulted in increased royalties. All these factors led to an increase in the revenue of Nigeria in 1917 over that of the previous two years.[102]

THE EMPIRE RESOURCES DEVELOPMENT COMMITTEE

As a result of the attention Nigeria had received during the war, first as an edible oil producing area and again as an area of immense economic potentialities following the debates over the sale of German property in Nigeria, coupled with the development of the idea of a United Empire which the war had fostered, many schemes for the economic development of Nigeria and other West African colonies came into being.

A propagandist body called the Empire Resources Development Committee was established, with the self-appointed duty of making the British people and government realise the vast opportunity in West Africa and particularly in Nigeria, the principal supplier of vegetable oils. The committee was an amorphous one but it included many important men in business and government and, not surprisingly, people connected with war-time control in the Ministry of Food. Lord Milner belonged to it.[103] Their idea was no less than that the vast territories of the Crown should pay off the British war debt. In order to realise this objective, the resources of the Crown territories would have to be developed by the 'state', not by the local colonial governments, not even by the imperial government but by corporations of practical businessmen acting on behalf of the imperial government and paying into the British Treasury an adequate share of the profits.[104]

The people behind this idea were influenced by their connection with chartered companies and their knowledge of the huge concessions granted to companies in the Belgian Congo and French Equatorial Africa. 'Think what it would mean', exclaimed Alfred Bigland, an important member of the Committee, 'if all the products of West Africa, mineral and vegetable were controlled for the benefit of the Empire as a whole, think how huge is the potential profit which could be devoted to the service of the Empire's debt! . . . it would be a splendid means of facilitating the civilisation of natives as their labour would be harnessed to the chariot of progress and productiveness.'[105] Wilson Fox, M.P., Secretary of the Empire Resources Development Committee, arguing for a more thorough utilisation of the man-power in British colonies wrote: 'the native population of our tropical possessions . . . may properly be included in any review of our undeveloped national assets.'[106] If natives were national assets just like property, he did not see why they should not be fully exploited to serve the Empire's needs.

The committee's proposal in essence was that Britain should adopt in the Crown Colonies and Protectorates, beginning with West Africa, a system of production, export and sale of tropical produce under concessions granted to businessmen. In what seems to have been a grandiose plan of state or imperial socialism, the businessmen granted concessions were not to be allowed a completely free hand in the disposal and accumulation of capital; rather, they were to be paid salaries and commissions and any surplus or profit was to be handed over to the imperial government. The committee even promised to reduce the working hours and increase the pay of the toiling masses of British labourers, apparently to secure the support of the Labour Party. The Labour Party was of course against any kind of exploitation of the colonies, as had been made known in the series of press releases they issued during the war; nevertheless, the idea of better pay for British labourers seems to have drawn some Labour sympathisers to the ranks of the committee. One of these was a certain Jesson, a Labour member of the London County Council who while supporting the programme of the committee said:

> the Empire Resources Development Committee has a scheme for paying for this war, without any increase in taxation, showing how we can develop wealth on a whole sale scale which will find work for everyone. That is the proposal that has been put to this meeting [the meeting was convened by the London Chamber of Commerce on 30 Jan. 1918 to hear an address by Alfred Bigland]. As a Labour man I want to see these problems dealt with peacefully and in the best interest of this country and the Empire.[107]

This movement is of particular importance to Nigeria because it was the unprecedented profits made on oil-palm products and groundnuts by private individuals that first attracted the attention of idealists and hard-headed imperialists. Had they succeeded, Nigeria with its abundant labour and land would have been the guinea-pig for their experiment.

The movement was resisted successfully by four groups, all of which had first-hand knowledge of West African conditions. These were the Association of West African Merchants, the Church Missionary Society, the Anti-Slavery and Aborigines' Protection Society, and literate Africans joined by the Governors of Nigeria and Gold Coast.[108] The British merchants, quite apart from any altruistic motives, opposed the committee since most attacks on the *status quo* were aimed at them. In one of a series of articles Wilson Fox, the Secretary, stated:

> ... my committee sees no reason in principle why the state should not be directly interested in selected commercial concerns which would stand in no different position in relation to the government of the territory in which the state has no direct interest. It is quite reasonable that in the natural development of the Empire as a whole the state should in the future retain for itself some of the profits which now go into the pockets of private individuals.[109]

The West African merchants had plausible arguments to counteract the effect of the propaganda of the Development Committee. They contended that to attain the goals aimed at would entail finding a huge working capital to start with, which meant that the National Debt would be increased by some hundreds of millions of pounds before Bigland, Fox and company could begin to reduce it. They claimed that even the control then existing went beyond reasonable limits and that the merchants were threatened

> with a most fantastic and gigantic trading monopoly ... the essence of which was a proposal to make West Africa a milk cow and out of it squeeze a huge profit ... the illuminating manifestoes emanating from the Empire Resources Committee might be treated with the contempt they deserved, were it not that nothing in these days seems too extravagant a fad to obtain a hearing. It seems extraordinary that just when the world was face to face with the greatest cataclysm known to mankind, it should seem to anyone to be an opportune moment to try and rearrange everything down even to their weights and measures.[110]

Sir Hugh Clifford had this to say about the movement:

> It appears to me as rather comic that any person connected with so unfortunate an experiment in Colonial Administration as the government of Rhodesia should aspire to teach Great Britain the principles upon which the Crown Colonies and Protectorates should be ruled and managed. When these are found on examination to be the principles to which the Dutch in the Malayan Archipelago have steadily adhered, but which the British discarded finally (except in the case of some chartered companies of modern origin) before the end of the 18th century the thing becomes more ludicrous still. I know of few people who, from my point of view, are more radically unsound on all questions connected with Colonial Administration than Mr. Fox, and I hope that it will only be across the dead bodies of all of us that his highly mischievous and I think immoral policy will ever be adopted.[111]

Lugard was no less contemptuous of members of the Committee than was Clifford. In a reply to Clifford's letter Lugard wrote that Wilson Fox and Bigland wanted to 'charterise' the colonies. He added: 'Had I thought that they would command any serious attention I might have gone further [i.e., in earlier criticisms], but I imagined that they were so manifestly opposed to all British

tradition . . . that I put them aside as unworthy of serious treatment . . . I now learn to my surprise that Milner claims to be their
originator. He like the others . . . have from their connection with
South Africa imbibed many South African principles which I have
opposed for the last 20 years or more.'[112]

The Empire Resources Development movement might have
succeeded, taking into consideration the important men involved
and its pseudo-socialist appeal, were it not that organised religion,
African opinion,[113] humanitarians and the colonial governors
were against it. In addition, the ideological trend of the post-war
era was decidedly not in its favour.

When finally the war ended in November 1918 Nigeria, in
spite of the post-war economic boom and the Allied powers'
demand for her exports[114] of vegetable oil producing nuts, was
faced with many economic problems. Public works and railways
had been starved of capital; their needs had become cumulative
and by the end of the war the government found itself confronted
with a programme of expenditure almost every item of which
taken separately could be shown to be a matter of pressing urgency,
and which collectively presented demands that clearly could not
be satisfied. Although Nigeria ended the war with its balance
sheet on the credit side,[115] this was achieved at a great price in
terms of the almost permanent damage done to the transportation
grid of the country. In view of the crying need for capital after
the war Lugard's successor, Sir Hugh Clifford, said Nigeria could
not honour the promise of six million pounds that Lugard had in
1916 committed Nigeria to pay as part of her share of the imperial
war debt. The Colonial Office accepted Clifford's disavowal with
the proviso that if Nigeria should decide she was financially
capable of honouring Lugard's pledge, the Colonial Office would
be happy to receive her contribution.[116]

The economic hardship caused by the war and the various
attempts by British monopolies and combines to depress prices
artificially and the advocacy by responsible British politicians of
what were considered racist policies in West Africa, particularly
those of the Empire Resources Development Committee, gave
added point to the criticisms of the colonial regime by educated
Africans.

Notes

1 C.O. 583/39/504, Harding's minute on estimates for 1916, 7 Feb. 1916.
2 C.O. 583/17/29836, A. J. Harding's minute, 12 Aug. 1914. One-third of Nigeria's total revenue came from customs duties which amounted to £1,138,305 in 1913. The total amount of spirits was over 4 million gallons, with Rotterdam accounting for 3 million, Hamburg 1 million and Liverpool 60,000 gallons.
3 C.O. 583/45/20906, A. J. Harding's minute, 17 May 1916. The actual revenue from direct taxation in 1914 was £299,002.
4 C.O. 583/33/36251, Lugard to Colonial Office, 19 May 1915. The German firms were (1) Behrens & Wehner & Co. (2) Bey & Zimmer & Co. (3) Deutsche Kamerun Gesellschaft (4) Oskar Kaiser & Co. (5) Paul Guericke & Co. (6) J. W. Jackel & Co. (7) W. Mertens & Co. (8) Paul Meyer & Co. (9) Niger-Benue Transport Co. (10) Holtman & Co. (11) Morin & Co. (12) Ring & Co. (13) Witt and Busch & Co. (14) German West Africa Trading Co. (15) L. Pagenstecher & Co. (16) G. L. Gaiser & Co. (17) Woermann Linie (18) Lohmann and Vietor & Co. (19) Sachse & Co.
5 C.O. 583/73/13284, undated August 1918, 'enemy firm in liquidation' memo on Charles Ungebauer by T. F. Burrowes. See also Ernst Hieke, *G. L. Gaiser: Hamburg-Westafrika: 100 Jahre Handel mit Nigeria*, Hamburg, 1949, pp. 5–37, hereafter cited as Hieke, *Gaiser*.
6 C.O. 583/33/28178, Lugard to Colonial Office, 25 May 1915.
7 E. Hieke, *Gaiser*, p. 38.
8 Cd. 8247, 1916, iv, 15: Report of Committee on Edible and Oil-producing Nuts and Seeds, pp. 12–13.
9 C.O. 583/33/28174, Lugard to Colonial Office, 28 May 1915.
10 C. A. Birtwistle (Commercial Intelligence officer in Southern Nigeria), Report on British trade in Southern Nigeria, 24 Aug. 1912, in Cd. 6771, 1913, lxviii, 361.
11 In 1911, for example, 197 German ships with a total tonnage of 339,507 tons visited Nigeria compared with 347 English vessels having a total tonnage of 476,175 tons. From this it can be seen that the German ships were larger than and superior to the British. See microfilm A9. V.68, *Denkschrift über die Bedeutung des deutschen Handels mit West Afrika*, Firmenarchiv – Hamburgisches Weltwirtschaftsarchiv, Hamburg, Germany.
12 C.O. 583/17/31122, Harding's minute of 10 Sept. 1914. The total value of all produce exported in 1913 was £7,097,646 of which £3,693,941 went to Germany, including £2,005,626 worth of palm kernels.
13 C.O. 583/19/44174, Harding's minute of 27 Aug. 1914.
14 C.O. 583/19/44174, Harding's minute of 27 Aug. 1914. 14 per cent of total imports came from Germany and 0·02 per cent from Austria

in 1913. The Commercial Intelligence Officer, A. Birtwistle, predicted in 1912 that the Germans would catch up with Britain in 1922; see Cd. 6771, 1913, lxviii, 361: Report on British trade in Southern Nigeria, p. 9.

15 *Ibid.*

16 Dane-guns were flintlocks, they were originally introduced into West Africa by the Danes around the 17th century and this gave the name 'dane gun' to the particular type of gun.

17 C.O. 583/19/44174, memo on goods of German and Austrian origin imported into Nigeria, by C. A. Birtwistle, 20 Oct. 1914.

18 *Ibid.*

19 C.O. 583/20/47126, Lugard to Colonial Office, 6 Nov. 1914.

20 C.O. 583/20/45046, Lugard to Colonial Office, 15 Nov. 1914.

21 C.O. 583/17/31122, Harding's minute, 10 Sept. 1914.

22 Cd. 8247, 1916, iv, 15, p. 7.

23 C.O. 583/17/29836, Lugard (writing from London) to Colonial Office, 10 Aug. 1914.

24 C.O. 583/17/31122, Strachey's minute, 21 Aug. 1914.

25 C.O. 583/19/44174, Lugard to Colonial Office, 27 Aug.1914.

26 C.O. 583/25/33348, Niger Company to Lugard, 2 Sept. 1914.

27 C.O. 583/25/33348, Harding's minute, 4 Sept. 1914.

28 C.O. 583/20/48789, Lugard to Colonial Office, 20 Nov. 1914; 'Estimates of revenue and expenditure' for 1915.

29 C.O. 583/18/42162, Harding's minute, 15 Nov. 1914. By 30 Sept. 1914, £790,013 had been spent on the eastern Nigerian railway project out of the estimated cost for the entire line of £3,927,260. Thus if work were to continue £3,137,000 would have to be found within the next three or four years. About £416,000 was needed to complete the Lagos harbour works and £98,000 still remained to be spent on the Lagos Water Works; the railway shops at Kaduna as well as water supply for both Kaduna and Kano were estimated to cost £310,000 and £117,800 respectively. The Kaduna capital had cost £31,949 9s. 8d. in 1913 and stores worth up to £125,000 had been purchased against 1914. The exact estimate for the Kaduna capital was not known.

30 C.O. 583/41/6774, Harding's minute of 23 Feb. 1915. On 31 Dec. 1913 the position of the Nigerian economy using round figures was that Nigeria had a public debt of £8,267,500. The amount spent from loan funds up to 31 Dec. 1913 was £5,755,823 for railway construction, £482,748 for Lagos Harbour Works, £81,301 for Lagos Wharfage Scheme, £213,576 for Lagos Water Works and £226,086 for other public works. Balance of loan funds available was £1,111,500, which was invested to await use; ordinary surplus funds also invested in stocks stood at £1,164,500, making a total of £2,276,000. The ordinary surplus funds were not easily realisable unless at a loss because they were invested in stocks; only the £1,111,500 unused loan funds were available. Before 1916 Nigeria would have to borrow about £4,223,000 to pay off the unconverted 5-year debentures issued in 1911. In short, Nigeria was over-

committed and since money could not be raised publicly, many of
the pre-war development programmes had to be shelved.

31 C.O. 583/17/29836, Lewis Harcourt, Secretary of State for the
Colonies, minute of 17 Aug. 1914.

32 C.O. 583/20/48789, Lugard to Colonial Office, 20 Nov. 1914. The
customs duties on tobacco rose from 8*d*. per pound to 1*s*. Rice was
taxed for the first time and the duty levied was 1*s*. per cwt. Stockfish
was also taxed and the duty was 1*s*. 6*d*. per cwt.; timber wood 1*s*.
per a hundred superficial feet. Duty on an imperial gallon of kerosene
also increased by 1*d*. A surtax of 25 per cent was imposed on all other
articles. Trade spirit, which in 1914 had a customs duty of 300 per
cent was left untaxed. A total sum of £170,000 was expected from
this increase.

33 *Ibid*. For instance the price of palm kernels jumped from £13 11*s*.
in 1908 to £23 5*s*. in 1913.

34 C.O. 583/45/20906, Foreign Office to Colonial Office, 8 April 1916.

35 C.O. 583/24/45997, Board of Agriculture and Fisheries to Colonial
Office, 21 Nov. 1914.

36 *Ibid*.

37 C.O. 583/26/34701, R. E. Dennett, Deputy Chief Conservator of
Forests in Southern Nigeria, gave a lecture to Royal Societies Clubs
on 'palm kernel trade and Great Britain', 11 Sept. 1914.

38 Cd. 8247, 1916, iv, 15, p. 21. In 1915 fifteen ships arrived at Hull
direct from Lagos for the first time with palm kernels valued at
£681,408, weighing 42,549 tons. London also took 8,729 tons valued
at £146,245, and Liverpool took 178,060 tons valued at more than
one million pounds.

39 Cd. 8247, 1916, iv, 15, p. 23. Members of the Select Committee
were:
Arthur Steel-Maitland (Chairman)
Sir George Fiddes (Colonial Office)
Sir Owen Philipps (Chairman, Elder Dempster & Co.)
G. A. Moore and T. Walkden (representing London, Liverpool
and Manchester Chambers of Commerce)
Sir W. G. Watson
Leslie Couper (Manager, Bank of Britain West Africa)
Professor Wyndham R. Dunstan (Director, Imperial Institute)
T. Middleton (Board of Agriculture)
T. Worthington (Commercial Intelligence Branch, Board of Trade)
T. Wiles, Liberal M.P. for Islington.

40 *Ibid*. Minority Report by T. Wiles, M.P.

41 *The Times*, 4 Aug. 1916; see also Parliamentary Debates (*Hansard*),
3 Aug. 1916, *v* 85, 529–66.

42 Cd. 8247, 1916, iv, 15, p. 23.

43 *Manchester Guardian*, 17 July 1916.

44 C.O. 583/31/15673, Lugard to Colonial Office, 13 March 1915.

45 *Ibid*.

46 *Ibid*.

47 *Ibid*.

48 *Ibid.* Grier (Resident of Ibadan) enclosure in Lugard to Colonial Office, 13 March 1915.

49 Sir George Fiddes, G.C.M.G., K.C.M.G., born 1858. Joined Colonial Office 1881; Imperial Secretary and accountant to Sir Alfred Milner (High-Commissioner for South Africa) 1897; Political Secretary to Lord Roberts at Pretoria 1900; Secretary, Transvaal Administration 1900; returned to the Colonial Office as Principal Clerk 1902; Assistant Under Secretary of State for the Colonies 1916; retired 1921.

50 *Ibid.* Sir George Fiddes's minute, 19 April 1915.

51 *Ibid.* Sir John Anderson's minute, 19 April 1915.

52 C.O. 583/39/504, Colonial Office to Lugard, 7 Feb. 1916.

53 C.O. 583/50/842, Lugard to Colonial Office, 17 Feb. 1917. The following table gives an idea of the fall in revenue up to 1916.

Year	Total Revenue	Expenditure
1913	£3,462,507	£2,917,602
1914	£3,048,381	£3,596,764
1915	£2,703,258	£3,434,213

This fall was due to the decline in revenue from trade spirits.
The following figures give an idea of the rate of decline. Revenue from trade spirits:

1912	—	£1,015,000
1913	—	£1,140,000
1914	—	£924,000
1915	—	£648,000
1916	—	£373,000

54 C.O. 583/45/20906, Lugard to Colonial Office, 8 April 1916. The following table gives an idea of the reduction in the prices paid and the profit made on Nigeria's main staples.

Pre-war price per ton

Produce	Nigeria (Lagos)		Liverpool	
	£	s.	£	s.
Palm oil	14	15	19	5
Palm kernel	21	11	29	11
Cocoa (per cwt.)	1	12	2	7
Groundnut	8	0	20	0

War-time per ton

	Nigeria (Lagos)		Liverpool	
	£	s.	£	s.
	16	17	44	0
	9	10	26	0
	1	17	3	8
	2	10	16	0

From this it can be seen that the profit made ranged from more than 100 per cent to over 700 per cent though allowance must be made for increased shipping freight rate and insurance.

55 C.O. 583/45/20906, Sir George Fiddes's minute, 25 July 1916.
56 *Ibid.*, Harding's minute, 17 May 1916.
57 *Ibid.*, Lugard to Colonial Office, 8 April 1916.
58 C.O. 583/48/41330, Lugard to Colonial Office, 30 Aug. 1916. Export duties of £2 6s. 8d. per ton on cocoa, £2 per ton on palm oil, £1 2s 6d. per ton on palm kernel were imposed and the revenue expected to accrue from this source was estimated at £276,000.
59 C.O. 583/53/37164, Lugard to Colonial Office, 4 Aug. 1916. The firms involved were Miller Bros. Liverpool Ltd, African Association Ltd, the Company of African Merchants, The African Traders Co. Ltd, Paterson Zochonis & Co. Ltd, John Holt & Co. Ltd, Holt Bros. & Co. Ltd, Thomas Welsh & Co., McNeil Scott & Co., H. B. W. Russell & Co., the Lagos Stores Ltd, G. B. Ollivant & Co., W. B. MacIver & Co. Ltd, F. and A. Swanzy Ltd, and a French company, Compagnie Française de l'Afrique Occidentale.
60 *Ibid.*
61 C.O. 583/30/2475, Lugard to Colonial Office, 15 Jan. 1915.
62 *Ibid.*
63 *Ibid.*
64 C.O. 583/38/59211, Lugard to Colonial Office, 4 Dec. 1915.
65 C.O. 583/43/57279, Lugard to Colonial Office, 11 Dec. 1915.
66 *Ibid.*
67 C.O. 583/49/55579, A. G. Boyle to Colonial Office, 31 Oct. 1916, enclosing a memo by A. S. Cooper, General Manager Nigerian Railway, 20 Oct. 1916.
68 *Ibid.*
69 C.O. 583/45/20906, Harding's minute, 25 July 1916.
70 *The Times*, 9 Nov. 1916. L. Scott, Unionist M.P. for Liverpool, to the Editor.
71 C.O. 583/53/54100, Association of West African Merchants to Colonial Office, 9 Nov. 1916.
72 Charles Wilson, *The History of Unilever: a Study in Economic Growth and Social Change*, London, 1954, i, p. 181.
73 *Ibid.*, p. 237.
74 C.O. 554/36/60567, Ministry of Food to Colonial Office, 7 Dec. 1917.
75 Wilson, *op. cit.*, p. 388.
76 *Ibid.*, p. 239.
77 *Ibid.*, p. 253. Lever Bros. bought the Niger Company for a sum of about £8,000,000 in July 1920, which Lever Bros. later found out was almost a ruinous price.
78 C.O. 583/55/14179, Lugard to Colonial Office, 29 Dec. 1917.
79 C.O. 554/35/47011, Harding's minute, 14 Sept. 1917. *Colonial Office List* 1919, (Waterlow & Sons, London), p. 294. Total value of exports for

1913	—	£7,097,646
1914	—	£6,420,461
1915	—	£4,946,228
1916	—	£6,029,546
1917	—	£8,602,486

80 Cmd. 468, 1919, xxxiv, 609: Lugard Report, p. 32.

81 C.O. 554/34/5777, W. A. F. Wickhart, assistant secretary, West African Currency Board, Nov. 1917.

82 Alfred Bigland (1855–1936), was one of the earliest adherents of Chamberlain's Tariff Reform League. He stood for parliament in 1910 as a Tariff Reformer in East Birkenhead and won; he retained the seat until 1922. He was Chairman of the Empire Development Parliamentary Committee (1921), Assistant Director of the Propellant Branch of the Ministry of Munitions to provide glycerine for cordite (1916). He became Controller of Oils and Fats under Lord Rhondda in 1917.

83 C.O. 554/35/47011, Harding's memo, 14 Sept. 1917.

84 *Ibid.*

85 C.O. 554/38/28949, H. J. Read, Assistant Permanent Under Secretary, Colonial Office, to Ministry of Food, 8 July 1918.

86 C.O. 554/35/47011, Harding's memo, 14 Sept. 1917.

87 *Ibid.*

88 *Ibid.*

89 C.O. 583/45/20906, Lugard to Colonial Office, 8 April 1916.

90 In the case of Australia and New Zealand the Dominions got half of the profits on wool assigned for non-military use. C.O. 554/35/47011, Harding's memo, 14 Sept. 1917.

91 C.O. 554/35/47011, Harding's memo on government control of oleaginous produce, 14 Sept. 1917.

92 *Ibid.*

93 C.O. 554/35/47011, Long to Lugard, 12 Oct. 1917.

94 C.O. 554/35/47011, Ellis minute, 17 Sept. 1917.

95 C.O. 554/33/56388, Lugard to Long, 21 Oct. 1917.

96 C.O. 554/39/35530, Ministry of Food to Colonial Office, 1 July 1918.

97 *Ibid.*

98 C.O. 554/41/61101, Ministry of Food to Colonial Office, 23 Oct. 1919.

99 C.O. 554/38/28949, H. J. Read (Assistant Permanent Under Secretary, Colonial Office) to Ministry of Food.

100 C.O. 554/37/5409, Boyle to Long, 20 Dec. 1918.

101 Cmd. 468, 1919, xxxiv, 609. Lugard's Report, p. 35. In 1913 £100,000 worth of coal was imported from United Kingdom and in 1917 it fell to £83,000, mainly imported by commercial houses and tin-mining companies. In 1913 £60,000 worth of timber was imported, reduced to £18,000 in 1917; £117,000 worth of iron sheets were imported in 1913, reduced to £19,554 in 1917.

102 *Colonial Office List*, 1919, p. 294.
Nigeria's tin production rose from 5,530 tons in 1913 to 9,966 tons in 1917, valued at £1,485,887. The total revenue rose thus:

> 1914: £6,420,461
> 1915: £4,946,228
> 1916: £6,029,546
> 1917: £8,602,486
> 1918: £9,511,970.

103 *West Africa*, 9 Feb. 1918, ii, 54, pp. 26–31. Alfred Bigland said Lord Milner was privy to the formation of the committee.
104 W. K. Hancock, *Survey of British Commonwealth Affairs*, ii, Oxford University Press, London, 1940. Part I, p. 107. The programme of the committee was published on 29 Jan. 1917 with 33 signatures.
105 Alfred Bigland, 'The Empire's Assets and how to use them'. *Journal of the Royal Society of Arts*, 30 March 1917, lxv, p. 358. The author was an M.P. and a member of the war-time government as Controller of Oils and Fats.
106 Hancock, *op. cit.*, p. 108. Wilson Fox was Managing Director of British South Africa Company which ruled Rhodesia until 1923. He wrote articles on the subject of Empire Resources Development in *The Times* of 28 Sept. 1917, *The Nineteenth Century and After*, Oct. 1917, and *United Empire*, Jan. 1918.
107 *West Africa*, 9 Feb. 1918, ii, 54, pp. 26–31.
108 *Lugard Papers*, i, pp. 121 and 123. Clifford and Lugard private notes of 7 Feb. 1918 (Clifford to Lugard) Lugard to Clifford, 21 May 1918. See also C.O. 583/88/29829, Clifford to Lord Milner, 29 May 1920.
109 H. Wilson Fox, Supplement to the *African World*, 9 Feb. 1918.
110 G. A. Moore, Chairman of the African section of Liverpool Chamber of Commerce, in *The African World*: Special West African Monthly Supplement, 8 Sept. 1917.
111 *Lugard Papers*, i, p. 121. Clifford to Lugard, 7 Feb. 1918.
112 *Lugard Papers*, i, p. 123. Lugard to Clifford, 21 May 1918.
113 See ch. 3.
114 C.O. 554/44/7252. Resolutions were adopted by French, Italian and British delegates at a conference held in Paris, 7–11 Dec. 1918, calling for an 'inter allied oil seeds Executive' to buy vegetable oils from Britain and French West Africa for distribution to the Allied powers according to their needs. The British later withdrew from the scheme, by forming a separate 'oils and fats council' in Jan. 1919 to look after British needs. See C.O. 554/44/7252, 29 Jan. 1919, Oils and Fats Council to Colonial Office.
115 C.O. 583/78/6883, Blue Book for 1918. In Dec. 1918 Nigeria had to her credit surplus funds amounting to £702,785 plus £321,482 belonging to the Native Administrations. Her public debt stood at £8,470,593 and accumulated sinking fund amounted to £580,071.
116 C.O. 583/79/69455, Clifford to Milner, 12 Nov. 1919.

3 The educated elite and the war

The attitude of educated Nigerians to British administration in Nigeria during Sir Frederick Lugard's Governorship can best be seen through their newspapers, various petitions to the Colonial Office and in the moderate opinions of the privileged few who were handpicked to represent the people either in the Legislative Council of the Colony of Lagos or in the Nigerian Council. These educated Nigerians were mostly lawyers and doctors but their ranks continued to be swelled by traders, skilled artisans and the products of the mission schools that proliferated in Southern Nigeria in the early twentieth century.[1] The number also increased in direct proportion to the economic opportunities which the opening up of Nigeria created, and by the influx of 'Creoles' from Sierra Leone and other 'Europeanised' Africans from the coast of English-speaking areas of West Africa, including Liberia. These people were heavily concentrated in Lagos, while a few others lived in Abeokuta, Ibadan, Calabar and Onitsha as well as along the coastal towns of the Niger Delta.

The educated Africans, as we have already noted, were totally against the policy of indirect rule to which Lugard was committed. When Lugard decided to 'up-grade' the Southern administration to the standard of that of Northern Nigeria, the *Lagos Weekly Record* commented, 'Lugard is a disappointment to Nigeria', and that he was 'A man whose walking stick is a pistol and whose thoughts by day and dreams by night are punitive expeditions and military patrols. Stirring tales were told of his negrophobia, his anti-black proclivities, his distant attitude to all men in general.'[2] In their opposition to specific policies of Sir Frederick Lugard and to the man himself, they could not conceal their admiration for British tradition and what they aspired towards was to become part of the Empire as full citizens enjoying equal rights with all others, white, brown or black.[3] One of the African lawyers criticising Lugard's sweeping judicial changes in Southern Nigeria brought out clearly how 'British' some of these people were. Lugard had argued that the English legal system was unsuitable for a primitive society like Nigeria. In answer to this Osho Davies, a lawyer, wrote:

> if that system stands condemned in Africa, why is it so much admired in every part of the habitable globe! Is the African not human, and is he so dense as not to be able to discern between what is evil and what is good? How many a time since, fifty years ago, Lagos was given the advantage of English justice, has a discordant tune been raised against the system; not once. Our cry is not against English justice, as we are bred to it, and love and admire it, but against the endeavour now being made to deprive us of that justice and relegate us back to the first ages of barbarism . . . for if English justice stands condemned in Africa it must necessarily be so in England herself, since, what is good for the goose is also good for the gander.[4]

The attitude of educated Africans to British rule was succinctly and sympathetically expressed by Sir William Geary when he wrote:

> the intelligentsia . . . is Christian and protestant mainly . . . still there is faithful and shrewd criticism of the administration. However, these African critics combine a hearty dislike and contempt for official methods with affectionate regard for England, just as many a good Christian has loathing for the clergy . . . the sound old system in West Africa was to consider the African as an 'English man with a black face' in return, the African used to talk of going 'home to England'. A snob might sneer: but this good feeling is the result of the statesmanship of Wilberforce and his friends . . . let us take care that no latter-day policy, or lesser man, and least of all any 'damn nigger' prejudice may undo the work of the great men of the past . . .[5]

It was precisely the bringing home to these people that they were not 'Englishmen with black faces' and that if they were, they had no right to claim to represent the illiterate Africans, that brought them into collision with the Lugardian administration.

It can thus be seen that an unbridgeable chasm lay between the educated elite and the Lugardian administration. One of the consistent points made by those opposed to the Lugard administration was that they had known better times under other governors and consequently considered Lugard as a reactionary bent on turning back the hands of the clock.

While the war softened the tone of criticism of the administration, 'patriotism' did not put an end to the vilification to which government officials, including the Governor-General and the Secretary of State himself, were subjected. The outbreak of the war coincided with the period of amalgamation which the press itself had championed with considerable enthusiasm, but the form of amalgamation and its manner of implementation filled them with dismay.

The reason for the belligerency of the Nigerian press is better understood when it is realised that the newspapers were all owned and edited by educated Africans in Lagos, the very element which was excluded deliberately from participation in government as a result of the indirect rule system. At the outbreak of war there were five weekly newspapers in Lagos edited and published by their owners, except the *Nigerian Pioneer* which was jointly edited by an English lawyer by the name of Irving[6] and Kitoyi Ajasa,[7] the owner of the paper. Other newspapers were the *Times of Nigeria*, owned and edited by James Bright Davies, the *Lagos Standard*, edited by George Williams, the *Lagos Weekly Record*, owned by the Liberian J. P. Jackson, but edited during the time of Lugard by his son, Horatio Jackson. The other newspaper was the *Nigerian Chronicle*, printed and published by Chris Johnson. Their appeal was directed to the whole country but only few could read outside Lagos Colony and a few Yoruba cities such as Abeokuta and Ibadan, while there were isolated pockets of readers scattered in coastal towns such as Warri, Sapele, Calabar and the Niger River port of Onitsha; the colonial administration at first took solace in this fact of limited readership.

The contempt for the administration as shown by the press attacks was matched by the administration's derision for the educated Nigerians. This can be seen in Major Lugard's writings; when describing the Durbar in Kano in honour of his brother, he wrote: 'the only type unrepresented here, I am thankful to say, is the trousered negro of the coast, the very black men in Bond Street attire – the black gentleman of Lagos who sends his laundry to England every week.'[8] There was just no point on which the educated people and the administration seemed to agree; the gap between the two was so wide that the 'truce' which prevailed at the outset of the war was soon broken.

This is the background against which the views of educated Africans had to be seen during the war years. The Governor-

General's notion that the newspapers' influence was confined to Lagos was a gross under-estimation of the influence of the press despite the limited readership. Lugard failed to realise the values illiterate Africans placed on the views of educated Africans. This was especially the case in Southern Nigeria of the time, when the ability to stand up to the rulers and exchange verbal blows in the imperial tongue enhanced a man's position and prestige in society. The extent to which information filtered into the interior of the country can be shown by the fact that events and issues concerning the southern provinces were known and discussed as far north as the Sudan.[9]

When war broke out Lugard seized the opportunity to press the Colonial Office to allow him to curtail the freedom of the press, which in his view amounted to scurrilous licence. He complained that even under the 'Defence of the Realm Act' enough provision was not made for the control of the press. He was of the opinion that the local newspapers had become too militant to be tolerated and that every week scrurrilous articles full of abuse of the King's local representatives were published. The whole tone of the Lagos newspapers, he asserted, was calculated to stir up racial enmity and to embitter the relations between Europeans and Africans. He went on to stress the danger of an uncontrolled press in such a partially educated community as that of Lagos. Lugard therefore asked for wide powers to deal with the situation because the officials so attacked were practically precluded from replying to 'wilful misrepresentations' and 'open letters' addressed to them by name, accusing them of incompetence and holding them up to derision.[10] Lugard fulminated 'that such letters should pass without replies and be read by half-educated youths', undermined the authority of the government.

Lugard therefore asked for permission from the Colonial Office to pass a law in Nigeria limiting the freedom of the press. Sir George Fiddes supporting Lugard minuted that he would agree with Lugard's proposals that he should enact an order, and send copies of it to other governors in West Africa telling them to pass similar laws. Sir George added '. . . at this juncture we ought not to add to our risks by allowing this poisonous press to inflame native minds'.[11] Sir John Anderson, while agreeing with Lugard and Sir George Fiddes, was of the opinion that there already existed sufficient legal provision[12] in Nigeria to deal with the situation. He went on to suggest that perhaps a law like that existing in India which obliged every newspaper to deposit a sum of money with the government which was forfeited if the newspaper published matters injurious to government might satisfy Lugard.[13] This was overruled in the best Liberal tradition by the Secretary of State, Lewis Harcourt, who minuted, 'I am not inclined to utilize war conditions for enacting press laws of a permanent nature which I should not assent to in peace time . . .'[14] This was not to be the end of the matter, however, for Lugard did not take defeat easily.

While this debate on press law was going on among the decision makers, the editors concerned, realising full well that censorship might be imposed, tried to sidestep direct control by offering a system of self-censorship. The editors met formally with F. S. James, the administrator of Lagos Colony, and assured him of their co-operation during the war. They also took the opportunity to pass the message to Lugard that he should not expect their co-operation unless he desisted from introducing 'vexatious measures'.[15] But since Lugard was not going to stop passing into law the 'Provincial Courts Ordinance and the Criminal Code over which educated Nigerians had differed, the *Lagos Weekly Record* took this as a sign that the administration was not ready to keep its word of honour. The paper commented, '. . . if we are under a moral obligation to refrain from criticising the government the latter is also under a moral obligation to refrain from springing any measures upon the people or adopting any actions calculated to evoke such criticisms'.[16] In another plea for moderation Bright Davies of the *Times of Nigeria* wrote that just as the hatchet was being buried for the time being in the agitation for Home Rule in Ireland until after the war, Nigerians would also desist from unnecessary agitation. He said, however, that the mere fact that British officials were not sure of African response to the patriotic appeal coming from the Governor-General constituted a clear condemnation of the regime, which he claimed had lost the confidence of the people:

> It would appear, from questions which were asked at the time when the declaration of war by England against Germany was announced here, that grave doubts were entertained in the minds of a few of our European fellow British subjects as to what our attitude towards themselves and the local administration is likely to be. This is not surprising, the fact that such ideas should occur to them is a clear

evidence that they were frightened at the grim spectre which the consciousness of their un-toward treatment of us as a subject people has brought up to their imagination ... the people of this country are not opposed to Sir Frederick Lugard personally . . . all our opposition is directed against his measures, not himself. It is because his legislative measures, his political administration, his educational policies, in fact the whole policy and principle of his administration bear such close resemblance to, or are in such intimate relations with German rule ... and they are so entirely un-British. The whole system is framed deliberately after the pattern of the German system. Herr Doctor Solf's declarations recently that Germany and Britain hoped to pursue the same policy in Africa, set the question completely at rest.[17]

It was the opinion of the *Times of Nigeria* that changes had taken place for the worse in the system of colonial administration. It lamented:

what a change has come over the British Colonial Office today! It was not so in the pre-Chamberlain era. Then the representations and complaints of grievances from the subject peoples under British rule in West Africa were treated with every consideration and dealt with on their merits and justice, strict justice was the rule, even Mr. Chamberlain was open to reason at times when faced with incontrovertible facts or unassailable arguments. The line of distinction between the present administration and that of German *Kultur* is hardly distinguishable, in fact it is imperceptible for the difference between its methods and its measures and those of German rule is merely one of degree and the cause of this is due to the present day laxity of control and restraint which were aforetime exerted to hold in check within the bounds of British traditional policy in the government of subject races, the vagaries of an administration and any exuberant and intolerant spirit of a governor which is working to the injury and oppression of the subject peoples over whom he is appointed to rule as the representative of the British government.[18]

The press was cleverly protesting loyalty and anti-German fervour and trying to tar Lugard with a pro-German brush, thus trying to create a situation in which the war-time psychology could be used to continue effective criticism of indirect rule and get changes in the direction of policy.

It was this kind of press attack that really hurt Lugard, yet there was much validity in the charge that he operated a 'legalised autocracy'. In their criticism of the government, the press called

for no violent opposition; in fact the most indomitable and
fearless of the editors, James Bright Davies, wrote:

> our agitation against the measures of the government is purely of a
> domestic character. We have the conception, that consciousness of
> our duty and our obligations to know and to have an intelligent
> appreciation that the larger interests of the Empire must prevail. If
> even we had need for an example, the warring elements in Ireland
> and in Parliament over Home Rule have set us a most admirable and
> excellent example. The only deplorable circumstance in this con-
> nection is that it seems uncertain that Sir Frederick Lugard will take
> the example of the Prime Minister in postponing the enactment of
> the provincial courts ordinance and other kindred ordinances until
> the present war is over. We take solace in the fact that the administra-
> tion of Sir Frederick Lugard will not last for ever. Who can forecast
> the results of this war? We hope the results would bring peace in a
> special degree for the peace of and contentment and freedom from
> oppression of the nations of Africa.[19]

While continuing to criticise the administration, some sections
of the Nigerian press like others in different parts of the Empire
waged verbal war against Germany. They denounced every
aspect of German life. They explained with considerable lucidity
the role the military establishment had played in German history.
In the rather flamboyant language of the West African press of
the time, the 'German mind', claimed the *Lagos Weekly Record*,
was

> diseased with and distorted by doctrines as regards the effectiveness
> of brute force and unspeakable terrorism . . . the bare mention of the
> name of Germany as a colonizing power in West Africa conjures up
> in the minds of the natives, a state of affairs which may be described
> as *pandemonium in mundo* and which invariably stirs from the depths
> of their souls the most repulsive feeling of horror, of intense disgust
> and acute bitterness against the fiendish orgies of German tropical
> rule.[20]

The *Nigerian Pioneer* writing on the same theme commented that
Germany's successes in the previous century made her drunk
with power and that 'with dreams of still greater greatness, she
suddenly and ruthlessly attacked with colossal strength and utter
disregard the very fabric of civilization'.[21]

The hard line taken towards Germany was not unusual for a
colonial press whose sale rose in accordance with the violence of
its language; moreover, the editors were no doubt genuine in

their belief that the British colonial system, if well applied, was more beneficial to the subject races than that of any other power. Educated Nigerians were convinced that the Lugardian phase was but a temporary aberration. Furthermore they were affected by British propaganda exposing the 'cruelty' of German soldiers in Belgium and those of German African troops in neighbouring Cameroons. The newspapermen also feared that if they persisted in attacking the British administration during the war, legislation might be brought in to suppress them.

The activities of the press were not confined to attacks on Germans, they also made positive contributions to the war effort, by encouraging a spirit of competition between the southern and the northern provinces in the donations and contributions of money to various organisations connected with the war. Following the refusal of some people in Egbaland and Lagos to contribute to the National Relief Fund because of the 'Ijemo massacre'* the *Lagos Weekly Record* in an untypical editorial came out praising the British colonial record. The paper commented:

> have we anything to offer in exchange for the benign influences of British imperial rule, whose watch words are liberty and progress? Do we not then owe a debt of deep gratitude towards Great Britain for the education, wealth and liberty she has so lavishly bestowed upon us at the greatest expenditure of men and money, and is not the balance sheet in her favour? . . . It is true we pour into her lap our rich resources of raw materials but she has paid for every pound of material thus exported. She did not extort by force these raw materials nor compel us to produce same at the point of the bayonet *à la mode congolaise* . . . It is only fair that we should always award them their full share of praise they may merit. Our policy should be that of 'give and take' and not that of 'confirmed growlers' especially as nothing is so instrumental in withholding the cup of mercy as base ingratitude. Therefore we are under a very heavy debt to Great Britain![22]

The paper also mentioned that the coast of Nigeria was being protected by the Royal Navy and that this had made it impossible for German marines to land and 'institute an inquisition; with which they are generally credited'.[23] This loyalty did not pass unnoticed by some members of the British administration in Nigeria: Major Lugard contemptuously commented 'the "civilized" tribes of the South including the trousered negro and our

* See chapter 4.

scurrilous Lagos press are busy praying for the success of British arms'.[24]

But not all sections of the press were transparently loyal to the British Crown. Before the war, Germans, because of their easy credit terms to African traders, were very popular in Lagos and in Yorubaland as a whole, and many Nigerians were sorry to see them go. It might be pointed out that British traders between 1880 and 1914 were often pro-German and anti-French, because of the protectionist policies of France in her Empire whereas the Germans, like the British, welcomed citizens of all nations to their colonies. In mundane terms, the expulsion of the Germans from Nigeria meant a loss of business and prosperity not merely to newspaper proprietors (who made money through German firms' advertisement fees) but to a large sector of the mercantile and agricultural communities. The press, in spite of the campaign against Germany, came out in defence of local German traders against any abuse of their persons or privilege. 'Amongst us,' commented the *Nigerian Pioneer*,

> 'are certain German subjects under the greatest misfortune that can fall upon people of martial race, that they cannot be in their own country when war has descended upon it ... Many of them have lived for many years in our country, engaged to the benefit of the population in missionary, medical and mercantile work, they are entitled to more than our chilvalry'

and that the attitude of Nigerians 'towards these Germans who for many years have been amongst us as our good friends ... should be one of studied politeness and courtesy'.[25] This plea for chivalry was of importance, because ignorant people might pounce upon Germans among them in the belief that they were helping the British.

Many questions not connected with the war, but with Lugard's policies in Southern Nigeria, continued to inflame African reaction against British administration during the war. There was a series of demonstrations and petitions against the imposition of water rate in Lagos and the passing into law of a Criminal Code applying to both the Protectorate and the Colony. This Criminal Code was a Northern Nigerian law, which Lugard wanted to extend to the whole country after amalgamation. The Lagos people were naturally opposed to any code that provided for corporal punishment in public. Lugard blamed the opposition to the water rate and the Criminal Code upon 'agitators' in Lagos, and asked the Colonial Office to permit him to enact a 'Deportation Ordinance' because it was feared that there might be bloodshed as a result of the intrigues of the 'returned convict Macaulay', one of the educated Nigerians most opposed to Lugardian principles of 'native' administration.[26] Lugard argued that the failure of the executive government to show itself able to cope with organised disturbers of the peace would be regarded as a triumph by the 'unruly and seditious elements and a defeat for the loyal minority who have endeavoured amid much abuse and possibly at personal risk of violence to uphold the traditions of good government'.[27] As in earlier decisions, the Colonial Office refused to allow Lugard to pass any such ordinance as the 'Deportation Ordinance', but he was asked to take appropriate measures to prevent violence.

Lagos opposition to government policies assumed greater dimensions towards the end of 1915. There were mass meetings in Lagos in August 1915 and A. G. Boyle, the Lieutenant-Governor of Southern Nigeria, wrote:

> the whole agitation has been engineered by its two leaders, Drs. Randle and Obasa, the latter was moved by an ardent desire to become a member of the legislative council . . . I have little hesitation in saying that the appointment of Mr. S. H. Pearse (as a member of the legislative council of Lagos) has not only caused him considerable heart burning, but has probably urged him into the present agitation. Dr. Randle stands alone as an agitator pure and simple. He is well off, but gladly leaves the placid atmosphere of law and order for the troubled waters of political disturbance which appears to be his main hobby in life.[28]

Bonar Law, after receiving a petition from these people on the questions of the Criminal Code and water rate, asked Lugard to suspend the two measures until after the war. Lugard refused and argued that while Lagosians wrote about the 'unswerving loyalty of Lagos and the great sacrifices for the war in men and money', they were actually being very disloyal. Lugard said troops employed in the war were not recruited from Lagos and that whatever monetary contributions Lagos people had made were voluntary. He added that there was a lively dread of German rule in Lagos and that no sacrifices however real would be considered too great to avert 'what to them would be an awful contingency'. Lugard implied that Lagosians were scaring everybody with the possibility of widespread disaffection and wrote that if there was any disaffection 'it will be entirely due to agitators from Lagos, who as in previous cases grossly and wilfully misrepresent facts in order to serve their own ends'.[29]

This sort of agitation did not continue for long before the people behind it were lumped with 'enemy agents' or people who were diverting the energies of the government from fighting the Germans to solving internal problems or grievances which ought to have been left unraised until after the war. Lugard, writing to the Colonial Office on the activities of Doctors Randle and Obasa, said that their pertinacity in agitating against the Criminal Code and water rate was to be largely accounted for by a desire to pose as popular leaders in antagonism to the African members of the Legislative Council. He added 'in the prosecution of this ambition they allowed themselves to act in a manner opposed to their loud protestations of loyalty' and that when Nigerian members of the Legislative Council convened a 'patriotic meeting in connection with the war, they countered it by holding a mass meeting to initiate their protest against the water rate and the Criminal Code'.[30] When in reply to one of the series of petitions coming from Lagos, the Secretary of State warned against 'seditious agitation', Obasa's reply verged on the point of giving the Colonial Office a choice between allowing Lagosians to follow the line of 'constitutional' protest and petition or violence. He wrote:

'we regret to hear that the exponents of the sorrows, distress and dissatisfactions of their fellow countrymen should be stigmatised as leaders of a seditious agitation ... this leaves us under the impression that it is not desired that we should make any further constitutional representation on matters affecting our vital interests'.[31]

Serious rioting broke out in Lagos in September 1916 over the water rate and Criminal Code, which Lugard had finally convinced the Colonial Office to sanction in 1915.[32] Over two thousand people were involved and the houses and property of known supporters of the government were damaged. Twenty-seven people were arrested and they were promptly charged with unlawful assembly.[33] None of the important Lagosians was arrested, but the stipends of the Oba of Lagos, Eshugbayi, and his chiefs were stopped for their alleged complicity in the affair.

When it became clear that Lugard was not going to allow educated Africans to dictate the policies to be followed in Nigeria just because the Empire was at war, the press came out with full rage. It was pointed out to Lugard that 'great as the indignation of the people was' at the outbreak of the war:

> they did not deviate from the path of constitutional agitation; nor was their imagination fed upon revolutionary propaganda, nor did their passions bitterly aroused seek unbridled expression in the frenzied acts of the suffragettes or of determined ulsterites, but on the contrary beneath their stormy protests and external indications of anger ran a strong current of unswerving devotion and . . . loyalty thus it will be conceded that if the people had been chivalrous enough to shelve their grievances . . . the administration was also under a great moral obligation to withhold the passing of all contentious measures that were calculated to . . . annoy the people and excite that very opposition which had been so honourably postponed on the grounds of political expediency and imperial unity. Under the circumstances need there be any wonder that the people should indulge in impassioned speeches . . . Has not the administration through folly broken the truce that was proclaimed on the outbreak of hostilities in Europe? Has it not by its indiscreet acts precipitated the undesirable state of affairs that now exists?[34]

One thing the war achieved for educated Nigerians was the increasing sense of confidence in themselves, and this confidence led to the ability to question long-standing assumptions, attitudes and even words used to describe subject races. A writer to the *Times of Nigeria* questioned the use of the word 'native': 'the word "native" is made to signify anything or any person not European'. He said,

> one hears of native clerks, native canoes, native doctors, native lawyers, native staff . . . But in England or Germany, I am not aware of the fact that there are similar phrases used when referring to natives of and things made in England or Germany. An African, a European, a white, a black, a native of a place or an alien of that place. These are phrases capable of comprehension, but to make the word 'native' to mean that not everybody is a native but only non-Europeans or non-whites are natives, is a bit too thick for one to understand.[35]

The Nigerian press, while striking this note of racial equality, was also involved in the process of redefinition of Africans' ultimate goals within their own society. What should educated Africans aspire to be, should they continue to be 'gentlemen' of Lagos dressed in 'Bond Street attire' – shoddy imitation of the white man – or be Africans combining what is good in their own culture with whatever cultural traits they had acquired through contact with their British rulers? Providing what seemed a reasonable answer, the *Lagos Weekly Record* commented:

> we believe that wholesale adoption of foreign customs without any regard to racial idiosyncracies, congeniality of climate and environment, is equally bad from an aesthetic point of view as the blind pursuit of ancestral customs – without any regard as to whether they have been outgrown by the necessities of modern existence. Furthermore western civilization is not the one possible and ideal civilization, but it is merely one of the persistent types. It cannot and has not said the last word upon civilization and consequently its *obiter dicta* need not impress ... it can only provide material for original development. We believe that while nations do borrow from one another yet the scientific process is best represented by a process of selection and assimilation, the most brilliant example of which has been furnished by the sudden rise of Japan into the forefront of world politics. Japan has a peculiar way of japanising western methods and still retaining her original customs and institutions, her religion, code of ethics, family life, dress, food, etc. Unfortunately with us matters are just the other way round, instead of emulating the brilliant example of Japan, by endeavouring to Africanise western methods and yet retain our individuality, we eschew everything native and strive fruitlessly to make our customs and institutions pitifully Anglo-Saxon.[36]

This development of racial or cultural pride was a reaction against the prejudice implicit in the colonial relations. The Africans' pride in Japan's power was a sort of counterweight against the white man's power and prestige. This cultural awakening of the educated Africans had for long been preached by E. D. Morel,[37] the *bête noire* of West African journalism. Since Morel favoured indirect rule and was opposed to the affectation of Western ways by the educated Africans he was much despised by Lagos press, but during the war it seemed the Africans were responding to some of Morel's condemnation of their attitude to their own culture. Morel had written in 1911:

> why cannot the administration and missionary societies combine in some practical, positive form to combat this curse of alien dress? There is absolutely nothing to be said in its favour. The West African looks better in African dress ... it is preservative of his racial identity ... that many members of the anglicised community would

be hostile, goes without saying . . . that is the fault of the wretched system everywhere at work.[38]

It seems the 'anglicised community' was having a second look at itself during the war. When the educated Nigerians found that being Anglicised and Christianised was not going to make them acceptable as the white man's equals, they began to reject many of the values that they had upheld before the war. As Morel pointed out in 1911, the reason why many Yorubas were becoming Muslims was the incompatibility of Christian doctrine of equality of all before God with the white man's rule.

> Since Christianity which taught natives about equality before God, which the English as 'an imperial race' could not concede to the Nigerian whom it subjugates and controls, between the race of the converter and that of the would-be convert there gapes an abyss of racial and social inequality which does not lessen, but if anything widens with conversion, it is the colour line. This accounts for Islam gaining ground in the western provinces among the proud Yorubas.[39]

While beginning to fight for a revival of African culture, the press nevertheless pursued its anti-government campaign, exploiting the war situation to settle old scores. First of all some sections of the press asked the government to remove Germans whom they claimed were serving in the administration. Before their campaign could reach a climax the Director of Education in the Northern provinces, Hans Vischer,[40] at whom the attacks were aimed, left and went to Europe and enlisted in the British Army. What the educated Africans really disliked about Vischer was not his 'German' background (in fact he was Swiss) but that he was the brain behind the northern educational system which had as its goal the training of the sons of emirs and their subordinates as good Arabic and Hausa scribes to work in the Native Administrations. The main idea of the system was that the education of Northern Nigerians should not produce 'denationalised, discontented, shoddy imitations of Europeans'.

> The system was not aimed at producing 'barristers to entrap their more ignorant countrymen into litigation and ruin, nor produce newspaper editors to preach sedition discontent and abuse of all constituted authorities, nor even primarily to train clerks for employment by government or European merchants'.[41]

This educational system in the north had been the subject of criticism before the war, and even the pro-government *Nigerian*

Pioneer was against it. The newspaper believed that unification would not be a reality until northerners were given the same 'liberal education' as the southerners, and asked:

> is it too much to expect that natives of the North should have such a liberal education as would fit them for the posts now occupied by clerks from the coastal towns? It is too late in the day, in the 20th century to attempt to stem the tide of civilization. If there is any race of people that should be given a liberal education, it is the Hausas so that they may be able to hold their own with their brethren from the South.[42]

It was the contradiction in aims of the administration of Lugard that baffled the educated Nigerians. Here was a Governor amalgamating two diverse regions, but instead of trying to bridge the gap between the two areas, he continued to emphasise what divided them rather than stressing what united them. The idea that the English type of education was unsuitable for Northern Nigerians, the practice of segregating southerners from northerners in Northern Nigeria, the creation of southern ghettos (*sabon garis*) all over the north, thus further accentuating the cultural differences, were all Lugard's and yet his mission was that of unification of the country.

As the war progressed and more and more troops were raised in Nigeria for imperial service, the Nigerian press began to pose the question of why educated Nigerians were not admitted to the commissioned ranks. The press was of the opinion that while the higher military commands should be retained by representatives of the imperial powers, the lower ranks should be dominated by educated Nigerians. They cited the example of India to justify their case. The *Nigerian Pioneer* wrote, 'as to the lower commands in India it has been found feasible to utilise native officers . . . now in Nigeria no such recognition exists except towards the European'.[43] The Nigerian press felt very proud of the role Nigeria was playing in the war, and of 'men of our own race' taking

> 'their place in the world struggle . . . men willing to leave their country for a voyage of 5,000 miles to East Africa, to join with others in upholding the honour of the flag by fighting the cruellest and most unscrupulous fighters ever seen on Earth'.[44]

On the conclusion of the Cameroons campaign one of the Nigerian newspapers, welcoming the soldiers home, commented:

... British subjects are remembering that the W.A.F.F. has succeeded in painting another little piece of red on the map, has added another jewel to the Crown of our British Empire and the W.A.F.F. have earned the undying gratitude of every place where the Union Jack proudly unfurls its folds. And what of the enemy? We may be sure that he remembers that the West African Frontier Force is largely responsible for the loss of another of his overseas possessions. Never will the Prussian Eagle raise its head and flutter its wings with defiance in West Africa. It has been brought to Earth ... and now lies crushed and dead beneath the claws of the British lion. – For this we owe deep gratitude to those fine fellows whose return we all welcome so gladly. And what of those who through the fortunes of war, will never see Lagos again? They have died in harness, fighting the battles of their King and Country, died for our safety and for the cause of British freedom. Would they have asked for, or could we have given them a nobler death?[45]

As hardship mounted, the initial enthusiasm of some sections of the press disappeared, and they demanded positive signs of change for the better as a gesture of good-will and compensation for Nigerians who had died for the imperial cause. Following Asquith's reference to the important roles the dominions would play in the future constitutional development of the Empire, the *Times of Nigeria* asked:

But what is Mr. Asquith and his government going to do with other colonies and in particular with the Crown colonies of West Africa? They too have borne their part ... nobly in the struggle of the British nation against the enemy who would smite it to dust. Are these Crown colonies not to have something more than the crumbs from the table? Are they not deserving of better treatment than that conventionally regarded as the portion of the poor relation? The time has not merely arrived, it is long past when what is known, as educated native population of our West African colonies should be given more direct voice in the government under which they live and thus an influence on the laws made for them and their fellow citizens. None has proved more worthy in the present period of stress and both justice and statesmanship demand that a practical recognition should follow.[46]

In this idea that service gave rights and deserved its reward the press was exploiting the war situation to further internal aims which had nothing to do with the war. The sort of reward they expected was contained in several articles published from 1915 onwards.

One thing that could be said for the educated community was that it was well informed about events in other parts of the Empire and outside it, particularly about events in England, India and the United States,[47] and events in these places tended to reverberate throughout the educated community in Nigeria. As early as 1915, a Nigerian wrote to the editor of the *Lagos Standard* that Nigerians should think seriously about events in India since

'for several years we have borne these restraints of Crown Colony oligarchy and our wants are identical with those of India . . . let it not be forgotten when the time comes to lay our petition before His most gracious King George V'.[48]

From this time article upon article aimed at forcing the government to adjust to what the educated elite considered as the changing world appeared in the press. Some sections of the press said they were no longer going to tolerate the 'high-handed tyranny of the present administration';[49] they wanted a Legislative Council popularly elected, if not for Nigeria as a whole at least for the Colony of Lagos. Under such a system of representative government, the *Lagos Standard* wrote:

the fatuous eccentricities of the present administration and the love of framing and passing ordinances for their own sake would never be. Any administration absurdly harassing the peace and destroying the good will and harmony of the community and people would soon through a popularly elected council know the relationship of ruler and subject. There is no race, no nation that is immortal, the result of the struggle we are today experiencing can hardly be doubted. Every year we shall become more democratic and consequently more independent in thought, freer in speech and nobler in action, taxations would be apportioned as they are necessary and as shoulders are able to bear them, education will be free and its scope enlarged because the people desire it. All privileges that are due to the ruler will be swept away, social lines of demarcation between classes will be less sharply defined. Economy will replace extravagance in public departments. Sinecures and excessive salaries will no longer exist. Africa will be rid of all exotics and foreign imposters.[50]

The influence of Americans of African descent introduced more openly than before the issue of race to Nigerian politics and at this particular time a Sierra Leonian 'Aku' (Yoruba) by the name of Orishatukeh Faduma appeared on the scene writing about pan-African unity and calling on all black peoples of the world to unite and take the opportunity of the war to assert their independence.[51] Faduma, who was educated in the United States and assumed the title of 'Professor', wrote series of articles in various Nigerian newspapers and his ideas soon pervaded the Nigerian press. The appeal to racial sentiments became a useful device for attacks on the government. Article upon article appeared in Nigerian newspapers praising the contribution of Africans to world history, and the press boldly declared that after the war the ruling powers in Africa would have, or be forced, to re-adjust their relationship with the ruled: that one day 'Ethiopia [Africa] ... shall stretch forth her hand unto God ... our belief in the ultimate consummation of this end, in the future realization of this hope is strong and unclouded as the brilliant sunshine of a noonday sun in cloudless sky in Western Africa'.[52]

As the war progressed and economic difficulties arose, the Nigerian press began to reflect the increasing frustration of all sections of the public. The press became covertly seditious, and letters complaining about the suffering caused by the expulsion of German traders from Nigeria began to appear in the press. They complained about the ruinous producer prices paid on cocoa and vegetable oils, and blamed this on lack of competition which had resulted from German expulsion from Nigeria. The *Nigerian Pioneer* writing about the collapse of Onitsha as a market commented:

> glory has departed from Israel ... Onitsha's fate is sealed, already nine out of every ten of the native shop keepers are bankrupt ... it is all very deplorable and one cannot wonder that the cry 'How long is this rotten war going to last' is being heard everywhere, semi-starvation, compulsory idleness, a discontented native population – these are not the conditions that make patriots.[53]

Many of the editors of Nigerian newspapers saw the war as an opportunity to force the hands of the government to grant concessions over the administrative policy in force in Nigeria. The most successful editor of them all, James Bright Davies, specialised in personal attacks and insults on Lugard and this was soon to land him in trouble. This editor was convinced that Lugard detested educated Africans and idealised the illiterate chiefs and emirs. Many educated Nigerians were convinced that Lugard was a negrophobist which, as far as the educated Africans were concerned, he no doubt was.[54] When Governor Merewhether of Sierra Leone was posted to the Leeward Islands on routine transfer, the editor of the *Times of Nigeria*, knowing that the educated class in Sierra Leone had been having trouble with their own Governor, rejoiced with the Sierra Leonians and went further to say that the

> people of Sierra Leone have our heartiest and warmest congratula-
> tions on the removal ... of this negrophobist Governor, who sat
> like an incubus on the genuine progress of their country ... the
> people of Nigeria will take courage from this fact that some day or
> other whether distant or near, their own relief from the iron and
> cruel rule of their own administration, is sure to come and we shall
> be freed from the galling yoke of its iniquitous measures and laws.[55]

For this article and others, Bright Davies was prosecuted for seditious libel by the Attorney-General of Nigeria in February 1916. Davies was accused of publishing articles in his paper that were designed to bring into hatred and contempt the government of Nigeria, and, by implying that government policy towards Lagos, especially the idea of moving the central capital to Kaduna, was an act of hostility to Southern Nigeria, of bringing the government to public odium. The words complained of were that the removal from Lagos of the capital to Kaduna 'threatens with ruin the progress and prosperity of the only town of importance in the Colony and Protectorate of Nigeria and which ... by austerities and severities of a continuous series of measures and enactments which could only have been dictated by a rancorous negrophobism and which apart from German rule could only flourish under the British Crown Colony System of government or under a constituted or authorised autocracy.'[56] Davies pleaded guilty and tendered an apology. Irving, his counsel, added: 'what-ever his [Davies's] faults, the accused is not a rogue or a scoundrel, not one of those demagogues who under the guise of standing up for oppressed brothers is really seeking his own interest and feathering his own nest ...'[57] He also said that Davies at sixty-eight years old was a dying war horse and that his imprisonment might result in widespread disaffection. The Chief Justice, Sir Edwin Speed, in delivering his judgement blamed Davies for using the war situation to deride the actions of the government. The Chief Justice said that in ordinary times of peace Davies's action might have been ignored but that the time when the

Empire was engaged in a life and death struggle, made his offence doubly serious. He added:

> it is a notorious fact that even the remotest parts of the King's dominions are full of, or if not full of, have been invaded by numbers of paid emissaries of the enemy seeking to raise strife and unrest in order to make an easier prey of the Empire which they have set to destroy and this is the time you have chosen to hold up His Majesty's representatives to public odium and contempt.[58]

Davies was fined one hundred pounds and ordered to enter into a personal recognisance in the sum of one hundred pounds, with two sureties each of a like amount that he would be of good behaviour for twelve months and in default of this he would be sent to jail for six months.

Bright Davies had come lightly out of a difficult situation, but not for long. He was a man of ideas who realised that he was growing old, and confronted with the alternative of writing about events as he saw them or keeping quiet to avoid official wrath, he chose the former. Although he devoted long articles in his paper to fund-raising for wounded soldiers and the families of the dead ones, he insisted that these funds should be spent on Nigerian soldiers – people of 'our own Kith and Kin' – rather than sent to England or to the Red Cross to be spent on Europeans. Almost scorning the consequences, Davies attacked the monopoly of British firms in such a way as to compromise the government. In August 1916 he wrote:

> the system adopted by the British firms in the produce trade since the war is responsible for the strong undercurrent of sympathy for the German cause which pervades the breasts of the majority of the native population, and the intensity of this feeling is such that one frequently hears the wish and the most sanguine hopes expressed in the daily conversations of the people about trade, that Germany should win this war, as they would prefer to come under German rule if only to escape and be saved from tyranny and exploitation of the British merchant.[59]

Lugard himself was against the practice of monopoly by the British merchants, but he felt that Bright Davies's attack was calculated to excite African disaffection. Davies was arraigned before the Supreme Court of Nigeria, tried for sedition, and sentenced to six months' imprisonment, to the jubilation of the Governor-General.[60] In sentencing Davies, the Chief Justice remarked that he could not ignore the fact that on two separate occasions within nine months Davies had 'chosen to publish wicked and malicious libels against the government of Nigeria at a time when every right minded man ought to give to that government his most strenuous and uncompromising support'.[61] The judge said that the publication illustrated the 'war' going on between the European and African merchants in Lagos, but that in order to emphasise his indictment of the merchants the editor of the *Times of Nigeria* did not shrink from making a statement which was obviously calculated to excite disaffection against the government. He said he could have sentenced Davies to seven years' imprisonment, but that he found it unnecessary since he was aware that the most ignorant Nigerian would surely not prefer German rule to British tutelage and that perhaps the editor did not have preconceived seditious designs before publishing his article. Sir Edwin Speed's leniency towards Davies showed that he apparently took Davies's age into consideration; and since he considered some of Davies's attacks as 'justifiable journalese comment' one should not perhaps be surprised by the leniency of these sentences, but the fact remains that they seemed extraordinarily liberal at a time when the same thing in Britain would have provoked a very harsh response.

With the incarceration of Davies, the government at least removed, if temporarily, one of the turbulent characters on the West African scene. But the educated class had many enemies to fight and causes to espouse. When it was learnt that E. D. Morel had been arrested for circulating illegally in Britain socialist pamphlets smuggled into Britain from Switzerland and for being an enemy sympathiser espousing pacifism in the interests of Germany if not in the pay of the German Empire, West African newspaper editors were jubilant. E. D. Morel, as editor of the *African Mail* published in Liverpool, had alienated the feelings of the educated class, because the *African Mail* had constantly opposed the aspirations of the educated class and supported the policy of indirect rule. For example, Morel had said in 1911:

> Our only conspicuous imperial failure was due to a misguided belief that we could and that it was desirable in our own interests that we should crush out nationality by violence ... elsewhere we are experiencing the discomforting reflex of a policy based upon the supposition that East is capable of assimilation with West under alien guidance. British India is rent with confusion and mentally unsettled

by a jumble of conflicting ideals . . . All the good work accomplished in Northern Nigeria can be flung away by a refusal to benefit from experience in other parts of the world.[62]

While Morel recognised that 'it is among the Yorubas almost exclusively so far as Nigeria is concerned, that the problem of the educated Native and what his part is to be in the future of the country arises and threatens already to become acute',[63] his solution left much to be desired – the same Lugardian solution of propping up the Alafin of Oyo into a sort of 'Sultan' of Yorubaland. In the verbal war carried on between the West African newspapers, Morel's *African Mail* once wrote, 'West African journalism to be successful, must be scurrilous and muddy'.[64]

With Morel in trouble, the Nigerian press found an occasion for character assassination. The *Lagos Weekly Record* wrote:

After many years of patient toil and unremitting effort on the part of . . . West African Press to expose the perfidy, duplicity and insincerity of E. D. Morel of the *African Mail* God . . . has now willed that the double dealings of this *soi-disant* oracle of West African affairs should be detected by his own people. We had intuitively indulged in the idea that all the hue and cry raised over the Congo Reform[65] rested on some solid basis of 'filthy lucre'. It was a 'rigging' of the philanthropic market; it paid to be a Congo reformer. Those who were initiated into the hidden mysteries of the Reform caucus saw the gilded fruits pouring into their laps . . . from the Congo market . . . Morel next transferred his indomitable energies into the land tenure market and startled all West Africa by his strange and stupid announcement that 'occupancy and not ownership is the fundamental principle underlying West African Land Tenure' – playing the capitalists' game for them.[66]

The paper continued that the reason why Morel supported the Lugardian system was to maintain a common and same policy which Herr Dernburg and Dr Solf, German Colonial Secretaries, had tried to achieve .The paper claimed that 'this system aimed at the elimination of the educated native proletariat . . .' and was strongly advocated by Morel. The paper added:

we can also understand why he was shedding crocodile tears over the spectacle of the white races jumping at one another's throats in Africa.[67] . . . By pretending to better the condition of Congo natives and plead their cause when in reality he was only bettering his own condition by filling his pockets with gilded coffers and pleading the cause of Germany[68] and one or two interested trading establish-ments. Again by defending the Nigerian system he was practically perpetuating those very conditions against which he had previously agitated under the misleading Congo Reform.[69]

The Nigerian press was no respecter of persons whenever it had a chance to indulge in invective against government officials; the press was so much against the Lugardian administration that editors risked imprisonment rather than maintain their silence.

When James Bright Davies finished serving his prison sen-tence, in 1917, he was a tired and dying man, but he continued his attack on the government as an old warrior who had seen much of battle and had overcome fear. When the news of Lewis Har-court's being raised to the peerage was announced, he com-mented: 'Lord Harcourt will always be remembered by the people of this colony as the Secretary of State, who drafted the constitution of Nigeria – the most peculiar, unhistoric and ante-diluvian administrative document in the colonial history of Great Britain.'[70]

When in July 1917 Lugard again appealed to the Colonial Office for permission to impose permanent press censorship in view of the violence of the attack on government officials and the former Secretary of State,[71] James Bright Davies also petitioned the Colonial Office arguing that 'the law establishing the censorship is a transient law called into being for specific purpose and under special circumstances and when the occasion which gave rise to it has passed, the law must expire automatically ... the censor-ship in England is not established upon a distinct or direct law, but upon regulations framed under the Defence of the Realm Act – a temporary measure called forth by the Great War which will cease to operate when the war comes to an end.'[72] The Colonial Office was sufficiently impressed by Davies's arguments to turn down Lugard's request on the grounds that there existed adequate provisions in the British Protectorate Order in Council 1916 to deal with the press, and that there was no reason why Lugard should want to 'muzzle the press' and no reason why Nigeria should take the exceptional course of including this provision in its permanent legislation.[73]

When in 1917 the Empire Resources Development Committee[74] launched its campaign for greater exploitation of the 'undeveloped estates' of the Empire, the Nigerian press, including even Ajasa's *Pioneer*, came out against the committee. This committee promised profits large enough to pay off the whole war debt and give to the British workers increased wages and a six-hour working day. Its propaganda laid special emphasis upon the great profits which could be raked in from the West African section of Britain's 'estate'. This greedy and hubristic conception of the Empire was resisted by all sections of the Nigerian press and by educated Nigerians in the Nigerian Council.[75] Because most supporters of the Empire Resources Development Committee, such as Lord Milner and Wilson Fox were connected with South African and Rhodesian business and finance, educated Nigerians saw racial prejudice behind the movement. The *Lagos Weekly Record* wrote:

> To endeavour to obliterate the old landmarks of British Imperial policy by the substitution of a coercive system of state exploitation is not only to court disaster or stir up a hornet's nest in West Africa, but also to anticipate ... destiny in creating the most favourable conditions of transferring political ascendancy and world leadership to some representative of the coloured races, a task for which Japan is most admirably fitted by virtue of her excellent spiritual order which has been the marvel of the old world and by the unique and dominant position she has enjoyed ... in the Far East, particularly through the present collapse of Russia.[76]

Others in more realistic and forthright way asked how the committee expected Africans to react to a scheme by which profits derivable from Africa would be sent 'to a distant country to pay the cost of a war before making which they were not consulted, but in the waging of which they have given both of their men and money', and that Nigerians had hoped that the effect of the war 'will be to break down old class privileges rather than to set new ones up and that effect will not be confined to the white peoples of the Empire ... the notion that West Africa consists of communities which would patiently win wealth to be exported as a tribute to Britain is a notion destined to be disappointed, if any imperial government acts upon it'.[77]

Many of the educated Nigerians felt that this idea would not have gained ground if the Africans had been given a say in the government of their various countries. They complained that, having been conditioned to think of the African as backward, the imperial government ignored the progress already made by Africans; thus a state of events was created by which a static system of rule was imposed upon a people who were making progress daily. Educated Nigerians had the support of a new and powerful force in the new weekly magazine *West Africa*,[78] which started publication on 3 February 1917. This magazine hoped that the discussions going on about Indian reforms would lead to a reappraisal of the system of government in which educated Africans had no part to play.[79] It also hoped that the importance being given to India would be bound to affect West Africa directly or indirectly and that India was in a position to champion the cause of the non-white races of the Empire.[80] The paper even suggested that the Colonial Office should seek the opinions of the educated and articulate section of the public in West Africa, by inviting some of them to present their views before the imperial parliament. The *Lagos Weekly Record* raised the banner of 'Africa for the Africans' and maintained that victory for the Allies must usher in an era of democracy for all peoples, regardless of race, creed or colour. The paper said that the Allied leaders had after all declared many times that they were fighting for the right of 'self determination' for all peoples. The paper asserted that 'no peace can last which does not recognise and accept the principle that governments derive their just powers from the consent of the governed'.[81] The paper added:

a free Africa will mean that Africa will no longer be exploited by a ruling caste of European overlords, that natives will no longer be crushed under the heel of alien rule imposed by unrighteous force, that civilization of Africa by machine guns and bad gin will cease and that government of the people by the people and for the people shall be the rule in Africa as in Europe, nor can self-government be longer denied certain peoples upon the fantastic pretext that there are superior and inferior peoples ... The pretence that superior have a moral right to impose their authority upon the inferior is a mere euphemism for the vicious idea that the stronger has the moral right to subjugate the weaker. Is it not this very idea that we are fighting in Europe? What difference is there in Germany trying to impose her authority over others and other nations trying to impose their rule upon Asiatics and Africans who have not yet learnt Europe's dominant philosophy of force. Wrong for one, it cannot be right for others.[82]

In the same vein the *Times of Nigeria* quoted enthusiastically Marcus Garvey's[83] speech in New York in 1919 on the Versailles Peace Conference, in which he said,

Africa must be returned to the negroes ... the world must be made safe for the race, Wilson, Clemenceau, Orlando, David Lloyd George, and the rest have signed the treaty of peace for certain class of whitemen, blackmen have nothing to do with this thing, for blackmen are not yet free. There can be no abiding peace until all men are free, so I ask that all negroes prepare now for the new world war twenty or thirty . . . years hence.[84]

Educated Nigerians welcomed the peace that followed the war and demanded that in recognition of the role played by Nigeria in the war, educated Africans should be treated humanely and that they should be considered as an asset to the Empire. The *Nigerian Pioneer*, as early as 1917, urged that African opinion should be sought on every matter that concerned Africans. The paper was of the opinion that the imperial government placed too much weight on the opinions and views of the 'man on the spot', and that in adopting new policies, the views of the 'man on the spot' were likely to be narrowed by the conditions of his life and interests. He might be invaluable for guidance on imperial questions but he was hardly the man to settle the general line of imperial policy. The paper claimed that opposition to making use of educated Africans arose out of a policy that

> it may be suicidal for the Empire to let the subject races into its secrets by having them employed in positions of trust . . . this objection would be true and sound as applied to localities newly settled whose loyalty would be a matter of great speculation . . . but Nigeria as a whole cannot be described as newly settled and not only is her loyalty undisputed . . . it is indisputable. An Empire that is only justified by views of policy and sentiment, such as segregation and whiteman's prestige, stands upon insecure basis, however great may be its show of strength, to such an empire the subject races are always foreign and the Empire is exotic to the subject races.[85]

When it was finally learnt in Lagos that Lugard was to retire and be succeeded by Sir Hugh Clifford, the *Lagos Weekly Record* came out with the most virulent attack on Lugard and his administrative record, while songs of praise were being sung for his successor, Sir Hugh Clifford. The *Record* as a parting shot thanked God

> for his tender mercies in delivering his children from the baneful effects of an inglorious administration which constitutes not only a standing disgrace to the cherished traditions of British colonial policy, but is also a positive libel upon the accepted principles of British culture. The Nigerian system is the most infernal system that

has ever been devised since the days of the Spanish inquisition for the express purpose of humiliating and depressing the loyal and progressive community. Its nefarious laws and ordinances read like weird contents of some musty-fusty documents unearthed in far-off Cathay. Its twenty-five lashes, its public floggings of general offenders, stripped naked in public markets ... bespeak an administrative system which is the exact prototype of German Kultur in Africa.

The paper went on to say that Lugard was

the victim of exaggerated personality induced by the autocratic power conferred upon him through the indiscretion of Lewis Harcourt ... so high was he in the clouds that he saw very little of the people he was called upon to govern ... Sir Frederick consciously or unconsciously endeavoured to intensify ... racial antipathies between Black and Whites, which had never been suspected ... during the palmy days of the old colony of Lagos and subsequently of the colony of Southern Nigeria. The three basic principles necessary for the successful working of the Nigerian system are ignorance, fear and military terrorism. The crass ignorance prevailing in the Northern provinces, the farcical show and studied mockery of the much vaunted Nassarawa[86] schools ... which constitute a disgrace to any decent educational or technical system, the respect paid to the ordinary *bature*[87] much more to talk of the *baban bature* ... the compulsory salutation, the summary jurisdiction of the provincial courts all these bespeak the methods of German rule in Africa.[88]

The paper accused Lugard of deceiving the emirs of Northern Nigeria 'by the fiction of indirect rule since the real authority lay in the hands of British residents'. The paper added that in trying to build a *cordon sanitaire* around Northern Nigeria, Lugard was leaning on broken reed since

For communication of thought, New York is nearer Lagos today than Lagos to Ibadan some twenty years ago ... When in the fullness of time the natives of the Northern provinces in spite of Sir Frederick Lugard's preventive policy shall taste the fruit of the tree of knowledge they shall be as gods, knowing good and evil, then the bogey of whiteman's prestige shall with increased knowledge among the masses die a natural death.[89]

Impracticable as were some of the educated Africans' demands, such as that of complete independence, these were forced upon them by the general frustration they suffered and by the seemingly hopeless situation into which the colonial government pushed them. What educated Africans really wanted was something like the 'career open to talents', removal of arbitrary ordinances restricting their freedom of movement and residence, and direct but enlightened government on the old-established colonial pattern. They did not actually ask for the removal of chiefs, in fact some of them wanted the institution modernised, hence the reference to Japan as an example of the successful modernization of indigenous political institutions. Even the most radical of them all, Herbert Macaulay, championed the cause of Eleko Eshugbayi[90] in the latter's effort to get himself recognised as the African ruler of Lagos. Herbert Macaulay's rise to fame as the 'grand old man' of Nigerian nationalism was actually built on his devotion to seeing justice done to an African ruler.[91] His ascendancy was derisively recognised when he was called by the *Nigerian Pioneer* 'the leader of the people; . . . by the people we mean that portion of Lagos, the turbulent elements'.[92]

The war-time activities of the Nigerian and other West African newspapers were to lead to the formation of the National Congress of British West Africa, which met in Accra, Gold Coast, in 1920 with representatives from all British West Africa being present. The idea of a conference was first mooted by the *Nigerian Chronicle* in 1915, when the paper called for a conference 'to formulate the lines which future development must take . . .'[93] When the conference met they placed on record resolutions which among other things embodied all the criticisms of the indirect rule system. The educated Africans called for the establishment of representative government and the abolition of the colour bar in civil service appointments as well as the introduction of compulsory education and the establishment of a university.[94] The conference also viewed with alarm the right assumed by European powers 'of exchanging or partitioning countries between them without reference to or regard for the wishes of the people [concerned]'.[95] The Congress resolved to maintain inviolate the connection of the British West African Dependencies with the British Empire, but asserted that this implied the choice between having full citizenship of that Empire or complete independence.

They did not stop in Accra, they sent representatives to London to lobby the League of Nations Union for support of their cause; and they also visited the House of Commons and met members of parliament, particularly Labour members in the House. The impact these activities had on the colonial officials on the spot and the home government was minimal. Sir Hugh Clifford, who was always sympathetic to educated Africans' opinion, nevertheless described the Congress as a

> self-appointed body ... and in no way representative of Nigeria ... neither of the *soi-disant* Nigerian delegates at present in England has any personal knowledge of more than insignificant portions of Nigeria ... their programme ... if it were possible of realisation which it today is not, would be subversive of all governments, would cause anarchy ... and probably sporadic insurrections in many parts of Nigeria.[96]

A. J. Harding of the Colonial Office minuted: 'the signatories on behalf of Nigeria are Mr. Shyngle, the black barrister – not a native of Nigeria, and that ridiculous petty chief Oluwa who is masquerading as a Nigerian potentate with his ex-convict secretary, Herbert Macaulay.'[97]

The Nigerian newspapers provided a medium by which the opinions and views of educated Africans were made known to the local colonial administration and the home government. Lugard failed in his attempt to muzzle the press because, in spite of the fact that the local press with the exception of the *Nigerian Pioneer* was considered subversive and their denunciation of the government 'noisy, scurrilous and personal' and was said to have fomented rebellions in Egbaland during the war,[98] yet the Colonial Office was against censorship because according to A. J. Harding, only 'an arbitrary government uses a newspaper censorship to suppress expressions of opinions'.[99] The home government, at least through cuttings from Nigerian newspapers by the Colonial Office, knew the feelings of the educated elite, though it did not necessarily respond to their demands. In their exploitation of war psychology Nigerian editors were able to write about things that they would not have had the audacity to write about in peace time, and in their condemnation of Germany and protestation of loyalty they cleverly likened the administrative policy of Lugard to that of German rule in Africa. In this regard they achieved some measure of success in that they forced Lugard to appoint, in 1917, Henry Carr,[100] an educated Nigerian, as Secretary of Native Affairs in the Colony of Lagos. Lugard thought Henry Carr's appointment might put a damper on the series of agitations against government measures by 'a group of native lawyers and their touts' and on 'the scurrilous and at times almost seditious and blasphemous native press which day by day published articles calculated to embitter racial feeling'. He felt this appointment would satisfy the 'native community . . . which has allowed itself to be dominated by persons who seek their own interest only and thrive by agitation and discord, chief of whom . . . is the extremely able ex-convict Macaulay'.[101]

The newspapers certainly reflected the frustrations and aspirations of the educated people, in spite of the limited readership, and the fact that most of the newspapers were based in Lagos gave the illiterate Nigerians in Yorubaland in particular, the impression that the editors were really *au fait* with the real meaning of all government schemes and policies; hence the newspapers had influence disproportionate to their circulation and readership. It is of great significance and an important victory for the newspapers that they were able to preserve their independence in spite of the onslaught of the Governor-General, but the credit actually belongs to the Colonial Office which upheld the freedom of the press throughout the war despite the fact that this freedom was taken for licence.

The war which ironically created the atmosphere for a relatively free discussion of grievances, whether actual or imaginary, gave rise to the beginning of agitational politics in Nigeria and the ideas thrown up by the world conflict made Kitoyi Ajasa's plea for the introduction of a system of education which would make Nigerians more loyal to the throne of Great Britain – 'a system which will not produce men discontented as in India and Egypt'[102] – out of date and out of tune with educated African opinion. These people, instead of using supplication and pleas, asserted that they must be accepted as equal members of the Empire or they would agitate to cut loose the ties that united Nigeria with the Empire. It was in the reflection of this mood that Herbert Macaulay became the dominant figure in post-war Nigerian politics. This fact was recognised by the Colonial Office clerks, for one of them minuted, 'Herbert Macaulay is, I am afraid, a dangerous man as likely as anybody in Nigeria to be leader of anti-European movement on American negro lines'.[103]

Sir Hugh Clifford, the new Governor of Nigeria, wrote on the same issue, that

> an almost superstitious belief in the supposed power and influence of the ex-convict Macaulay is entertained by the more seditious sections of the indigenous population of Lagos . . . It is seriously

expected by many of them that he would . . . return in triumph from England armed with a mandate for the expulsion of the colonial government and with authority to proclaim *Eleko*, King of Lagos, if not of Nigeria.[104]

This recognition of the importance of the man who was later to launch a political party – the National Democratic Party – and a newspaper – *Lagos Daily News* – with the aim of achieving self-government for his people, brings one to the conclusion that the war was an important milestone in Nigerian history. It was the articulate few who made this so, and a far more significant fact was that Macaulay's emergence as a leader, partly as a result of his championing the cause of a 'native' ruler, contradicts the generally accepted assumption that all educated Africans wanted to get rid of their 'natural' rulers.

The effect of this agitation and the introduction of unpopular administrative and fiscal measures and the ineffective British hold on the country occasioned revolts even if it did not cause them directly. In some cases the revolts were directly related to some of the issues raised by the educated Nigerians, such as the granting of too much or illegitimate power to traditional rulers. In other areas the economic hardship caused by the war led to revolts. The recruiting of labour gangs as well as the recruiting of combatants and carriers for various theatres of military operations had unsettling effects in the country and made rebellion more attractive to otherwise docile suffering peoples.

Notes

1 James S. Coleman, *Nigeria: Background to Nationalism*, University of California Press, Berkeley and Los Angeles, 1958, p. 141. Coleman estimated that by the early 1920s Nigerian university graduates numbered 30, and that 200 Nigerians had post-primary school education.
2 *Lagos Weekly Record*, 8 March 1913.
3 *Times of Nigeria*, 14 July 1914.
4 Osho Davies to Travers Buxton, 20 Oct. 1914. The Anti-Slavery and Aborigines' Protection Society Papers, G. 236, quoted in M. Perham, *Lugard: The Years of Authority, 1898–1945*, Collins, London, 1960, pp. 585–6.
5 Sir William Geary, *Nigeria Under British Rule*, Methuen, London, 1927, p. 14.

6 C.O. 583/15/23865, Lugard to Colonial Office, 29 June 1914. The *Nigerian Pioneer* was a pro-government newspaper edited by a certain Irving, who was a close associate of Kitoyi Ajasa, the owner of the paper.

7 Kitosi Ajasa was born in Lagos and unlike many of the earlier educated Nigerians was a 'proper' Yoruba and not one of the sons of the repatriates from Sierra Leone. Ajasa was a supporter of the administration and he was consequently made a member of both the Lagos Legislative Council and the Nigerian Council. He had a highly successful legal practice and used his newspaper, the *Nigerian Pioneer*, to champion the cause of indirect rule and the administration's policy in Southern Nigeria. He was one of the two Nigerian lawyers included in the commission that looked into Aba tax riots in 1929. Subsequently knighted.

8 *Lugard Papers*, i, p. 59, Major Lugard to his wife, 1913.

9 C.O. 583/83/3057, H. R. Palmer, account of his journey from Maiduguri to Jeddah in Arabia, August 1919. Palmer said 'I found that one of the leaders of the so-called Christian Obgoni Society in Lagos – the Rev'd T. A. J. Ogunbiyi was known in Khartoum. The Fellata communities in the various Sudanese towns and even in Jeddah in Arabia were quite up to date in all the happenings in Nigeria – even down to Abeokuta Outbreak.'

10 C.O. 583/17/30139, Lugard to Harcourt, 12 Aug. 1914.

11 *Ibid.*

12 The Act referred to was 'The Seditious Offences Ordinance' – Southern Nigeria Ordinance No. XXII of 1909, which provided *inter alia* for heavy punishment for any person who 'makes, publishes or circulates any statement, rumour or report with intent to unite any class or community of persons to commit any offence against any other class or community or who by words either spoken or written . . . promotes or attempts to promote feelings of enmity or hatred between different classes of the population'. This is an interesting piece of legislation and anticipates Race Relations legislation in Britain and Canada.

13 C.O. 583/17/30139, Sir John Anderson's minute, 27 Aug. 1914.

14 *Ibid.* Harcourt's minute, 27 Aug. 1914.

15 C.O. 583/18/38609, Lugard to Colonial Office, 15 Sept. 1914: this meeting was on 13 Aug. 1914.

16 *Lagos Weekly Record*, 12 Sept. 1914.

17 *Times of Nigeria*, 15 Sept. 1914. The reference to Herr Dr Solf, the German Colonial Secretary, was to his declaration in the Reichstag about the wisdom of Lugard's indirect rule. In a personal letter to Lugard on 16 June 1914 Dr Solf wrote: 'At various occasions I have quoted Nigeria in connection with the future development of the Cameroons and pointed out the wonderful achievements of your work in West Africa. I think I have profited a great deal from the valuable information received during my interesting stay in your colony and have already put it into practice in several instances of

our West African administration.' *Lugard Papers*, i, p. 47, Herr Dr Solf to Lugard, 16 June 1914.

18 *Times of Nigeria*, 30 Nov. 1915.

19 *Times of Nigeria*, 15 Sept. 1914.

20 *Lagos Weekly Record*, 7 Oct. 1916.

21 *Nigerian Pioneer*, 30 April 1915.

22 *Lagos Weekly Record*, 10 Oct. 1914.

23 *Ibid.*

24 *Lugard Papers*, i, Major Lugard, 19 Oct. 1914. MSS British Empire, S. 72.

25 *Nigerian Pioneer*, 28 Aug. 1914.

26 C.O. 583/33/30188, Lugard to Colonial Office, 18 May 1915.

27 *Ibid.*

28 C.O. 583/35/40131, Boyle to Bonar Law, 10 Aug. 1915.

29 C.O. 583/43/36259, Lugard's memo on 'Lagos opposition and disaffection during the war', 6 Aug. 1915.

30 C.O. 583/39/547, Lugard to Colonial Office, 13 Dec. 1915.

31 C.O. 583/38/54783, Dr Obasa to Colonial Office, 18 Nov. 1915.

32 C.O. 583/39/547, Colonial Office to Lugard, 13 Dec. 1945.

33 C.O. 583/49/44741, Boyle to Colonial Office, 19 Sept. 1916.

34 *Lagos Weekly Record*, 28 Aug. 1915.

35 *Times of Nigeria*, 1–22 Dec. 1914.

36 *Lagos Weekly Record*, 8 Jan. 1916.

37 E. D. Morel, 1873–1924, was an author, journalist and politician. He founded the Congo Reform Association in 1904 and was its secretary 1904–12. He published with Pierre Mille, the French West African explorer, *Le Congo léopoldien*. He was a member of the West African Lands Committee of the Colonial Office 1912–14; editor of *African Mail* for ten years; a vice-president of the Anti-Slavery and Aborigines Protection Society; secretary and part founder of Union of Democratic Control; Labour M.P. for Dundee, 1922–4 and author of more than fifteen books.

38 E. D. Morel, *Nigeria, its Peoples and its Problems*, London, 1911, p. 219.

39 *Ibid.*, p. 216.

40 Hans Vischer, the Swiss Director of Education, Northern Provinces of Nigeria, was hated by educated Nigerians for his stiff condemnation and ridicule of the southern Nigerian educational system and for his insistence on educating Nigerians along their own lines.

41 C.O. 583/96/2064, Harding's minute on education in Northern Nigeria, 15 Jan. 1920.

42 *Nigerian Pioneer*, 31 Sept. 1915.

43 *Nigerian Pioneer*, 13 Oct. 1916.

44 *Ibid.*, 7 Nov. 1916.

45 *Ibid.*, 7 April 1916.

46 *Times of Nigeria*, 1–8 Aug. 1916.

47 *Lagos Standard*, 18 Aug. 1915. In a letter printed in the *Standard* Dr W. E. B. Dubois urged 'Africans like ourselves' to press for

'compulsory education, representation at all levels of government and resistance to oppression'.

48 *Lagos Standard*, 23 June 1915.

49 *Ibid.*, 11 Aug. 1915.

50 *Ibid.*

51 *Times of Nigeria*, 7–28 March 1916.

52 *Ibid.*

53 *Nigerian Pioneer*, 16 Nov. 1917.

54 C.O. 583/32/26256, 15 April 1915. When Sir Hugh Clifford said he was going to establish a Gold Coast medical staff (of European and African doctors) separate from the West African Medical Service which barred Africans from their association and service, so that the Gold Coast could employ qualified African doctors, Nigerian officials said they would have nothing to do with such a scheme. A. G. Boyle wrote, 'Just as it is so often said that an Irishman out of his own country is a very different man to an Irishman in Ireland so is the case with the natives who have qualified well in England but deteriorate on coming home', and Lugard in his comment of 15 April 1915 wrote: 'there are many men who with a life long sympathy with the negro, would yet regard it as intolerable that their wives should be attended – say in childbirth – by a negro practitioner – I am myself such a man.' Lugard wrote that discrimination existed in Ceylon and India too, the Straits Settlements, Hong-Kong and Wei-hei-wei. He added, 'these considerations lead me to the conclusion that in the matter of the medical service the existence of racial prejudice and racial disqualification must as between the European and the negro be recognised'.

55 *Times of Nigeria*, 7 Dec. 1915.

56 *Times of Nigeria*, 15 to 19 Feb. 1916.

57 *Ibid.*

58 *Ibid.*, 1–16 Aug. 1916.

59 *Nigerian Pioneer*, 1 Dec. 1916, Reporting the Rex *vs.* Bright Davies case.

60 Perham, *Lugard: The Years of Authority*, p. 598. Lugard probably influenced the Chief Justice's decision. When he showed the Chief Justice Davies's article, the judge, Lugard wrote, 'argued that it was justifiable journalese comment. I wholly disagree and I am glad to say that the editor was tried and is "doing time" in gaol'.

61 *Nigerian Pioneer*, 1 Dec. 1916.

62 E. D. Morel, *op. cit.*, p. 152.

63 *Ibid.*, p. 77.

64 *African Mail*, 7 Aug. 1914.

65 In his fight against King Leopold over the cruelty of his rule in the Congo, E. D. Morel published *Red Rubber: the Rubber Slave Trade on the Congo*, London, T. Fisher Unwin, 1906.

66 *Lagos Weekly Record*, 20 Feb. 1915.

67 *African Mail*, 7 Aug. 1914. Morel at the outbreak of the Great War wrote, 'there are however still lower depths into which the rulers of

Europe can fall if they are bent upon doing so. They can launch their African levies at one another on tropical African soil.'

68 *The Christian Commonwealth*, 23 Dec. 1914, 'Revealed' that Germany coveted the Congo and E. D. Morel aided them. The paper wrote that though again and again Morel was challenged to disclose the sources of the immense funds which must have been necessary to carry on the Congo Reform agitation he had consistently refused; and that Morel's 1912 book *Morocco in Diplomacy* was written to advance the cause of German imperialism.

69 *Lagos Weekly Record*, 20 Feb. 1915.

70 *Times of Nigeria*, 17 April 1917.

71 C.O. 583/59/45852, Lugard to Long, 3 July 1917.

72 *Ibid.*, enclosure (I) in Lugard to Long, 3 July 1917.

73 C.O. 583/59/45852, Colonial Office to Lugard, July 1917.

74 See ch. 2, pp. 52–6.

75 C.O. 583/55/14179, Proceedings of Nigerian Council 28 and 29 Dec. 1917. Kitoyi Ajasa criticised the Empire Resources Development Committee's programme on the grounds that it would create a big monopoly and that Nigerian labourers would be confined to one employer and that labourers would be enslaved by the monopoly, since there would be no room for selling labour freely if no other firms existed.

76 *Lagos Weekly Record*, 27 Oct.–3 Nov. 1917.

77 *Times of Nigeria*, 5 June 1917.

78 When Morel's *African Mail* on 5 Jan. 1916 announced that it was going out of business, it became necessary for a non-official magazine published in England to replace it. Lugard tried to get Liverpool merchants interested in launching a new magazine in 1915 but nothing came of it until 1917, when *West Africa* appeared. The paper was owned by the 'public' but especially by those interested in West Africa and its first editor was Albert Cartwright.

79 *West Africa*, 2 June 1917.

80 *West Africa*, 9 June 1917.

81 *Lagos Weekly Record*, 5–12 Oct. 1918.

82 *Ibid.*

83 Marcus Garvey was born in St Ann's Bay in Jamaica in 1887, he emigrated to the United States as a boy. In the years immediately following the First World War he founded the Universal Negro Improvement Association (U.N.I.A.), which flourished in the 1920s and 1930s before it collapsed because of dissension and corruption. It achieved immense success in 'uniting' Negroes of the New World and those of Africa at least ideologically, and the nationalism of Dr N. Azikiwe and Dr Kwame Nkrumah, ex-presidents of Nigeria and Ghana, owes its origins partly to their contact with Garveyism. See Edmund David Cronon, *Black Moses: The Story of Marcus Garvey and the Universal Negro Improvement Association*, University of Wisconsin Press, Madison, 1969; and Amy Jacques-Garvey, *Philosophy and Opinions of Marcus Garvey*, New York, 1969.

84 *Times of Nigeria*, 3–24 Nov. 1919.

85 *Nigerian Pioneer*, 7 Sept. 1917.
86 Nassarawa Schools were founded in Northern Nigeria to teach sons of emirs and chiefs Hausa and Arabic and some accounting so as to prepare them for positions in the 'Native Administration'.
87 *Bature* – Hausa word for a white man, *Baban bature* for father of white man, i.e. Governor.
88 *Lagos Weekly Record*, 1 Feb. 1919.
89 *Ibid.*, 22 Feb. 1919.
90 Eleko Eshugbayi was chosen in 1901 as head of Docemo (Dosumu) House (ruling dynasty in Lagos) after the death of Oyekan in 1900. Eshugbayi was deposed by A. G. Boyle, Lieutenant-Governor, Southern Nigeria in 1918, but he was reinstated by Sir Hugh Clifford in 1919 and later deposed in Dec. 1920 when he refused to accept Clifford's advice that he should dissociate himself from Macaulay's utterances by sending 'criers' round Lagos for the purpose.
91 For further details see M. Perham, *Lugard: the Years of Authority*, pp. 584, 592, 596, 600.
92 *Nigerian Pioneer*, 12 Dec. 1919.
93 *Nigerian Chronicle*, 26 Feb. 1915.
94 C.O. 554/49/46935. Thirty-three resolutions of the National Congress of British West Africa were passed at the Accra Conference of 11 to 29 March 1920 and sent to Lord Milner. See also G. Eluwa, 'National Congress of British West Africa and the Colonial Office Reforms of 1922/1923', Ph.D. thesis, 1967.
95 C.O. 554/49/46935, Resulutions of the National Congress of British West Africa, 29 March 1920.
96 C.O. 554/46/58090, Clifford to Milner, 26 Nov. 1920.
97 *Ibid.*, Harding's minute, 4 Dec. 1920.
98 C.O. 583/37/33183, Boyle to Milner, 10 May 1919.
99 C.O. 583/65/18486, Harding's minute, 28 Feb. 1918.
100 Henry Carr (later Sir) was a Lagosian by birth. He was the highest paid African civil servant during the time of Lugard. He was Inspector of Education, Southern Provinces, until 1917, when he was appointed Secretary of Native Affairs, and was promoted Resident of Lagos Colony in 1918.
101 C.O. 583/59/56467, Lugard to Colonial Office, 25 Sept. 1917.
102 C.O. 583/84/7580, 29 Dec. 1919. Proceedings of Nigerian Council meeting.
103 C.O. 583/94/63713, Harding's minute, 11 Jan. 1921.
104 *Ibid.* Clifford to Milner, 12 Dec. 1920.

4 Disaffection and revolts in Southern Nigeria 1914–18

The period of the First World War coincided with the time not only of administrative innovation in Nigeria but with the period when the weight of the colonial connection began to be felt particularly in the demand either for taxes or for military recruits.

Many of the revolts in Nigeria were partly an expression of rebellious spirit against the colonial imposition as well as a defence of traditional ways of life. In the unsubjugated areas the revolts were strictly speaking resistance movements, in the sense that those resisting were fighting against what they anticipated the white man's rule would involve, unlike those who mounted full-fledged rebellion against the constraint and exaction of the first phase of colonial domination. In essence, resistance and rebellion form different stages of the anti-colonial movement, which eventually was to pass through the more refined constitutional and in some cases ideological and revolutionary stages of rebellion against imperialism.[1] The question of resistance and rebellion during the period of the First World War when the full impact of colonial rule began to be felt has not been adequately discussed.

The general impression one has from existing literature on the situation in Southern Nigeria during the war is not a balanced one. While several writers have recognised the fact that there were revolts in certain parts of the south, no attempt has yet been made to give a picture of their extent and significance. Margery Perham in her biography of Lugard wrote that 'Lugard was never alarmed by them [the revolts] but only worried by the demands they made for troops or police who could be ill-spared'.[2] This was not the case; the Governor-General did not feel so secure as his biographer would have us believe.

Southern Nigeria went through a period of considerable turmoil. British weakness and understaffing gave opportunity for the assertion of resistance. Suppression of rebellion was in most cases violent; this was because available forces had to be rapidly concentrated to inflict a heavy blow on dissidents before troops were rushed to another part of the country where there was trouble. In some cases the war in itself was not a cause of revolts but an occasion for them. They essentially arose from resistance to British administrative policies, especially to Lugard's indirect rule. Secondly, the revolts were the result of the general *malaise* created by the war and the lack of effective British control of the country which followed the withdrawal of some of the administrative staff for war service. Coupled with this was the economic slow-down created by the disruption of the normal flow of trade, the effect of which on ignorant farmers who could not sell their palm produce was disastrous. The demands of the imperial government on Nigerian peoples as soldiers, and the recruitment campaigns carried out in many parts of the country, further unsettled the society.

THE FIRST EGBA REVOLT

The first sign that there was something wrong in Nigeria became apparent in Egbaland just at the onset of the war. These events were concerned with opposition to government policy in Egbaland. The revolt against the Egba government, whose existence depended on British support, took place because of the widespread belief that the war had left the government in a position in which it could not spare troops to suppress insurgents.[3]

Egbaland was a difficult place to administer since it was riddled with factions. There were four distinct groups pulling the states in different directions. There was the 'church party' headed by ministers and educated members of their congregations. Their influence was greatest in Abeokuta, but the existence of rural churches and schools gave them some influence in the countryside. They also relied for support upon 'non-resident Egbas' who formed such societies as the Egba Society in Lagos under such men as Coker and Savage, and the Egba Citizens' League of Ibadan led by Sowemimo, who had been deported from Abeokuta in the time of Sir H. M. McCallum.[4] This church party was wealthy and was able to 'buy a good deal of support and to inculcate into the uneducated chiefs that government was exploiting them purely for its own purposes'.[5] The church party pursued rather contradictory policies of supporting the chiefs, while opposing at the same time the Ogboni, whom they were anxious to destroy in order to take over its powers.[6] The church party saw Edun, the Egba Secretary, as a stumbling block in their way and they worked for his removal.

Another pressure group in Egbaland was the Ogboni[7] – a secret society of great influence, but also a religious as well as a judicial organisation possessing traditional rights of settling disputes and performing burial rites of its members, and non-members whose relatives generally paid for such favours.

There were the Muslims, who were subservient to Egberongbe, their leader who had failed to secure the Alakeship and had consequently become an inveterate enemy of the reigning Alake. This group was always prepared to act in any way that would upset the *status quo*.

There was lastly the 'Women group' under the leadership of their *Iyalode*[8] (leader of women in civic affairs). This group was split in two; one faction was led by the accredited leader, but the more militant and subversive faction was led by one Subuola, 'a rich and unscrupulous trader' and daughter of Egberongbe. Her faction was therefore pro-Muslim and was consequently hostile to the Egba government.

In the face of all these factions it should hardly be a surprise that the position of the Alake was very shaky.

Some of the shortcomings of Egba socio-political organisation go far back in their history. The Egba people were organised into four sections each under its own head chief. These sections were and are still called Egba-Alake, Oke-Ona, Gbagura and Owu, each ruled by its Oba respectively called *Alake, Oshile, Agura* and *Olowo*. At first each Egba group inhabited a distinct part of the country, but as a result of wars in the nineteenth century the Egbas were driven into a corner of their country where they founded Abeokuta in 1830. In founding Abeokuta the Egba reproduced the original divisions of their country for each group had its own distinct quarter in the town under its own chief. The Alake, coming from the largest of the four sections of Egba people, was recognised as senior chief, but he was by no means paramount and according to the 'constitution' of Egbaland he was *primus inter pares* in relation to sectional Obas.

When the people expanded into the adjoining farmlands around Abeokuta their chiefs remained in the city. This allowed authority to be centred in the defensible city with constant and quick adjustment of any inter-sectional dispute without civil strife.

In addition to the Egbas, there were the Egbados and people grouped around Otta in the south-west of Egbaland. They recognised the overlordship of Abeokuta. The whole political and ceremonial life of the people was centred on Abeokuta. People in the town had farms in the country to which they went for long or short periods, those in the villages came to Abeokuta at some time or another during the year.

The festivals were held in Abeokuta, the graves of the dead were located there and it was the custom for every Egba, unless a pauper or a small child, to be brought to Abeokuta for burial in the section of the town to which he belonged. Each section managed its own affairs and the affairs of the group of villages and farmlands which looked up to that particular quarter as its home. This was done through the sectional Oba and his chiefs, the latter including members of the Ogboni. Every chief had to join the Ogboni before he could be made a chief and the Ogboni was the body that nominated chiefs. Occasionally the head chief might happen to occupy a lesser position in the Obgoni hierarchy than other chiefs. The Ogboni was intimately associated with the religious as well as with the political life of Egbaland. This organisation provided a check on the growth of the absolute power of chiefs. The judicial system was also associated with the Ogboni, as their hall was the court house. The chiefs sat there to hear cases and they took fees and imposed fines. These formed the main revenues of the chiefs; as the Alake put it, 'when a man became a chief the Ogboni house was his farm'.[9] This was the system replaced by the Lugard-inspired 'Native Court' system. On these new courts created by the white man sat a certain favoured number of 'chiefs', but not the Ogboni.

The greater part of the revenue of Egbaland was derived from tolls collected on goods entering the land and those in transit. When Egba 'autonomy' was abolished as a result of the Ijemo affair in 1914 the colonial government decided to phase out the system of toll collection. The government advised Egba province to substitute direct taxation for tolls and Edun, the Egba Secretary, went to the northern emirates to study the system in 1914.[10] After his return he recommended that the Northern system with scarcely any modification be introduced into Egbaland. This scheme, however, was shelved for three years for fear of the reaction of the people.

The Ijemo rising had long been in the making and many grievances had converged to spark off the explosion in August 1914. A
certain Shobiyi Ponlade was arrested towards the end of July 1914
on the order of the Egba government, not the colonial government,
since Egbaland was by treaty an 'independent' political unit
within British Nigeria. This was an anomalous situation, which
was only tempered by the fact that the British Commissioner in
Egbaland wielded so much power that it made nonsense of the
autonomy of Egbaland. Ponlade, who was about 90 years old, was,
however, arrested on the orders of the local government of
Egbaland, for failure to join and order his people to construct and
repair roads in his area, without pay.[11]

Ponlade was a chief of a section of the Egba people called
Ijemo. He was a somewhat truculent old man who had not much
respect for the Alake. Ponlade was arrested because the Ijemo
section of the Egba people, to which he belonged and of which he
was a minor chief, had been known to treat the Egba government
with contempt. Right from the start the case was a political one,
with the Egbaland government determined to assert its authority
in the face of growing erosion of its power. The mystery of the
whole situation is why the Egba government decided to put on a
show of strength in a case involving such an aged man. When
policemen were sent to bring Ponlade from his village to Abeokuta,
he was said to have resisted arrest, and in the process the old man
was seriously bruised. After this Ponlade and his cousin Odebiyi
were taken to Abeokuta to face humiliating treatment at the hands
of the British Commissioner, P. V. Young, and the Egba government secretary, Adegboyega Edun. The fact that Ponlade was
brought before the British Commissioner and not the Alake, the
head of the Egba government, is a clear indication of the hollow-
ness of Egbaland's independence. Edun and Young behaved in
the most inhuman way in their treatment of Ponlade and Odebiyi.

Whatever was the offence committed by Ponlade, Young and
Edun went beyond reasonable limits in inflicting punishment on
him. According to Duncombe, the district officer of adjacent
Ijebu Division who was an eye-witness of Ponlade's ordeal, after
his arrest Ponlade was brought before Commissioner Young and
made to remain in a prostrate position in the sun outside Young's
house for a considerable length of time; after that he was beaten
with 'stout sticks' by the Commissioner's carriers without any
attempt by the Commissioner to stop this. Edun also joined in the

beating and after that Shobiyi Ponlade was secured to a tree where he was left until the following morning.[12]

Young, defending his very callous behaviour, said that Ponlade was tied to a tree because there was no 'lock-up' in the immediate neighbourhood, and that he had to do this to prevent the old man from committing suicide as he had threatened to do. He defended his order that Ponlade's legs and hands be tied on the grounds that this was done to prevent his escape 'since native guards could not be trusted'.[13] Adding insult to injury, the court convicted Ponlade and his cousin Odebiyi for assaulting the police, and they were ordered to pay a fine of two pounds each or go to prison for two weeks. Ponlade was separately fined for an offence under the Road Construction Ordinance.[14] Ponlade refused or was unable to pay this fine and was sent to prison.

Immediately after the arrest and imprisonment of Ponlade rumour got abroad that he and his cousin had been arrested and severely beaten by order of Adegboyega Edun, the Egba government secretary, and the 'seditious' Lagos newspapers, especially the *Nigerian Chronicle*, gave great prominence to these events in Egbaland.

Ponlade later died in prison and fortune seemed to have played into the hands of the enemies of the Egba administration. In order to defuse the highly explosive situation, the Egba government called in its medical officers to perform a *post-mortem* examination on Ponlade's body and to give the result as 'death due to natural causes'. In the light of the torture inflicted on such an old man, the Egba government must have been totally out of touch with reality if it expected the Ijemo people to believe their doctors' evidence.

The Ijemo people, having been worked up by the death of Ponlade and the refusal of the Alake to dismiss his secretary, Edun, whom they held responsible for Ponlade's death, took to the streets to stage a demonstration with the purpose of forcing the Alake to dimiss Edun.[15] The Alake refused, confidently trusting that if things got too bad he could ask for military support from Lagos. Before the Alake actually took the next step, he tried to placate the Ogboni[16] (which could make and unmake an Alake) by bribing[17] them to support him against the Ijemo people; but the Ogboni refused to be bought over and they threatened to depose the Alake if he did not get rid of Edun.

At this juncture the Alake lost control of events and left affairs in the hands of the British Commissioner, P. V. Young. The Alake wrote to the British Commissioner asking him to provide the necessary protection to enable his police to arrest the recalcitrant Ogboni chiefs, especially those in the Ijemo quarter of Abeokuta led by the Oluwo (one of the leaders of the Ogboni). The Alake was told by the Governor's Deputy, A. G. Boyle, that he would be risking the autonomy of Egbaland. But the Alake had no other choice, and there was not much to lose in Egba 'autonomy'.

When serious rioting broke out on 5 August 1914, Lugard set his eyes on the abrogation of the 1893 treaty preserving Egba autonomy.[18] The Governor-General had always seen the Egba state as an embarrassment and an inconvenience too,[19] because the state levied tolls on goods in transit through its territory and even charged the colonial government dues for the railway that passed through Egbaland. When rioting broke out in Abeokuta Lugard wrote to Boyle that the Alake must be told to renounce the 1893 treaty and place Egbaland under Britain as an ordinary province in Nigeria. There was no time for all these legal niceties in the face of a breakdown of law and order. Troops were ordered into Abeokuta on 6 August 1914 by the British Commissioner, who by now had assumed control. In fact Egba independence was lost from the time the control of affairs passed into Young's hands on 5 August. The logical thing was to abrogate straightaway the 1893 'independence' treaty and Lugard telegraphed from England, whence he was administering Nigeria 'continuously', urging this line of action:

> It is obvious that if the head of state says publicly that he is compelled to appeal for the assistance of armed forces of the colonial government, the state can no longer be deemed capable of standing alone as an independent state. It is also obvious that the existence of such a state in the middle of the British western provinces becomes a source of danger to government. Again the colonial government cannot be called upon from time to time to support the authority of a native ruler unless the government has had full opportunity of investigating the cause of the disturbances endeavouring by its own authority to secure peace without the loss of life. This it can only do if the state is under its control. Finally it is imperative that a stop should be put to the possibility of riots breaking out and troops being required, at a time when England is at war or troops are needed elsewhere. If it is true that advantage was taken by the malcontents to provoke hostilities purposely at such a time, measures must be adopted to render such action in future impossible.[20]

The loss of Egba independence was almost inevitable, but the measures adopted in putting down the revolt in Abeokuta went far beyond a reasonable and humane limit.

Following the series of demonstrations in Abeokuta from 5–8 August, the British Commissioner decided that the revolt needed to be firmly suppressed before it got out of hand. Instead of employing force straightaway the Commissioner first temporised by summoning the Oluwo, the leader of the disaffected area, to his residence and asked the Oluwo to call a meeting of his people where the dispute would be resolved.[21] This was precisely what the Oluwo did, but it seems the British official went back on his promise. According to Lieutenant D. E. Wilson, the military officer who was sent to put down the disorder in Abeokuta, the Commissioner simply told him on 8 August 1914, to make twenty arrests in the disturbed Ijemo quarters.[22]

Lieutenant Wilson said that when he got there he found 1,500 men assembled in the compound of the Oluwo, and ordered them to disperse immediately and to hand over their chiefs. If it was true that the Commissioner had asked these people to assemble in the first place, the order to disperse from soldiers must have come as a rude shock to the men, who were expecting to meet a British civilian officer. Secondly, it was expecting too much, and showed a gross misunderstanding of the positions of chiefs in a a traditional society, to ask ordinary peasants to hand over their chiefs for arrest. Lieutenant Wilson said the people 'absolutely' refused to obey orders and when one Oguntayo made an attempt to assassinate him, he instantly shot his assailant; this was the signal for a general fusillade upon a panicstricken and unarmed crowd. Wilson said he ordered his troops to shoot because he thought his life was in danger. During the shooting that followed, the Oluwo, a man of 70 years, and six other chiefs as well as twenty-nine others were killed.[23] Among those killed were two wives of the Oluwo and a twelve-year-old boy.[24] This was a clear illustration of the uncontrolled official violence unleashed on an assembly summoned at the instance of the colonial government. No inquest was held on the victims and their bodies were buried without identification in a single trench by a party of prisoners. This action constituted a great injustice, bearing in mind the respect for the dead and the elaborate burial ceremonies the Yoruba always had for their departed elderly relatives and especially chiefs. Lieutenant Wilson was directly responsible for what Sir John Anderson later said looked like a massacre.[25] When his troops opened fire on the crowd, the British officer made no effort to check the killing of men and women who were in flight and who were offering no resistance. A maxim gun was used, which was totally unnecessary for the situation, and soldiers entered the Oluwo's house to shoot down people in their rooms.[26] On the following day, after most inhabitants of Abeokuta had deserted the town for their farms, Lieutenant Wilson and his troops went about 'destroying houses and collecting property'.[27] Justifying this action P. V. Young, the Commissioner, said it was done at the Alake's request and he commented: 'I quite concurred in it as being a necessary and salutary lesson for them which all their people would be able to see for themselves as showing the power of the Alake'.[28] It is interesting to note that when power was slipping from the hands of the Alake, with the loss of Egbaland's autonomy, the British Commissioner continued to justify every action in terms of giving the Alake more power. The reality of the situation was that the British Commissioner was actually following a thinly disguised policy of turning Egbaland into a sort of southern 'emirate' where the policy of indirect rule could be more suitably applied.

The whole episode was a sad beginning for Nigeria during the war and it showed how irresponsible those involved in the whole affair were. P. V. Young, the British political officer, at whose instance the troops had been summoned and under whose directions the military officer acted, neither accompanied the troops, as was usually the case, nor did he send his assistant. Neither Edun, the Egba secretary, nor any other responsible representative of the Egba government in whose support the troops were sent was present. If the normal procedure had been followed in such an operation, the province would have been spared the bloodshed and the hostility which this engendered, which remained thinly concealed until it blew up into a greater explosion in 1918.

Scapegoats were inevitably found for the serious bungling in Egbaland, in the persons of Anthony Green, who was formerly the president of the Egba mixed court, and Soyemi Alder of Lagos. These two men were subsequently arrested and charged with the crime of inciting the Ijemo people to riot. The two men were severely beaten after their arrest, and paraded handcuffed like common felons round the town while their homes were destroyed by soldiers.[29] The British Commissioner did not conceal his hostility towards these two men, who 'are to a certain extent educated and would like to have the government in their own hands'.[30] Since this class of Nigerians was regarded as enemies of the Lugardian administration, it is hardly surprising that they were rushed to judgement and sentenced to one year's imprisonment by the Chief Justice, Sir Edwin Speed; he had suffered quietly the virulent press attacks on him by the same class of people. The Chief Justice in sentencing them said the two men:

> were themselves nursing private and personal grievances against the Egba administration and particularly the government secretary ... they made use of the unfortunate incident which caused such profound discontent and dissatisfaction among the Ijemo section as a lever to obtain their own objects, chief among which was the dismissal and disgrace of the government secretary.[31]

The Chief Justice erred in his analysis of the role of these two men in the Ijemo affair. There is no doubt that Edun was very unpopular in Egbaland and the attempt to maintain him in power by the British was again to cause trouble in the future. If Green and Alder had manipulated the Ijemo people to achieve whatever ends they had in view – an allegation which was not proved – they certainly did not create the occasion making this possible. The situation in Abeokuta was more complex than the Chief Justice perceived.

The issue in Egbaland was how to maintain 'independence' and modernise without falling under the British administration, as well as how to resolve internal conflicts under the shadow of the surrounding British overlordship. These were very difficult problems, and the men in control of affairs were hopelessly unsuited to cope with them. The Alake and Edun were more interested in maintaining themselves in office than in upholding Egba independence, which was why they quickly surrendered their powers to the British Commissioner after the outbreak of violence in August 1914. As a result of their weak position it was easy for the Nigerian Government, which had always wanted to annex Egbaland, to nullify the 1893 treaty of Egba independence on 30 September 1914.

The Ijemo 'massacre', as it was called, was investigated following pressure put on the Colonial Office by the Anti-Slavery and Aborigines' Protection Society and the Church Missionary Society, but the report was never published.[32] The Ijemo affair was a prelude to the turmoil into which the whole of Nigeria was to be thrown. Its pattern, first of defiance of 'native' authority or agents of the colonial government, and then open rebellion against both African and British rulers and finally brutal suppression with little attempt to discover the grievances, was one to be repeated in other areas.

Just as the embers of revolt were dying out in Egbaland a very serious rebellion broke out in the Central and Eastern Provinces, first of all in Warri Province. One of the most important factors in the uprising here was the great dependence on German trade, but it was not the only one, since the Germans were unable to use their economic dominance in Yorubaland to disturb the peace there. The reason for the trouble in Warri Province therefore must not be sought in the economic strength of the Germans, but in the nature of the change of administrative policy which lent itself to easy exploitation.

The rebellion started in Kwale district, where many government messengers and court clerks were murdered. These clerks had been greatly resented by the people because of the way they had manipulated the Native Court System created by Lugard to serve their own pecuniary ends. The rebellion spread westwards into other parts of Warri Province, where the Kwales were joined by the Urhobos and Ika-Ibo in killing not just court clerks but Yoruba and Hausa traders who were seen as 'foreigners'.[33] They also attempted to burn the factories of English firms, most especially those of John Holt & Company, in the area. The revolt was so serious that the government was compelled to withdraw some troops from the Ikom column on the Nigeria–Cameroons border and to bring those occupying Egbaland to deal with the rebellion in Warri Province.

The government tried to find out the causes of this sudden uprising by sending F. S. James, who was credited with the gift of understanding the peoples of this area and similar areas east of the Niger river, to investigate the reasons for the trouble. After suppressing the rebels militarily, F. S. James called their leaders together and tried to solicit their loyalty. He told the men that they should not imagine that because Nigeria was at war, they could take laws into their own hands. He said the government was strong enough to carry on war against the Germans and also see that law and order prevailed. The Kwale uprising led the government to start questioning some of its administrative methods without actually changing the direction of policy. It was not realised that the extensive use of warrant chiefs[34] as agents of the administration was one of the causes of the uprising.

It was believed that the chief cause of the rebellion was the resumption of trade by the Germans, who were temporarily stopped from trading at the outbreak of war. F. S. James wrote:

> The presence of the German traders – more especially ... their resumption of trade had had disastrous effect on the native mind. If we accept the theory that the idea of the government leaving the country had been gradually growing in the minds of the people, an idea ... not confined to the ignorant Urhobos and Kwales ... the presence of the Germans has done everything possible to foster and confirm it. The native mind cannot grasp how we English can be at war with Germany and yet German subjects are allowed to compete against their English rivals.[35]

That the Germans were not allowed to trade when war broke out seemed logical to the people of the area, James commented, though their freedom to move about, he felt, must have seemed surprising to Nigerians, but when the Germans were allowed to resume trading operations, the chiefs and the common people felt Germany must have won the war in Europe.

The Lugardian institution of native courts presided over by warrant chiefs, or government agents, without the close scrutiny of British officers who formerly sat on these courts, was an unsettling innovation. F. S. James said the removal of the white man from the native courts was misunderstood; and that further withdrawal of military and political personnel from the area following the outbreak of war was interpreted as clear evidence that the government was actually leaving. It was the fear or expectation of this, said the British official, that was one of the causes of the rebellion. F. S. James claimed that the people preferred what they had been led to believe was the British judicial system – which amounted to no more than the presence of the district officers in native courts. This presence at least prevented unscrupulous court clerks and warrant chiefs from cheating and extorting money from their fellow Africans. It was this change that the people had been protesting against since Lugard removed the district officers from the courts. In a way the rebellion was against changes in administrative policies, as witnessed by the merciless slaughter of court messengers and warrant chiefs.

The Nigerian authorities underestimated the penetration of the Germans into the hinterland and the dependence of the native economy in this area on the German market. This was a palm oil and palm kernel producing area and the Germans probably used their economic goodwill and influence against the government. The sudden stoppage of German commercial operations in the first place must have hit the producers hard, and when they were allowed to resume trading, the hostility of their English rivals made it impossible for them to trade. Thus the resumption of trade itself did not benefit the producers, who now found that the Germans who used to buy their stock were not allowed to do so, while the English merchants were not buying produce because of the uncertainty of the times.

The fact still remains that the withdrawal of personnel must have left the room wide open to German intrigues. The British knew the risks they were taking in withdrawing men from their posts. Some of them were convinced that if rebellion broke out it would not last, as evidenced in a letter by one of them:

> We are seriously depleted and have unrest and risings amongst the ignorant pagans in many directions . . . these low type pagan tribes are wholly incapable of combination and if it is the will of heaven that they should cut one another's throats for a bit of pastime because 'the whiteman have all gone to war' well they won't be greatly missed![36]

According to F. S. James's Report on the rising in Warri Province, the Germans were accused of having incited the people to rebel against the British. The Germans protested against the allegation in a series of notes to the Governor-General. In a note jointly signed by agents of G. L. Gaiser and other important German firms in the area, the Germans wrote:

> while we are patriotic Germans we emphatically dissociate ourselves from any persons of our nationality who may have sought to trouble or inconvenience the government in any way whatever and we have frequently . . . remonstrated with such persons on their attitude.[37]

This note at least made it clear that some Germans were hostile to the government and such persons would naturally exploit the war-time situation to inconvenience the government.

The local British authorities were, however, not unanimous in attributing the Kwale rising to German intrigue. One district officer wrote:

There is not the smallest doubt that there are numberless wild rumours circulated among illiterate natives to the effect that German success is assured and that our government is powerless, and this idea has been fostered by the recent permission to allow the enemy factories to reopen. To the uneducated native our attitude in this matter is inconceivable unless forced upon us by a successful foe. . . . I am informed that these rumours (of German victory) emanate from the German factories and are distributed through the shop boys and native employees . . . the fact remains that these rumours are having serious effect at a time when owing to the peculiar circumstances it is not possible to properly visit the district regularly and keep the people up to the mark.[38]

Another British officer commented:

I would not go so far as to say that any German subjects have deliberately incited the natives against the government . . . but they have doubtless spoken to their boys or others concerning the war from their own point of view, probably also in a very exaggerated tone. In this way various ridiculous rumours have spread through the country.[39]

These British officials were positive that the Germans had spoken to their employees from their own point of view, which was to be expected, and that the Africans must have felt that since the white men were fighting themselves, they would probably leave the country. The anti-German feeling of British officials was instigated by British merchants. The Germans had never been liked by their commercial rivals before the war, which must have come to some of the British merchants as welcome news. They expected the German traders to leave the country or be imprisoned, so that when the local people rose against the British, the merchants were quick to identify the cause of the rising as the German presence in the country. One of the merchants wrote:

We are strongly of the opinion that allowing the Germans to trade again has had a great deal to do with this rising as the natives think that the Germans have won . . . and are assisting them by rising against us. In any case it shows that they are ripe for a rising if only they get a leader and there is nothing to prevent them getting a German for a leader in view of the liberty that these Germans are allowed here.[40]

Some of the articulate African leaders in the areas of the rebellion were interviewed and they too came up with different

versions of the story of German involvement. Chief Ogbe of
Warri told F. S. James that he had not heard any German speak
any words against the government or anything to make people
believe that Germany was getting the best of the war. He added:
'I cannot say what has been the cause of the recent troubles ... I
think some people who wish to have nothing to do with the
government, but to do just as they feel inclined fancied that the
government was too busy with war against Germany ... to
punish them if they did wrong.'[41] One educated Nigerian trader
in the area said that he was told that the Germans were doing so
well in Europe that the British sent to the President of United
States of America to intercede on their behalf as they could not
continue the war. The same trader also said that the agents of
some German firms were boasting publicly that after their
masters had won the war, life would be much easier for Nigerians
under German rule.[42] Chief Dore, who represented the area in
the Nigerian Council, said the Kwales, Urhobos and Itshekiris
believed the Germans had won the war and that when a government messenger was sent to Ogidigbe near Burutu the people there
said 'we don't recognise the government, the government is
finished, we hear the Germans have beaten them'.[43] One British
police officer summarised the German involvement or non-
involvement when he put it succinctly thus:

> the most sinister feature underlying all these revolts is the repeated
> statements one hears proving that in many cases the towns have been
> intrigued into disaffection either by German agents immediately or at
> least by dissemination of lies by strangers from other parts of the
> province as to the effect of the war upon the position of the govern-
> ment in the colony. I have not been able to trace these reports to any
> definite source and they appear at present to be widely published as
> the result of general rumour, but one is forced to the conclusion on
> hearing the same fables retold again and again that they all have a
> common seditious origin.[44]

In assessing the cause of this rebellion the factor that was not
taken into account was the vulnerability of the society to intrigue,
being largely 'chiefless' in the Hausa–Fulani or Yoruba sense;
there were no leaders on whom the people could focus their
grievances except government appointed 'chiefs' and the educated
court clerks, who were sometimes from other parts of the country,
so that when revolt broke out it was directed against the British
administration which had created the dummy chiefs and delegated

powers to them. When the people found out that the delegating power was weakened by the war, they tried to assert themselves and forcefully remove the agents of the colonial power such as court clerks and 'alien natives' who were suspected of being part of the colonial establishment. The Germans probably lent support to the insurgents, but their support could not have been decisive, for their influence in this area was after all not as much as in Yorubaland, where the revolts were not German-inspired; this is not to minimise the influence of the Germans, who were far more popular than their British counterparts because of their generous credit system.[45] Some of the Africans in this area definitely felt that the Germans must have won the war and in rising they thought they were aiding the Germans; at the same time it was a rebellion, given opportunity by weakened British forces, to even up old scores with the hated court-clerk types and warrant chiefs. As if to disprove the alleged German complicity, revolt broke out in the South-eastern provinces in the later part of the year 1914.

The resentment here was directed against the same class of 'alien Africans' as in the central provinces. In November 1914 rebels forcibly released prisoners from the local jail in Onitsha, and the houses of unpopular native clerks and court messengers were razed to the ground.[46] Between 1914 and 1916 there were serious revolts in Okigwi District, Afikpo, Bende and Aba Districts in Owerri Province. There were revolts in Udi District of Onitsha Division and in Ogoni District in Calabar Province. The causes of these revolts were as varied as the areas of their occurrence, but the common denominator was that court clerks and warrant chiefs were killed.

During the disturbances in Udi District the government clerks and the artisans working on the railway from Port Harcourt to the Udi colliery were killed. The villagers succeeded in driving police-men out of their district, and in holding their own against the policemen sent to put down the revolt from October 1914 to February 1915.[47] The Nigeria Regiment was engaged in the Cameroons at this time and could not be employed against the rebels. The situation was saved by a volunteer force of European officials and non-officials assisted by local police, which succeeded in putting down the revolt by killing 252 rebels. The revolt in Udi District was due partly to the fear of the people of the area that their land was going to be taken from them by hundreds of men engaged in railway construction.

The revolts in Owerri Province continued until July 1915 and sporadically afterwards; one of the causes of revolt there was opposition to recruitment of people as carriers.[48] The rebellion in the Eastern provinces was not actually a novelty. The area had not been completely brought under government control before the war broke out, and in a sense the revolt was simply initial resistance to the imposition of colonial rule. But because of the fear generated by the war, the colonial officials saw every revolt as an attempt by the native population to overthrow the colonial government. It was felt that punitive measures and heavy casualties would bring the people to their senses. One official commented: 'The necessity for punitive measures, while raising the prestige of the government caused its sincerity to be fully understood by natives.'[49] Many of the rebels told their fellow Africans that the government forces were in the Cameroons and that the government was therefore not in a position to impose its authority on the country. The government, fearing that if this rumour were allowed to spread unchecked a dangerous situation might be created, decided to strike heavily at the rebels, hoping that the punishment meted out would have the 'salutary effect of impressing upon the natives that in so thinking they were labouring under a delusion and that government is in a position to quell a local disturbance . . . when the necessity arises'.[50]

In the suppression of the revolts in the Eastern provinces the government placed emphasis on the policy of massive infliction of casualties on the rebels. R. C. Cavendish, the assistant police commissioner in the area, commented: 'the lesson administered by the patrol lies in the number of casualties the enemy suffers in the course of the hostilities . . .'[51] Lugard also commented, 'I do not regret the loss of life among the aggressors, for these people hold life so cheap that the only way to prevent a recurrence of the outbreak is to make them understand that it will be severely dealt with'.[52] Lugard persuaded his officers with this rather absurd reasoning since none questioned him about whether, if the men held life so cheap, they would care about the casualties inflicted. The revolts in some of the provinces in the eastern area were easily contained because of the lack of combination and co-operation among the rebels. The government's massive retaliation policy did not pay off, however, because sporadic outbreaks of violence continued to occur until the end of the war.

Resistance to British rule during this time was not always

martial or violent, occasionally it was literary and sometimes apocalyptic, as happened in the Niger Delta during the first half of 1916 when a serious threat to British administration came from a semi-religious movement, This movement was led by one Garrick Sokari Braid who was a member of the C.M.S. in Bakana, New Calabar. Bishop Oluwole Johnson of Lagos described him as 'a humble man of quiet disposition, full of zeal and energy for preaching. . . . He was instrumental in converting thousands of people to christianity.'[53] Braid was said to have indulged in psycho-physical faith-healing practices which had apparently brought him many admirers and followers. This movement was described by *The Times* of London as 'a dangerous pseudo-christian movement'; the paper claimed that the movement was spreading throughout Southern Nigeria and that it was of such a dangerous character that it upset the normal course of administration in the Delta.

Braid proclaimed himself Elijah II and preached that power was soon to pass from whites to blacks. The British authorities viewed the whole movement as a sort of 'negro mahdism', and *The Times* commented that the movement had affected trade and threatened government authority and Christian influence while the 'fanatics have made a holocaust of a great number of articles and valuable ivory'.[54]

Another paper, the *African Mail*, remarked:

the native mind is such that but little is necessary to sway the more ignorant section of the community into paths which are inimical to good government. At the same time we do not go so far as some of our popular Dailies who see in this false prophet another *Mahdi* under whose banner are flocking millions of natives ready to attempt to overthrow the British *raj* . . . we must confess that there are dangerous elements in this new cult. A type of this new Elijah might so work upon the emotional side of the native mind as to constitute a real danger . . . it is strongly advisable to nip this evil flower in the bud . . . there may be political motives behind it and before it is a real source of trouble it ought to be effectively crushed.[55]

The movement was no doubt a dangerous political one, but with religion as the motive force behind it, it attracted so many people partly because of frustration over the temporary depression in the palm oil trade, which hit the Niger Delta.[56] The movement became a political one when Braid started preaching independence for the Delta peoples, which he felt would come after mutual destruction of each other by the British and the Germans in the war. His revivalist Christianity almost wrecked the little liquor trade, that was still very lucrative because the demand exceeded supply, since Braid advised his followers to abstain from alcohol. For this reason many European traders looked at him with apprehension, Braid was later arrested and jailed for receiving money under false pretences. There is no doubt that the movement's importance was greatly exaggerated. It must be said that before Braid was jailed, he did more within a short time to stop the liquor traffic in his area than all the international conventions and the anti-gin lobby had been able to do in decades; his only sin was the challenge he posed to constituted authority, which could not take anything lightly in view of the chaotic happenings all over the country.

The Elijah II affair made Nigerian authorities very suspicious of unorthodox Christian sects in Nigeria. It led to censoring of the correspondence of a mission such as the Seventh Day Adventist Mission, which had as its head in Nigeria a black American named D. C. Babcock. This mission had stations at Shao in Ilorin Province, at Erunmu, near Ibadan, and Ipoti in Ekiti Division. The church congregation were mostly dissenters from the C.M.S., and most of the staff were educated Africans from the Gold Coast and Sierra Leone – that class of Africans repugnant to Lugard. Lugard felt that Babcock's personal sympathies were certainly pro-German, but that the mission was not carrying out subversive activities in Nigeria. The Colonial Office, with the experience of the Chilembwe[57] 1915 rising in Nyasaland, pointed out to Lugard: 'In Nyasaland the Mission's doctrine or its results if spread among uneducated coloured races by persons with more enthusiasm than wisdom were regarded . . . as likely to unsettle the minds of the natives.'[58] The Colonial Office asked the Governor to close down the mission at the first sign of any suspicion of subversion.

As if all these problems of revolts and their subsequent suppression were not enough, other groups in other parts of the Southern provinces tried to exploit the war-time situation to manifest their opposition to government policies, as happened in the Okeogun rebellion.

The Okeogun rebellion took place in the 'back yard' of the Alafin of Oyo, whose influence and power the government was committed to bolstering up. The cause of the revolt was deep rooted and connected with innate Yoruba disregard for over-bearing authority, especially when that authority did not have grass-roots support or traditional sanction. In an attempt to make indirect rule work in Yorubaland the traditional respect which Yoruba people had for their Obas, including the Alafin, was being eroded by the fact that the Yoruba increasingly saw Alafin Ladigbolu as no longer serving the interests of the people but as allowing himself to be turned into an instrument of the colonial government.

The Yoruba, like the Hausa–Fulani, were marked out by the administration as a proud and haughty people whose loyalty should be cultivated by strengthening their traditional political in-stitutions and trying as much as possible to separate the 'natural' leaders from the *parvenu* leaders who made their way to the top through education. The Yoruba were admired and loathed at the same time. They were seen as the most difficult people to ad-minister because a sizable fraction of them had become 'de-nationalised' through their affection of Western civilisation, and in the tide of rising expectations this minuscule group was demanding too much from the administration.

The government was not sure of the appropriate policy to follow in Yorubaland until Lugard in 1912 decided that Yorubaland possessed the essential qualifications for indirect rule. In attempt-ing to apply 'orthodox' indirect rule in Yorubaland, the first mistake was made. Each Yoruba town was a 'kingdom', though it might acknowledge its subservience to another powerful 'kingdom' and pay tribute to its ruler; it was not truly analogous to the northern emirates where the powerful emirs controlled and even chose district heads of adjoining areas. It was unfortunate that the policy of indirect rule and 'native treasury' had to be tried here during the unsettled time of war. Lugard failed to recognise that Yoruba society, in spite of the 'chiefly' and monarchical institu-tions, was basically constitutional, in the sense of existence of various pressure groups whose interests had to be reconciled and balanced with those of others in the society; pressure groups like the Ogboni and the guild of hunters (and war chiefs), some of whom resented the large Hausa settlements in Yorubaland as a licence which the white man had given to their former enemies from the North. It is in the light of this medley of interests, sentiments and resentments that the Okeogun rebellion of 1916 can be understood. It is also important to note that beneath the apparent progressive culture of the Yoruba lay a sort of inherent conservatism which contact with the white man and the presence of educated Yorubas had failed to change.[59]

The signal for the revolt in Oyo province came when the Onjo (head chief) of Okeiho and his relatives were killed by the 'war chiefs of Okeiho in October 1916'.[60] The Onjo's position was analogous to that of the Alake of Abeokuta, who ruled over what essentially was a federation of separate groups each with its own head chief. Okeiho was a creation of the Yoruba wars of the nineteenth century, when several groups moved south in reaction to Fulani incursion and Dahomey raids into northern Yorubaland. Each of the groups that founded Okeiho retained their separate identities, as evidenced by the fact that each area of the town was peopled by separate groups of Oyo–Yoruba who owned allegiance to their different head chiefs. These head chiefs regarded the Onjo, on whose land Okeiho was situated, more than just *primus inter pares*, although there were occasions when the Onjo was deposed by these guest-chiefs.[61] In other words, the opposition to the Onjo by sectional leaders in Okeiho had some precedence. The events of 1916 were therefore a culmination of a trend begun at the onset of British rule in the area. The rebels also went further, burning down the Onjo's house as well as the court house where he sat as a judge. They were not just bloodthirsty criminals but genuine traditionalists who had from 1909 sought to remove the unpopular chief from office, but were blocked by the British administration.

In 1914 the 'war chiefs' gave orders that nobody should be recruited as soldiers or carriers in Okeiho, but this was overruled by the Onjo with the backing of the Resident at Oyo. The Onjo also used the new 'Native Court', in which his powers were un-trammelled, to suppress his opponents.

After the killing of the Onjo and his relatives the African government clerks who fled in the face of violence were pursued to Iganna, a town of about 12,000 inhabitants, and shot. The rebels also burnt the government rest house where the visiting white man always stayed and they uprooted the cotton which the government had encouraged the district to plant for sale to the British Cotton Growing Association. The Okeiho incident set in motion a train of rebellions in which the war chiefs played pro-minent roles. This group historically had profited from chaos in Yorubaland and like medieval war lords in Europe they had always taken pride in the prestige and wealth that accompanied every victory. They thought they could recall the 'glorious' past and come to their own while the white men were fighting among themselves.

The rebel leaders sent messages to neighbouring towns to join in and get rid of the native courts. About a thousand young men from neighbouring towns of Ilero, Iganna and Otu rallied to the cause. The ranks of the rebels were swelled by sympathisers from Iseyin, a town of about 50,000 inhabitants. Iseyin had its own grievances against the colonial administrative policy, which completely subjected Iseyin to the Alafin of Oyo's control and meddlesomeness. The reigning Aseyin was therefore a willing tool in the hands of rebels who claimed to be fighting for Iseyin's autonomy from the British-backed Alafin. Before the rising, Iseyin politics had been dominated since the advent of the British by a struggle for mastery between the pro-Alafin and the anti-Alafin factions. The local people were also against the British-inspired judicial system which made divorce easier for African women, who were more or less their husband's property before the advent of British colonialism. Other grievances centred on opposition to vaccination and the digging of latrines near every house, which the people considered less hygienic than their custom of defecating in the bush! Lastly, the people were against forced labour (*corvee*), which was resorted to by the administration for public purposes.

The burning of government houses was repeated in Iseyin as well as in each of the other towns. The joining of the rebels by many people in Iseyin introduced a dangerous element into the whole crisis because of the size of population of the town. The rebels became very confident after their ranks had been increased, and they went about the district setting ablaze the telegraph office and blowing up bridges along the Iseyin–Oyo road. Trees were felled along the road to hamper fast movement of government troops and the rebels dug trenches which they manned with their dane-guns.

The Aseyin (Oba of Iseyin) seems to have tried to calm his excited subjects, but he too was driven into the hands of the extremists by the impolitic action of the Resident of Oyo, Captain Ross, who in spite of the delicate situation set out to humiliate the Aseyin, perhaps without knowing that he was doing so. He asked the Aseyin to meet him at the gate of the town to discuss the crisis. This was an order which no self-respecting Oba could comply with. The Aseyin had no choice in face of the stiff opposition of his people and the proud nature of Yoruba obas but to refuse to meet Captain Ross unless the latter were prepared to come to the Aseyin's place, which would have been hazardous in view of the people's will to resist the government.

Alafin Ladigbolu tried to intervene but he too had become very unpopular with his people. To most of them Ladigbolu was the white man's Alafin – a member of the Nigerian Council. The Alafin himself, seeing the people in Oyo were becoming increasingly fascinated and impressed by these events in the distrct, felt very insecure and asked the Resident to bring troops to Oyo itself and parade them through the town so that his subjects might know he had the support of the government.[62] Thus he symbolically paraded his own weakness and dependence upon British support – he whom the British regarded as pseudo-'sultan' of Yorubaland.

Troops were eventually rushed to Iseyin and the other rebellious towns, but they were ambushed and some lost their lives. The nature of the resistance necessitated asking for some companies of the first expeditionary battalion of the Nigeria Regiment, which was about to proceed to German East Africa, to be brought in. In the meantime, influential men were sent from Oyo to warn the towns of Otu, Shaki, Iwo, Ibadan and Ogbomosho, which were showing signs of unrest, not to join the rebels.

The rebellion was brought to an end when government troops killed many of the war chiefs – that breed of men whom Yoruba folklore had always surrounded with mystery and invincibility. Their followers became demoralised and by the beginning of November 1916 the whole movement collapsed after approximately two hundred men had died in the fighting.

The rebellion was so widespread and the signs of latent uprising in adjacent areas were so visible that the administration began to look for deeper roots of the unrest in Oyo Province, which had hitherto been held up as the best organised of the Southern states, ranking with the Islamic emirates of Northern Nigeria as an example of African capacity for political development and organisation. Apart from the Onjo of Okeiho's tyranny, which was the immediate occasion of the rebellion, the government felt the cause lay deeper and that the Okeiho situation simply provided an excuse for giving vent to a rebellious attitude that had remained latent for some time. One cause of the rebellion was an appeal from the Alafin to all the Bale (head chiefs) of Okeiho, Shaki and Iseyin to collect Red Cross Funds from their subjects at the rate of a shilling per man and six pence per woman. The people, whose political horizon was limited to their immediate relation with the Alafin as their king, could hardly have been expected to understand the purpose of the Red Cross Fund; and little effort was made to tell them the reason for the levy. The malcontents said that the Red Cross Fund was a tax to which there might be no end.

Iseyin people had a history of opposition to the Alafin, now being built up as paramount ruler of Yorubaland by the British. Between 1899 and 1905 arrests of principal chiefs had been made by soldiers following their disobedience to the Alafin. In November 1914 supporters of the Aseyin had stormed the court house and stopped the proceedings, saying they would no longer have anything to do with it. The fact that the Aseyin was not the president of the court itself constituted a flagrant departure from the Lugardian principle in this matter; rather than make the Aseyin the court President, the Alafin's men from Oyo were handpicked by the Resident and imposed on the local population. In 1915 Captain Ross gave a warning to the government that Iseyin was probably the only town in Oyo division that would resist any form of direct taxation. In March 1916 there was great dissatisfaction with the native courts. The court judges, who ought to have been loyal to the administration, were also not satisfied with the pay of £2 a month. Chiefs from Iseyin, who were excluded from the courts and who formerly maintained their positions and authority by receiving fees, fines and bribes, were forbidden to exercise authority, and were punished for trying cases in their homes contrary to the Native Courts Ordinance imposed by Lugard. Those formerly accustomed to receiving money, exercising authority and entertaining their followers found themselves without the usual means, and discontent brought them to the state of revolting against a system that they considered had impoverished and belittled them and put all the power and influence they were accustomed to exercise into a few hands of government-appointed 'foreign' judges, educated court clerks and messengers from Lagos and Abeokuta.

In a rather 'Lugardian' way of reasoning, the Resident, Captain Ross, argued that, had a 'tribute' tax been instituted at the same time as the native courts, the principal chiefs concerned would have had employment and remuneration as well as influence. The point that was overlooked was that these people would have resisted and did resist any system of direct taxation or any other form of levy, as shown in their attitude to the Red Cross Fund. The argument that the estranged chiefs would have had influence if they had been paid by the government disregarded the fact that the government-paid chiefs were the ones who had lost influence because they had been cut off from their traditional roots – from gifts freely given, homage duly paid and respect properly earned without resort to force.

During the rising about a thousand Hausa people in Iseyin barely escaped being massacred. Luckily they caught wind of the news and got away before the plan for their slaughter was ready for execution. The reason why the Hausa were marked out for extermination could have been historical, commercial or religious. The northern Yorubas never really trusted Hausa–Fulani people for historical reasons.[63] Secondly, the Hausa were used by the British as 'spies' and 'political agents' all over Nigeria, and although Yoruba and Hausa predominated in the Nigeria Regiment, the British had always sent Hausa detachments to Iseyin in the past to shoot down rebels.

In order to prevent similar outbreaks led by the same 'hunter-warrior' class in Shaki, Ogbomosho, Ibadan and other 'Oyo' towns, the Alafin was said to have insisted that no mercy should be shown to the ringleaders. The government imposed collective fines on all the towns involved in the uprising. The inhabitants of the towns were forced to rebuild and widen their roads, as well as build camps for troops stationed in their towns. The government introduced compulsory registration of all inhabitants in the area and prohibited the sale of fire-arms. The most revolutionary and perhaps potentially explosive feature of the measures taken was the novel idea that district heads would now be appointed from Oyo to supersede the existing ones, in an attempt to enforce centralisation of power in the hands of the loyal Alafin, whose influence with his people was being undermined in direct proportion to the government favours being showered upon him. The policy of inflating the position of the Alafin was thus not seen as one of the causes of the revolt. The inhabitants of Okeiho (a town of about 20,000) as instigators of the rebellion were told to move their entire town to a more easily accessible location.

The shock of the Okeogun rebellion moved Lugard to embark on a tour of Oyo Province so that he could see things for himself.[64] Before visiting the Alafin, he interviewed *en route* the Bale and chiefs of Oshogbo, Ogbomosho and Ibadan, and warned the Bale of Ibadan in particular of the severe consequences of collaboration with anti-government forces. Lugard brought in more troops to Ibadan to augment the garrison normally stationed there. He also sent troops to Ijebu Ode to overawe opposition, which was manifesting itself there. In a despatch to the Colonial Office Lugard summed up his impression of the situation in these words: 'the disturbances were originated by seditious and lying counsels emanating from a thoroughly disloyal clique in Lagos led by the ex-convict Herbert Macaulay'.[65] This certainly was not true. It was claimed by some of the rebels that the Red Cross Fund was similar to the water rate,[66] which Lagosians had refused to pay, and that consequently they too would not pay the Red Cross Fund. But apart from this tenuous connection, the 'clique' of educated Lagosians were not involved in the rising, which was a purely traditional revolt expressing strong hostility to the educated scribes of Lagos and Abeokuta who lorded it in the new native courts.

Eight of the ringleaders were tried by a 'court-martial' and sentenced to death, including the Aseyin. Lugard ordered that the sentences be carried out publicly so that the people could draw the moral from the punishment. Delegates from all over Oyo Province were invited to witness the hanging of the eight men, including an oba who, according to Yoruba custom, 'does not die but simply fades away'. To crown it all Lugard decided to strike while the iron was still hot; he introduced direct taxation into Oyo Province, but this was done over the dead bodies of the Aseyin and his chiefs.

Following these draconian measures the *Lagos Weekly Record* alleged that officials were going round Yorubaland frightening the obas and 'terrorising and bullying people ... by holding up to their gaze the tragic fate of the Aseyin and his chiefs'. The paper went on that their action was:

> not calculated to inspire any degree of respect but rather of contempt and dislike for the administrative methods and capabilities of those who to all intents and purpose ... are painfully afflicted with megalomania, that they should even go further ... to lay a hard and fast rule that henceforth every native of the district on accosting any

European, be he a gutter-waif or what not so long as he can boast a pink coloration, should prostrate before this descendant of the gods of white prestige is assuredly adding insult to injury.

In what seemed to mirror the resentment of educated Nigerians about the Okeogun rebellion, the paper concluded:

there can be no question, that the high-handed policy that is being adopted in Yorubaland savours more of the destructive rather than the constructive way of imperialism. . . . For it is too late in the day, at least in Yorubaland to endeavour to foist upon the people obnoxious rules and regulations that bespeak a recrudescence of dark and unenlightened days . . . wherein they derived their origin.[67]

As if to say that unless the Lugardian policies were abandoned in Yorubaland, there would be more trouble. The rigidity and inflexibility of the government in its enforcement of indirect rule finally led to a disastrous second rebellion in Egbaland in 1918.

THE SECOND EGBA REVOLT OF 1918

The second Egba revolt was intimately connected with the first, but it was more widespread and better organised. The refusal of the government to publish the report of the commission set up to probe the causes of the first rising had led to great misunderstanding and wild exaggeration of the Ijemo affair. The popular belief of Yoruba people about the Ijemo incident was that a government official summoned hundreds of people to the Oluwo's compound in Abeokuta promising to discuss their grievances, but ordered them to be slaughtered in cold blood.[68] The publication of this Report had been opposed by the Colonial Office on the grounds that only the educated Lagosians would read it and that

'these agitators . . . would probably use it as a means to unsettle the political peace of Egbaland and would also claim, not perhaps altogether unjustifiably, that publication was tantamount to an admission that the criticisms of the government which it contains are well founded'.[69]

Direct taxation was imposed on Egbas on 1 January 1918. The Egbas were told that 'compulsory unpaid labour' would cease as from 1918. Every adult Egba was to pay not less than five shillings, which the people complained was too heavy in view of the depressed state of the economy.[70] Edun, the government secretary, refused to reduce the taxes and consequently the Egba were forced to pay what they said they could not afford.

When direct taxation was introduced an important constitutional change was made at the same time by the division of Egbaland into seven districts each under a district head.[71] The district heads were the three principal chiefs next to the Alake – the Oshile, Agura and the Olowu (who later refused to co-operate); the others were the Olotta of Otta, the Olu of Ilaro and one Seriki Onatolu – who was not a prince but Edun's man. Seriki Onatolu and the post he was chosen to fill had no *locus standi* from the point of view of Egba custom. Edun also appointed native courts' judges not from the Ogboni chiefs, but put his own stooges in office, thus virtually dispossessing the Ogboni chiefs of their traditional powers. The sectional obas who were made district heads were forced to leave Abeokuta town and reside in the villages where their districts were located. All these changes coming at the same time were too much for the people to swallow.

As from May 1918 signs of unrest began to manifest themselves in the rural areas of Egbaland. The government made attempts to look into the causes of the grievances. In May 1918 A. G. Boyle, the Lieutenant-Governor of Southern Nigeria, accompanied by the Alake and Edun, toured Egba Division in order to meet leaders of the disaffected areas, but they were ignored, especially at Papalanto where the people brandished their dane-guns as a sign of defiance.[72] A. G. Boyle felt insulted and went back to Lagos after having told the men in the area that if the Alake could not settle the problem, the government would use force to settle it. Boyle apparently thought this threat would end the agitation, but it never did. Boyle gave Edun and the Alake a few days to settle the crisis, thus abdicating his responsibility as Lieutenant-Governor.

Serious discontent showed itself first in the Western District under Seriki Onatolu. The Eastern District under the Oshile was equally disturbed and Abeokuta itself showed signs of tension. As a result of all these incidents the Egba government decided to reduce the taxes to placate the people, but this was too late to save the situation. Discontent grew and assumed formidable proportions. By the end of May 1918 troops were rushed from Kaduna to Abeokuta and Wasimi.[73]

The Egba people struck on 13 June 1918 from the countryside and divided into three columns with Abeokuta as their final objective. Although the rebellion had been in the air for some time, the actual outbreak took everybody by surprise, especially its size and the efficiency of its organisation. Trouble was expected in a localised form in Papalanto and not over such a wide area. The rebels, whose number was put at 30,000,[74] were led by the traditional warrior class. It was rumoured however that among the leaders were educated people from Abeokuta and elsewhere and that some Egba regular soldiers belonging to the Nigeria Regiment joined in the rising.[75] The rebels were apparently joined by malcontents from other parts of the country, particularly from Ibadan and Ijebu Divisions.[76] Some people from French Dahomey crossed the border and assisted the Egbas. This is an interesting commentary on the effect of European colonisation of Africa, that people under different colonial administrations should find common cause in resisting European domination. The Dahomeyans crossed the border in large numbers as fugitives fleeing from French reprisals after an unsuccessful attempt to kill the Governor of Dahomey.[77]

The rebels tore up railways and destroyed telegraph lines; railway stations were set ablaze and thousands of pounds' worth of property was destroyed or carried away. The Nigerian authorities, not realising how serious the uprising was, sent a small force which the rebels quickly drove away. They then continued pulling up railway lines throughout Egbaland, apparently to paralyse all communication and the movement of troops. They were also marching on the water works, perhaps with the intention of unlocking the dam and flooding a considerable area of Egbaland.

The rebels intended wrecking and sacking Abeokuta and nearly succeeded in taking the city. All Europeans, hearing that one Ashworth, the agent of John Holt & Co. Ltd, had been killed by the rebels, fled to the residency, whilst the Alake hid himself in the Roman Catholic mission house at Abeokuta.[78] The road to the residency was mined with quarry blasting charges in case an attack might be launched against the Europeans hiding there. The village of Oba, eight miles from Abeokuta, where the Oshile resided as district head, was one of the most seriously hit by the rebellion. The Oshile, the second in rank to the Alake, was killed after he had been given a chance of either championing the cause of the rebels or facing death for refusing to join. The rebels marched towards Abeokuta, surprisingly with the Oshile's own son leading them.

The rebellion extended over the southern part of Egbaland to Alagada in the north, near Otta in the south, its eastern limits being the valleys of the Ogun and Ore rivers.[79]

The Egba rising came at a particularly favourable time for the government. Nigeria had a superfluity of soldiers now that campaigning was over and the rising took place in an easily accessible area, making suppression easy. About 2,600 soldiers were engaged in the operation.[80] The scale of the operation was quite considerable and government troops suffered 100 casualties,[81] and about 1,000 rebels were reported killed.[82] Active resistance came to an end on 22 July 1918, terminating the most widespread rebellion in Nigeria during the war.

The bloodshed was on such a large scale that humanitarian circles in Britain and the C.M.S. hierarchy both in Britain and Nigeria as well as educated Nigerians demanded a full inquiry into the causes of the rebellion.

The reasons for the rising were so intricately tied up with the changes introduced into Egbaland between 1914 and 1918 that it is difficult to say what was the immediate cause. In A. G. Boyle's view the whole crisis was caused by the Edun–Alake maladministration. He commented:

> the former Administration of the province ... combined all the worst forms of injustice and misrule covered by a veneer of apparently advanced methods at the capital of Abeokuta. The Alake, a Constitutional monarch and Edun his prime minister presided over a large council who directed the affairs of the country ... the Alake an illiterate ... chief ... was well disposed but weak and a mere tool in Edun's hands. His council consisted of a number of very old men who rarely or never left the capital and whose only nature was to acquire personal gain by extortion from the peasantry.[83]

The Resident of Egbaland could not think of any other cause but the influence of outside agitators. He wrote to Lugard that:

> there was no opposition from resident Egbas – opposition came from outside the province especially by educated natives from Lagos ... at once suspicion is aroused and the people cannot understand that advice from so-called well wishers and supporters in Lagos may not always be unbiased or that their Lagos friends resent not being taken into confidence before schemes are embarked upon. Furthermore, the idea of Lagos being the headquarters of the government always carries great weight and advice from Lagos sounds to people

as advice from those who are really *au fait* with the real meaning of all schemes and would be listened to with much respect.[84]

A Commission of Enquiry was set up to look into the causes of the Egba rebellion. The Commissioners were James Crawford Maxwell, A. Duncan Atholl, both of whom were senior Residents, A. Macgregor, a police-magistrate, Reverend Oliver Griffin, a Wesleyan missionary, Frederick Lowe, agent of John Holt & Co. Ltd, and an educated Egba lawyer Eric Olawolu Moore.[85] The inclusion of Moore itself was significant, in that it gave the commission a balance, and an opportunity to know the Egba side of the story. The commission blamed the rebellion on the continuation of compulsory unpaid labour after the introduction of taxes. The opposition to this kind of labour had been felt as a hardship for some time and Ponlade's arrest of 1914 and the subsequent 'Ijemo Massacre' arose out of the opposition of the people in the rural areas to this system. Even before the Colonial Office knew the outcome of the commission, A. J. Harding minuted: 'It is hardly possible to acquit the resident of *mala fides*. He did give a definite undertaking that this should cease at the end of 1917 and he did enforce its continuation beyond that date.'[86]

The commission also blamed the division of Egbaland into seven districts with district heads who had general administrative control and were also tax collectors as one of the causes of the rebellion. The change was too revolutionary and it ought not to have been done during the war. The idea of sectional obas being appointed district heads was contrary to tradition and the appointment of Seriki Onatolu as a district head was resented by sections of the Egba people. Seriki Onatolu was tactless, threatening the people that if they did not pay their taxes they would be treated like the Ijemos – an unwise action since the killing of people during the Ijemo affray 'still rankled in the breasts of many Egbas and was a potent factor in the distrust of the government officer'.[87] The Commission of Enquiry found out that many people in the rural areas were asked to pay double taxes – one on their farms and one in the town – and these farmers were also made to pay electricity taxes in spite of the fact that electricity was available only in the city.

The prolonged duration of the war and the constant recruiting of troops from Nigeria to take part in distant campaigns had a cumulative effect in weakening the prestige of the local government while they inspired the hope among disaffected sections of the people that 'now, if ever, had arrived the time when armed rebellion might prove successful'.[88]

Edun, the Egba secretary, was hated personally by many sections of the community; according to Lugard he was an 'unscrupulous man who is said to have improperly acquired some lands'.[89]

The treatment of the Ogboni was found to be one of the causes of the rebellion. The government abolished what was vaguely called 'death duties' payable to the Ogbonis by the children of a deceased member. The commission reported that there was no justification for government interference in this, since people were not coerced to join the society and if a man were not an Ogboni his children need not have paid; the fees were used for burial rites which were based on tradition and the people and their chiefs had vested interests in its continuance. One witness at the enquiry commented:

> Parakoyi [the traders' guild] has been done away with and to do away with Ogboni would be to deal a death blow to the tradition of the Egbas. The British government has abolished slavery but we are being reduced to servitude. .... I mean that all our old customs are being interfered with up till today you hear *Oro* in Lagos but in Abeokuta it is prohibited.[90]

The Resident of Egbaland argued that the Egba situation would have been brought under control were it not for shortage of staff; the Commission of Enquiry, however, criticised this argument. It was pointed out that shortage of staff was:

> no justification for the introduction of new schemes and constitutional changes ... An officer who knows that he and his staff cannot carry on current work efficiently and who not withstanding this introduces new and far-reaching schemes, is inviting trouble and he cannot plead that he did not have the staff to supervise efficiently.[91]

Because of the irresponsibility of the British Resident and the Governor in forcing these changes on the people, about a thousand unfortunate people lost their lives, £55,637 11s. 2d. worth of property was lost and in addition there was the aftermath of bitterness and distrust that was to hamper administration for years to come. In a strong indictment the commission concluded that 'the actions as a whole were contrary to the best tradition of good government'.[92] The responsibility for the Egba riot which marred the achievement of Lugard in Nigeria was laid on the shoulders of the Governor by *West Africa*, the London weekly magazine, which commented:

> Today Nigeria has a black mark upon its record, like Ireland, part of South Africa and part of Quebec, it is one of those portions of the Empire which have added to the anxieties of Great Britain by having civil disorder within their boundaries. Unlike the other three places named it is a country whose people are not at all as yet sufficiently developed as to be able to govern themselves ... therefore responsibility for what has happened rests firstly and mainly upon its practically autocratic government ... the man on the spot cannot have in his hands all the machinery of government and then if that machinery be so used that a breakdown occurs escape adverse criticism. The first job of the man on the spot is to see that the King's business is done, that order and peace prevail ... and in so far as he does not do this he is a failure ... needless to labour the point that Sir F. D. Lugard ... must feel it as something of a personal humiliation that during his Governor-Generalship, normal courses in Nigeria should be violently interrupted at this time of all times.[93]

Lugard himself accepted the blame which he knew would come.[94] The Colonial Office however did not accept the entire findings of the Commission of Enquiry, especially the strong condemnation of all government actions being contrary to the best tradition of good government. The commission did a good job in pointing out the unwisdom of the British in introducing revolutionary and sweeping changes during the war. Lugard should be held responsible for his hasty action in connection with the introduction of direct taxation in Yorubaland. Had the Colonial Office allowed him he would have introduced this measure at the outbreak of war. This rising strengthened the hands of the incoming Governor, Sir Hugh Clifford, to make modifications of the indirect rule system. Clifford even went so far as to propose that all the taxes collected in Egbaland be spent there without the colonial government taking its share of fifty per cent. This however was disallowed by the Colonial Office.[95] But the Egba rebellion made the British look at the Lugardian administration with a more critical eye.

The basic cause of these movements of resistance and rebellion was not the war itself. The war provided the occasion by visibly weakening the military presence of the British, while at the same time creating administrative understaffing which loosened administrative control and lessened the amount of hard information the

British could command on the state of local and regional feelings and opinions. The causes however lay in the attempt to introduce concepts and practices of native administration, in political re-organisation (especially in Yorubaland), direct taxation and native courts.

The bitter hostility was everywhere directed at illegitimate chiefs or illegitimate powers given them, and at the native court clerks' and messengers' abuses of power. The British may be justly accused of unwisdom and irresponsibility in trying to introduce such profound changes exactly at the time when their contact with popular feelings was weakened by understaffing and their police control weakened by the war's demand for troops.

The movements were essentially movements of resistance to colonial rule. They represent a stage between the 'primitive' or 'initial' African resistance when the Europeans were first trying to occupy African territories, and the 'nationalism' of the post-1930s. It is significant that the series of revolts and rebellions in the Southern provinces were led by the 'traditional,' often illiterate warrior-class and not by the educated 'native' who hardly had any nerve for such resistance, or probably felt the pen was mightier than the sword – the educated native resistance movements were boldly written in flamboyant language on the pages of their newspapers.

It should however be noted that while the British were con-cerned with revolts, resistance or rebellion in the Southern pro-vinces of Nigeria and about the possible political consequences, they at no time imagined that the challenge to their authority could be so serious as to threaten their hold on Nigeria. It was realised that the rebellions in the south were rather isolated sporadic outbursts against alien rule lacking organisation, and that there was neither cohesion nor co-ordination. There was no unity as such, unity which the force of Islam could provide in the Northern provinces. The fear of a general rebellion with Islam as an instrument of cohesion haunted the British throughout the war and they were always out to root out 'Mahdism' wherever it was suspected. This is why the matter of any kind of revolt in Northern Nigeria attracted more than the usual attention.

Notes

1 See Robert I. Rotberg and Ali Mazrui, *Protest and Power in Black Africa*, Oxford University Press, New York, 1970, p. xx of Introduction.

2 Margery Perham, *Lugard: the Years of Authority, 1898–1945*, Collins, London, 1960, p. 542; see also Michael Crowder, *The Story of Nigeria*, Faber and Faber, London, 1962, p. 223; Alan Burns, *History of Nigeria*, Allen and Unwin, London, 1929; M. Perham, *Native Administration in Nigeria*, Oxford University Press, London, 1962, pp. 75–79; see also Akinjide Osuntokun, 'Disaffection & Revolt in Nigeria during the First World War', *Canadian Journal of African Studies*, ii, 1971, pp. 171–2.

3 C.O. 583/43/36642, P. V. Young (Commissioner in Egbaland) to Colonial Office, 9 Aug. 1915. See also the pro-government newspaper *The Nigerian Pioneer* of 21 Aug. 1914.

4 Sir H. M. McCallum, Governor of Lagos 1897–9.

5 C.O. 583/75/33183, Boyle to Milner, 10 May 1919.

6 *Ibid.*

7 See Samuel Johnson, *The History of the Yorubas*, Routledge and Kegan Paul, reprinted, London, 1969, pp. 22–7.

8 Women in Egbaland had always played a rather interesting role in the society. They had joined in the defence of Abeokuta in the nineteenth century and the legendary Tinubu (after whom Tinubu Square in Lagos was named) had been one of the most famous of Egba women in public life. See S. O. Biobaku, *The Egba and their Neighbours*, pp. 48, 51, 57, 86. In recent times one Egba woman, Mrs Ransome-Kuti, headed a movement which led to the exiling of the late Alake of Abeokuta, Sir Ladapo II – and she has also been active in local and national politics. The role of women in Egbaland deserves special recognition in a country where the status of women has been little better than that of a slave or property.

9 C.O. 583/72/12803, Boyle to Milner, 21 Jan. 1919.

10 *Ibid.*

11 C.O. 583/33/32243, Lugard to Colonial Office, 12 June 1915.

12 C.O. 583/33/32243, Duncombe's letter enclosed in Lugard to Colonial Office, 12 June 1915.

13 C.O. 583/43/36642, Young to Colonial Office, 9 Aug. 1915.

14 C.O. 583/30/4294, R. M. Combe's memo 4 Jan. 1915.

15 C.O. 583/25/34071, Bishop Herbert Tugwell of Lagos to Lugard, 9 Sept. 1914.

16 C.O. 583/25/34071, Young to Lugard, 24 Dec. 1914.

17 *Ibid.* The Alake actually offered a bribe of £50 to the Ogboni.

18 See S. Johnson, *op. cit.*, pp. 651–2. After the first four clauses of the Anglo-Egba 1893 treaty had provided for freedom of trade, etc., the 5th clause states: 'It is . . . agreed . . . that so long as the Provisions of this treaty are strictly kept, no annexation of any portion of Egba country shall be made by Her Majesty's Government without the

consent of the lawful Authorities of the Country, no aggressive action shall be taken against the said country and its independence shall be fully recognized.'

19 Perham, *Lugard: The Years of Authority*, pp. 434–6.
20 C.O. 583/19/42181, Lugard's minute, 30 Sept. 1914 (later sent to Boyle as a despatch).
21 C.O. 583/25/34071, Bishop Tugwell to Lugard, 9 Sept. 1914.
22 C.O. 583/25/34071, Lt D. E. Wilson to Commandant, Nigeria Regiment, Kaduna, 4 Jan. 1915.
23 *Ibid*. cf. *Nigerian Chronicle*, 14 Aug. 1914, which reported that over 100 people were massacred: an unpublished Report of a Commission of Enquiry put the figure at 38 to 55 (C.O. 583/34/32247, Lugard to Colonial Office, 21 June 1915).
24 C.O. 583/34/32247, Lugard to Colonial Office, 21 June 1915.
25 C.O. 583/34/32247, Sir John Anderson's minutes, 30 July 1915.
26 *Ibid*. Unpublished Report of the Commission of Enquiry into the Egba riots of 1914. Members of the Commission were Messrs Bedwell (Ag. Administrator of Lagos), Dunlop (legal adviser), Henry Carr (educated Nigerian civil servant who was Inspector of Education for the Colony).
27 C.O. 583/25/34071, Wilson to the Commandant, Nigeria Regiment, 4 Jan. 1915.
28 *Ibid*., Young to Lugard, 24 Dec. 1914.
29 *Nigerian Chronicle*, 14 Aug. 1914.
30 C.O. 583/25/34071, Young to Lugard, 24 Dec. 1914.
31 C.O. 583/30/4924, Lugard to Colonial Office, 4 Jan. 1915.
32 C.O. 583/25/3407, Secretary of the Anti-Slavery and Aborigines Protection Society to Colonial Office, 7 Sept. 1914.
33 C.O. 583/30/4960, Report of the Kwale rising by F. S. James (Administrator of Lagos Colony) to Lt-Governor, Southern Provinces, 30 Nov. 1914.
34 For detailed study of the warrant chiefs, see A. E. Afigbo, *The Warrant Chiefs: indirect rule in South-Eastern Nigeria 1891–1929*, London, Longman, 1972, ch. 2.
35 C.O. 583/20/48783, F. S. James to Lugard, 7 Nov. 1914.
36 *Lugard Papers*, i, MSS British Empire 72. 'Extracts from Rough Journal Jottings' written by Major E. J. Lugard from Nigeria to his wife in England for her interest only, 19 Oct. 1914.
37 C.O. 583/20/48783, Paul Meyer and R. Breitenbach (agents for Witt & Busch), Karl Note (G. L. Gaiser) to Lugard, 6 Nov. 1914.
38 C.O. 583/20/48783, J. Davidson (D.O. in charge of Forcados) to Lugard, 26 Oct. 1914.
39 *Ibid*. F. B. Adams, D.O., Warri, to Lugard, 31 Oct. 1914.
40 C.O. 583/27/44386, John Holt's agent in Warri to Lugard, 17 Oct. 1914.
41 *Ibid*. Chief Ogbe's interview with F. S. James, 2 Nov. 1914.
42 *Ibid*. I. T. Palmer (an educated Nigerian trader) said he heard his story from agents of Behrens & Wehner in Warri and Sapele. I. T. Palmer told F. S. James all this on 2 Nov. 1914.

43 *Ibid.* Chief Dore's interview with F. S. James, 2 Nov. 1914.

44 C.O. 583/38/55086, R. C. Cavendish (assistant police commissioner) to Boyle, 4 Nov. 1915.

45 Cmd. 468, 1919, xxxiv, 609, Lugard Report, p. 41.

46 C.O. 583/20/4874, Lugard to Colonial Office, 19 Nov. 1914.

47 C.O. 583/32/23453, Lugard to Colonial Office, 29 April 1915.

48 C.O. 583/19/45292, Lugard to Colonial Office, 28 Oct. 1914.

49 C.O. 583/49/58210, Boyle to Colonial Office, 7 Nov. 1916.

50 *Ibid.*

51 C.O. 583/38/55086, R. C. Cavendish's report enclosed in Boyle to Colonial Office, 4 Nov. 1915.

52 C.O. 583/33/28160, Lugard to Colonial Office, 29 May 1915.

53 *Times of Nigeria*, 15–22 Aug. 1916, p. 6.

54 *The Times*, 22 June 1916.

55 *African Mail*, 30 June 1916.

56 Michael Crowder, 'West Africa and the 1914–1918 War'. *Bulletin de l'institut fondamental d'Afrique noire* (I.F.A.N.), xxx, Janvier 1968, 1, p. 230. See also Crowder, *The Story of Nigeria*, p. 223.

57 See for further details: George Shepperson and Thomas Price, *Independent African, John Chilembwe and the Origins, Setting and Significance of the Nyasaland Native Rising of 1915*, Edinburgh, Edinburgh University Press, 1958.

58 C.O. 583/50/3521, Colonial Office to Lugard, 27 Dec. 1916.

59 The Okeogun rebellion was led by the Baloguns (hunter-warrior guild), whose strength in Yorubaland was great. It is interesting that at the same time the French in Dahomey were also fighting 'les chefs de guerre ou Balogouns' in the Yoruba-speaking part of Dahomey. See *L'Afrique française*, Aug. and Sept. 1916, pp. 303–4.

60 C.O. 583/55/10824, Captain Ross, Resident of Oyo, to Lugard, 4 Feb. 1917.

61 See J. A. Atanda, 'The Iseyin-Okeiho Rising of 1916: An example of socio-political conflict in colonial Nigeria.' *Journal of the Historical Society of Nigeria*, iv, 4, June 1969, pp. 498–9.

62 C.O. 583/55/10824, Captain Ross, Resident of Oyo, to Lugard, 4 Feb. 1917.

63 See Johnson, *op. cit.*, pp. 197–202.

64 C.O. 583/55/10824, Lugard to Colonial Office, 4 Feb. 1917.

65 *Ibid.* Herbert Macaulay (1864–1946) grand old man of Nigerian nationalism, jailed by the Lugardian administration for embezzlement. He was one of the greatest critics of the government and championed the cause of restoration of the dynasty of Lagos (the House of Docemo or Dosumu). He founded the *Lagos Weekly News* in 1922 as well as the first political party in Nigeria (the Nigerian National Democratic Party); published a book entitled *Justitia Fiat: The Moral Obligation of the British Government to the House of Docemo*, Lagos, 1921.

66 C.O. 583/48/49544. There was a riot in Lagos in September 1916 over the water rate issue; 2,000 people participated and burnt down houses

belonging to two chiefs (Obanikoro and Ojora) sympathetic to the
government.

67 *Lagos Weekly Record*, 17 Feb. 1917.
68 C.O. 583/77/55483, Clifford to Colonial Office, 29 Aug. 1919.
69 *Ibid.* L. S. Amery to Clifford, 8 Jan. 1920, quoting Colonial Office's
   official stand on withholding the report in 1915.
70 C.O. 583/68/59455, N. C. Syer's (Resident of Egbaland) memo
   enclosed in Boyle to Milner, 21 Jan. 1919.
71 C.O. 583/75/33183, C. W. Alexander's memo, 10 May 1919.
72 C.O. 583/68/59455, Boyle to Milner, 21 Jan. 1919.
73 C.O. 583/71/41944, from an unnamed Nigerian official to Walter
   Long, 28 Aug. 1918.
74 *Ibid.*
75 C.O. 583/69/44321, H. J. Read to Secretary, Liverpool Chamber of
   Commerce, 5 Dec. 1918.
76 C.O. 583/83/21289, Lugard to Colonial Office, 5 April 1919.
77 The Yorubas in Dahomey had been giving the French administration
   there a hard time since the beginning of the war. Chiefs of Ijofin on
   the Nigeria side of the border had from 1916 given one Sohingbe
   from Dahomey support in organising a refugee camp for deserters
   from the French army and for organising pro-British demonstrations
   in Porto Novo to the utter embarrassment of both Allies. The Lt-
   Governor of Dahomey reported in 1916 that 'Une groupe d'une
   soixantaine de jeunes nagots (Yoruba) musulman tous vêtus d'un
   boubou blanc et d'un bonnet vert et porteurs de petits drapeaux
   anglais parcourut les rues de la ville ... chantant ... "le drapeau
   anglais flottera ici dans six mois, nous en avons déja reçu la nouvelle
   ... c'est sous l'autorité du drapeau que nous portons à la main que
   nous allons rester".' See L.A.O.F. (Affaires Politiques) Carton 575
   Dossier 3, 'Dahomey: repression de troubles survenus dans diverses
   regions 1916–1917'. The Dahomeyan Yorubas no doubt wanted to
   enlist the support of the British in their effort to avoid conscription
   and probably to join with their kinsmen in Nigeria, but they were to be
   disappointed on 11 March 1918. In spite of some Colonial Office
   officials like Harding opposing this French recruitment, which
   Harding called 'a peculiarly objectionable form of slavery', and
   Strachey's saying that 'we must be judges of our necessities and
   possibilities and the French can no more tell us to recruit compulsorily than we can tell them to stop doing so, although there is
   much more reason for the latter ...' See C.O. 445/45/7565, 12/2/1918.
   The French demanded repatriation of Yorubas of Porto Novo and
   Ketu origin: C.O. 445/45/6688. M. le ministre des colonies to Foreign
   Office, undated. It was perhaps the attempt by Nigerian officials to
   aid the French in Dahomey by repatriating Dahomeyans in Nigeria to
   Dahomey, which angered the pro-British Yorubas there and made
   them join in the Egba rising, seeing that there was not much to choose
   between France and Britain.
78 C.O. 583/66/35056, T. J. Waters (acting chief surveyor Northern
   Nigeria) to Lugard, 20 June 1918.

79 C.O. 583/71/41944, unnamed official to Long, 28 Aug. 1918.
80 C.O. 583/67/44709, Harding's minute, 16 Sept. 1918. Forces which took part in the operations were (a) 2 Battalions of West African Service Brigade, (b) 220 rank and file Nigeria Regiment from Ibadan, (c) 1 company First Battalion Nigeria Regiment from Kaduna, (d) 2 platoons of 1st Battalion West Africa Service Brigade, (e) 50 men and officers of 4th Battalion Nigeria Regiment at Ede, (f) 33 rank and file Nigeria Regiment and 50 armed police, from Lagos.
81 C.O. 583/68/59455, Brig. General Cunliffe to Lugard, 9 Dec. 1918. The 100 casualties were listed as 'dead and wounded'.
82 C.O. 583/71/41944, unnamed official to Long, 28 Aug. 1918.
83 C.O. 583/67/44709, Boyle to Colonial Office, 15 Aug. 1918.
84 C.O. 583/66/24819, W. C. Syer (Resident of Egbaland) to Lugard, 6 Aug. 1918.
85 C.O. 583/72/12803, Report of Commission of Enquiry into the Egba rebellion 1918, enclosed in Boyle to Milner, 21 Jan. 1919.
86 C.O. 583/83/21289, Harding's minute, 5 Aug. 1919.
87 C.O. 583/72/12803, Report of Commission of Enquiry into the Egba rebellion, enclosed in Boyle to Milner, 21 Jan. 1919.
88 C.O. 583/77/55483, Clifford to Milner, 29 Aug. 1919.
89 C.O. 583/66/35056, Lugard to Colonial Office, 21 June 1918.
90 C.O. 583/72/12803, Boyle to Milner, 21 Jan. 1919, enclosing Report of Commission of Enquiry into the Egba rebellion.
   Oro is a secret cult and members perform the rites at night. Women are not allowed to see the members, any woman who sees Oro may be killed. The Oro referred to here is the shrill sound produced by a flat piece of iron or stick with a long string attached to it which when whirled swiftly in the air produces this sound. Oro is sacred among the Egbas and Ijebus and was responsible for executing criminals.
91 *Ibid.*
92 *Ibid.*
93 *West Africa*, 24 Aug. 1918, 2, 82, p. 493.
94 See M. Perham, *Lugard: The Years of Authority*, pp. 451–6.
95 C.O. 583/85/17703, A. J. Harding's minute of 6 Jan. 1920.

5 The North, Muslim loyalty and the spectre of revolt

With the entry of the Turkish Caliphate, the head of the Islamic world, into the war on the side of the Central Powers, the British administration in Nigeria was gripped with the fear of possible pan-Islamic revolt. The administration was particularly concerned about the reaction of the Muslim emirs and their subjects in the big and well-organised emirates of Northern Nigeria. The *Lagos Weekly Record*, without knowing it, was reflecting the official mind when its editor wrote: 'It is only in the Northern provinces that some erratic visionary might look upon the present opportunity as one favourable for the proclamation of a Jihad.'[1] The fears of the British authorities arose out of the knowledge of Hausa–Fulani fanaticism in religious matters, and the 'colonies' of Tripolitan Arabs in the north formed potential centres of Islamic insurrection. The British did all they could to win the loyalty of the Muslims in the north, by continuing to exclude Christian missionaries from the Islamic emirates, and by giving more freedom to the native administrations during the war, yet the threat of a Jihad hung over the administration like the sword of Damocles. This fear was underscored later in the war by the pan-Islamic revolution that swept through French Sudan, partly caused by African resistance to the French *recrutement intensif* and the opposition of militant Islamic Tariqa such as the Senusiyyah to alien 'infidel' rule.[2]

It is generally known that indirect rule and other policies pursued by the British created a community of interests between the British and the Muslim hierarchy in Northern Nigeria, for which the British were rewarded with Muslim loyalty during the war. What is not generally known is that below the British-supported ruling class were significant resistance movements, occasioned by the war but not necessarily caused by it.

To forestall any hostile anti-British propaganda the Nigeria

Government published during the first few months of the war a *Gazette Extraordinary* in Lagos, explaining how England had always upheld Turkish independence since 1878.[3] Lugard followed this up on 8 November 1914 when he called a meeting of representatives of Muslims in Lagos, including chiefs and town Imams and explained to them how Muslim princes like the Sultan of Zanzibar and the Aga Khan had begged the Ottoman Caliph

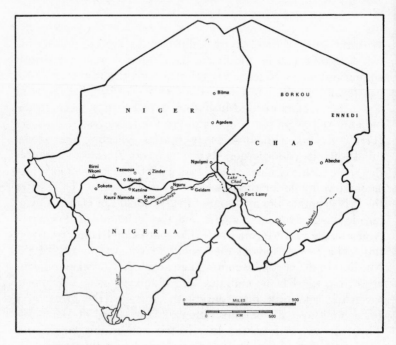

Nigeria and French Saharan territories of Niger and Chad

not to fight Britain, but to no avail. He also told the Muslim leaders that their co-religionists in Tunisia and Senegal were fighting on the side of France and that millions of Indian Muslims were also fighting under British banners. He added that the Egyptians had revolted against the Turks and they too were on the side of Britain against Turkey. He later convened a meeting of Muslims in Lagos and solicited their support for Britain in the time of the world crisis. A similar meeting was held in Ijebu Ode and addressed by the Governor-General's representative.[4] No such meetings were held in the north, where one might have expected mammoth gatherings to be organised. Lugard apparently was prepared to trust the northern emirs' competence to keep their people in line; this could not be said of the south, where the Muslims did not constitute a state but formed part of a society that was religiously variegated.

To consolidate the already existing loyalty to the British in the north, Lugard caused the Aga Khan's message in support of Britain to be translated into Arabic and distributed over wide areas of Northern Nigeria. The Aga Khan, whom Lugard described as the head of Indian Muslims, claimed that

> No Islamic interest was threatened in this war, our religion was not in peril for the British . . . had offered solemnly to guarantee Turkey and all her territories in complete independence if she had remained at peace. Turkey was the trustee of Islam and the whole world was content to let her hold our Holy citities in her keeping, now that Turkey has so disastrously shown herself a tool in German hands, she has not only ruined herself but has lost her position as trustee of Islam. . . . All men must see that Turkey has not gone to war for the cause of Islam . . . thus our only loyal duty as Moslems now is to remain . . . faithful and obedient to our temporal and secular allegiance.[5]

The upper classes in Northern Nigeria had everything to lose and nothing to gain by any kind of disorder. Many of the chiefs, especially those who owed their positions entirely to the British administration in Nigeria, were extremely uneasy about the war. The Muslim hierarchy was steadfast in its support for the British and one might say that their loyalty arose out of enlightened self-interest. They showed their support by contributing large sums of money to the Imperial war chest. Individual Muslim rulers like the Sarkin Musulmin Attahiru II contributed a thousand pounds[6] to the Prince of Wales' Fund, and others, seeing the 'Commander of the faithful' (Amir-al-mu'minin) making this friendly gesture, followed suit. The emirs of big and small emirates sent contributions with Arabic letters to the government as a proof of their loyalty. In a letter accompanying his contribution the Emir of Kano, Sarkin Abbas, wrote:

> . . . Because we hear you send many men to guard the boundaries of the land in the region of the Cameroons that they may not allow the Germans to come into the land to despoil us and to take us unawares . . . we thank you for the work you have done . . .

wherefore I wish if you agree to help you with a gift of money from Native Treasuries of £6,542.[7]

The Shehu of Borno, Bukar Garbai bin Muhammad Lamino el-Kanemi, wrote:

> the war is close to us at Mora, who knoweth the ways of Allah. We are warring against proud and stiff-necked people as the Germans are. In such a case Allah is on our side ... prophet Muhammad saith 'those who break friendship kill them like pagans, if you kill them perhaps they will repent'. We know that Governor Lugard wants money for this year. I remember last January I gave him £4,000 for schools public works and sanitation ... I should like this money to be changed and given for the war ...[8]

In another letter Sarkin Abega of Lokoja wrote to the Governor saying:

> we are not a great province, we are a small town. The Emirs give great gifts, they are great people, we give small gift, we are a small people, see now we give £100 from our Native Treasury ... if the King makes war we follow him, we are Mohammedans.[9]

By the end of the first year of war £38,000 had been placed at the disposal of the Governor-General, with a promise of £45,000 annually until the end of the war.[10] The Governor-General in notifying the Colonial Office about the generosity of the emirs noted that the whole movement was entirely spontaneous and that the opportunity of contributing to the war expenditure had been most popular and a matter of intense pride to the emirs and chiefs. The Colonial Office was somewhat sceptical about the spontaneity of these contributions in view of the attempts by Lugard before the war to encroach on the financial independence of the Native Administrations. One Colonial Office official minuted:

> if this offer is spontaneous it is satisfactory but looking at the pertinacity with which Sir F. Lugard has tried to raid this particular henroost I am anxious to know whether it is not a cleverly conceived move to get by hook what he has failed to get by crooks.[11]

There is no doubt that the emirs were being pressed to contribute money to offset Nigeria's revenue losses during the war; furthermore, the contributions, except in the case of that of Sarkin Musulmin, Attahiru II, were not personal funds, but public funds taken with the residents' permission from the native treasuries. But this is not to say that the emirs were not loyal. As can be seen from the letters of the Emir of Kano and the Shehu of Borno, the campaigns in the Cameroons meant more to them than those elsewhere and most of the emirs must have felt the war was first and foremost between Nigeria and the Cameroons. This is not to imply that these intelligent Muslim rulers were not aware of developments in other parts of the world, but like the 'Southern Dominions' which first disposed of the German colonies near them, the emirs felt the Cameroons needed to be reduced so as to guarantee the security of their emirates from external attacks.

The Shehu of Borno and the Lamido of Yola were unceasing in their support for the British. Their actions illustrated very well the point that the Muslim rulers were most concerned with the security of their states. These two rulers' territories ran coterminously with the German Cameroons border and in spite of the danger involved, the Shehu was ceaseless in his efforts to meet the extra demands caused by the war, providing transport, mail runners, remounts, escorts and gifts to the Nigerian troops. The Lamido of Yola with his council and chiefs, although placed in a very trying position on the Nigeria–Cameroons frontier where the early military operation by Nigerian forces had begun in disaster, still remained steadfast in his support. He rendered assistance in obtaining information as well as providing transport and supplies of food and material for the troops.[12]

The loyalty of the emirs manifested in their financial and 'military' assistance to the British is not as remarkable as it may appear to be. These emirs were very unsure of themselves, the security of their positions was threatened. German agents had promised nearly all deposed emirs and other chiefs out of office a speedy return to power should the Germans be successful locally.[13] It was in the interests of the emirs to see that the Germans, who were no less their adversaries as they were of the British, should not succeed.

The emirs were paid 'princely salaries' by the administration, and other members of their administrations also were handsomely remunerated. As long as these Muslim leaders continued to be well treated, they were certainly not going to be leaders of any Jihad against their benefactor, but this did not rule out the possibility of revolt from below, as was pointed out by H. R. Palmer.[14]

Native rulers and *Ulema* are not an absolute guarantee against fanatical outbreaks but they are the most effective buffer that can be devised and in their absence there is much more open field for the fanatical type ... the politics of the senusiyyah can do little in the West [i.e. Northern Nigeria with the exception of Borno] while the judicial councils of the Emirs, the Cadis and Imams are in receipt of substantial salaries from the Native treasuries.[15]

Although the British-sustained Hausa–Fulani establishment remained sound in its loyalty, below the establishment we find significant resistance movements. The causes of resistance lay in British policies and the administrative system. These movements were led by disaffected and often deprived or deposed elements of the Hausa–Fulani hierarchy or religious leaders. Their followers were *talakawa* expressing wider resentments.

Revolts broke out first in the semi-isolated areas of the North as early as September 1914. The attempt to merge small tribes into bigger coalitions under paramount chiefs or honorific emirs for administrative convenience very often led to resistance by unwilling subjects. In this connection revolts broke out in Kabba and Ilorin divisions, where British policies had attempted to override local particularism in favour of more centralised political organisation.[16] The Igbirra revolted when rumour reached them that they were to be ruled by the Attah of Idah rather than be left alone under whatever petty chiefs they had.[17] The Mada of Nassarawa Province also resisted the centralising tendencies of the government when they resorted to murdering Hausa traders, political agents and tax collectors among them. The Mada hated the splitting of their district into three units which were incorporated into the emirates of Jemaa, Keffi and Lafia.[18] The Mada had never recognised the authority of these emirs, with whom they had little in common. The Mada wanted to be left alone as a group, but since they had no important chiefs, the government had put them under 'foreign' emirs whom they naturally resisted. But no matter how widespread some of these revolts were the government always managed to suppress them.

Other revolts broke out in September 1914 in Nassarawa and Niger Provinces involving the Bassa of the two provinces. The Bassa rose against the Hausa and Nupe traders and native administration officials in their midst. The direct cause of the revolt was the improper conduct of Sarkin Umaisha, who ordered Bassa village heads to bring in large quantities of grain required for war supplies.[19] On their refusal to do this he ordered some of them to be arrested. Once the revolt started it fed on rumours such as the idea of an imminent withdrawal of the British from the country.

This was said to have been put about by Herr Walter Wiemann, an agent of the German firm of Pagenstecher & Co. Ltd. Captain Byng-Hall, the Resident of Bassa Division, alleged that Wiemann told rebels that the Germans would be in their country in three months. He was reported to have told the people:

> Why do you pay taxes to the English? We set up stores and give you goods in exchange for your produce, but the English government officials take money from you and give you nothing. When the Germans arrive, you will be given things you want, don't pay taxes.[20]

The Bassa–Nge chief, Taru Shidi, accepted the German story and urged his people to resist the government which was 'being defeated by the Germans who would shortly take over the country'.[21]

Disturbance occurred in various parts of the north in 1915. In Kontagora Province, trouble started in Kaiama emirate of Borgu Division. The trouble here was centred on Bussa following the deposition of the emir, Kitoro Gani, and his replacement by a pro-government emir who happened to have been a slave. Added to this were administrative neglect and lack of supervision and low visibility of British officialdom. On top of all this and perhaps most crucial was the elevation of ex-slaves and commoners to positions of authority following the deposition of the Sarkin Bussa.[22] In other words, the revolt here was a legitimist revolt against British-backed usurpers. This revolt was further compounded by recruitment of kinsmen of the Borgawa by the French in neighbouring Dahomey, thus leading to an influx of French subjects into British Nigeria, consequently upsetting the delicate peace there. The rising in this area was led by a certain Sabukki, a brother of the ex-Sarkin Bussa. Sabukki appeared at the head of a force of about six hundred warriors armed with poisoned arrows to attack the British-backed 'native administration'. After a feeble resistance by Bussa native administration authorities, Sabukki occupied the town of Bussa, driving out all members of the administration.[23] Following his success the *talakawa* rose up against their various district heads and other officials in Borgu. Two district heads, three district mallamai and the Alkalin Bussa were killed.[24] The Sabukki revolt, though a serious threat, was suppressed by troops after a tour of the area.

The Sabukki revolt was by no means caused directly by the

war, a grievance that had remained dormant only exploded at the opportune time. The ex-emir of Bussa (i.e., Sabukki's brother) had been removed because he and his relatives resisted 'progressive' measures, such as tax assessment, railway labour and collection of taxes, while on the other hand the emir chosen to replace him had worked loyally for the British.

There was also considerable unrest in 1915 in the technically Islamic emirates of Kano and Borno as well as in the semi-Islamised Bauchi province. The revolt against the native administration was concentrated on Fika, Katagum and Biu districts of Borno.[25] The revolt started in Biu district bordering on Yola Province in May 1915. The immediate occasion for this was a call to assist in some building work at Biu, at a time when reports had been received that the British forces had suffered reverses in the Cameroons and Europe. The rumour led to widespread uneasiness, particularly among the rulers. Most of the towns on the Yola side of the Borno–Yola border were quite out of control because of the war and the shortage of administrative personnel. The Fulani district heads in these areas had earlier fled their stations, fearing that they might be killed. The leader of the revolt was a certain Maina Gwanki, a Yola man who for many years dodged back and forth over the Nigerian–Cameroons border; he was suspected of German sympathies. After initial successes by the rebels, the revolt was put down by soldiers after about fifty people had been killed.[26]

In the same month of May 1915 another revolt having Pankshin District of Bauchi Province as its centre broke out. The rebels killed government mail-runners and tried to paralyse the communications system. They boasted that they would have nothing to do with the administration and that the British political officer could do nothing to them except burn down their huts and that to save him that trouble they would oblige him by doing it themselves. They told government emissaries sent to them to sue for peace that they had decided not to follow anyone but themselves for the foreseeable future. They warned that any Sarkin following or obeying the government's orders would be killed and any white man who dared to come to their town would also be killed. This was a challenge which the government could not allow to pass unnoticed. Although Pankshin was a difficult area topographically, government troops were rushed in to put down the rebels and about a hundred of them were killed.[27]

A bigger revolt covering Kano Province and north-eastern Bauchi as well as western Borno (i.e., the Borno–Dambam–Katagum–Hadejia area) broke out in the same year as these lesser ones. Lugard believed the reason for it to be mainly the paucity of administrative staff, and that as a result the area affected had 'afforded an asylum for political malcontents and professional highway robbers. Fulani herds were raided and the meat served to swell the ranks of the malcontents.'[28] Lugard's assessment was a gross distortion of the facts. The rebels in Bauchi were led by the ex-district head of Potiskum in Fika emirate backed by a large number of *talakawa*. This rebel leader no doubt felt he had been wronged by being dismissed from office, and the apparent weakness of the British made him attempt to regain the power that had been taken from him. The rebels succeeded in capturing Potiskum in January 1915.

At about the same time the revolt spread to Dambam. The Emir of Dambam was found to have secretly encouraged this rising, an offence for which he lost his position in the administration. The promptitude with which the situation was handled prevented revolt spreading to other areas. Most of the rebels – 'disorganised and yelling war cries' - lacked any sense of combination and co-operation. They were easily shot down by the few government soldiers that were available. *Dogorai* from Kano and Maiduguri were, for the first time in the history of native administration police, issued with guns to help Nigerian regular troops put down the rising in Potiskum and Dambam.[29] This action is significant and showed clearly that the rebels not only threatened British interests but also those of the emirs who willingly sent in their help in the form of the *Dogorai*, whom Governor Hugh Clifford later described as 'a mob of scarlet clad native police armed with swords and whips – the local representatives of the corrupt lictors of antiquity'.[30]

From May 1915 to the beginning of 1916, Muri Province was also in a state of considerable turmoil. The province, situated close to the fighting zone in the Nigeria–Cameroons border, naturally suffered from the restlessness and panic caused by the war. The people of the emirate exploited this situation by withholding their taxes, and they went further by asserting that they wanted the white man out of their country. To make it clear to the authorities that they meant what they said, they surprised the British assistant district officer of Ibi Division of Muri Province and fifty-eight other local employees of the government in an ambush by armed men and most of the party including the British officer were killed.[31] The Muri people also killed some missionaries along with the political officer and his agents. The inevitable British reprisal followed. The army and police were sent in, destroying crops and seizing cattle as well as killing about a hundred people in retaliation.[32]

Sokoto emirate, the most closely watched of all the emirates as headquarters of the disbanded caliphate, because of its historical importance as the home of Usman dan Fodio the nineteenth-century Islamic revolutionary, also passed through a period of unrest in 1915. The Nigerian authorities believed that the unrest in Sokoto was due 'apparently to the apprehensions of forced military service in consequence of action by the French over the border'.[33] The revolt in Sokoto emirate, which was led by 'three minor chiefs', was put down by a combined force of Nigerian troops, Sokoto native administration's *Dogorai* and the emir's 'horsemen'. The revolt was said to have been confined to the peasantry.[34] One might add that in the state of things in that part of Northern Nigeria the peasantry, being the most oppressed, was the most likely class to revolt, given the chance and the leadership.

During this period Nigerian authorities always dreaded the possibility of the emergence of a self-proclaimed Mahdi who might possess enough charisma to attract a large following. In 1916 this happened, but on a rather small and inconsequential scale. A certain Mairigan Karfi,[35] or the 'invulnerable one', declared himself a Mahdi in Donga District of Ibi Division of Muri Province. He quickly collected a band of fanatics like himself and raided surrounding villages until a force was sent to crush them, thus scotching the movement before it had any chance of growing. With the death of Mairigan Karfi, Mahdism petered out during the war, but the fear of Islamic revolt continued to haunt the government.

During this difficult period most of the important emirs and their officials were steadfast in their loyalty to the British, but as has been shown, Northern Nigeria did pass through an anxious time. In fact, not all emirs were as loyal as had been previously accepted, and in addition to using force to suppress rebels the government also resorted to deposing and exiling unco-operative rulers. At the end of 1916 emirs who were known to have tried to cause trouble were deposed and exiled, including Sarkin Mamuda, from Bauchi; Sarkin Muhammadu, Emir of Atchari in Niger province; and Sarkin Saibu of Sankwolo, who were all sent to exile in Ilorin,[36] far removed from their subjects and bases of power.

As expected, the Germans tried to exploit their connection with the Caliph, the religious leader of the Islamic world, to disturb the peace in Nigeria, but without any noticeable success. Arabic letters purporting to come from the Sultan of Turkey were smuggled into Yola and Borno emirates during the early months of the war. The letters claimed that Germany was fighting to prevent the British from giving Constantinople to pagans. Later in the war, before the fall of Garua in 1915, another Arabic letter was found in a Yola mosque, written by one Hauptmann Kariyesimu, an African who was being used by the Germans for propaganda purposes. Kariyesimu asked all Fulani rulers and their subjects to support the Germans, who were winning in Europe. He warned in the letter that since Germany was going to take over Nigeria after the war, all rulers who failed to rally round Germany would be punished.[37] Still another letter turned up late in 1915, addressed this time to the Emir of Yola. The letter as usual was said to have come direct from the Sultan in Istanbul; it ran thus:

> the Sarkin Musulmin has sent to the Kaiser to tell him what the English are doing. The English intend to take all the Fulani country when they have conquered them. They will stop them from praying. He the Sultan is one with the Kaiser . . . those who help the Germans are helping the Sultan. If he dies, he dies a Muslim, he who helps the English when he dies, he dies a *Kaffir* . . . I the Sarkin Musulmin tell you Muslims that he who follows Allah follows me, I believe they will meet Allah in peace.[38]

When the Germans sent a raiding party into Muri Province in May 1915 they left thousands of Arabic letters exhorting the people to rise against the British and the French in a holy war:

> Verily Allah has given us the banner of a Jihad to enable us to fight these people [the English and the French] not of the faith, who have stirred up strife between us in order to confiscate our wealth, our homes, our wives and all that Allah has bestowed on us. It is our duty to take up our guns and arrows and go to the great water [the River Benue] and man our boats and fight a Jihad with them. The holy book of *Islam* said 'if you are Mohammedans I command you, make

war on the unbelievers . . .' to all of you who have any authority I command you to help Germany . . . in this holy war . . . he who helps them verily helps the religion of Islam, he who helps the religion of Islam . . . shall find great reward from Allah. . . . You Mohammedans in English territory, if this letter reaches you, though you be soldiers, if you have any fear of the wrath of Allah in your hearts, I order you to desert and come to German country.[39]

Nigeria was provided with good ammunition to counter the German propaganda in 1916. When the Grand Sharif of Mecca proclaimed himself the guardian of the holy land of Islam and declared that Arabia was a separate political entity independent of Turkey, the Nigerian Government seized this opportunity to point out that Turkey was no longer the spiritual head of the Islamic world. The copy of the Grand Sharif's statement declaring himself as the sole guardian of the holy land of Islam was translated into Arabic and distributed in posters all over Islamic Nigeria.[40]

The two areas affected by German propaganda were Yola and Muri Provinces, but although there were revolts in those areas, they were not German-inspired and the German effort did not amount to more than a nuisance to the Nigerian Government.

The series of revolts in the north during the war were widespread enough to cause the administration some anxiety. The fact that no revolt was led by any of the great emirs or an important religious leader was a vindication of indirect rule, but not a justification for the maintenance of the *status quo* indefinitely. The revolts had shown a need for the modification of some aspects of policy such as taxation in relation to the ability or willingness of the *talakawa* to pay. It is also significant that few of the revolts in the north were caused by resistance to military service.

DANGER FROM WITHOUT

The Senusi movement and threat can be better seen as a test of the strength of the British hold on Northern Nigeria or, to put it the other way round, of Northern Nigerian loyalty to the British. From the beginning of the war to November 1916 the effect of Turkish and Senusi propaganda was negligible and reception to it cold. Certain persons were captured late in 1915 who declared that they were Turkish agents, but on close scrutiny it was doubted whether they actually were and whether their professions were not induced by an 'inherent love of Charlatanism and the ordinary motives of a mendicant'.[41] As far as Muslims in Hausa–Fulani emirates and most of Northern Nigeria were concerned, with the exception of Borno, the only Khalif (Amiral-Mum'inin) who really mattered was the Sultan of Sokoto. Furthermore, the religious and political horizon of most of the Muslims here did not go beyond their immediate loyalty to the Sultan of Sokoto, so that even if a few Turkish agents were captured they did not make any difference to the Muslims, nor did they undermine their loyalty to the British via their own leaders.

As soon as the Allies achieved victory in the Cameroons the emirs felt more secure and were little concerned with developments elsewhere in the Muslim world. The only places where events in the Muslim world were followed with keenness were the large centres like Kano and Katsina, where there existed fairly large Tripolitan 'colonies'. There was undoubtedly a certain undercurrent of sentiment among the Tripolitans for the Turks, and a pious hope that they might recover North Africa. In this connection the Germans were viewed merely as the instrument by which the Turks might come back to their own.[42] But since Nigeria was not isolated, events in the whole Sudan belt were bound to have effect.

> From Darfur to Senegal and from Yola to Agades the chiefs exchanged presents and news and were often united by marital and other ties. While they were not intolerant Muslims as a rule they were far more fervid believers in and votaries of the essential tenets of Islam than the average Turk or Arab of North Africa. They would be quite capable under certain circumstances of fighting for their faith ... Up to the time of the war the pride of the Fulani in their own position and history had entirely discounted the political influence of external sects. The Emirs have usually dismissed Senussi agents with presents and nothing more, not because they disapproved of their aims, but because they will not be patronised by Sidi Ahmed [Sayyid Ahmad-al-Sharif, the Grand Senusi] or anyone else.[43]

Two events, the Italian evacuation of the Tripoli hinterland and French conscription of their colonial subjects in the Sudan for service in Europe, altered the whole situation. These two events produced an immense moral effect all over the Sudan and especially in Kano, which was so closely connected with Tripoli commercially. The French conscription embittered and envenomed not only the majority of the Muslims to the immediate North of Nigeria, but a very large number of Nigerian Muslims who were in many ways related ethnically (like the Hausas in Nigeria and French Niger) to them. People were heard saying: 'here have these *Nasara* [Christians] been for twenty years preaching and legislating against slavery and now they themselves are slave raiding our villages and taking away our children to fight for them'.[44] The French by their compulsory military conscription had made the local leaders of the Tijani Tariqa (a sect generally considered most friendly to Europeans) extremely hostile and anti-French. People in Kano were also saying that the French wished to wipe out the Ulliminden Tuareg. All these happenings in French West Africa and the Sahara reverberated throughout Northern Nigeria, because relations between Sokoto, Katsina, Kano and Borno and such places as Agades, Bilma and Tawa (Taoua) were constant and intimate. The failure of the French to preserve order in their territory could not but react on Northern Nigeria. Once the atmosphere of unrest was created it was feared that the immediate occasion of trouble was more likely to be some petty local affair rather than any large question of world-wide importance.

From 1916 onwards a 'storm cloud' seemed to gather on the northern and north-eastern horizon and Senusi emissaries were traversing Nigeria from Wadai encouraging a general rising.[45] These Senusi emissaries came from disaffected French territories of the *Territoire militaire du Niger* and the Chad to the north and north-east of Nigeria. A pan-Islamic movement spearheaded by the militant *Senusiyyah* was sweeping through these two territories as a reaction to French policy.

Most of the Northern authorities – emirs, kadis, imams and mallamai – followed the rather conservative Qadriyyah Tariqa, but in Borno as well as some pockets of Hausaland most people belonged to the more egalitarian and forward-looking Tijaniyyah Tariqa. In Borno and Kano there were Senusi *zawiyas* (lodges) here and there so that penetration into Nigeria through them was possible.[46] Although there were different Islamic brotherhoods or Tariqas in the north they were not mutually antagonistic sects.[47] In fact it was not the practice of the Senusi to destroy other Tariqas; rather, they even allowed members of other Tariqas to belong to the Senusiyyah,[48] so that there was minimal room for conflict and ample room for co-operation between them and Northern Nigerian Muslims. Even if there were no adherents of militant Islam within the borders of Nigeria, this could not be said of returning pilgrims from Mecca and Medina and from the various *Fellata* (Fulani and Hausa) 'colonies' in the Anglo-Egyptian Sudan. The great number of these pilgrims made keeping watch on their activities almost impossible. For example, between 1913 and 1918, 20,601 pilgrims left Northern Nigeria for Mecca and within that period 24,633[49] returned, so many who returned had been away for several years and might have become members of some subversive Tariqa. The heads of the *Fellata* (Fulani, Hausa, Kanuri) 'colonies' in the Anglo-Egyptian Sudan were leaders with whom the returning pilgrims were associated, while there were sheikhs who were brothers or sons of emirs who had failed to secure a throne in Nigeria. The most influential was Mai Wurno, the son of Sarkin Musulmin Attahiru I. Mai Wurno was a religious fanatic and his possible influence on these returning pilgrims and its consequences were feared in Nigeria. Through such links with the Sudan ideas spread westwards into Nigeria. It was feared that it might be difficult to prevent a well-organised and properly led rebellion directed against *Nassara*.

In view of this, Nigerian authorities watched with interest any religious movement in the Muslim areas north and north-east of Nigeria. What made the authorities more apprehensive of the situation was the change in the attitude of the Senusis to the British in 1915. Sayyid Ahmad al-Sharif, having been ordered to declare war on all infidels by the Ottoman Sultan in 1915, attacked West Egypt (Egypt was proclaimed a British protectorate after the outbreak of the war in 1914), and this brought in Britain against the Senusis. The British imagined that the Grand Senusi declared a holy war against them to synchronise with the revolt of Ali Dinar, Sultan of Darfur. This is doubtful, since Ali Dinar had never been friendly with the Senusi,[50] but the possibility of a link-up remained. With this turn of events Nigerian authorities in February 1916 rushed reinforcements to the frontier between Chad and Nigeria.[51] This strengthening of the frontier was necessary to prevent Senusis from getting supplies of food and to prevent these reaching them in the Chadian districts of Borkou and Wadai where they were operating. Nigeria put her soldiers in these frontier districts on the alert and sent a maxim gun and ammunition to help the beleaguered French in the Chad.[52]

The situation in French Chad however continued to deteriorate. Ali Dinar had been opposed to the French occupation of Wadai since the French tried to make their hold on the sultanate effective in 1912.[53] Though he was pacified by generous gifts from the French, when the occasion seemed opportune in 1915 he declared a Jihad on them. Within a short time his *mujahidin* (soldiers fighting a holy war) overran the French Chadian 'Sultanates' of Dar Tana, Dar Massalit and Dar Sila. After Ali Dinar's success the revolt soon spread to Kibet and Salamat, and Wadai itself was about to fall to the forces of the Senusis and Ali Dinar.[54] This posed a serious threat to Borno, which was near enough to Wadai and had a large Arab and Tuareg population who could be expected to join any popular Islamic uprising against the colonial powers.[55]

The situation became very serious and the British in the Sudan feared that the success of Ali Dinar might lead to further insurrections. Hence they decided to co-operate with the French to put the rising down. The British rushed reinforcements from the Sudan and Egypt to Nehoud, the terminus of the railway from Khartoum which was only five days' march from Ali Dinar's stronghold of El-Fascher in Darfur.[56] Luckily for the French and British, by the time Ali Dinar got to Wadai the fighting in the Cameroons had ended and French troops under General Largeau were rushed from there in February 1916 to stem Ali Dinar's march on Fort Lamy.[57] While this was happening the British covered Ali Dinar's path of retreat into the Sudan. Ali Dinar was eventually killed in action in November 1916 by the British attacking from the Sudan.

Towards the end of 1916 the tension caused by the situation on the frontiers eased a little as a result of Ali Dinar's death, and the success of Egyptian troops against the Senusis. This led Nigerian authorities to hope that there was no immediate danger to be apprehended from the commotion in neighbouring French colonies. Thus in reply to an instruction from the War Office, half of the Nigeria Regiment was sent to East Africa.[58] This force included the very flower of the regiment with almost all officers in the country accompanying them to East Africa. Lt-Colonel Jenkins, the acting commandant, was left with a completely disorganised force, consisting mainly of those unfit to go to East Africa.[59] The only exceptions were three well organised units of the Nigeria Regiment left at home in Sokoto, Maiduguri and Dikwa in the Cameroons. The infantry companies at Birnin-Kebbi, Katagun and Nafada were seriously depleted and there were no troops whatever in Kano, the mounted infantry company there having left for Ibadan to deal with the disturbed situation in Yorubaland in 1916. Other troops in the country were scattered. There were 250 recruits in Kaduna, about 100 in Zungeru and the rest in Iseyin, and the company in Lagos could not be moved to another place because it was feared that withdrawal of troops from there could give rise to a revolt.[60]

This then was the delicate military situation and disposition of troops in Nigeria when Lugard received warning from Dakar on 23 December 1916 of the invasion of French Sahara by Senusis.[61] A day before the Dakar telegram reached Lugard information was received from the French Commandant at Zinder, some sixty miles from the Nigerian frontier, that Agades had been invested by Senusi Sheikhs with a strong force including guns and machine guns. Subsequently Lugard received a message from M. Fournier, the Colonial Secretary of French West Africa in Dakar, that he was despatching a force from Dakar and asking that facilities should be granted for their rapid transportation to Kano *en route* to Zinder. M. Fournier told Lugard that he had instructed the French Commandant at Zinder to call on the nearest British military garrison for support should the necessity arise.[62]

The hands of the Governor-General seem to have been tied; the French had committed him without even asking, apparently taking the view that the Senusis if not stopped might well enter Nigeria, thus making it seem that it was in the interests of both colonial powers to stop them. What added to the anxiety was the fact that the Resident of Sokoto took a serious view of the situation and admitted the possibility of an attack on Sokoto itself. A regulation was passed under the colonial Defence Ordinance empowering the Governor-General to requisition private motor vehicles.[63] On 3 January 1917 reservists were called up and all leave for European military staff except on medical grounds was cancelled. In spite of the still unsatisfactory position in Ibadan, troops had to be moved from there and all available troops in the vicinity of Sokoto and Birnin Kebbi were concentrated in Sokoto. Light motor vehicles were commandeered for use on the Zaria–Sokoto and Kano–Katsina roads, and 200 policemen were armed and concentrated in Kano. Nigerian troops were pushed up to the frontier and roads leading from Sokoto and Kano provinces to the French territory were saturated with Hausa sentinels and patrols to watch people who might pass messages to sympathisers on the Nigerian side of the border.

While Nigeria was still taking precautionary measures on her borders, the revolt spread across the whole of French Sudan from Timbuctoo to Lake Chad. The forces of the Senusis under Sheikh Abdul Salaam and the Tarqui Tuareg chief Muhammad Ahmad ben Kaossen, who styled himself 'the servant of the Grand Senusi and Governor of the Fezzan Valley', pressed down on French forts.[64] Their ranks were swelled by the Oullimunden Tuaregs under their chief Firhoun and also by the desertion to their side by Sultan Tegama of Agades.[65]

The French reacted to the serious situation by creating a Saharan military high command under the experienced 'desert warrior' General Laperrine of Algiers on 13 January 1917.[66] Before the French were properly organised Agades was reported to have fallen. The French Commandant at Madawa (Madaoua) also relayed the message that strong columns were marching on Tawa (Taoua) and Madawa with the possibility of invading Nigeria through Sokoto.[67] The Governor-General at Dakar raised another spectre by saying that the French Government was of the opinion that the Senusis might intend to go to the Cameroons via Borno with the object of allowing the Germans to contest the conquest of their colony and 'drawing the argument there to'.[68]

Lugard was perturbed by the news and he immediately wrote the Colonial Office that further reinforcements would not be sent to East Africa until things became normal. The Secretary of State did not contradict him; Walter Long asked Lugard to be in constant touch with the Governor-General of French West Africa but warned him that he should not send any military assistance to the French unless instruction was obtained from the home government authorising such a step.[69]

Not satisfied with the security arrangements already made, Lugard asked Lieutenant-Colonel Jenkins, acting Commandant of the Regiment, to send an urgent message to all available Europeans – officials and civilians – in Nigeria to assemble in Kaduna ready to go to the frontier and defend Nigeria. Lieutenant-Colonel Jenkins said this was impracticable. Lugard also suggested, rather naïvely, that some arms should be sent to Sokoto so that the Resident might arm any 'reliable natives' to assist the frontier garrison. The Lieutenant-Governor of Northern Nigeria and the Resident of Sokoto opposed this suggestion, fearing that undisciplined Muslims could not be trusted and that they might make common cause with their co-religionists.[70] Lugard at the same time cabled the Governor of Sierra Leone asking him to despatch all available troops to Nigeria. This last decision met with opposition from Lieutenant-Colonel Jenkins, who said that the West African Regiment (i.e., the Imperial Garrison in Freetown), because of their bad reputation and indiscipline, might cause more harm than good and possibly behave in such a way as to provoke Muslim revolt in Northern Nigeria. Lugard promised Jenkins that the Sierra Leone troops would only be used to replace companies of the Nigeria Regiment stationed in the south, so that the latter might proceed to the north. This promise was not kept when actual fighting north of Nigeria started.

Meanwhile the situation on the northern frontier was deteriorating. On 3 January 1917 before the French had brought in General Laperrine to take charge of the Saharan front, Lugard received a telegram from the Resident at Kano saying that the French Commandant at Zinder, Captain Faulque de Jonguières, requested reinforcements of Nigerian troops to support the French against the Senusis who were marching in three bodies on Tawa, Madawa and Maradi. On receiving this information, Lugard cabled the Secretary of State for authorisation and informed Lieutenant-Colonel Jenkins to take whatever steps were necessary in the defence of Nigeria.

At the request of the Governor-General of French West Africa, Lugard informed French authorities in Equatorial Africa and the Cameroons of the suggestion that the Senusis might contemplate a raid on the Northern Cameroons. The forces at Katagum, Nafada, Maiduguri and Dikwa were augmented in case the Senusis might try to invade the Cameroons through Borno, as surmised by the French. Construction of a telegraphic link between Kano and Zinder (in French Niger) proposed some years before the war was begun during the crisis, with the intention that it would facilitate communications if the operations became protracted.[71]

Two British columns moved into French territory on 8 January 1917. A British column from Kano under Colonel Coles consisting of two mounted infantry companies, one 2·95-inch gun and one maxim reached Maradi on 12 January and at Tessawa on the 19th, while the column from Sokoto under Captain Randall, consisting of 65 infantry, 85 mounted infantry, and two maxim guns, arrived at Madawa on 10 January and was due at Tahoua on the 20th. Several civil officers were detailed to do intelligence and transport work for the W.A.F.F. (Nigeria Regiment). The Nigerian infantry companies stationed at Abinsi and Udi were asked to proceed to Lokoja to act as Reserve. Others were brought from Calabar to Lagos, while the Lagos company was sent off to Sokoto and the Sierra Leone troops were stationed at Zaria as reserves.

The effect of the arrival of the Nigerian troops in French territory was immediate and far-reaching. They relieved the French garrisons in the towns near the Nigerian border, thus liberating troops for the relief of Agades. The Senusis had put considerable pressure upon the Kel Gress Tuaregs around Madawa (Madaoua) to induce them to rise, and the attitude of this tribe was very uncertain, but on the arrival of Captain Randall's column, to quote the words of the Sultan of Sokoto, 'they sat down again'.[72]

French reinforcements continued to arrive in Lagos and were speedily despatched to Kano by rail and then to Zinder, at times by motor vehicles, but most often they had to trek from Kano to Zinder. Except for a short distance from Sokoto, motor vehicles were almost useless because of the sandy nature of the waterless country. By the middle of January 1917 the French had about two thousand *tirailleurs*, eight machine-guns, six artillery guns, 394 camelry, 109 mounted guns and 17 tons of war material converging on Agades from Niamey, Bilma, N'guimi, the Chad, Filingue and Tahoua.[73]

With the presence of sufficient French forces in the Sahara, Lugard told his field commanders not to get too involved in the Saharan war. Lugard also wanted to know whether the French would allow the British to use planes in the Sahara, if the British War Office would supply them.[74] He felt the Sahara was a place where planes could be effectively used against the insurgents, instead of sending troops that Nigeria needed for maintaining internal law and order.

During the crisis Lugard toured the emirates, because the Residents felt his presence would have some political and moral effect on the people. When rumour reached Nigeria early in February 1917 that the Senusi–Tuareg forces were capable of fighting their way to Sokoto, the Resident of Sokoto declared a state of emergency. The Sultan and his immediate relatives were offered refuge in the residency in expectation that the emirate was indeed going to be invaded.[75] But nothing came of the scare.

The West African Regiment from Sierra Leone was eventually given a taste of battle north of the border, because of shortage of troops. They proved, as expected, grossly unsuited for the task. They demanded tinned beef and biscuits from England and the small detachment involved in the fighting could not move with less than a thousand carriers recruited from the sensitive Muslim population around Katsina and Sokoto.[76] Added to this, sickness broke out among them and on the whole they were inferior to the W.A.F.F.

The danger faced by both Allies did not diminish the rivalry and antagonism which had bedevilled Anglo-French relations in almost every theatre of operations during the war. Though relations were cordial on the surface, day-to-day contact was beset by mutual suspicion and unnecessary jealousies. First of all, Nigeria's military aid was accepted grudgingly by the senior French Commandant, Colonel Mourin, who had told the Governor-General of French West Africa, M. Clozel, at the initial stages, that he did not want Nigerian troops on French soil![77] The French also refused to allow British aeroplanes to be used in French Sahara despite the fact that the War Office was prepared to supply them.[78] The British officials felt the French were afraid of losing prestige by allowing the British to impress Africans with their technology;[79] the French emphatically maintained that if aeroplanes were to be used they must be French.[80] Nigerian authorities towards the end of March 1917 demanded that all Nigerian troops should return, but without any positive response from the French side.

Agades itself had been relieved on 3 March 1917 by troops under Colonel Mourin, and Muhammad Ahmad ben Kaossen was being pursued towards Air by Mourin, but the Tuareg chief remained at large until the end of the war.

By this time the Senusi movement was losing much of its force. The leadership had been split towards the end of 1916 with Sayyid Muhammad Idris, the cousin of Sayyid Ahmad al-Sharif the Grand Senusi, being recognised as the Amir of Cyrenaica whilst the Grand Senusi became merely the head of the religious order.[81] Thus political and religious factions were created, following which the Grand Senusi left the country never to return; he died in Medina in 1933. His cousin Muhammad Idris reached a *modus vivendi* with Italy and the Allies in 1917 by which the *status quo* was preserved at least until after the war, with the Italians controlling the coastal towns and the Senusi the hinterland. This accord was not completely respected by the more fiery Senusis, who felt they owed no allegiance to Idris, and they continued fighting but with diminishing effectiveness because of lack of ammunition. The Ulliminden (Oulliminden) Tuaregs who rose in sympathy with Kaossen against the French were brutally suppressed and their chief, Firhoun, was killed; a collaborationist chief called Ag-Korakor was installed in his stead in 1917.[82] The new Amir of Cyrenaica was also helping the French in the pacification work in the Sahara. He sent emissaries to Chad and other areas bordering on Nigeria stating that he wanted his followers to live at peace with the Allies.[83] In spite of this co-operation by Idris-el Senusi, Muhammad ben Kaossen and another Senusi leader Muhammad Erbemi continued the struggle until 1919, when the latter was captured by the British in the Anglo-Egyptian Sudan.[84] But since the middle of 1917 they had ceased to present a threat to the British and the French.[85]

Throughout the period of the fighting the only time Nigeria was threatened by the presence of 'enemy' subjects on her territory was in February to March 1917. During this period armed Tuareg camel-men fled to Nigeria and remained in Hadejia and some other towns near the border. The local chiefs were warned not to encourage or give them support. In spite of French pressure that the government should expel them, the Nigerian authorities did nothing, for several reasons. The government did not expel them for fear of provoking sympathetic support from their Nigerian co-religionists; in any case the government did not have a sufficient number of troops to do the job, since most of the Nigerian troops were still bogged down in the desert and nothing was thought necessary or practicable until the troops returned. These Tuaregs threatened nobody and the government was disposed to let them stay, since it was understood that the French were adopting extremely drastic measures which appeared to be little short of extermination.[86] But later when a hostile force of a thousand Tuaregs concentrated near Nguru in Northern Nigeria an Anglo-French force drove them out of the place.

The British forces did a splendid job in the Sahara. They were assigned the task of patrolling the country between Gangara on the east through Tarkass to the north to Gibban-al-Moktar on the west. The troops under Col. Coles established headquarters at El-Hassan. Farther to the west the British forces were engaged in patrolling the country north and east of Tahoua on a radius of about 30 miles, while the remainder of the forces patrolled from

Madawa with a post established at Guidambado.[87] The Nigerian troops remained on French soil until 5 and 18 May 1917, when the two columns were withdrawn, because the situation was by then under control, in the immediate neighbourhood of Nigeria at least. Meanwhile Nigeria had despatched the West African Regiment back to Sierra Leone in April, and the authorities had regained their confidence so much that by 1 April 1917 a newly trained force of 500 left Nigeria as reinforcements for East Africa.[88] But the French still continued to make demands. Following strong representations from the French Government Lugard in June 1917 ordered that the Tuaregs who had been allowed to remain in Northern Nigeria be expelled, if necessary by force. The reason the French gave for this appeal was that they were facing serious difficulties in the matter of camel transport and they wanted all the French Tuareg subjects and their camels to return. These nomads were considered by the French to be in league with the rebels and to be anxious to remain in Nigeria until an opportunity would present itself for them to join the Senusi forces operating against the French.[89] They were consequently expelled and about a thousand of their camels were seized by Nigerian troops in and outside Nigeria and handed over to the French towards the end of June 1917.

Nigeria managed to come out of the serious crisis with the loyalty of the Muslim leaders behind the government, but the French were not too sure that some aid and intelligence had not been given to the rebels on their side of the border by some of the Muslim dignitaries in Northern Nigeria. They mentioned in particular that according to information in their possession, the Sultan of Sokoto was constantly in touch with Muhammad ben Kaossen and had promised a joint effort against the Europeans if he (Kaossen) succeeded in entering Sokoto.[90] This accusation was investigated but no evidence turned up which could have incriminated the Sultan; however, the suspicion cast over his character led Lugard to order a closer watch on his activities.

As a climax to the whole episode on the northern frontier the new French Governor-General at Dakar, Monsieur J. Carde, suggested to Lugard that they should embark on a railway link between Zinder and Kano. The British Colonial Office, while in sympathy with the project, felt that the desire of the French for a railway connection between Kano and Zinder might conceivably be a useful counter with France in the peace negotiations after the war, since, according to them, to obtain such a railway link the French might be prepared to make concessions elsewhere, possibly in the Cameroons.[91]

Throughout the war period the British maintained their hold on Northern Nigeria in spite of some disruptions from within and the much more serious threat from without. The steadfastness in the loyalty of the emirs revealed an essential alliance between the Northern Nigerian ruling class and British overlordship. In order to preserve this alliance the Nigerian Government continued to resist Christian missions' attempts to use the war to penetrate the north, where they were barred. The Nigerian authorities felt that the proven loyalty of the emirs deserved to be recognised and that there could be no better reward than to ban Christian propaganda in Northern Nigeria, indefinitely if not forever.[92] The anti-missionary attitude of the Northern Nigerian administration since 1906 was given legitimacy by an ordinance passed in 1916 which prohibited missionary enterprise of any kind in Muslim emirates.[93] The Christian missions, exploiting the war situation, argued that while men were dying on the battlefronts all over the world in order to guarantee the freedom of His Majesty's subjects, freedom of movement was being denied to Christian missionaries in Northern Nigeria. The Nigerian authorities replied that there could be no more striking vindication of their policies in Northern Nigeria than the loyalty of the emirs during the war. H. R. Palmer fulminated:

> ... it is a matter of extreme surprise to me that philanthropists and old ladies in England – unable as they are to secure acceptance for missionary teaching among their own sons, nephews, cousins and brothers – think that they are justified to force this same teaching on poor native Muslims.[94]

Whatever the good intentions of the missionaries, the time chosen to press the government for a change of policy was very inopportune and showed that they possessed more enthusiasm than wisdom. The government, which had refused missionaries the right of Christian propaganda before the war, found it relatively easy to enforce the continuation of the policy, in view of the demonstrated alliance between the Hausa–Fulani ruling class and British colonial establishment.

Notes

1 *Lagos Weekly Record*, 7 Nov. 1914.
2 See 'Jide Osuntokun, 'Nigeria's Colonial Government and the Islamic Insurgency in French West Africa, 1914–1918'. *Cahiers d'Études Africaines*, 57, xv–1, pp. 85–93.
3 W.O. 158/517, Lugard to Dobell, 10 Nov. 1914, see also *Nigeria Gazette Extraordinary*, Lagos, 6 Nov. 1914.
4 C.O. 583/20/45592, Lugard to Colonial Office, 19 Nov. 1914.
5 W.O. 158/517, Lugard to Dobell, 10 Nov. 1914.
6 C.O. 583/20/44928, Lugard to Colonial Office, 14 Nov. 1914.
7 C.O. 583/21/4925, 11 Feb. 1915. Translation of Arabic letters of loyalty for press release.
8 *Ibid.*
9 *Ibid.*
10 *Lugard Papers*, i, MSS British Empire, S. 75. The Native Administrations contributed in 1914 – £38,000; 1915 – £45,000; 1916 – £54,000 1917 – £51,000 to the Nigerian war effort.
11 C.O. 583/20/43098, A. J. Harding, 5 Nov. 1914. Lugard had tried to reduce the financial power of the native administrations by bringing some of their funds under protectorate budget. This had been resisted by the Colonial Office – see C.O. 583/7/1314, Charles Strachey to Colonial Office, 12 Jan. 1914.
12 C.O. 583/21/4925, Colonial Office press release, 11 Nov. 1915.
13 C.O. 583/63/14785, H. R. Palmer, attitudes of the Muslim provinces of Nigeria, 2 March 1917.
14 Richmond Palmer (later Sir) 1877–1958. Third-class Re ident Northern Nigeria 19c3; Commissioner (later supervisor) of Native Treasury Revenue 1912–15; second-class Resident 1916; Lt-Governor Northern Nigeria 1925; Governor, Gambia 1930–3; Governor Cyprus 1933–9.
15 C.O. 583/83/3057, Palmer to Colonial Office, Aug. 1919.
16 C.O. 583/20/48784, Palmer to Colonial Office, Aug. 1919.
17 C.O. 583/19/43995, Lugard to Colonial Office, 20 Oct. 1914.
18 C.O. 583/5757/22564, H. S. Smith (on revolts in Northern Nigeria) to Lugard, 6 March 1917.
19 C.O. 583/19/43995, Lugard to Colonial Office, 20 Oct. 1914.
20 C.O. 583/20/810, Lugard to Colonial Office, 16 Dec. 1914.
21 *Ibid.* Captain Byng-Hall, enclosure in Lugard to Colonial Office, 16 Dec. 1914.
22 See Michael Crowder, *Revolt in Bussa*. Faber and Faber, London 1973, ch. 5.
23 C.O. 583/38/57478, Hamilton-Browne (Resident of Kontagora) to Secretary, Northern Provinces, 14 June 1915.
24 *Ibid.* For a detailed study of this revolt see Crowder, *op. cit.*
25 C.O. 583/38/57474, C. L. Temple to Lugard, 23 Nov. 1915.
26 *Ibid.*

27 C.O. 583/32/26230, Lugard to Colonial Office, 14 May 1915.
28 *Ibid.*
29 *Ibid.*
30 C.O. 583/78/66560, Clifford to Viscount Milner, 31 Oct. 1919.
31 C.O. 583/50/1457, Lugard to Colonial Office, 16 Dec. 1916.
32 *Ibid.*
33 C.O. 583/31/9936, Lugard to Colonial Office, 5 March 1915.
34 C.O. 583/32/19349, Lugard to Colonial Office, 3 April 1915.
35 A. H. M. Kirk-Greene, *Adamawa, Past and Present*, Oxford University Press, London, 1958, p. 163.
36 C.O. 583/56/12673, H. S. Goldsmith to Lugard, 10 Feb. 1917.
37 C.O. 583/30/7842, translation of Arabic letter found in a Yola mosque on 29 Jan. 1915.
38 C.O. 583/30/7842, letter found in Yola, 23 Dec. 1915.
39 C.O. 583/34/34607, 26 July 1915, translation of pamphlets distributed by German raiding parties in Muri province.
40 C.O. 583/49/47652, Lugard to Colonial Office, 3 Oct. 1916.
41 C.O. 583/63/14783, Palmer to Lugard, 2 March 1917.
42 *Ibid.*
43 *Ibid.*
44 *Ibid.*
45 W.O. 158/517, Lugard to Dobell, 25 Jan. 1916.
46 C.O. 583/83/3057, H. R. Palmer's Journey from Maiduguri to Jeddah in Arabia, Aug. 1919. See also E. E. Evans-Pritchard, *The Senusiya of Cyrenaica*, pp. 22–5. The Senusiya (Senusiyyah) order was founded in Mecca in 1837 by an Algerian scholar named Al-Sayyid Muhammed bin Ali al-Sanusi-al-Khattabi al-Idrisi-al-Hasani (known as Al-Sanusi al-Kabir, i.e., the Grand-Sanusi). The Tijaniyyah and Qadriyyah were older Moroccan Tariqas, the latter being the older of the two. Both had adherents in West Africa; the Tijaniyyah made the greatest gain in West Africa during and after the Jihad of Al-hajj Umar-al-Tall in the nineteenth century. The Qadriyyah was a conservative order believing in a hierarchical structure of society and preaching maintenance of the social order – as being Allah's wish; while the Tijaniyyah believed in more egalitarian society and material improvement of the society. It therefore enjoined its followers to engage in trade and to be 'friendly' with Europeans, the purveyors of civilisation. The Senusiyyah was a trading order which combined the militant aspect of the Tijaniyyah with the hierarchical doctrine of the Qadriyyah. It was much more militantly opposed to alien infidels. See J. S. Trimingham, *A History of Islam in West Africa*, pp. 150–60.
47 All Muslims were united, no matter what Tariqas they belonged to, by their recognition of three common documents or beliefs as being binding on all. These are the *Koran* – the Allah-inspired document of the faith; the *Sunna* (way or example of prophet Mohammed which supplements the Koran), made up of collections of the sayings of Mohammed; *Ijma*, which provides basis for compromise between warring doctrines since it recognises that any belief entertained by the greater part of Muslims in history is infallibly true and that a

practice such as cult of saints allowed by most Muslims over a long period must be legitimate and good.

48 Evans-Pritchard, *op. cit.*, p. 8.
49 C.O. 583/83/3057, H. R. Palmer, Report of Journey from Maiduguri to Arabia, Aug. 1919.
50 Evans-Piritchard, *op. cit.*, p. 128.
51 C.O. 583/44/13029, Captain Badham, O/C Nigeria Regiment, Maiduguri, to Lugard, 1916.
52 C.O. 445/36/11059, Lugard to Bonar Law, 12 Feb. 1916. The Governor-General lent the French a Maxim gun and 18,000 rounds of ammunition to fight the Senusis in Chad and he was also prepared to assist the French militarily should the situation in French Chad threaten Nigeria's security.
53 L.A.O.F., XII/58, Lutte contre le Senoussisme, 1914. Les Archives nationales, Ministere des affaires étrangères.
54 L.A.E.F. (affaires politiques), Carton 338, Dossier 2, M. Merlin, Territoire du Tchad: Rapport d'ensemble pour l'année 1916.
55 C.O. 583/73/15668, C. F. J. Tomlinson, Resident of Borno, to Lugard, 9 Dec. 1917, on attitude of Muslims in Borno.
56 L.A.O.F. XII/58, M. de France (French Minister in Egypt) to M. Doumergue (President du conseil, Ministere des affaires étrangères) 3 Feb. 1914. The British railway had reached Nehoud from Khartoum in 1912, thus making it possible for the British to establish a presence in Ali Dinar's Darfur.
57 L.A.E.F. Carton 338, Dossier 2, M. Merlin, Territoire du Tchad: Rapport d'ensemble pour l'année 1916.
58 See ch. 8.
59 C.O. 583/56/13956, Lugard to Colonial Office, 23 Feb. 1917.
60 *Ibid.*
61 *Ibid.*
62 C.O. 445/40/1332, French Military Attaché in London to War Office, 6 Jan. 1917.
63 C.O. 583/56/13956, Lugard to Colonial Office, 23 Feb. 1917.
64 Augustin Bernard, 'Le Sahara français pendant la guerre,' pp. 3–9. See also, 'La pacification du Sahara: Nigeria-Nord,' *L'Afrique Française*, July and August 1917, pp. 267–8.
65 Bernard, *op. cit.*, pp. 3–9.
66 L.A.O.F. (affaires politiques), Carton 170, Dossier 8, M. le ministre des colonies to Conseiller d'état: Directeur de l'Afrique, 20 Nov. 1918: 'les mouvements et agitations indigènes en Afrique occidentale française au cours de la guerre'.
67 C.O. 583/56/6243, Lugard to Colonial Office, 10 Jan. 1917.
68 *Ibid.*
69 C.O. 583/55/55761, Colonial Office to Lugard, 4 Jan. 1917.
70 C.O. 583/55/43, Lugard to Colonial Office, 10 Jan. 1917.
71 C.O. 583/55/3863, Lugard to Colonial Office, 19 Jan. 1917.
72 C.O. 583/58/43044, Lt-Col. Jenkins, Report on the situation on the Northern frontier, 25 July 1917.
73 *Ibid.*

74 C.O. 583/55/8754, Lugard to Colonial Office, 23 Jan. 1917.
75 C.O. 583/55/10756, Lugard to Colonial Office, 7 Feb. 1917.
76 *Ibid.*
77 L.A.O.F. (affaires politiques), Carton 2081, Dossier 6, 'L'Affaire d'Agades 1916–17 et Nigeria. M. Clozel to Ministère des colonies, 13 March 1917.
78 C.O. 583/55/5610, Walter Long to Lugard, 7 March 1917.
79 C.O. 583/56/13687, Strachey's minute, 14 March 1917.
80 C.O. 583/58/43044, Lt-Col Jenkins, Report on the situation on the Northern frontier, 25 July 1917.
81 Evans-Pritchard, *op. cit.*, p. 135.
82 *Je Sais Tout*, 15 June 1918. Jean Tilho, 'Sur le front du desert Libyque', pp. 642–53. See also *L'Afrique Française*, July and August 1917, pp. 267–8.
83 L.A.E.F. (affaires politiques), Carton 338, Dossier 2, Tchad: Rapport trimestriel, Premier Trimestre 1917, by M. Merlin, Governor-General of L.A.E.F., who said Muhammad Idris el-Sanusi assured him through his emissaries that 'il est toujours animé d'intentions pacifiques vis-à-vis des français et des Aliés'.
84 L.A.E.F. (affaires politiques), Carton 338, Dossier 4. Col Ducarre, Rapport sur la situation du Territoire du Tchad. 2ᵉ Trimestre, 1919.
85 C.O. 583/58/38008, 28 July 1917. The French said they defeated Kaossen 80 miles north of Agades.
86 C.O. 583/56/27083, Lugard to Colonial Office, 31 March 1917.
87 C.O. 583/58/43044, Lt-Col Jenkins, Report on the situation on the Northern frontier, 25 July 1917.
88 *Ibid.*
89 C.O. 583/60/62016, Mourin to Lugard, 6 Nov. 1917.
90 *Ibid.*
91 C.O. 583/65/18476, Colonial Office to Lugard, 6 June 1918.
92 C.O. 583/63/5806, Charles Temple's letter to C.M.S. enclosed in G. T. Manley (secretary to the C.M.S.) to Arthur Steel-Maitland (Under Secretary of State), 30 Jan. 1917.
93 C.O. 583/70/31307, Rev. Ernest Jones, Secretary, Sudan United Mission of Toronto, Canada to Secretary of State, 24 June 1918, protesting against the 1916 ordinance. For policies before the war see E. A. Ayandele, *The Missionary Impact on Modern Nigeria 1842–1914*, Longman, London, 1966, pp. 117–52.
94 C.O. 583/67/57558, Palmer to Lugard, 27 July 1917.

Part II
Nigeria abroad – external aspects of the war

6 Nigeria and the war in German Cameroons 1914–16

Nigeria, the biggest of the British dependencies in West Africa and the most populous of all her tropical possessions except India, found herself involved in the First World War barely eight months after the amalgamation of the Southern and Northern Provinces of Nigeria. The country naturally did not have time to digest the administrative changes that had just taken place. As a stroke of good luck the administrative unification also led to a considerably better organised 'national' army.

By the end of 1913 the armed forces of both Southern and Northern Nigeria were merged into one single brigade of five battalions known as the Nigeria Regiment.[1] Three of these battalions (including the only mounted infantry battalion) were stationed in the north and the remaining two in the south. The Nigeria Regiment consisted of two batteries of artillery each armed with 2·95-inch mountain guns, a mounted infantry battalion of three companies with a total strength of about 380 men, and four infantry battalions each with an establishment of about 1,200 men; each infantry battalion had eight machine-guns. In all, the total number of combatants was about 5,000 and 320 reservists, and there were about 400 gun carriers.[2] The entire force was under the command of 172 British commissioned and non-commissioned officers.

In addition to this military force there was also in Nigeria a police force of 33 British officers and 2,100 Africans, excluding of course the *Dogorai*, or Native Administration police. The Nigerian police had a semi-military training and were armed with carbines. There was also a marine department with about 90 British officers and 1,000 Nigerian ratings. The marine department had over 60 steamers, launches or pinnaces for work in the inland and coastal waterways; many of these steamers could be fitted with light, quick-firing machine-guns.[3]

For a small colony with a few million people the forces available would have been more than adequate, but in the case of Nigeria the forces were hardly sufficient for maintaining internal law and order, and were widely scattered because of the size of the country. The headquarters of the infantry battalions were Kaduna, Lokoja, Calabar and Lagos, while the mounted infantry battalion had its headquarters in Kano. The first battalion at Kaduna had eight companies, three of which were stationed in Kaduna, and one each in Sokoto, Kano, Bauchi-Pankshin, Birnin Kebbi and Katagum. The second battalion at Lokoja also had eight companies, with two companies stationed in Lokoja, one each in Womba, Yola-Pirambi, Maiduguri, Ankpa-Boje, Zungeru-Zuru and Nafada. The third battalion based at Calabar consisted of eight companies, two of them at Calabar and one each in Ukpo, Owerri, Obudu, Ogoja, Okigwi and Abinsi-Katsena-Allah. The fourth battalion in Lagos had seven companies, two of which always remained in Lagos, and one each in Okwoga, Onitsha, Udi, Agbor and Ibadan. The fifth mounted infantry battalion based in Kano had just three companies, one each stationed in Kano, Sokoto and Geidam.[4]

In the past, members of the Nigeria Regiment had been recruited almost entirely from Hausa and Yoruba, but with the generally increased security in the country and with the completion of the Kano–Lagos railway in 1912, trade offered greater inducements than military service and by 1914 increasing difficulty had been experienced in obtaining Hausa and Yoruba recruits.[5] To circumvent this Colonel Carter, the Commandant, suggested that reintroduction of deferred pay or a corresponding gratuity would have a good effect, as this capital sum would enable 'a soldier on discharge to purchase a small stock in trade . . . which is the ambition of every Hausa and Yoruba'.[6] The authorities, however, were not unduly worried about shortage of suitable manpower for the army, and in fact the Commandant had always favoured recruitment among the 'excellent pagan tribes' such as Munshi (Tiv) and Dakkakeris, who easily acquired Hausa, the language of command. The Commandant argued that, because these 'pagan' tribes were not Muslims, they were not 'so liable to be infected by any wave of fanatical religious sentiment, such as the temporary success of some *Mahdi* may any day excite'.[7] This new doctrine had not gained much ground before the outbreak of war, so that only a few of these 'pagan' tribes found their way into the army since their 'backward state of civilization' militated against their enlistment in large numbers.[8] At the time of the Cameroons expedition three-fifths of the Nigeria Regiment was still composed of Hausa and Yoruba.[9] It can thus be seen that Nigeria, with an area of over 335,000 square miles and a population of about 20 million, was not a fertile ground for military recruitment. The main reason for this was that only a small proportion were educated or 'civilised' enough to be suitable for military service and even then the educated ones were considered unsuitable for political reasons.[10]

In spite of the emergence of a 'national' army by January 1914 following the amalgamation, the Southern and Northern Nigerian military establishments had remained out of contact for fifteen years. There had not been joint manœuvres; the Governor-General did not believe in them. He had said:

> I do not feel fully convinced of the necessity of these manœuvres. The unit of the W.A.F.F. in the conditions of Nigeria is, at most, the Company and not the battalion, and whatever the magnitude of the operations in which the force was engaged, the Company would remain the unit.[11]

The Governor-General felt that manœuvres involved too much expense and that while they might help in training officers, could not be justified as improving efficiency of soldiers themselves. General Dobell, the Inspector-General of the West African Frontier Force (W.A.F.F.), disagreed with Lugard. He minuted:

> unless units are systematically trained together under peace conditions they cannot be expected to act with mutual cooperation which makes for success in war. . . . The W.A.F.F. is required to be trained to such a standard as to render it fit, to meet an enemy capable of using arms of precision with effect in fairly open country . . . owing to the fact that there are so many isolated stations in Nigeria, the training of the Regiment even under the most rigorous form of inspection is apt to get into a groove unless troops are occasionally brought together to be exercised in their higher formations (battalions or batteries).[12]

Once it was accepted that the W.A.F.F. must be prepared to meet forces of neighbouring European colonies, Nigerian authorities were told by General Dobell that they should not be satisfied that the standard of training which sufficed in the past was high enough for 1914. Consequently, manœuvres were planned for January 1915, but of course this plan was overtaken by events of August 1914.

The rearmament programme which commenced in 1913 and was scheduled to end at the end of 1915 progressed rather slowly, with the result that when war broke out not all the soldiers had their new Short Lee Enfield rifles and had to use their old long rifles.[13]

After the amalgamation an entirely new Defence Scheme for Nigeria was formulated and given to Lugard, who was holidaying in England. The Governor unfortunately misplaced or lost the plan. As a result of this the local civil authorities had generally little idea of what would be required of them, while the military establishment, not knowing whether the views they had put forward in the draft scheme had met with approval, were uncertain about what preparations to make.

However, Nigeria was not totally unprepared, there were contingency plans existing for such emergencies. This did not mean that Nigerian authorities had plans for aggression against any of the neighbouring colonies. In fact, it was a cardinal principle of British policy in her dependencies that military forces were mainly organised for internal policing and defence.[14]

British policy-makers had always thought that if there was any threat to the security of British West Africa, that threat was not from the Germans but rather from the French, who maintained far larger forces in West Africa than did the British. Therefore, when war broke out in Europe between the Central Powers and the Allies, the decision to carry the war to Africa had to come from the French and the British. Historically Britain had always benefited from a European war by seizing the colonies of her enemies because of her supremacy on the high seas. Britain saw no need to abandon the well established strategy.

As early as 1904 it was decided that:

> a war between Germany and Great Britain would in some ways resemble a struggle between an elephant and a whale, in which each although supreme in its own element would find it difficult in bringing its strength to bear on its antagonist. ... Our power of defence against Germany is limited to:
> (a) the destruction of her seaborne trade,
> (b) the seizure of her colonies.[15]

Germany was of course against carrying the war to Africa where she would be at a disadvantage in face of an Anglo-French military combination. It was clear to the Germans that the British would use their superior navy to cut German colonies off from sources of military supply. The responsibility of extending the European war to Africa lay more with the British than with the French.[16] On this point the British had stated that the principle of imperial defence affecting overseas colonies and protectorates revolved around her naval supremacy over the:

> naval forces or any combination of naval powers likely to be arrayed against us . . . so long as British naval supremacy is maintained the power of reinforcing oversea garrisons will be assured to us and denied to the enemy. . . . In a war with France or Germany observance of articles X and XI of the Berlin Act of 1885 [the Neutrality clauses] would be in the interest of France or Germany. Consequently, Britain does not intend to abide by it.[17]

At the onset of the war the same policy was restated by the War Office:

> It has been regarded as a moot point whether in the event of a European war the tropical possessions of the contending powers should remain neutral, but as no decision has been given on this question . . . it was presumed that Great Britain was free to act in such a manner as to best safeguard her own interests.[18]

It was in Britain's interest that the Germans should be driven out of the Cameroons. It was simple prudence that Germany should be attacked wherever she was weak, and she was definitely weak in the Cameroons.[19] *The Times* in a comment on British strategy put the reason for seizing German colonies very succinctly:

> Our invariable practice in a great war against a Power possessing territories oversea has been to occupy these territories as soon as practicable, not only, and sometimes not mainly, in a spirit of acquisitiveness, but in order to have in our hands something with which we can bargain in case our enemy conquers territory in Europe and refuses to release it at the peace. . . .
>
> Germany aims at throwing the whole of her manhood into the field in order to destroy her enemies speedily, and if a peace comes soon, and we have not in our hands the means of bargaining, we are too late. . . .
>
> In the case of Togo and the Cameroons measures must be concerted between us and the French, who will of course, reoccupy the strip of the French Congo which was torn from them as the price of the Morocco settlement.[20]

On 23 August 1914 the German Government approached the

American Government, through its ambassador in Berlin, urging the United States to persuade the British, French and Belgian Governments not to allow hostilities to extend to the conventional basin of the Congo, which included the major part of the Cameroons and technically some part of German East Africa.[21] After first refusing the Americans finally transmitted the German plea to the belligerents without making any comments.[22]

This plea was rejected by the Allies. The British and the French argued that the neutrality of Belgium guaranteed by the whole of Europe had been violated by Germany and inferred that Germany had no right to remind any nation of its treaty obligations. France claimed that neutralisation was not in the interest of the Allies, and that the fall of Togoland and the destruction of the powerful transmission station at Kamina between 23 and 25 August 1914, which made communication between Germany and her African colonies impossible, was the sole reason why Germany asked for United States intervention.[23] M. Renkin, Belgian Minister for the Colonies, said the same Germany which had described the treaty guaranteeing Belgian neutrality as a *chiffon de papier*, could not morally blame the Allies for violating the neutrality of the conventional basin of the Congo.[24]

The country which the Allies decided to invade had a common boundary with Nigeria running from the Atlantic Ocean in the south to Lake Chad in the north, a total distance of about a thousand miles, with the important Nigerian provinces of Calabar, Adamawa and Borno being vulnerable to possible German counter-attack. When the Allies decided to seize the Cameroons, they expected a short campaign like that in Togoland, but they were to be disappointed. The country covered some 300,000 square miles; it was about 530 miles wide at its equatorial base and tapered to a point nearly 1,000 miles north at Lake Chad.[25] From here down the eastern part of the country ran French Equatorial Africa (i.e., the French territories of Chad, Ubangi-Shari, Gabon and Congo Brazzaville). As a result of the Franco-German accord of 1911 following the Agadir crisis, French Equatorial Africa lost to Germany 100,000 square miles of her Congo territory. This gave Germany a foothold on the Congo River and common frontier with the Belgian Congo. French Equatorial Africa by this 1911 cession of territory to Germany had been strategically weakened, with German Cameroons having 'deux fenêtres ... ouvertes sur le Congo et sur l'Oubangui'.[26]

French anger about this humiliating concession was aptly described at the time by the Comte de Mun, who said, 'it is not only a question of national pride, but it means the shattering of a splendid plan which offers to national pride the grand spectacle of a French Africa stretching without break from the Mediterranean to the mouth of the Congo'.[27]

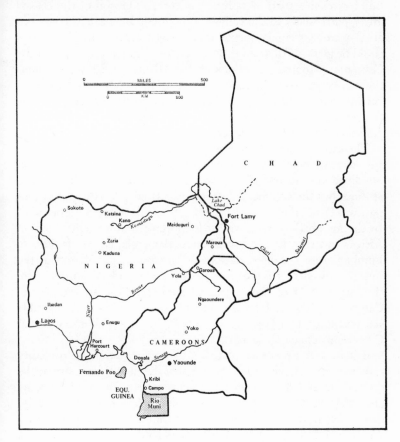

Nigeria, Cameroons and Chad

The Cameroons presents a great diversity of physical features. The whole of the southern area including the basins of the Sanaga, Dachang and Njong rivers lies within the region of the African tropical forest and is covered with dense forest presenting great difficulties to military operations. The central area is a high tableland with a magnificent climate. The northern area, including the upper basins of the Benue and Logone rivers, is a rich district falling northwards towards Lake Chad. Communication was very poor in the central and northern parts of the German colony because up till 1914 the Germans still left the local Fulani and Kanuri chieftains in full control,[28] and had not found the need to build extensive road or railway networks. The soil of the coastal areas, particularly in the valleys of mountain ranges in the western area, were extremely fertile and many valuable tropical crops could be grown. All around Buea, Victoria and on the slopes of the Cameroon Mountain overlooking the Atlantic Ocean were plantations of cocoa, coffee, rubber, cloves, vanilla, ginger and tobacco. Private and public capital had been heavily invested in the Cameroons between 1894 and 1914 by individual German companies and the imperial government.

The estuary of the Cameroon river provided at Duala-Bonaberi an excellent port with a fine floating dock, broad streets, good buildings and up-to-date sanitation. The seat of government was at Buea, but the commercial capital was Duala. Another important port was Kribi, the commercial outlet for south-eastern Cameroons. In the far north, Garua was an important trading centre and an African town on the navigable Benue. Bamenda, Kontscha, Banyo, Fumban were considerable African centres of population in the western district. In the south-east, Nola and Molundu were thriving centres of the ivory and rubber trades. In the central Cameroons, Tibati, Joko and Yaunde were towns of considerable size and important German stations.[29] This was how the German Cameroons appeared in 1914.

Britain and France emphasised that it was strategic necessity rather than territorial covetousness that dictated the seizure of the Cameroons and all German oversea possessions. But it will become clear that strategy alone as a determining factor of British naval or military moves is not convincing. Strategy after all is not just a mirror of interests which needs to be defended but in a way it is a register of the hopes and memories which go to determine a strategist picture of the world. The British decided that the capture of Duala was a particularly valuable military objective. Its value lay in the fact that it could afford a harbour of refuge to German warships, commerce raiders and destroyers, and from Duala it was believed vital British trade routes could be threatened. Its importance was further increased by the fact that there was a wireless and telegraph station there which maintained communication with Europe *via* Fernando Po and Kamina in Togoland.[30] Information thus transmitted could then be disseminated to German ships and men-of-war. At this time it was rumoured that the German gunboats *Panther* and *Eber* might be in West African waters. In addition to all this, Duala was a large European centre with stores and coal which could be seized as loot. Resistance was not expected since the British, drawing conclusion from the short campaign in Togoland, felt that German strategy appeared to be one of abandoning the coastal ports of their colonies after destroying everything of value and retiring inland, on the assumption that no effective pursuit would be undertaken and that at the conclusion of hostilities Germany could claim continuous occupation of the colony.[31] The War Office in one of the series of plans argued that an attack on Duala without naval co-operation would have to be made from the direction of the Cross river and Calabar, but it later dawned on the War Office that the difficult nature of the country, and absence of reliable information as to communications beyond Nigeria, would render movements of columns of the size necessary too hazardous an undertaking. The British therefore decided that when the time of attack on Duala came, it would be a joint naval and military operation.

Meanwhile it was being considered what interpretation should be placed on the Anglo-French *Entente* in relation to British territorial ambitions in the Cameroons. One of the experts on Nigerian affairs at the Colonial Office, Charles Strachey,[32] believed and convinced others to agree with him that for various reasons Germany could be persuaded to give up the Cameroons without a fight.[33] Because of the general resentment of the French following the territorial cession to Germany in 1911, Strachey asserted that the Germans would find it more honourable and easier to surrender territory to Britain than to France. He adduced as evidence the readiness with which the Germans surrendered Lome and South Togoland to British forces coming from Gold Coast in the first few days of the war. He therefore concluded that Britain would have a better chance of attaining the surrender of Cameroons, or at least Duala, the coast and a certain distance inland, if she proceeded alone. It was felt that the Germans would realise that it was in their interest to surrender in view of the widespread rebellion in the Cameroons which started in October 1913 and continued till August 1914, resulting in the deaths of a

German civilian and Lieutenant von Raven.[34] An Englishman in the Cameroons at this time wrote: 'we can rest assured of one thing, the natives throughout the country, are in an excited state and they will revenge themselves on the Europeans who have in the past caused them so much misery if they see the least chance of doing so'.[35] Further intelligence reports claimed that the *Schutztruppe* itself had mutinied and that the government was not issuing ammunition to the troops. This source claimed that the German authorities were afraid that their subjects would rise in support of the enemy.[36] All these reports coming from the Cameroons actually caused the British some anxiety for the safety of the Germans it was felt that an appearance of British forces might lead to Germans being massacred – 'such an occurrence is to be deprecated', minuted an official at the Colonial Office – and that owing to the large proportion of Europeans in Duala an attack using black troops would in a great measure 'be a conflict between black and white, and from an ethical point of view, should if possible, be avoided'.[37] It was assumed that the French were, however, insensitive to this kind of argument. The British saw a potential seed of discord which could germinate into mutual recrimination between the two Allies, 'the method of our gallant allies with black troops in the field against Germans will not I fear, please our officers at all',[38] said Charles Strachey.

The British authorities were prepared to wait for the opportune time before making a decisive move; this would be when the Cameroons had been totally cut off from Berlin. Up till 25 August 1914, the Cameroons was still in contact with Germany by means of their shore-to-ship wireless, which was still receiving messages from the Kamina station in Togoland. It was consequently suggested that as soon as the Kamina station was captured a telegram should be sent to the Governor of the Cameroons from Lagos to the following effect:

I am commanded by H.M. the King, to call upon you to surrender to His Majesty the territory of the Cameroons. In view of the geographical situation of the country which renders impossible a successful defence against the military and naval forces of Great Britain and France, His Majesty trusts that your excellency will recognise that this is compatible with honour and it will avert unnecessary bloodshed. I am authorised to state that in the event of your assent H.M.G. will arrange for the conveyance of yourself and your personal staff as well as all non-combatants, women and children to Genoa or some other suitable neutral port in Europe. I have to request that you will furnish me with a reply within 24 hours.[39]

Strachey advised that the letter be signed 'Lugard' because of the Governor's reputation as a man of determination; and hoped the result would be 'a finely successful example of bluff'.[40]

A *parlementaire* to summon the surrender of the Cameroons was accordingly sent to Governor Ebemaier after the destruction of the Kamina station by the Germans themselves. It was expecting rather too much for the German Governor simply to surrender his Colony without instruction from his home government. Failing to get that instruction from home, he had no alternative but to fight a war described by Hauptmann von Crailsheim as the most 'unequal warfare' ever fought in history.[41]

The Colonial Office of course did not base all hopes on this gamble, the Nigerian authorities had been instructed to put everything in order in case the Germans refused to surrender voluntarily. A proclamation was issued on 5 August by A. G. Boyle, the Governor's Deputy, for the formation of a Land Contingent.[42] It was composed entirely of Europeans. Companies were enrolled in Ibadan, Abeokuta, Lagos, Lokoja, Ebutte Metta, Calabar, Warri, Zungeru, Naraguta (Jos) and Port Harcourt. Throughout Nigeria Europeans took the oath, though outside the large centres there was no opportunity or necessity to arm, equip and drill those who enlisted.[43] In addition to being members of the land contingent, the officials as well as the 'non-officials' had to carry out their civil responsibilities either as administrators, miners or traders. During the first critical months of the war, the energy, enthusiasm and application of the force were unbounded. It was not possible to supply the requirements of all the detachments, some of the members had to equip and clothe themselves at their own expense; but most of the recruits were armed and equipped from the Nigeria Regiment stores and the old long Martini Enfield rifles lately belonging to the disbanded Southern Nigeria volunteer corps were issued to the companies and sections in important centres. Daily parades, later reduced to weekly parades, were held during the first months of the war. The contingent was trained in 'bush fighting', signalling and in the use of machine-guns. The force was initially used for escort duties of German prisoners of war and at Ibadan the force supplied for several months guards for the European internment camp at the Moor Plantation. Both at Calabar and Lagos the companies were called out to man the trenches during alarms and periods of anxiety and uncertainty.[44] At Calabar the force was constantly on duty in the trenches, 'their presence being of the greatest value in reassuring the European ladies and the Nigerian Community'.[45] A considerable number of members of the force were attached to the Nigeria Regiment and some became company commanders and assisted the depleted military staff in training Nigerian recruits.

At the same time as the Land Contingent was formed, the Marine department was also constituted into a Marine Contingent. This consisted of British naval officers and Nigerian mates; thus the Nigerian Marine became a combatant force.[46] On this force devolved the work of preparing the various harbours for defence against attack from the sea. Dredgers and an old branch boat of Elder Dempster & Co. were moored in such a position that at short notice they could be sunk in the Lagos channel in order to deny ingress to any hostile gun-boats that might attempt to land marines. All vessels at Forcados were ordered to proceed to Sapele and those at Bonny to Degema and the approaches to Sapele and Degema were mined. A fast launch was detailed to patrol the coast around Calabar.[47] British vessels were ordered out of Lagos port for their own security and the street lights in Lagos were put out, while the light-houses temporarily switched off their lights. As with the Land Contingent, a number of officers were eventually sent to the Cameroons to assist in the operations there. On the reduced numbers left behind fell the task of carrying out the ordinary services of the Marine department, and the special duties due to war such as the joint Marine-Land Contingent work of manning the naval guns loaned by the Admiralty for the defence of Lagos.[48]

Nigeria's defence was further augmented by putting into force an order legalising censorship of letters and telegrams received or sent at the terminal telegraph stations of Yola, Maiduguri, Calabar, Bonny, Forcados and Lagos. Arrangements were made for extra telegraph lines to be fitted to the cable house and to the signal station at Lagos, and the telephone exchange was kept open all night.[49] A strict watch was kept on the acts of all German residents in Nigeria.

F. S. James, the Administrator of Lagos, in an interview with Nigerian newspaper editors asked them not to publish any information about military movements and also to refrain from over-dramatising events so as not to cause public excitement. On 5 August a proclamation was issued calling on the educated inhabitants of Lagos to enlist as special constables, so that the police could be released for military duties. The educated Nigerians quickly volunteered because they too feared that their lives were threatened.[50]

Instructions were received from the Colonial Office on 5 August 1914 that German and Austrian consular officers should leave Nigeria, and that all German naval and military reservists should be arrested and interned.[51] This was done, and the men were locked up in Lagos prison, as it was impossible to put them anywhere else; but instructions were sent to Ibadan asking authorities there to prepare a prisoners' encampment at the Moor Plantation. The Secretary of State for the Colonies later left the question of releasing the German prisoners of war to the discretion of the Governor's Deputy[52] and consequently it was decided that heads of firms and their clerks should be released. Other Germans were released if their good behaviour was guaranteed by well-known German residents in Nigeria. Those who had nobody to stand for them as sureties were sent to the Ibadan camp.

Smooth as the war preparations appeared, military miscalculation or adventurism on the part of Colonel Carter, the Commandant of the Nigeria Regiment, almost upset everything.[53] Colonel Carter decided to attack the Cameroons before he was ordered to do so. He took this action because of the breakdown of communications between Kaduna, his headquarters, and Lagos, the seat of government. There was lack of co-ordination between the civil and military high commands and the absence of Lugard from Nigeria, thus leaving direction of affairs in an emergency to his Deputy, A. G. Boyle, generally regarded as a weak man for such a serious situation, must have added to the cause of the fiasco.[54] Colonel Carter ordered three columns of the Nigeria Regiment operating on the Nigeria–Cameroons border to advance from Maiduguri in the extreme north, Yola on the Benue, and Ikom in the south to capture the German hill fortress of Mora, German Garua on the Benue and Nsanakang in the south respectively.[55] On 29 August a mounted infantry detachment of the Nigeria Regiment crossed the border and occupied the German frontier town of Tepe, then attacked Garua and succeeded in capturing one of the German forts there. The Germans counter-attacked and inflicted severe blows on the Nigerian detachment, killing

Lieutenant-Colonel Maclean, the commanding officer. A similar fate befell the Nigerian troops trying to capture Mora; but the greatest disaster was suffered in the south. Between 30 August and 6 September 1914, Nigerian troops under Lieutenant-Colonel Mair succeeded in capturing Nsanakang but they could not hold it in the face of a strong German counter-offensive. The Germans inflicted severe losses on the British force, killing three officers, capturing four and wounding one mortally. Seventy-one rank and file were killed, nineteen wounded and twenty-four captured. Eighteen carriers were killed, five gun carriers wounded and another five were captured.[56] A considerable amount of ammunition was lost to the Germans as well as two 2·95-inch quick-firing guns and five machine-guns.

Following this disaster there was discord among the British officers, and the senior civil servants became very critical of Colonel Carter, who was accused of sending orders and counter orders to columns in the field and the Residents in frontier provinces without consulting anyone.[57] In order to avert trouble and further disaster Colonel Carter was removed and recalled to England.[58] A new commandant, Lieutenant-Colonel Cunliffe,[59] was appointed. This appointment proved to be the best that was made during this difficult period when the morale of the Nigerian troops was at its lowest ebb. One of the side results of the Carter affair was that it undermined Anglo-French co-operation for some time because the French felt that the English sought French collaboration only after they had single-handedly failed to invade the Cameroons successfully.[60]

While Nigerian forces registered a failure on the Nigeria-Cameroons border, hostilities had begun between the French and the Germans long before the Carter adventure. These took place in the area ceded to Germany by France in 1911,[61] thus confirming the notion that strategy was a register of the hopes and aspirations of a power and was not shaped only by military or naval considerations, as the Allies frequently claimed. The French claim that their fear that the neutrality of the conventional basin of the Congo would not be respected led the Governor-General of French Equatorial Africa to order a general mobilisation on 1 August 1914. French troops from Moyen-Congo and Oubangi-Shari moved towards Bonga and Zinga,[62] two strategic points on the frontier, even before serious fighting began in the German colony.

THE ANGLO-FRENCH EXPEDITION

After the fiasco on the Nigeria-Cameroons border, Lieutenant-Colonel Cunliffe was asked to withdraw to a defensive position until a joint Anglo-French expeditionary force was ready to reduce the Cameroons. The British approached the French on this in August 1914 and towards the end of the month the French agreed to the British proposal. The British had proposed that the expedition should be commanded by General Charles Dobell,[63] Inspector-General of W.A.F.F. While accepting this, the French made it clear that their acceptance of the British officer's command was based upon the recognition of General Dobell's peculiar fitness for the job and that French acquiescence must be taken as being without prejudice to the future division of the country.[64] This was the beginning of the rivalry and petty jealousies which almost ruined the marriage of convenience between the French and the British during the war, especially in their wrangling over the division of the spoils of war.

The Anglo-French expeditionary force numbered initially about 7,000 men, of which three battalions (3,000 men) of infantry came from French West Africa,[65] the remaining troops came from the British West African colonies of Gambia, Sierra Leone, Gold Coast and Nigeria, the bulk of them from Nigeria.[66] At the same time another French force of about 3,000 under General Aymerich operated outside the joint expedition. The reason for this unnecessary confusion was the seniority in rank of the French General over General Dobell. In order not to complicate the command he chose to operate from the south-eastern part of the Cameroons adjoining the Congo and Gabon territories. From October 1914 three companies of the Belgian Congo's *force publique* were incorporated into General Aymerich's force and the Belgian Congo forces were commanded by three Belgian captains, Bal, Marin and Weyemberg.[67] Besides this force under General Aymerich another French battalion of about 1,000 men was organised in French Chad and placed under General Largeau and Colonel Brisset.[68] This latter force was incorporated with much difficulty into the Nigerian force under General Cunliffe in spite of the almost implacable detestation of the British by Colonel Brisset.[69] The force under Cunliffe operating on the Nigeria–Cameroons frontier from Ikom in the south to Maiduguri in the north, numbered 2,224 troops made up exclusively of the

Nigeria Regiment with 134 British officers and 21 medical personnel as well as many carriers.[70]

From this it can be seen that there were over 6,000 British troops and over 7,000 French troops in the Cameroons, but technically only the 7,000 in the joint expeditionary force were under the command of General Dobell and this created a lot of problems, especially over jurisdiction and area of command.

Facing this array of forces from all the territories of the Allied powers were 2,000 German *Schutztruppe* and 2,200 policemen with para-military training.[71] The German Cameroons was completely encircled, and the Commandant of the German force, Lieutenant-Colonel Zimmermann, had to make the best of a bad situation. A simple comparison of the German strength with that of the Allies makes the German position appear hopeless; the fact that they fought for so long was a credit to German soldiery. One thing was in favour of the Germans, however: they knew the country very well and their command was unified. The quality of the *Schutztruppe* was superior to that of the Allied African troops, because of better and longer training.[72] The Germans believed that five years were needed to train a good African soldier, while the training given French and British soldiers hardly lasted more than a year. Because of this training, German African troops were much more professional than their counterparts in Nigeria, for example.

On the side of the Allies, instead of unity of command, there was petty jealousy and lack of co-ordination, but even so the conquest of the Cameroons was only a matter of time. After the initial reverses on the Nigeria–Cameroons border the Allies scored their first victory when Duala surrendered on 27 September 1914 to Captain Cyril Fuller[73] commanding the battleship H.M.S. *Challenger* and about a dozen vessels of the Nigerian Marine.[74] Duala, in one of the greatest surprises of the war, surrendered even before Dobell's forces were landed. After the surrender Marines from H.M.S. *Challenger* were landed and occupied Duala and Bonaberi. Eight steamers of the Woermann Linie and one of the Hamburg–Amerika line, with a total tonnage of 30,915, were seized.[75] By the end of 1914 the important district of Buea-Victoria where over one million sterling was invested in cocoa, rubber and tropical fruit plantations, had fallen to the Allies.

The British were struck not so much by the amount of money

expended as by the fact that so much had been accomplished within such a short time. One British political officer commented:

> Much of the work appears almost unnecessarily perfect . . . no money has been spared in regard to machinery, plant or housing accommodation for the European and native staff throughout the plantations. One cannot fail to see the evidence of the wonderful forethought and method with which the work has been planned, nothing has been left to chance and there is no sign of that lack of continuity in the management which so seriously affects . . . British firms on the West Coast.[76]

The seizure of Duala-Bonaberi, and then the productive Buea-Victoria district so early in the war made the Allies over-confident that total conquest of the Cameroons would follow quickly; but the Germans simply withdrew inland when a position was over-run, to carry on fighting until it became futile to continue resisting.

With Duala surrendered, the work of the Navy became that of patrolling the coast to prevent ammunition from being smuggled into the Cameroons from neighbouring and friendly Spanish Equatorial Africa.[77] Owing to the absence of good roads in the areas conquered around Duala and because of the complex network of rivers, communication by river became the most reliable, and because of this dependence on the rivers as a means of communication, the closest co-operation and mutual understanding between the naval and military services became essential to the success of the expedition. When there was an attempt to withdraw British warships from the area, General Dobell was particularly bitter against such a move and he made it clear he was not prepared to work with French naval officers who failed to display an eagerness in 'allowing the men under their command to leave their ships. Even if they do, so frequent complaints which are entirely out of place in war, are made as to the discomfort experienced.'[78] The Admiralty in the end withdrew H.M.S. *Challenger* but left Captain Fuller and H.M.S. *Cumberland* to continue the work begun in the Cameroons, to the immense satisfaction of General Dobell, whose co-operation with Captain Fuller had been particularly fruitful. General Dobell's refusal to work directly with French naval officers and his condemnation of the French warships *Bruix* and *Pothanu* as unsuitable for operations in the Cameroons demonstrated the thinly concealed dislike for the French which most of the British officers harboured.

From January 1915 General Dobell refused officially to assume overall responsibility for the campaign in northern Cameroons, because of communications difficulties. Lugard immediately responded by asking that Lieutenant-Colonel Cunliffe be promoted Brigadier-General[79] so that he would be senior in rank to Colonel Brisset, the French Commandant from the Chad who was operating in northern Cameroons, and could then assume command in the north. Lugard was full of hopes that Cunliffe could do this without friction with the French. The dreaded French antagonism to Cunliffe was based in the first place on national pride which neither the French nor the English were prepared to forget in the interest of a common goal. Colonel Brisset could not have been unaware of the reason for Cunliffe's sudden promotion. The French felt that the number of white troops in W.A.F.F. was too small,[80] and argued that this was bound to detract from the effectiveness of the British forces. One of the French officers declared: 'les habitudes de nos Alliés sont fort opposés aux nôtres'.[81] The French ridiculed the British African troops, who marched on bare feet, compared with their Senegalese who wore combat boots. The French also criticised the British officers for stopping at every convenient place to have tea or whisky.

The recrimination was, however, mutual; some of the Englishmen serving with the force were positively anti-French. In a typical comment a British officer, blaming the French for military ineffectiveness wrote, 'the French appear to be an idle lot and never push on a bit on their side . . . we may have to go and finish it off for them'.[82] Following an attempt by the British Admiralty to withdraw some naval officers serving with General Dobell, the British General, casting doubt on French capability, demurred:

> Owing to the complex nature of the operations it would be a matter of very grave difficulty to any British officer to act in consort with an officer of a different nationality . . . my experience of the French temperament leads me to believe that much of the methodical work that has to be performed at all hours of the day and night does not appeal to the characteristic displayed by that nationality.[83]

In spite of the mutual suspicion and denigration coupled with the fragmentation of authority and unmitigated scorn for each other, the Allies had in abundance what the Germans lacked, soldiers and ammunition.

Apart from lack of ammunition and the relatively small numbers of their soldiers compared with those of the Allies, the Germans were further handicapped by the internal rebellion, which they had to contain in some parts of the Cameroons. As soon as fighting broke out, the Dualas, one of the most virile and largest ethnic groups in the Cameroons, became very hostile to the Germans after their king, Manga Rudolf Bell, was executed for treason.[84] The hostility of the Dualas towards the Germans arose from the attempt to dispossess them of their lands and move them to another part of the area in order to make way for properly segregated European and African townships. The King of the Dualas from May 1914 was in constant touch with other African potentates in the hinterland such as King Joja of Fumban, urging a concerted effort to drive out the Germans from the Cameroons.[85] He had also told other African rulers that English support would be forthcoming. Apparently this hapless man knew nothing of the gathering clouds in Europe, but when war broke out, the Duala king was tried and publicly executed for treason. This action turned all Dualas into German enemies and they co-operated with the English against their former colonial masters. The Germans retaliated by declaring all Dualas as 'active combatants' who were to be shot on sight.[86]

Some of the Sultans in the north were also unco-operative. The Sultan of Gulfei on the Shari river who was a relative of Shehu Garbai of Borno supported the British because of the dynastic ties existing between Borno and Gulfei. The same was true of Sultan Bokhar of Mandara, a Muslim ruler who ruled over largely pagan subjects. Bokhar maintained close ties with the Shehu's court at Borno, and when the Germans discovered that he was passing secrets of German military movements to the British in Maiduguri, he fled to Borno towards the end of 1914 to avoid German wrath.[87]

Not all German subjects in the Cameroons were disloyal, in fact some of the Fulani Ardo and Lamido backed the Germans militarily until the instinct of self-preservation made it necessary for them to go over to the Allies.[88] The Yaundes, led by their very vigorous Chief Atanga,[89] supported the Germans in the south; they collected a force of about 8,000 and fought bravely on the side of the Germans. They used spears and poisoned arrows against the Allies, and Colonel Mayer, the Senior French officer in the expeditionary force, protested against the employment of this 'horde of savages' by the Germans; but the Germans were too hard pressed to bother about his protest.

The Germans also received support from Spanish subjects in Rio Muni and the strategically important Island of Fernando Po off the coast of Nigeria. This support was in the form of ammunition smuggled into the Cameroons by Spaniards to replenish the dwindling German supply. Before the war Germans had always enjoyed special privileges in Fernando Po. They had a high-powered wireless transmission station on the island, which they continued to use with Spanish connivance after the outbreak of war. This led to a flurry of exchanges between the Allies and the Spanish Government.[90] Failure to secure Spanish co-operation led to the blockade of Fernando Po and Rio Muni by the British and French Navies towards the end of 1914.[91] The blockade was not completely effective but it checked the rate of smuggling of ammunition by Spaniards into the Cameroons.

This action led to strained Anglo-Spanish relations. Suspected Spanish vessels were intercepted and in one case a senior Nigerian naval officer seized a Spanish vessel and confiscated goods destined for the Germans.[92] This led Lugard to comment that 'the action of the Spanish authority has been open to suspicion ever since the outbreak of the war. . . .'[93] Merry del Val, the Spanish ambassador in London, described the action of the British naval officer as 'a grave abuse of authority'. The ambassador wanted British officials on the spot to be warned seriously to desist from 'interference of the kind referred to which undoubtedly prejudices the cordial relationship and mutual sympathy existing between the two powers which it is our endeavour to conserve and develop'.[94] What worried Lugard most was not the overt sympathy for the German cause shown by the Spanish authorities, especially Angel Barrera, the Governor-General of Spanish Equatorial Africa (Fernando Po and Rio Muni), but the danger of the conversion of the island into a German naval base from which raiding parties could be sent to Nigeria or the Cameroons. If this were to happen, the security of Nigeria would be threatened. When General Dobell ordered another Spanish vessel on its way to Fernando Po to be detained because it was suspected the ship was carrying ammunition destined for the Germans, Governor Angel Barrera fumed: 'I fail to understand the reason for this fresh annoyance and violation of the law of Nations, for I am ignorant of any Hague convention which authorises the detention of a neutral ship, in this case a Spanish vessel'.[95] He warned Dobell that this kind of action 'might bring about a serious conflict which I wish to avoid'.[96] This was a dangerous situation, and it was feared that a local clash could conceivably bring Spain into the war against the Allies. General Dobell pleaded with Barrera that the 'highest military consideration' was behind every action he had taken against Spanish vessels and that his action should not be construed as an attempt 'to lower the prestige of the Spanish flag'.[97]

While the coast of Spanish Equatorial Africa remained blockaded, the war continued to be fought in the Cameroons. Throughout the entire period from November 1914 to July 1915 the Germans were active on the Nigerian frontier and Nigerian forces were constantly marching and fighting. In March 1915 the Germans were reported to be aiming at capturing Yola and invading Nigeria through that corridor.[9] Between 10 and 13 April 1915 a strong German raiding party actually succeeded in breaking through the Nigerian defences and reached Mutum Biu on the Benue river in Nigeria. They burnt the government quarters there, destroyed the telegraph line and temporarily uprooted British communications in that area.[99] As a result of this German military incursion, the Emir of Yola and members of his Native Administration as well as the British district officer fled the area. This was disastrous politically and psychologically: this German show of force might have persuaded the Emir that he could achieve his own distinct territorial ambitions by co-operating with the Germans. Before the Germans drove him out of his emirate the Emir of Yola had been of immense help to Nigerian forces operating from his capital. He had provided the infantry companies with hundreds of horses, rifle slings, several head of cattle and tons of grain to feed the army. He had also recruited more than 500 of his own people as carriers, and provided border patrols on his own initiative.[100] It can thus be seen that it was in the interests of the Nigerian Government that the Emir remained loyal. The Emir was of course not doing all this because of his love for the British; he was motivated by the desire to restore his rule over the whole of Adamawa – most of which was in the Cameroons.[101]

In the raid in Muri and Yola emirates, the Germans struck terror into the hearts of the people there, and the Nigerian Government felt compelled to do something dramatic that would impress the fear-stricken Nigerians. General Cunliffe moved some of his troops back to Muri and Yola emirates in May 1915 and started to drive out the Germans. By 11 June 1915 he had succeeded in driving out the Germans and had pursued them to their Benue river port of Garua, which he took with the assistance of the French that same month.[102] After the fall of Garua the siege of Mora, which had been on since the previous year, continued, but not as effectively as it should have been, because of the problem regarding the overall command of Allied troops in northern Cameroons. The French troops under Colonel Brisset which had co-operated in the capture of Garua were apparently placed under the command of Cunliffe only for the duration of the attack on Garua, because afterwards Cunliffe's orders fell on deaf ears.[103]

The fall of Garua was, however, happy news in Nigeria. The tension on the border eased; the Emir of Yola went back to his capital and presented a thousand head of cattle to the victorious soldiers.[104] Although Mora remained in the hands of the Germans, the northern part of the Cameroons was quiet for some time. The whole of Dikwa, which the Germans had held ineffectively before the war, was completely clear of the Germans. The northern situation was so encouraging that Cunliffe sent 300 Nigerian troops back home to recuperate.[105] Lugard also took the opportunity of the lull to seek permission from the Secretary of State to leave Lagos at the end of June for vacation in England. Since the heavy rains had completely halted fighting in the south, it was felt the Governor-General could take his leave, and by the end of June Lugard, full of hopes for a quick reduction of the German colony, left for England.

Efforts continued to be made to agree to a *modus vivendi* with the French in connection with the problematic question of the northern command. There was a sudden prospect of final resolution of this thorny question when General Largeau at Fort Lamy in July 1915 placed all forces commanded by Colonel Brisset under Cunliffe.[106] But Brisset refused to comply and a crisis point was reached in September 1915 when Cunliffe gave Brisset clear orders to remain in Garua, but the latter refused to obey and marched off to Ngaundere with all French troops under him.[107] He would also have taken with him the British troops left under his command in Garua had it not been for Cunliffe's veto. Cunliffe again referred the case to General Largeau, but Colonel Brisset rebuffed both his own superior officer and General Cunliffe by saying he was no longer under General Largeau, but under direct orders of General Aymerich.[108] Lugard, on learning about this in London, urged the Secretary of State to protest vigorously to the French Government so that 'this dual or triple command subject to counter orders from Brazzaville' should cease immediately.[109] Following direct intervention of the home governments, Cunliffe was confirmed as Commander.

Firmly in the saddle, Cunliffe succeeded before the end of 1915 in clearing the Germans from that portion of the Cameroons which lay between Lake Chad to the north and the Nachtigal rapids on the Sanaga river to the south, with the exception of the isolated German hill fortress of Mora which remained still unsubdued. What forced Garua to surrender was also eventually to lead to the capitulation of Mora: having been cut off from the rest of the world, the Germans had to subsist on African food and eventually had no choice but to eat all 'the horses, donkeys and camels'[110] in their desperate effort to stay alive. By the time the Germans in Garua surrendered to Cunliffe they were mentally and physically exhausted by what one of them referred to as the 'unequal warfare'[111] in the Cameroons.

Military operations in the equatorial forest of the south were more difficult. The distance which had to be traversed was immense and transportation was by head porterage since horses and camels were unsuitable because they would have died from the bites of tsetse flies. The forces under General Aymerich and those under Dobell were separated by a distance of over 400 miles.[112] In order to overwhelm the Germans by sheer numbers Allied forces under Dobell were increased in July 1915 to 9,700, including the 5th Light Indian Infantry battalion normally based in the Straits Settlements.[113]

While General Dobell's forces began to press south-eastwards, General Aymerich's forces also started sweeping the Germans from the south after the rains had stopped in October 1915. Pressed from all sides by the Allies, the German military effort seemed to be collapsing but nobody was sure of where the Germans would dig in and make their last stand. General Dobell thought it was likely to be Yaunde in the south-east, where Governor Ebermaier was rumoured to have been towards the end of December 1915 trying to bolster the fighting spirit of his army by telling them to hold on since the war in Europe was about to end.[114] On hearing this, several columns of the Allied force advanced towards Yaunde and when Yaunde was eventually occupied by

Colonel Haywood commanding a Nigerian battalion, the Germans had already evacuated the town.[115] The Germans were by this time tired, short of food and ammunition and completely demoralised. It was stated by one of the British prisoners of war in the Cameroons released when Yaunde was occupied, that the prolonged resistance of the Germans was due mainly to uninterrupted communication with Spanish Muni, to Ebermaier's strong personality and to the influence and example of German regular officers.[116] After withdrawing from Yaunde the Germans fought their way straight for the Spanish Muni border, stopping to engage the Allies in fierce fighting until they finally slipped into Spanish Muni on 15 February 1916.[117] On 17 February, at the request of Governor-General Angel Barrera of Spanish Guinea, General Dobell forwarded a telegraphic message from Governor Ebermaier to the German Government reporting his surrender and evacuation of the Cameroons.[118]

After the collapse of German resistance in the south, General Cunliffe left the Cameroons for Lagos to collect a Howitzer and European gun crew to storm Mora, the only remaining German foothold in the Cameroons. Lugard, moved with pity for the isolated German garrison in the north of Cameroons, suggested to Cunliffe that in view of the very gallant stand made by the German garrison at Mora and the fair and soldierly way in which they had fought, it would be advisable to offer them terms if they would surrender.[119] Lugard told Cunliffe that the capture of this impregnable fortress by assault would involve a heavy loss of life and he feared that Nigerian troops might disobey if ordered to go back to Mora after the difficult campaign that had just ended.

Cunliffe agreed with Lugard and a message was sent to the Germans holding Mora that the rest of the German forces had been defeated, and were told that if they surrendered, officers would be allowed to retain their swords and the African soldiers would be given safe passages to their homes, while the Europeans would be sent to England as prisoners of war.[120]

In one of the most honourable deeds of the Germans in the Cameroons during the war, Captain von Raben, the German officer commanding the fort, accepted the terms but with the proviso that £2,000 be lent him to pay his African soldiers.[121] Lugard advanced him the money from the credits of liquidated German firms in Nigeria, for which Captain von Raben accepted responsibility. The garrison which surrendered included eleven

Europeans, 145 African soldiers, 232 women and servants with 183 rifles, 4 maxim guns, 37,000 rounds of ammunition.[122] This capitulation completed the conquest of the Cameroons.

After the conquest, the territory was garrisoned by eight infantry companies of W.A.F.F. and another 230 rank and file from Nigeria. The area garrisoned by the British was one-third of the country and this included important districts such as Dikwa, Kontscha-Jabassi, Victoria-Buea, Rio Del Rey, Duala-Bonaberi, Ossidinge, Bare and Bana. A mixed French and British garrison was stationed at Garua because it was jointly conquered by the two forces. The French also provided eight companies from their Equatorial African possessions to garrison the remaining part of the country until the time of the provisional partition in March 1916.[123]

With the defeat of the Germans and their withdrawal into Spanish territory another problem arose. Angel Barrera, the Governor-General of Spanish Guinea, promised the Allies that the Germans and their African troops would be interned in Fernando Po. Barrera then followed this promise by evacuating them from the mainland of Muni to Fernando Po. Out of the 16,000 Cameroonians taken to the Spanish Island, 6,000 were soldiers.[124] Barrera made no effort to intern the Germans as he had promised. The British consul in Fernando Po wrote that the ex-Governor of the Cameroons, Herr Ebermaier, wielded so much influence in the Spanish Island that he appeared 'to hold the governor [Barrera] in his hands'.[125] The Germans were also said to be drilling their troops and were poised to attack and reoccupy the Cameroons after their soldiers had fully recuperated from their wounds. It was feared in Allied circles that the Germans might actually take over Fernando Po if Barrera proved unamenable to their demands.

Sir Arthur Hardinge, the British ambassador in Madrid, was again compelled to plead with the Spanish Government concerning the large number of 'native' troops and their German officers in Fernando Po. He complained that the presence of these soldiers constituted a threat to the security of Allied territories and especially to the newly conquered Cameroons. The British ambassador alleged that German ammunition had been smuggled into Fernando Po in Spanish vessels to re-arm the soldiers supposedly interned there.[126] The Spaniards were unimpressed by all these remonstrances and their intransigence was to continue until after the war and continued to divert the attention of the

Allies from more serious problems. This was particularly so in the case of Nigeria, where the authorities continued to expect attack from German cruisers using Fernando Po as a base,[127] but the fears and anxiety proved baseless, since nothing came of the marine scare.

GERMAN PRISONERS OF WAR TAKEN DURING THE CAMEROONS CAMPAIGN AND THEIR TREATMENT

One aspect of the war which attracted much attention was the question of European prisoners of war, in an African campaign. From the time Duala surrendered a stream of prisoners of war began to pour into Nigeria from the Cameroons. The Germans claimed that they surrendered because General Dobell promised that their surrender would be with honour and without any precondition.[128] The Germans complained that this bargain was not kept and that their property was plundered and looted by troops under General Dobell. They also bitterly resented the fact that they were not allowed to take any kit with them before being shipped out of the Cameroons, which led to unnecessary suffering, especially by women and children.

German colonial officials complained that Europeans were escorted by African soldiers and that while passing through Duala they were laughed at and insulted by their erstwhile subjects. Dr Dix, Assessor of the Imperial German Government of the Cameroons, even complained that he was made to carry his luggage while Dualas laughed at him. He found this particularly humiliating in view of the fact that before the war both his luggage and he himself would have been carried in a hammock by these same laughing Africans. Dr Dix said that in spite of the fact that he had given his *parole d'honneur* as an officer, a French officer angrily removed his sword which he had been allowed to keep by his English counterpart, and that the French officer told the English officer not to treat any German with respect. Dr Dix alleged that all this drama took place in front of an 'insulting lot of Duala natives'.[129]

The German officers claimed that missionaries were manhandled by soldiers and they ended their petition by declaring, 'we can only still mention that ourselves and with us, all our country people got the impression that these occurrences refer in the first way to orders of the French Captain who was in charge of the transport on the 28th of September 1914'.[130] There can be no doubt that the French for historical reasons were much more hostile to the Germans in the Cameroons, a fact which General Dobell himself recognised.[131]

In reply to the German charges General Dobell said that when the Germans left Duala, they were allowed to take away such baggage as the exigencies of the military situation permitted. He claimed that there were several hundred Germans, practically all combatants, in Duala at the time of Allied occupation and that the presence of such a large number constituted a menace that could only be removed by immediate deportation.[132] As to their private property, the Allied commander said that everything was being done to collect and store what could be found. He agreed that prisoners naturally suffered some discomfort in the rapid deportation that was necessary for security reasons. As far as the missionaries were concerned, the General said he found their case most complicated. While agreeing that some were badly treated, he said the discovery of hidden arms together with cast-off army uniforms in the Basel Mission justified the steps taken against them.[133]

The Colonial Office was less sympathetic towards the Germans. It was claimed that no less than four hundred packages were forwarded from Duala to Lagos and restored to their German owners, and that even Dr Dix's two dogs were recovered and brought to him in Lagos.[134] Lewis Harcourt commented that not much luggage was transported for British prisoners of war in Germany. Others in the Colonial Office said that the Germans had better be shown the Belgian reports of the treatment meted out by their fellow countrymen to Belgians.[135] Sir George Fiddes ridiculed the Germans by minuting: 'Kultur squeaks if even a coin is trodden on'.[136]

The German Government made representations to the American Government on alleged British maltreatment of missionaries, apparently to gain the sympathy of an influential neutral power. The British Foreign Office drew the attention of the United States envoy in London to the fact that the attitude adopted by certain of the German missionaries in Nigeria had not been such as to encourage the view that they should be treated as non-combatants adhering strictly to their proper duties, taking no part, active or otherwise, in the war; and in proof of this A. G. Boyle, the Governor's Deputy in Nigeria, stated that the daring attack made on H.M.S. *Dwarf* by 'a launch carrying an infernal machine was conducted by a missionary'.[137] When the culprit was questioned by Nigerian authorities he was said to have replied that he was 'a soldier first and a missionary afterwards'.[138]

Other incriminating evidence brought against the missionaries was that they interfered with 'native spies' sent by British field commanders to collect information about German military movements in the Cameroons.[139] General Cunliffe said he found a letter from Colonel Zimmermann asking to have in writing, the terms under which missionaries were serving with his forces.[140] Another letter from Zimmermann was found in which he regretted that he could not free these missionaries serving with him as the fall of Garua had deprived him of many Europeans. Cunliffe wrote that when the missionaries were to be arrested the officer in command of the detachment sent to fetch them stated that they endeavoured to lead the detachment into an ambush by asking the officer to enter the Mission House to discuss the matter at a time when a party of German soldiers were concealed in the long grass round the Mission.[141]

There can be no doubt that in the heat of battle, individual Germans suffered in the hands of their enemies. Stories of German atrocities in Europe further inflamed passions, although British prisoners of war taken by the Germans in the Cameroons were well treated; but when the Germans mentioned this, they always got back the answer, 'Germans had committed outrages on the wounded in Flanders'.[142] Those Germans who were prisoners of war taken in battle were less fortunate than those who were incarcerated in Nigeria as reservists living in enemy territory. Although one German died in prison in Ibadan, many of them claimed to have been well treated and one of them, writing to his wife about his experience, commented:

> the English are already a little bit ashamed of their way of locking us up in criminals' cells . . . we tease them on every occasion, we do not often but our English friends call on us fairly often and always assure us that the war ought not to make any difference to our personal relations. It is firmly asserted by the English that our arrest is only a consequence of bad treatment of Britishers . . . in Germany.[143]

These complaints as far as Nigeria was concerned ended with the shipment of these Germans to England to be interned there, thus releasing much-needed time for solving the administrative problems of the newly conquered territory of Cameroons.

THE AFRICAN SOLDIER AND THE CAMEROONS CAMPAIGN

The role of the African fighting man deserves some comment because of the uniqueness of the situation in which he found himself, fighting well-trained Africans like himself as well as Europeans all armed with the best that modern weaponry could provide. The Germans maintained that they were defeated in the Cameroons because of the shortage of ammunition and the complete lack of artillery.[144] This seems almost self-evident and beyond dispute. Secondly, the Germans claimed that 'honest fighting was rendered practically impossible' because of the system of widespread espionage which the English carried on and also because of 'native treachery and betrayal'.[145] The Germans also blamed their defeat on the Dualas 'aided by British funds'. It was alleged that 'English rule was presented in the most glowing colours' and that a strong prejudice against the Germans existed in many parts of the country.[146] Yet they still acknowledged that 'some chiefs and their people remained true to us until the enemy occupied the country'. Some Germans blamed unfairly their African troops, who could not stand the enemy's artillery, and in the face of shelling of their positions, they were said to have got out of hand and 'the wild bush negro in them broke out'.[147]

But by the victorious Allies the African soldiers were showered with praise. The French, who had always considered their black subjects more of a military asset than anything else, were extravagant in their praise.[148] The success of the campaign was attributed to the African soldier, particularly troops of the Nigeria Regiment.

> whose gallantry and willing endurance of real hardships have been remarkable, who were plunged suddenly into a form of fighting of which they could not possibly have had any conception, but who responded magnificently to all the calls made upon them and to whom must for ever be credited a large portion of the success achieved.[149]

Another officer writing about soldiers in the field commented:

> ... they are good fellows and work splendidly; of course they stand things no white man ever could and ... They are good fighters, too,

and, considering they have never been up against rifle fire before, they are marvellous, as the black man generally has an unholy fear of a gun. It's an extraordinary experience for them, unlike anything that has ever happened to them before, and when they return to Nigeria again they will be full of swank as to what they have done and seen.[150]

Brigadier-General Cunliffe in his appreciation of the efforts of each component part of the force also remembered the 'transport carriers who have toiled incessantly under heavy loads and at times also under heavy fire to keep the troops in the field supplied with food and ammunition'.[151] On the achievement and problems of the Nigeria Regiment Cunliffe wrote:

their characteristics, traditions and even their languages differ as widely as does the food to which they are accustomed. They were called upon to take part in a great struggle the rights and wrongs of which they can scarcely have been expected dimly to perceive. Their rations have been scanty, their barefoot marches long and trying and their fights at times extremely arduous, yet they have not been found wanting either in discipline, devotion to their officers or personal courage.[152]

General Dobell proudly commented:

the troops of the W.A.F.F. have realised my fullest expectations, to them no day appears to be too long, no task too difficult, with a natural aptitude for soldiering they are endowed with a constitution which inures them to hardship.[153]

Before the war in the Cameroons ended the British had suffered total casualties of 1,668 killed and wounded and the French 2,567.[154] Cunliffe recommended that distinguished conduct medals (D.C.M.) or money be given to thirty-eight survivors of the soldiers cited for courage and bravery under fire,[155] but one of the most unfortunate elements in the history of the W.A.F.F. as far as the African serviceman was concerned was that they were not allowed to bear their proper last names, so that those who distinguished themselves during the war were remembered with such names as 'Sambo Kano', 'Gama Bida', 'Usman Yola', 'Adegbite Offa', 'Amusa Ibadan', 'Musa Bauchi', 'Tanko Zaria', 'Oke Modakeke', 'Agbe Owo', 'Umoru Bornu'.[156] Since these last names were the names of towns where these soldiers came from and not their proper names, their outstanding performance was merged in the names of their towns; this knotty question was finally resolved by building cenotaphs in Ibadan and Kano, the main centres of recruitment in Nigeria.[157]

As if to forestall the imperial government's action of sending Nigerians to fight in other theatres of war, Brigadier-General Cunliffe warned against employing the troops 'in any theatre of war far distant from their homes'. He added that in officering West African troops:

> the personal element stands for almost everything ... the present dearth of British officers who are in close touch and sympathy with the men renders it impossible to contemplate employing the Nigeria Regiment outside its own country.[158]

But it was just around this time that questions were being asked in the British parliament why Britain was not raising a black army of millions from the 'soldiering peoples of her African possessions like the Hausas and the Zulus'.[159] Nigeria did not have to answer the question immediately after the Cameroons campaign; the problem of administration in the conquered colony took precedence over oversea service for a while.

Notes

1 C.O. 583/6/44563, Lugard to Colonial Office, 31 Dec. 1913.
2 F. J. Moberly, *History of the Great War. Military Operations: Togoland and the Cameroons 1914–1916*, H.M. Stationery Office, London, 1931, pp. 43–4.
3 *Ibid.*
4 C.O. 445/34/8785, General Charles Dobell (Inspector-General of W.A.F.F.) on distribution of forces, 1 Feb. 1914.
5 C.O. 445/34/24258, Colonel Carter (Commandant of the Nigeria Regiment) to Lugard, 3 July 1914.
6 *Ibid.*
7 *Ibid.*
8 Moberly, *op. cit.*, pp. 43–4.
9 C.O. 445/34/8785, General Dobell to War Office, 18 Feb. 1914. There were 1,800 Hausa, 1,156 Yoruba, 380 Kanuri (beri-beri), 351 Fulani, 91 Nupe, 21 Ibo in the Nigeria Regiment. Others were categorised as 'unclassified pagans'.
10 C.O. 583/6/44563, Lugard to Colonial Office, 31 Dec. 1913. The Southern Nigeria Volunteer Corps of educated Nigerians was abolished in 1913.
11 C.O. 445/34/16467, Lugard to Colonial Office, 4 May 1914.

12 *Ibid.*, Dobell's minute, 11 May 1914.

13 *Ibid.*

14 C.O. 537/395, Memo on Imperial Defence by J. R. Chancellor, Secretary, Colonial Defence Committee (C.D.C.), 24 Jan. 1911.

15 W.O. 106/46, C.I.D., 20 March 1904 memo on the military policy to be adopted in a war with Germany by intelligence department, War Office. See also Paul Guinn, *British Strategy and Politics, 1914–1918*, London, 1966, pp. 6–7.

16 Lt-Col Jean Ferrandi, *La conquête du Cameroun-Nord, 1914–1916*, Charles Lavauzelle et Cie, Paris, 1928, p. 17. Ferrandi wrote that the invasion of the German colony of Togo by British forces from the Gold Coast was the signal that war would extend to Africa.

17 C.O. 537/395, Memo on Imperial Defence by J. R. Chancellor, Secretary, C.D.C., 24 Jan. 1911.

18 W.O. 106/643, 2 Aug. 1914.

19 *Ibid.* According to H.M.'s Ambassador in Berlin, there were 2,400 trained soldiers in the Cameroons compared with well over 5,000 in Nigeria alone of the British possessions in West Africa.

20 *The Times*, 9 Aug. 1914.

21 'La Conquête du Cameroun: la neutralité du Congo', in *L'Afrique Française*, March 1916, pp. 61–6. See also W. O. Henderson, *Studies in German Colonial History*, London, Frank Cass & Co. Ltd, 1963, pp. 96–7. For the neutrality clauses of the 1885 Berlin Act see Sir E. Hertslet, *The Map of Africa by Treaty* (3 vols), London, 1909, ii, pp. 474–5 for General Act of Berlin Conference, 26 Feb. 1885, ch. III, Article X.

22 G. L. Beer, *African Questions at the Paris Peace Conference*, reprinted London, 1968, p. 264.

23 *L'Afrique Française*, March 1966, pp. 61–6.

24 General Aymerich, *La conquête du Cameroun: 1er Août 1914–20 Fevrier 1916*, pp. 26–8.

25 Beer, *op. cit.*, p. 65. See also M. Perham, *Lugard: The Years of Authority*, p. 29.

26 Henri Mailer, 'Le rôle des Colonies françaises dans la campagne du Cameroun 1914–1916', *L'Afrique Française*, June 1916, pp. 187–224.

27 Beer, *op. cit.*, pp. 65–6.

28 H. R. Rudin, *The Germans in the Cameroons 1884–1914: A Case Study in Modern Imperialism*, reprinted Archon Books, 1968, p. 155.

29 W.O. 106/645ª (undated), military operations in the Cameroons.

30 W.O. 106/643, 2 Aug. 1914.

31 *Ibid.*

32 (Sir) Charles Strachey, 1862–1942. Foreign Office 1885–99; Colonial Office, visited Nigeria in 1913 when he was principal clerk 1900; represented Colonial Office at the Paris Peace Conference 1919; Assistant Under Secretary for the Colonies, 1924–7.

33 C.O. 537/123, Strachey's memo of 14 Aug. 1914 brought before the sub-committee of Imperial Defence.

34 *Ibid.*

35 C.O. 537/123, Nigeria, secret 76. John Holt & Co. Ltd, to Colonial Office, 9 Sept. 1914 (enclosing letter from their agent in Duala, James Deemin, 3 Aug. 1914).

36 C.O. 537/135, 15 Aug. 1914, Report by Krooboys from the S.S. *Marina*. An official at the Colonial Office minuted 'Krooboys are notoriously intelligent and plucky sailors. Their information is much more likely to be sound than that from most natives.'

37 W.O. 158/518, Colonial Office to Secretary, Offensive Sub-Committee of Imperial Defence, 16 Aug. 1914.

38 C.O. 537/135, Strachey's minute, 24 Aug. 1914.

39 C.O. 537/123, Strachey's memo, 14 Aug. 1914.

40 *Ibid.*

41 C.O. 583/35/38554, letter from Hauptmann von Crailsheim to his father, intercepted by Cunliffe, 24 June 1915.

42 C.O. 583/35/38256, Major C. T. Lawrence, O/C Nigeria Land Contingent, 30 June 1915.

43 C.O. 583/56/17919, Major C. T. Lawrence, 14 March 1917, on work done by the Land Contingent: the strength of the Land Contingent was 1,134 rank and file divided as follows:
   (a)   Lagos Company, 3 officers, 147 rank and file
   (b)   Ebutte Metta Company, 3 officers, 65 rank and file
   (c)   Calabar Company, 2 officers, 90 rank and file
   (d)   Ibadan Section, 1 officer, 30 rank and file
   (e)   Abeokuta Section, 1 officer, 25 rank and file
   (f)   Warri Section, 1 officer, 34 rank and file
   (g)   Port Harcourt Section, 1 officer, 50 rank and file
   (h)   Northern Provinces (number of officers not given), 671 rank and file.

44 C.O. 583/35/38256, 30 June 1915. At 1 a.m. on 17 Oct. 1914 owing to alarm being given of possible German landing in Lagos, the force came out in combat dress ready to fight.

45 C.O. 583/56/17919, 14 March 1917, Major C. T. Lawrence's Report on Land Contingent.

46 C.O. 583/19/44167, Lugard to Colonial Office, 19 Oct. 1914.

47 C.O. 583/30/4984, Lugard to Colonial Office on the situation on the outbreak of war, 9 Jan. 1915.

48 C.O. 583/56/17919, 14 March 1915. Role of the Marine department in the Defence of Nigeria, by Captain Percival (acting director of Nigeria Marine).

49 C.O. 583/30/4984, Lugard to Colonial Office, 9 Jan. 1915.

50 *Ibid.*

51 *Ibid.* Secretary of State, telegram of 5 Aug. 1914.

52 *Ibid.* Secretary of State, telegram of 12 Aug. 1914.

53 C.O. 583/20/47149, Lugard to Colonial Office, 8 Nov. 1914.

54 C.O. 483/30/4984, Lugard to Colonial Office, 9 Jan. 1915. While Lugard was away in England A. G. Boyle acted as Governor. In the crucial moment, instead of Carter coming to Lagos to consult with Boyle he remained in Kaduna, thus leaving the Acting Governor completely ignorant about the military situation.

55 C.O. 583/20/47149, Lugard to Colonial Office, 8 Nov. 1914. See also Alan Burns, *History of Nigeria*, Allen and Unwin, 1929, reprinted 1963, p. 226.

56 C.O. 583/20/47149, Lugard to Colonial Office, 8 Nov. 1914.

57 C.O. 537/123, Nigeria, Secret 72, Lugard to Colonial Office, 8 Sept. 1914.

58 *Ibid.* Nigeria, Secret 124, Lugard to Colonial Office, 15 Sept. 1914.

59 Frederick Cunliffe entered the British Army in 1889, joined W.A.F.F. in 1904, commanded Nigeria Regiment in the Cameroons and East Africa 1914–1918. He was promoted Brigadier-General in 1915, died in 1955.

60 Aymerich, *op. cit.*, p. 14.

61 Henri Mailier, *op. cit.*, pp. 187–224.

62 Aymerich, *op. cit.*, p. 19.

63 (Brigadier-General Sir) Charles McPherson Dobell. Entered the British Army 1890; served in W.A.F.F. 1905–6; General Staff 1907–11; A.D.C. to the King 1910–13; Inspector-General, W.A.F.F. 1913.

64 W.O. 106/644, French military attaché to War Office, Aug. 1914.

65 Aymerich, *op. cit.*, p. 14.

66 C.O. 445/34/7714, 4 March 1914. Total strength of W.A.F.F. in 1914 was 7,733 rank and file and 242 British officers and 116 British N.C.O.s. Of these 5,426 troops, 172 officers and 103 N.C.O.s were in Nigeria. The Gold Coast had 1,553 troops, 39 officers and 11 British N.C.O.s, while Sierra Leone had 617 enlisted men, 28 British officers, 2 British N.C.O.s; Gambia had 137 troops, 3 British officers, 2 British N.C.O.s. At the commencement of the Cameroons campaign about half of the Gold Coast force was occupying German Togoland.

67 Aymerich, *op. cit.*, p. 189.

68 Ferrandi, *op. cit.*, p. 16.

69 C.O. 583/34/35933, Lugard to Colonial Office, 15 July 1915.

70 W.O. 158/539, undated, military operation in the Cameroons.

71 W.O. 106/643, 2 Aug. 1914. H.M. Ambassador in Berlin, intelligent guess of German military strength in the Cameroons. See also Aymerich, *op. cit.*, p. 14.

72 Armand Annet, *En colonne dans le Cameroun: Notes d'un Commandant de Campagnie, 1914–1916*, Paris, 1949, p. 123.

73 (Admiral Sir) Cyril Thomas Moulden Fuller, 1874–1942. Served with Togoland and Cameroons expeditionary forces as Senior Naval Officer 1914–16; Head of the British Naval Section, Paris Peace Conference 1919–20; Chief of Staff Atlantic Fleet 1920–2; Sea Lord and Controller of Navy 1923–5; Second Sea Lord 1930–2.

74 W.O. 106/645ᵃ, Conquest of the Cameroons. See also Sir Julian S. Corbett, *History of the Great War: based on official documents. Naval Operations*, ii, Longmans, Green and Co., 1921, p. 232.

75 W.O. 106/645ᵃ.

76 C.O. 583/29/4917, F. C. Stobart (chief political officer, African Expeditionary Force), to Dobell, 12 Dec. 1914.

77 CAB 137/12/No. 144, 'Intelligence Report' from Madric, 14 Oct. 1914.
78 C.O. 583/29/50748, Dobell to Admiralty, 6 Nov. 1914.
79 C.O. 583/30/9936, Lugard to Colonial Office, 23 Jan. 1915.
80 Ferrandi, *op. cit.*, p. 49.
81 *Ibid.*, p. 251.
82 C.O. 583/21/50756, Captain W. A. Ross to Charles Strachey (Private and Personal), 17 Dec. 1914.
83 C.O. 583/29/50748, Dobell to Admiralty, 6 Nov. 1914.
84 Rudin, *op. cit.*, p. 413.
85 *Ibid.*, p. 413.
86 C.O. 583/29/52206, Captured letter from Lt von Engelbrechten to Hauptmann Caisser, 7 Oct. 1914.
87 Ferrandi, *op. cit.*, pp. 42–62.
88 *Ibid.*, p. 193.
89 Annet, *op. cit.*, p. 120. See also C.O. 583/29/4916, Col Mayer's protest enclosed in Dobell to Harcourt, 26 Dec. 1914.
90 ADM/137/162M 15862/14, H.M. Ambassador at Madrid, Sir Arthur Hardinge, met the Spanish Minister of State, Marques de Lema, on 15 Aug. 1914 to protest about German use of Fernando Po.
91 ADM/137/162 M.O. 4419/14, Captain Fuller to Admiralty, 11 Nov. 1914.
92 C.O. 583/32/23370, Lugard to Colonial Office, 1 May 1915.
93 *Ibid.*
94 C.O. 583/41/10745, undated, 1915, Merry del Val to Sir Edward Grey.
95 ADM/137/29, Governor-General Angel Barrera to Dobell, 26 March 1915.
96 W.O. 158/517, Angel Barrera to Dobell, 20 May 1915.
97 ADM/137/29, Dobell to Barrera, 26 March 1915.
98 C.O. 445/36/11059, Lugard to Colonial Office, 12 Feb. 1916.
99 C.O. 583/33/26209, Lugard to Colonial Office, 19 March 1915.
100 *Ibid.*
101 C.O. 583/50/842, Lugard to Colonial Office, 2 Dec. 1916.
102 C.O. 583/33/27149, Lugard to Colonial Office, 12 June 1915.
103 C.O. 583/34/32561, Lugard to Colonial Office, 24 June 1915.
104 A. H. M. Kirk-Greene, *Adamawa, Past and Present*, Oxford University Press, London, 1958, p. 78.
105 C.O. 583/34/32561, Lugard to Colonial Office, 24 June 1915.
106 C.O. 583/34/35933, A. G. Boyle to Colonial Office, 15 July 1915.
107 C.O. 583/35/43293, Lugard (writing from Abinger Common, Surrey) to Colonial Office, 17 Sept. 1915.
108 *Ibid.*
109 *Ibid.*
110 C.O. 583/35/43293, Hauptmann von Crailsheim's notes seized by Cunliffe – written in Garua on 27 March 1915.
111 *Ibid.*
112 C.O. 583/52/23584, Dobell to Colonial Office, 1 March 1916.
113 *Ibid.*

114 Moberly, *op. cit.*, p. 394.
115 *Ibid.*, p. 393.
116 *Ibid.*, p. 406.
117 *Ibid.*, p. 420.
118 *Ibid.*, p. 420.
119 C.O. 583/44/13028, Lugard to Colonial Office, 18 Feb. 1916.
120 *Ibid.*
121 C.O. 583/44/8229, Lugard to Colonial Office, 18 Feb. 1916. See also Erich Student, *Kameruns Kampf 1914–1916*, pp. 332–4.
122 C.O. 583/44/8229, Lugard to Colonial Office, 18 Feb. 1916.
123 Aymerich, *op. cit.*, p. 197.
124 ADM/137/28/, Lieutenant de Vaisseau, Commandant Boissarie, to Captain Fuller, 8 March 1916.
125 ADM/137/380 MO 1803/16, 25 Feb. 1916, Captain Fuller to Admiralty.
126 ADM/137/339, Sir Arthur Hardinge to Foreign Office, 8 March 1916.
127 C.O. 445/3227, War Office to Colonial Office, 16 Jan. 1917.
128 C.O. 583/28/47131, Dr Dix (Assessor of the Imperial German Government of the Cameroons) and Herr L. Botcher (comptroller of customs) Lagos, to Lugard, 14 Oct. 1914.
129 *Ibid.* See also *Lugard Papers*, i, p. 122. Major Edward Lugard wrote: 'It is very gratifying to hear how intense is the [German] desire to be told off as a P.O.W. to the English and not to the French – down on their knees in supplication to go to the English and not to the French who are very bitter and remember the explosive bullets of Togoland.'
130 C.O. 583/28/47131, Lagos, Dr Dix and Herr L. Botcher's petition to Lugard, 14 Oct. 1914.
131 C.O. 583/28/47131, Dobell to Lugard, 2 Nov. 1914.
132 *Ibid.*
133 *Ibid.*
134 *Ibid.*, A. J. Harding's minute of 8 Dec. 1914.
135 *Ibid.*, Sir John Anderson's minute of 10 Dec. 1914.
136 *Ibid.*, Sir George Fiddes's minute of 9 Dec. 1914.
137 C.O. 583/41/40660, Foreign Office to U.S. Ambassador in London, 1 Sept. 1915.
138 M. Perham, *op. cit.*, p. 536.
139 C.O. 583/44/11061, Cunliffe to Lugard, 12 Jan. 1916.
140 *Ibid.*
141 *Ibid.*
142 W.O. 106/656, 24 March 1916. Herr Erich Scherte's statement as to the treatment of German P.O.W.'s by General Cunliffe's troops.
143 C.O. 583/28/47131, letter of W. Brunger from Lagos, 25 Sept. 1914, intercepted by the Home Office.
144 W.O. 106/656, Herr Bode (prisoner of war), 15 Feb. 1916.
145 *Ibid.*
146 W.O. 106/656, Ober-Jager Adler, German P.O.W., 24 Feb. 1916.

147 C.O. 583/35/38554, Ober-Leutnant Suren, P.O.W. taken at Garuaï, 24 June 1915.
148 *Ibid.*
149 C.O. 583/44/13051, Cunliffe to Lugard, 18 Feb. 1916.
150 *The Times*, 6 Feb. 1915, 'Letters from the Front' column.
151 C.O. 583/45/18334, Cunliffe to War Office, 20 March 1916.
152 *Ibid.*
153 C.O. 583/52/23584, Dobell to War Office, 1 March 1916.
154 W.O. 158/516, Dobell to War Office, 19 Feb. 1916.
155 C.O. 445/35/40221, Cunliffe to Lugard, 12 Aug. 1915.
156 C.O. 583/93/58894, Clifford to Milner, 9 Nov. 1920.
157 *Ibid.*
158 C.O. 445/35/40221, Cunliffe to Lugard, 12 Aug. 1915.
159 *The Times*, 26 July 1916. Lt-Commander Wedgwood, Liberal M.P. for Newcastle-under-Lyme, asked for 2½ million black soldiers to be raised from the fighting races of Africa.

7 Administration and Franco-British rivalry in the Cameroons, September 1914 to March 1916

Events in the Cameroons, from the fall of Duala in September 1914 to the provisional partition in March 1916, in every way showed that the rivalries, colonial ambitions and the mentality of partition and scramble were the driving motives behind almost every action. Initially the British as represented by their men on the spot staked out a 'maximum' demand for territories in the Cameroons, but as happened during the partition era, Britain eventually gave ground in the Cameroons in order to preserve her hegemony in the Middle East and East Africa.[1] The events in the Cameroons also demonstrated the inter-departmental rivalries within the British Government, with the decisions of the Colonial Office and the Admiralty being overridden by the Foreign Office in the name of British world-wide interests, as contrasted to the 'provincial' outlook of a department like the Colonial Office. It is probably true that the Asquith Cabinet was a coalition of in-dependent departmental heads,[2] dominated by the Asquith, Grey and Haldane triumvirate, with the effect that decisions of this group, particularly those of Grey, tended to carry more weight than those of his colleagues in the Cabinet.

British colonial ambitions in the Cameroons took some time to develop, but as they unfolded it became clear that the principal object was the regaining of all territories which Britain had lost to Germany by default in the period of partition and delimitation of boundaries between 1882 and 1894. Under this broad aim the Nigerian Government wanted to secure the lost territories of the Emir (Lamido) of Yola and the Shehu of Borno, who were victims of the arbitrary European mapping of African boundaries during the partition era. This aspiration to regain what was lost was not confined to the British; the French too never forgot the cession of territories in French Equatorial Africa to Germany in 1911, forced on them by the Moroccan crisis; besides yearning to recover what they had lost, the French also revived their dream of a French empire stretching uninterrupted from Algiers to Brazzaville. It is in the light of these general national ambitions that the administration and the provisional partition of the Cameroons can be understood.

The most urgent problem when Duala surrendered was to have a sort of workable administrative system established without paying too much attention to national differences and ambitions. In order to strike a national balance, the political staff attached to the expeditionary force was composed of two British and two French officials.[3]

They were charged with the duty of pacification and civil administration of the areas conquered by the Anglo-French force. This apparent sinking of national differences for the overall military success of the Allies soon broke down, with the result that French political officers worked in areas where French troops predominated, and the British likewise. In spite of this, General Charles Dobell continued to have full authority over all the expeditionary forces, with the exception of those under General Aymerich, which were technically outside the jurisdiction of the commander of the joint expeditionary force but no doubt called into question the extent of Anglo-French co-operation and the faith the French had in such co-operation. This manifestation of national rivalry was to bedevil the relations between the two Allies throughout the course of the war in the Cameroons. The emergence of seperate administration though under a not too effective unified control created vested interests that were very difficult to ignore during the negotiations preceding the provisional partition.

The first job of the administrative staff was restoring law and order in and around Duala, which was by no means easy. These white officers and their African subordinates were very impressed by the way the Duala people behaved. They did not take the laws into their own hands, especially during the confused situations when white men fought each other with the help of African soldiers. Although the Duala people insulted the humiliated Germans, they did not physically assault them. There was a good deal of looting, chiefly by labourers thrown out of employment, but this was quickly brought under control after effective occupation by Allied troops. The administration around Duala was beset with war-time dislocation and mass movement of people caused by panic, but the occupying powers were at least not confronted with having to deal with resistance movements. The Dualas welcomed the downfall of the Germans in the Cameroons and they actively co-operated with the new regime. They were quickly persuaded to open their markets, but this did not prove successful because the Dualas (who were traders) could not go into the hinterland and procure food for sale since Germans, who naturally regarded them as active combatants, were still in occupation of the surrounding markets. Food consequently became scarce in Duala and many resorted to petty thieving in order to avoid starving. To improve conditions the English commercial houses which had traded in the Cameroons before the declaration of war were encouraged to recommence their operations.[4] These firms were given the promise that the British Government would redeem the German currency in circulation in the occupied areas at the rate of one mark to a shilling pending a final decision on the currency problem. The firms sought and got this definite commitment because while the British authority accepted the mark as equivalent of a shilling, the French exchanged the mark at its bullion value, which was sixpence. Since it was not in the interests of the Allies to make the Cameroonians suffer a fifty per cent devaluation, a Franco-British agreement on the redemption of the mark at a shilling per mark was reached.[5] All the marks brought to the British 'sphere' were subsequently shipped to Britain to be melted down and recoined as shillings. In order to ease the financial transaction in Duala further, a branch of the Bank of British West Africa (B.B.W.A.) was opened in Duala in December 1914.[6]

Efforts were made to keep essential services in Duala and environs functioning and to maintain some form of administration, at all levels. The five hospitals, two of which were for Europeans and the rest for Africans, were refurbished and taken over by British doctors coming from Nigeria. The hospitals themselves were a credit to the Germans; they were copiously supplied with medical and surgical equipment as well as drugs, so that the patients there continued to receive attention while wounded soldiers were also brought in for treatment. Apart from the hospitals, the government offices and officers' quarters were quickly converted into officers' messes, and the headquarters for the army was located in the spacious government house in Duala.

As far as Duala was concerned the Germans had planned everything with the thoroughness for which they were generally known.

They had a 'model' prison just at the outskirts of the town and there were 478 prisoners there at the time of the occupation; forty-seven of them were released by the British because they were political offenders; all the prisoners looked in excellent physical condition. One of the British political officers attached to the expeditionary force wrote, 'I may say I have never seen a more healthy looking and better fed lot of prisoners elsewhere'.[7] This comment by an English officer to a certain extent showed that German rule in Africa, though often harsh, was not always cruel. An English ex-prisoner of war was installed as temporary superintendent and all forty-seven warders, still wearing German uniforms, were re-employed. Other former African officials in the German civil administration were also brought back into the service, primarily to stave off disaffection and possible revolt as a result of loss of their means of livelihood. Most important of all, postal services were restored and Nigeria and Duala postal links were thus re-established.

In order to salvage the enormous capital invested in the Cameroons, especially in plantations and the harbours, it was absolutely necessary that Nigeria should spare some of its much depleted civil staff for all kinds of work in the German colony. 'The plantation question presents a difficult problem', wrote Lugard, 'which urgently demands solution if these most valuable estates are to be saved.'[8] The owners of the plantations had been deported for security reasons by General Dobell and their houses and property were at the mercy of the labourers. These labourers, numbering about ten thousand, were deserting and leaving for their homes, and there was a real possibility of the plantations simply dying away as a result of lack of care. This urgent situation made Lugard send administrative officers to Buea and Victoria districts just across the Nigerian border, which were exclusively occupied by British troops. These British officers were told to reorganise the area and re-employ the labourers as well as to pay them from proceeds which might accrue from the sale of produce from the plantation.[9]

The Nigerian marine department in co-operation with the Royal Navy was engaged in raising from the bottom of the harbour in Duala the floating dock and ships, sunk by the retreating Germans in order to block the Allies' entry into the harbour. The Nigerian Marine also had the job of rebuoying and dredging the main channel of the Cameroon river in order to keep it navigable for

Allied boats, which were used extensively in patrol work against Spanish gun-runners from Fernando Po and Rio Muni.[10] The department also provided crews for captured craft, all of which were used in the operations in the southern creeks of the Cameroons. The Nigerian Marine was so absorbed in the Cameroons expedition that its work in Nigeria was consequently abandoned. The entrance to Lagos channel began to silt up since no dredging work was being done; all reclamation work on Lagos harbour ceased and the normal transport services along the creeks were abandoned, with consequent loss of considerable revenue which Nigeria could hardly afford to lose.[11]

Nigerian customs officials were brought into the Cameroons to reorganise the custom services of Duala and Victoria. All these activities of various departments of the Nigerian administration in the Cameroons left a British stamp on the reorganisation of the areas conquered from the Germans. The reason for the predominance of the British at this time was the proximity of all the areas first occupied to Nigeria, and the fact that Duala itself surrendered to the British Navy and the Nigerian Marine even before Dobell had landed any of his joint expeditionary forces. It was the great dependence on Nigerian personnel that made Lugard play such a vital role in the disputes with the French over 'spheres of influence' in the Cameroons.

While the British were busy setting up administration in areas near their border, the French were also preoccupied with re-annexing the territory which Germany had forced out of their hands in 1911. The French were not just involved in temporary administration of these areas, they embarked upon their incorporation into French Equatorial Africa as an integral administrative unit.[12]

Initially it seemed as if the policies of the Colonial Office and the local British representatives were vastly out of sympathy in the Cameroons, but gradually a united front was forged after exchanges of views. At the beginning of the Allied campaign in the Cameroons, Lewis Harcourt, Secretary of State for the Colonies, privately made known to Lugard his views. He had assumed that practically the whole of the territory would go to France and that in return for this 'generosity' Britain would demand the whole of Togoland and the French colony of Dahomey so that British possessions could stretch uninterrupted from the Gold Coast to Nigeria. Harcourt also had an alternative plan to put to the French in case the first one did not go down well with them; this would have involved Britain's giving up her share of Togoland in exchange for the French half of the condominium in the New Hebrides, plus some pieces of the Cameroons, especially Victoria, Buea and the Cameroon Mountain.[13] The idea of an exchange of territory was an old Colonial Office policy. From 1875 up to the outbreak of the Great War, the small British colony of Gambia had always featured in one of these schemes by which territories were to be exchanged for advantages in other parts of the world. In fact, in 1908 Sir Edward Grey apparently agreed that Gambia might be ceded to the French in exchange for some compensations in the Pacific and Asia.[14]

Lugard could not understand how Harcourt could even conceive a plan to give the entire Cameroons to the French; he was unimpressed by the idea of territorial exchanges in the first instance. Lugard no doubt saw himself as an empire builder of the greatest magnitude, and it was natural for him to think of expanding the boundaries of Nigeria, and the only direction in which Nigeria could expand was the Cameroons. Lugard told Harcourt that if he was thinking of using Buea as headquarters of the southern provinces because of its mild climate, the idea should be dropped because Buea was too far from Lagos and Port Harcourt, the future commercial emporia of Nigeria. Secondly, Lugard believed that Buea and Victoria without the railways and Duala would be useless; he wanted the Colonial Office to stake out claims for the whole of Adamawa, which formerly belonged to the Lamido (Emir) of Yola, and German Borno or Dikwa which was severed from the ancient kingdom of Borno during the partition. He specifically demanded annexation of Garua on the Benue 'so that the French should not have an access on the navigable Benue', which was very important since British annexation of Garua would set Britain free from the obligations of the Berlin Act as regards the navigation of the Niger and Benue; he added, 'we need then no longer maintain Yola as a port and need not worry about the height of the Benue bridge'.[15] All this was the old Royal Niger Company's ambition in this area.[16] His association with the company during the 1893–4 period of Goldie's effort to keep out the French from this area by bringing in the Germans (who later let him down by opening up the area to the French through the Franco-German agreement of 1894), must have left a permanent impression on Lugard, who apparently felt he must not allow the opportunity of making Britain master of the navigable stretch of the Benue to slip from British hands a second time.

On Harcourt's plan to acquire Dahomey and Togo so as to link Nigeria and the Gold Coast, Lugard saw one of the advantages in the abolition of the preventive service against liquor smuggling from Dahomey into Nigeria, thus saving the government the trouble and money involved in patrolling the frontier. He also admitted that annexation of Dahomey would rectify the 1898 division of Borgu between France and Britain and that this would prevent the Dahomey railway becoming a threat to Sokoto trade, by diverting the trade of Sokoto Province. Lugard was harking back to the partition period and was determined, if possible, to use the war to upset the earlier partition.

The Nigerian Government wanted the whole of the nineteenth-century amorphous emirate of Adamawa ruled by the Lamido of Yola to be reunited and given back to the Emir. When the boundary of Adamawa was originally drawn by the partitioning powers, the capital town of Yola with a certain radius round it was left in British hands, while the Germans managed to secure the greater part of Adamawa. This amputation of the emirate, said Lugard, had always been bitterly lamented by the Emir of Yola 'whose loyalty in the trying circumstances of late deserves recognition. He has looked on it as certain, that if the British win he will come into his own again, the restoration of that part of Adamawa which is now German would have a good effect in Nigeria.'[17] Lugard apparently did not want to let the Emir of Yola down as Sir George Goldie had done in 1893.[18] Lugard thought satisfaction of Fulani territorial aims would strengthen indirect rule, but on the other hand the cession of German Adamawa to France would have a damaging effect on the British, because the emirs would consider that France had forced Britain to give the territory to her and thus regard France as the more powerful of the two. This was an important issue in an area adjoining Northern Nigeria, where British control depended on prestige and power. The result of a deflation of this British almightiness might be accompanied by disastrous consequences.

The precise area of Adamawa which the Emir wanted was about half the Cameroons.[19] Before 1890–3 when Adamawa was divided between the Germans and the British, all the Fulani chiefs from Mandara in the north to Bayo and Tibati in the south, and from Minder and Rei-Buba in the east to Garbabi in the west were actually under the Emirs of Yola and acknowledged their suzerainty.[20] In addition to the districts under Fulani administration the pagan chiefs of Lere and Lame paid tributes to the Lamido of Yola. The powerful 'Sultan' of Bafum (Fumban) in the south was also tributary to Yola through his immediate overlord the Fulani ruler of Banyo. The reigning Emir of Yola during the period under consideration acknowledged that enforcement of his claim to suzerainty over Bafum could create difficulties 'as the Bafumawa had adopted more or less European ways'.[21] But the Emir was positive that the 'Sultan' of Bafum would acknowledge the claim, as he always sent an ambassador to Yola every year to salute the Lamido, a practice also maintained by the Emir of Ngaundere. The latter's ambassadors were actually in Yola at the outbreak of hostilities. Enormous as these claims were, they were confirmed by some of the chiefs concerned and also by French and German officers with whom the Resident had discussed the matter academically before the war. The Emir of Yola was keenly aware of the injustice done him by European powers, as he ruefully commented to the Resident, 'they have left me merely the latrines of my kingdom, they say they have left us the head, but they have cut off the body'.[22] There is no doubt that the Emir of Yola had historic claims to the areas wanted by him, but most of the *ardos* in Marua, Garua and other places had raised themselves into *Lamido* and the idea of losing the prestige they had enjoyed under the Germans, by becoming subordinates of the Emir of Yola, was resented by them, particularly by the Lamidos of Marua and Garua.[23]

As for Borno, Nigerian authorities wanted the restoration of German Borno (Dikwa Emirate) to British Borno, from which it was severed during the partition. The area demanded was the piece of territory lying in the delta of the Shari and Logone rivers bounded in the east by the Gulfei and Logone Districts, in the south by the Mandara District, in the north by Lake Chad and in the west by British Borno.[24] This area was ruled by Sheikh Umar Sanda,[25] a great-grandson of Sheikh Lamino-el-Kanemi, the great Islamic reformer in nineteenth-century Borno. As if this would make the British Government strive more to see German Borno annexed, Ruxton, the British Resident in Maiduguri, wrote to the Colonial Office that the percentage of semi-Arabs (Shuwa Arabs) in Dikwa was greater than that in British Borno.[26] This meant more to Lugard, who during his administration could not coneal his sense of affinity for the Fulani and Shuwa Arabs who, according to Charles Temple,[27] were 'Caucasians' and therefore of more importance to the administration than were Negroes. As far as Lugard was concerned the restoration of the lost territories of Borno and Adamawa to their rightful owners was the 'minimum' demand. In the position he took Lugard reflected Fulani and Kanuri historical claims to Adamawa and Dikwa respectively, and he thought satisfaction of these claims would strengthen indirect rule. In the pursuit of these aims Lugard hoped he could redress the failures of the 1890s, and go on to secure more realistic ethnic boundaries.

Being more concerned with the local situation and less with British world-wide interests, Lugard suggested that as soon as the Germans were defeated the Cameroons should be partitioned into two equal sections administered by France and Britain; a partition was necessary to avoid conflict with the French, who had shown their hand by seizing the Emir of Gulfei, a cousin of the Shehu of Borno (Bukar Garbai), and deporting him to Fort Lamy because he favoured British 'protection'.[28] As a result of the uncertainty about their future the Muslim rulers in the north were using all their ingenuity to play off the local authorities in Fort Lamy against those in Maiduguri.

In the south of the Cameroons, Lugard suggested that the area from the Nigeria–Cameroons frontier to the Sanaga river, up to fifty miles from the sea, should, without prejudice to the disposal of the remainder of the country, be permanently assigned to Britain.[29] The remainder of the seaboard, Lugard suggested, should be assigned to the French with the seaport of Kribi as the administrative headquarters. This arrangement, it was hoped, would not interfere with Allied forces' co-operation and would in fact solve the difficulty in the naval command, with the senior French naval officer remaining on French-controlled seaboard, while the British naval officer would remain attached to the general officer commanding and his staff.[30] In suggesting this division, Lugard wrote that there might be considerable unrest if suspicion got abroad that the French and not the British were to take over Duala. He felt a general exodus of African labourers from the area might follow such a French take-over and that the substitution of the French for the British might lead to arguments as to whether the French should share in the prize vessels and the valuable property at Duala captured by the Royal Navy and the Nigerian Marine.[31] Lugard said also that Britain should retain Duala with its eighty miles of railway which might be linked with the Nigerian railway system in the future.[32] He urged the British Government to take immediate decision over these matters, since apart from having a most quieting effect on the Dualas, such a decision might also have some positive effect on the Germans still fighting in the Cameroons jungle. He was of the opinion that if the Germans saw that a civil administration had been set up along the coast, they would recognise that guerrilla war in the interior of Africa was a hopeless and futile effort.[33] A civil administration would furthermore greatly facilitate the military operations, for such an administration would speedily get in touch with the Cameroonians and would ensure that no German raiding parties would penetrate the area without their movement being reported.

Officials in the Colonial Office were sharply divided on the issue of who should administer the Cameroons. Some of them, always too eager to suspect Lugard of wanting too much power, said General Dobell should have the responsibility for the administration of the British 'sphere' in southern Cameroons, if dividing into spheres was acceptable to the French. They conceded one point, however; that it would be open to Dobell, if he found it desirable, to hand over the administration of the area occupied by British troops to the government of Nigeria.[34] The Colonial Office decided that until the French had suggested concrete proposals General Dobell should administer the areas conquered and that Lugard's functions should be those of giving advice and supplying the materials the British general might ask for.

No consensus of opinion emerged in the Colonial Office over Duala, at least up to the end of 1914. Sir George Fiddes in an interesting minute wrote:

> it is a curious thing that we looked with indifference on the occupation of Duala by our declared enemy [referring to the partition period] but are up in arms at the idea of its passing to our ally. I earnestly hope H.M.G. will take heed of the desperate efforts now being made by Germany to sow discord between the Allies before doing anything to assist their designs.[35]

He continued that he knew the Admiralty would be all for 'grabbing' Duala, but Sir George was reminded by his superior Sir John Anderson that 'the enemy pursued an open port policy, our ally insists on preference for his own trade'.[36] With this last comment one can see how highly-placed British officials, in spite of the war, saw that Germany was commercially more liberal in her colonies and had more in common with Britain than Britain had with France. As no policy emerged from all the arguments and debates in the Colonial Office a policy of 'wait and see' was adopted at the beginning of December 1914 and the local officials in Nigeria and the Cameroons were left on their own to face the problems of their prickly relations with the French. Meanwhile the British Government decided to sound the opinion of the French on Lugard's suggestion for an equal partition of the German colony.[37]

Lugard, so as to be fully in command of his facts, accepted an invitation from General Dobell to visit Duala, and after seeking permission from Lewis Harcourt, left Lagos on 22 November 1914 and returned on the 29th of the same month.[38] His visit and report were very interesting and revealing. In Duala he observed, 'the native population appears to be a difficult one to deal with, having no chiefs of ability and influence and possessing many of the undesirable characteristics of the population of the whole West African coast'.[39] Perhaps this explains why Lugard was not particularly keen on the southern part of the Cameroons becoming British as compared with his avid desire to get the north with its Fulani and Shuwa Arabs and Kanuri, with whom he had come to develop some sort of camaraderie. This is not to say that Lugard did not want any part of the south; the part he wanted was limited to Duala plus a corridor behind it to Yola and Garua.

In advocating that the British should annex Duala, Lugard said he was surprised at seeing a large number of the people speaking English rather than German and that the Dualas not only spoke passable English but spoke it with 'much fluency'. Lugard was told by John Holt's agent (who could not have been impartial) that the coinage in the Cameroons was practically British, the mark being treated as a shilling when used.[40] In his discussion with General Dobell as to the future of the Cameroons, he was strengthened in his convictions about what he had earlier communicated to Harcourt.

General Dobell was all for British annexation of Duala. He pointed out that, situated midway between Freetown and Simonstown (in South Africa), Duala, as a naval base, coaling station or harbour of refuge:

offers peculiar advantages despite the fact that it is somewhat removed from the main trade routes ... lying as it does some 20 miles from the open sea, Duala is protected by the nature of the country on either bank of the Cameroon River from any form of attack other than one made by the river itself. On the land side ... it is equally well protected as the country in its vicinity is intersected by numerous creeks which traverse a large area covered by impenetrable bush.[41]

He added that the Cameroon river, being only about five miles wide at its mouth and flanked on the north-west by Cape Cameroon and on the south-east by Suellaba point, could easily be defended by 'guns of position' which by their fire could cover the whole area of water at the entrance to the river. The approach to the river was further protected by a bar at its mouth. This bar was so situated that while it formed no obstacle to direct access to the fair way, it would seriously increase the difficulties of attack from the sea. At a time of war an anchorage of 28 feet of water was available at Suellaba capable of accommodating a large fleet of ships that could be practically immune from sea attack. The depth of water in the Cameroon river precluded vessels of more than 18 feet 6 inches draught from using it, but even this was the best Lagos could boast of, and the Cameroon river channel could be vastly improved by dredging since it was known that 'the water deepens opposite and about Duala to a depth of 30 feet'.[42]

From a commercial point of view too the town of Duala was most favourably situated. It was not only the terminus of the existing railways, but it was also connected with the hinterland by waterways by which the naturally valuable products of the country would be cheaply brought down to Duala for export. General Dobell sounded a note of 'Duala or nothing' when he wrote, 'the power which possesses Duala must necessarily hold the hinterland'.[43]

Captain Cyril Fuller backed by the Admiralty had even more plausible reasons why Britain should not part with Duala; he lamented that everybody in England was necessarily too fully engaged with other more important things connected with the war to be bothered with the questions of the Cameroons. Harking back to the partition era, he warned:

Duala with the northern half of this colony may slip out of British hands for a second time, for which there will be many regrets in the future. ... Rumour has it that the British government are not keen on taking over any of this colony except small pieces to round off the Nigerian frontier; if our government does not take Duala and the Northern half, they will make a grave error, which they will be made to pay for years to come. At present the navy has won for them Duala ... its magnificent harbour, wharfs, town, etc. ... it is quite possible we shall be at war with France in say ten years time and if she is given Duala now she will prove a dreadful thorn in our side when she is our enemy, by sending out cruisers from here to harry our West Coast possessions and trade ... the French themselves who are out here have quite made up their minds that Great Britain is to have Duala and the Northern half whilst they get the Southern half of the colony including pieces Germany stole from them after Agadir ... in fact the campaign has been worked on these lines to a great extent.[44]

Captain Fuller went on to say that the Cameroonians in conversation with the officers of the expeditionary forces did not conceal their hostility towards the French and that several French officers had even remarked that the Francophobia exhibited by the Dualas was due to British intrigue.

In a sort of *addendum* the Admiralty maintained that 'the importance evidently attached to Duala by the Germans as a future naval base is a fact to be kept prominently in view of any negotiations relating to the colony at the conclusion of peace'.[45] The Admiralty was concerned that Britain had no naturally strong base upon the West African coast whereas France had Libreville in Gabon. It claimed that the geographical position of Duala gave it more strategical importance than most of the other 'river towns' on the West African coast; but the Admiralty, unlike the War Office, was not inclined to give undue weight to the comparative ease with which Duala could be defended since according to them, ease of defence was not in itself a consideration of primary importance.[46] What was important was the strategical location of Duala. The Admiralty was realistic enough to know that the settlement of conflicting claims would have to be resolved on the principle of 'give and take', 'if we retain Duala and the territories to the North, the French may ask for Togoland, and if such should be the case Duala with the surrounding territory is from a naval point of view a better bargain than Lome and Togoland'.[47] The Admiralty went on to say that the possession of Duala by the French in addition to Corisco Bay and Gabon would in case of future hostilities between Britain and France put Britain in a

very disadvantageous position in West Africa; whereas its possession by Britain would bring her to a par with France, and that the
exact comparison would depend on the steps taken by either
power to strengthen the natural defences of their ports. The
Admiralty declared,

> 'hitherto the French have shown no disposition to spend money on
> fortifying their West African coast harbours, but the experience of
> the present war exemplified by the capture of Duala may bring home
> to them and others, the desirability of being able to defend their
> possessions more effectually than is done at present'.[48]

Lewis Harcourt, the Secretary of State for the Colonies, was
puzzled by all this welter of information coming from all directions,
but he was also struck by the unanimity of their demand for
annexation of Duala. He minuted, 'as to Duala it is not easy to
explain to an ally that you must keep a particular port for the
purpose of a future war with her, but if we are to keep Duala, I
think it ought now to be placed in our sphere . . . we might adopt
the division suggested in the Lugard and Dobell despatches'.[49]

The British Foreign Office then took up the matter with the
French Government. After Sir Francis Bertie, the British ambassador in Paris, had discussed the question of the equal division
of the Cameroons with M. Delcassé, the French Foreign Minister,
he reported back to the British Government the French rejection
of the plan. Delcassé was in favour neither of equal division nor
of the administration of each half by British Nigeria and French
Equatorial Africa. Delcassé was of the opinion that an arrangement of division now would tend to solidify and prevent overall
bargaining throughout the world after the war.[50]

Delcassé suggested that instead of dividing the territory and
setting up two different administrations, a kind of condominium
arrangement would be preferable. This would see to provisional
administration until definite decisions could be reached. The
system would assure the Allies 'une unité de direction' since the
entire country would be placed under the administrative control of
the General Officer commanding the joint expedition. This French
plan was rather a clever way of allowing events in other parts of
the world to take shape so that if necessary they would demand a
larger share of, if not the entire, Cameroons.

The Foreign Office immediately recommended the French
proposal for adoption. The Colonial Office was told that in spite

of the inherent disadvantages in a condominium it was the only reasonable thing that could be done at the time. The Foreign Office argued that the arrangement would be temporary and under the circumstances in the Cameroons had certain advantages of simplicity. Furthermore, the Foreign Office contended that since the Cameroons campaign showed signs of lasting longer than expected, division into spheres of influence might acquire a character of permanency in Cameroonian eyes.[51] This the Foreign Office felt would be avoided by a condominium on the lines suggested by the French, which would leave matters in suspense. The Foreign Office and the Colonial Office were pursuing contradictory policies with regard to the Cameroons. Sir Edward Grey saw the issue in terms of diplomacy, and was using the Cameroons to gain advantage in areas where Britain's vital and security interests might be at stake.

The Colonial Office did not immediately bow to Foreign Office 'instructions'. The department stated that it was prepared to agree with the French proposal provided that the General Officer commanding the Allied force would have full powers of administration including the power of appointment and dismissal of officials and a free hand in dealing with all matters civil and military.[52] The Colonial Office also wanted to be assured that if General Dobell were to die or leave the Cameroons, the French would agree that should the next senior officer be British he would automatically succeed to the administration. If he should be French the Colonial Office believed a somewhat anomalous situation would be created, that the change of staff would necessarily cause discontinuity in civil affairs thus losing the 'unité de direction' to which M. Delcassé attached great importance. It was the view of the Colonial Office that a 'friendly understanding' should be reached with the French, that if Dobell were to leave or die, he should be succeeded by a British military officer. The Colonial Office promised that it would in such a situation make sure that the officer so appointed would be acceptable to the French and suitable for the job, and that such an officer would be senior to any French officer in the Cameroons, even if his rank was achieved by temporary promotion.

As for the expenses of the administration, the Colonial Office agreed that the pay, allowance, and other expenses of maintaining troops should fall on the government to which the troops belonged and that 'general expenses' of government, so far as they were not covered by revenue and receipts, should be divided in a proportion having some relation to the manner 'in which the territory is eventually divided between the two governments'.[53]

If the French Government accepted these amendments to its original condominium proposal, the Colonial Office argued that the French Government should instruct its officials in West and Equatorial Africa to accord the General Officer Commanding every possible assistance for which he might apply to them, whether in materials or information. The Colonial Office added finally that certain areas in the Cameroons near the Nigerian border were occupied solely by Nigerian troops who, owing to difficulties of communication, were not under the direct control of General Dobell but under the control of the Governor-General of Nigeria, in the same way that the area near the eastern and southern boundaries of the German colony was under the control of the Governor-General of French Equatorial Africa.[54] In a rather clever way the British Colonial Office stated that these two areas would no doubt continue to be administered so far as some form of administration could be set up by the adjacent governments 'until circumstances permit their being handed over to General Dobell'.[55] This was deliberately designed to render null the French re-annexation of the area ceded to Germany in 1911, or at least to put the areas on the same basis as the area under British administration in Dikwa and some parts of Adamawa, bordering on Nigeria.

These almost impossible conditions about the condominium wrecked any chance of an agreement until the proposal was laid to rest without any trial on 21 February 1916.[56] The French remained quiet on the condominium issue but did not agree either to an equal division of the Cameroons; so in a sense the field was open for all the rivalry that was to follow since no agreement was reached by the two home governments. Meanwhile French colonial organs continued to write about a railway from Brazzaville to Algiers passing through 'French Cameroons',[57] which meant that annexation of the Cameroons was kept alive by influential Frenchmen; but the situation in the Cameroons stayed as it was before, Dobell remained in control and consequently continued to draw most of his administrative personnel from Nigeria.

In the initial effort to give every assistance to Dobell in the Cameroons, Nigeria overstrained herself. It was not long before the administration began to see its own fragile hold on the country disintegrate following a wave of widespread rebellion all over the country, particularly in the Southern provinces.[58] Lugard naturally began to complain that he had not known that his officers would be retained indefinitely in the Cameroons. He said that most of the officers were considerably overdue for leave and were not in good physical shape. Furthermore, while the civil establishment in Nigeria was short of officers due to unfilled vacancies, the strain thrown on officers remaining in the country was almost crippling. Lugard was particularly worried about the drain on the political staff, to whom he looked to preserve internal order in the country, since it was their ineffectiveness due to lack of members that had partly led to the series of civil commotions in the country; to make matters worse, it was from the same class of political officers who were said to know the 'working of the native mind' that General Dobell drew his political staff. Lugard was so worried about the situation that he issued a thinly veiled threat that if relief could not be sent from England or from some other British colony, he might be forced to withdraw some of his administrative officers from the Cameroons in order to save Nigeria from collapse. The Colonial Office prevailed on him to be more co-operative and not to withdraw any of his men except in case of 'absolute necessity', and even then withdrawal should be effected only with General Dobell's concurrence.[59]

Lugard however felt the point of 'absolute necessity' had long been reached. He found the Colonial Office's order for consultation with General Dobell before he could withdraw his men not only galling, but evidence of a complete lack of understanding of the turmoil into which Nigeria had been thrown by the war. The Governor-General was particularly irked by the continual emphasis by the Colonial Office that he should leave all military matters in the hands of General Dobell, in spite of the fact that Nigeria was providing the bulk of the fighting force in the Cameroons as well as the civil staff of the administration. Lugard could not understand how the Colonial Office could ignore the fact that events in the Cameroons had direct bearing on the political stability of Nigeria. The Colonial Office went beyond what Lugard could take when he was told not to have anything to do with the administration of any part of the Cameroons overrun by British troops except to provide the staff that might be needed.[60] Lugard, who always felt that the Colonial Office was manifestly hostile to him, wrote back in annoyance demanding that he should have some control over the men he might send to the Cameroons: 'I feel sure,' he said, 'that it cannot be your wish that a civil administration should be set up in that country, the staff of which should be provided and paid for by Nigeria but over which the government of Nigeria should have no control whatever.'[61] What led to this firm stand taken by Lugard was a fresh demand by General Dobell for several men from the Nigerian public works and railways departments, needed to make the Cameroons railways function so that produce, especially from the plantations, could be moved to the coast and shipped to England in order to pay some part of the cost of the administration. Reasonable as this might seem, it would have been unwise to close down remunerative traffic, yielding a large revenue on the Nigerian railways on which Nigerian administration depended financially, especially in the absence of the large customs receipts on trade gin. This action, if taken, would have been most foolish because only a fraction of the administrative cost of the Cameroons could have been realised.

Lugard furthermore regarded the kind of administration General Dobell contemplated as too elaborate and consequently premature since no decision as to the future of the Cameroons had been reached. Even if General Dobell needed these men and if they could be spared by Nigeria, Lugard was of the opinion that Dobell had his hands very full with the conduct of a military campaign fraught with exceptional difficulty and with a force consisting of large numbers of detached units operating in widely separated theatres. It was not humanly possible, according to Lugard, for Dobell to conduct the civil administration of the Cameroons, and even if it were possible, he did not feel Dobell had any experience of or capability for such work. Apparently trying to put pressure on the home government to take the political decision on annexation, Lugard said a decision as to the future of the German colony should be the starting point and that after this he would submit the minimum requirements necessary to carry on the administration for such a period as might be considered necessary. Colonial Office officials, always distrustful of Lugard, felt he was interested in annexing some parts of the Cameroons to Nigeria, and one of them minuted,

'the thing which is no doubt at the bottom of all this is that Sir F. Lugard wishes to be given the control of the administration of the part of the Cameroons occupied by British forces in the same extent as the Governor of the Gold Coast has over Togoland; with any other governor it might be a good thing to do this but with Sir Frederick Lugard it is impossible.'[62]

In spite of the apparent lack of sympathy for Lugard's views, the Colonial Office accepted his analysis of the local situation and concluded that there was a limit beyond which it would be impossible for men to be spared for service in the Cameroons without undue harm being done to Nigeria, and that if Nigeria could not release men, the War Office would have to find the staff to send to Dobell since administration should rest in the hands of the British General, who was in any case under direct orders of the War Office. As a sop to Lugard, the Colonial Office informed him, as they had done before, that all territories captured by Brigadier-General Cunliffe's troops should be administered by the latter officer according to such general instructions he might receive from the Governor-General.[63]

The problem here was that the territories captured by Cunliffe and his Nigerian Regiment were being hotly contested by the French. In some cases, some of these territories had been captured with French military assistance. The situation was further worsened as far as Lugard was concerned by the rather spineless support he got from the British Government in his attempt to keep northern Cameroons safe for British enterprise. To consolidate British influence in Dikwa, Lugard sent Captain Foulkes with some Nigerian soldiers to help Sheikh Umar Sanda put down some rebellious fanatics.[64] The mission was conceived with the plan of showing both the Emir of Dikwa and his subjects that the British were the stronger of the two contesting powers. This signalled the beginning of local active 'scramble' for territory and influence in northern Cameroons.

The French were not inactive; on the contrary, they displayed great vigour locally and diplomatically. On 19 March 1915 the French in their first move since their suggestion of the condominium took up the question of the Cameroons again. Their military attaché in London handed to the British Director of Military Operations at the War Office, some papers on the Cameroons which contained substantially a criticism of General Dobell and British policy in the Cameroons.[65] The attaché complained that despite the initial agreement that equal forces were to be placed in the field, the British forces actually employed were considerably less than the total of the French troops. It was also stated that General Dobell appeared to be more anxious for the security of the Nigerian Frontier than for the reduction of the German colony. The French attaché complained that in spite of the fact that it was evident that the greater part of the burden of the conquest of the Cameroons was being borne by France, General Dobell in his despatches made little reference to the value of French co-operation, and he went on to say that General Dobell's plan of campaign assigned to the French contingent of the ex-peditionary force a task too great for its strength. He showed a report by Colonel Mayer, the officer in charge of French forces in the Cameroons, in which he stated that the greater share of the work appeared to be left to the French contingent, which was in danger of exhaustion. He also complained that the absence of French troops in Duala was likely to create special rights for the British in that port. Some of these complaints were justified: there is no doubt that the French committed more men to the Cameroons campaign and that the British excluded them from Duala, and that they did most of the dying, as borne out by their greater number of casualties in the war.[66] However, they were more interested in retaking the areas ceded to the Germans in 1911 and their obsession with this was a handicap to Allied operations.

The Colonial Office was furious with the French for claiming that they were doing more of the fighting. The department im-mediately suspected French motives as being the desire to equate military effort with the proportion of the country they wanted to claim. The Colonial Office insisted that a statement on military effort of the French could not be compared with British effort without taking into consideration the role played by the British Navy, without which the French would have been unable to do anything. The British Navy kept the colony cut off from fresh supplies of ammunition from Germany, which was the deciding factor in tilting the balance of power in favour of the Allies. Sir George Fiddes, who in all debates over British co-operation with the French had stood out as the most pro-French official in the Colonial Office, was moved to say that the French would make capital out of their claim if not challenged immediately and that she might make 'extravagant bids for territory' on the basis of her assumed greater military effort.

At about this time the Colonial Office saw another omen that was not likely to augur well for Anglo-French understanding. General Aymerich had been in the Cameroons from the beginning of hostilities without much friction between him and Dobell, but with the impending collapse of German resistance and the increased rivalry between the Allies, the Colonial Office was rather anxious over the presence of the French General. General Aymerich had held the rank of *Général de Brigade* since 1912, a rank which was equivalent to the British Major-General.[67] He was therefore the senior of General Dobell. This was important at that time, since the question of seniority of rank was closely tied up with that of the interim military administration of the occupied territory and of the ultimate division of it between the two Allies. The problem did not reach insurmountable dimensions because, first of all, Dobell and Aymerich did not meet until the end of the campaign, and although there were orders and counter-orders, no serious conflict developed between the two generals.

As the ring closed on the Germans, the local scramble resumed with much intensity and the French sometimes appeared to be more interested in spreading their influence than in fighting, especially in the northern Cameroons so dear to Lugard. While Cunliffe and his Nigerian troops were sweeping the northern Cameroons clean of the Germans, the French were busy consolidating their political hold at the rear of advancing British troops. With the exception of Dikwa, the French were succeeding in making their presence felt in the areas south of Dikwa and north of the Benue. Towards the end of 1915 their influence was becoming paramount in this area, as evidenced by the fact that when Cunliffe was marching on Mora with his troops and asked the local chiefs to assist him with transport and supplies, he was curtly told to seek first permission from a French captain in the district.[68] The French success in this respect was due to their system of 'living on the country' and relying on it for carriers, thus necessitating a close touch with the villages, backed up by a form of administration to ensure that demands were met. It was becoming increasingly clear that something had to be done to stop the complete takeover of the area by the French. The Colonial Office approached the French Government, arguing that the half of northern Cameroons bordering on Nigeria was needed for the supply of Nigerian troops and that the French had better forage on their side of the country. 'The French can't expect us to do all the giving and leave them to do all the taking',[69] commented one official at the Colonial Office.

Since nothing could stop the 'scramble' Lugard took the law into his own hands and instructed the Lieutenant-Governors of the Northern and Southern Provinces of Nigeria to detail political officers from the nearest contiguous province to move across the frontier and set up the nucleus of an administration.[70] These officers were told to try to assist the military forces operating in their areas in every way, and to refer any administrative difficulties to the nearest provincial Resident or Commissioner on the Nigerian side of the border. Political officers were sent from Maiduguri to Dikwa, from Yola to Garua, Kontscha and Tingere and from Ogoja to Bamenda. They were told to include as large an area as possible in the British sphere, subject to the proviso of avoiding friction with the French. How this could be done without friction with the French remained unexplained.

On 24 January 1916 Lugard issued a proclamation for temporary administration of the area of the Cameroons occupied by troops under Brigadier-General Cunliffe.[71] The administrators were empowered to hold courts with full jurisdiction in civil and criminal matters in which Africans were concerned, administering the laws of the Cameroons[72] in so far as they were known, and if not the laws of Nigeria.

At this time Cunliffe had his headquarters at Fumbam (Bafum) with detachments of his troops at Garua, Kontscha, Banyo, Bamenda and Mangan. Cunliffe grudgingly allowed the French to occupy Ngaundere-Joko area where the Sarkins of Rei Buba and Ngaundere were said to be anxious to become British.[73] The local British officers wanted the Ngaundere plateau because of its mild climate, which was said to be good for European settlement. The plateau also was the grazing ground for the innumerable head of Fulani cattle, and the Lugardian administration was particularly sensitive to questions affecting the Fulani. It was felt that this plateau could support a large number of cattle with room still available for European ranchers who had unsuccessfully sought land for their enterprise in Nigeria since 1912. The French had more or less 'dug in' and the problem of dislodging them from this area was one of the issues to be resolved by both powers.

It was very difficult to be on friendly terms with the French and still be influential in the area, said Lugard. The loyal chiefs of Yola who had assisted British forces so greatly in the war were naturally at a loss to understand British subservience to the French. Lugard added that it was by yielding to the French in everything that friction could be avoided. This was an intolerable situation, and Lugard was further irritated when he heard that the French had established themselves at Garua, just thirty miles up stream from Yola, and were imposing fines, imprisoning and deposing chiefs who were suspected of pro-British sentiments. Lugard decided to send some civil officials to Garua with the special mission of asserting, more forcefully than before, equal jurisdiction there, but to his surprise General Aymerich protested,[74] thus giving credence to the view that the French high command was behind the action of their junior officers in northern Cameroons. Lugard wondered if he could simply sit still and watch the French rule over areas overrun by Cunliffe and Nigerian troops. The Governor-General wrote in very clear terms that if the Colonial Office was not going to take any action the French were provoking his men and that they were at their wits end what to do.[75]

The Foreign Office then began to find other ways of administering the Cameroons besides the condominium arrangement the French had suggested earlier on. In a comprehensive memorandum Lewis Harcourt proposed, on the assumption that Britain was entitled to half the Cameroons, but that she did not need or could not usefully occupy more than one-fourth of it, that Britain would demand from France:

(a) their share of the condominium in the New Hebrides,
(b) their small settlement of Jibuti opposite Aden which controls the mischievous arms traffic to Abyssinia and Central Africa.

He went on:

to obtain these we can offer France:
(c) three-fourths of the Cameroons (instead of one-half) plus our share of Togoland,
(c) or if we wish to retain all Togoland and acquire Dahomey, we can offer France all the Cameroons except Mount Cameroon and Duala, and in such a wide settlement we could throw in the Gambia, which is an object of great desire by the French, but the cession of the Gambia would be very unpopular in this country, and arouse much public and parliamentary criticism and agitation. Alternatively we might surrender to France our share of the New Hebrides Condominium as compensation, with nearly the whole of the Cameroons, for our possession of Togoland and Dahomey.[76]

This memorandum revived the idea of trading in the Gambia for other areas, which had been constantly mooted by both the

Colonial Office and the Foreign Office, since 1869 down to 1912,[77] with the exception of the inclusion of the Gambia, Harcourt was more or less going back to his original proposal at the beginning of the war.

The Foreign Office as from February 1916 took over the negotiations with France. M. Cambon, French Ambassador to Britain, met Sir Edward Grey, the Foreign Secretary, and told him the French 'colonial party were very excited over the Cameroons' and that Britain had not always been sincere to the French in other areas. He complained that the French were edged out of participation in the campaign against German East Africa in spite of the fact that France had assembled a large force in Madagascar for the East Africa campaign.[78] M. Cambon said that Britain seemed to be afflicted by a 'land hunger' disease and that while France was bleeding to death on the Western Front, Britain was collecting the spoils of war all over the globe. He therefore demanded that Britain should hand over Duala to the French since that port was the only possible port for French Equatorial Africa, whereas Britain had several outlets in Nigeria. M. Cambon said France would agree to the incorporation of Dikwa into Borno if Britain gave up Duala and that the French would drop their demands for a share in German East Africa.[79]

The matter was then taken to the war cabinet and a conclusion was reached that since the Union of South Africa was already in possession of German South-West Africa Britain would accede to the French demand with as little qualification as possible. The British Government declared that Britain reserved the right for her merchant vessels and warships to make use of Duala at least for the duration of the war. With little modifications on the Nigerian frontier, the Cameroons was provisionally partitioned on 6 March 1916. The boundary was fixed after conferences between Generals Dobell and Aymerich, and a line running from Garua to Ngaundere, Tibati, Joko and Nachtigal rapids, formed the provisional boundary.[80] Thus the French received almost the whole of the Cameroons, with Asquith and Bonar Law's (the new Secretary of State for the Colonies) tacit agreement. Harcourt was outraged. In a letter to Asquith he fulminated:

> I am aghast at the decision of the War Committee (of which I only became aware yesterday morning) to hand over Duala as well as the rest of the Cameroons to the French ... it is all the more amazing that no attempt seems to have been made when making to France this

tremendous gift, to settle any of the other outstanding questions, such as Togoland, the New Hebrides and Jibuti . . . I cannot tell you how strongly I feel upon this matter, and it is for this reason I felt it necessary to write this letter in order to record in permanent form my utter dissent from the decision which has been arrived at without any consultation or concurrence on my part.[81]

Harcourt was told that the partition was provisional, but he knew better than that. Many officials in the Colonial Office and those on the spot felt themselves let down.

General Dobell was recalled by the War Office towards the end of March 1916 after having settled all outstanding questions connected with the Cameroons, and Nigerian officials were instructed to carry out on-the-spot negotiations. Lugard was later instructed to set up an administration in the small British sphere – a narrow little strip varying from forty to eighty miles broad, south of the Benue and of course including the greater part of Dikwa. The whole of Dikwa was agreed to as being in the British sphere, but because of a misunderstanding by local officials of the Franco-British agreement arranging for provisional partition, some part of Dikwa (which was later returned after the war) was taken over by the French.[82] Lugard was asked to provide such garrisons from the Nigeria Regiment as might be necessary for effective occupation of the British sphere, and on 1 April 1916[83] Duala, to the disappointment of the British local officials in particular, passed into the hands of the French. Lugard described the British sphere as 'an insignificant little strip, that it was hardly worth reserving at all'.[84] Captain Fuller and General Dobell were not less disappointed by the partition, as Lugard revealed when reflecting on the whole episode:

Poor Fuller is desperately disappointed. He has worked for a year and a half improving the harbour of Duala, perfecting the workshops and so on (and I am told he is a desperate hard worker). It was his child. He alone captured it, now he had to hand it over to the French. Dobell is no less sick and most anxious to get out of the country. I do think that it would have been a far better business to have handed the whole Cameroons provisionally over to the French till the end of the war, instead of sticking to this wretched little strip smaller than most of the provinces of Nigeria. By creating two 'spheres' we appear to have made a sort of bargain and no one in England stops to look at the size of each . . . it is a wonderful country, and from the French point of view almost worth a war to obtain it. . . .[85]

Humiliated by the home government, Lugard and his lieutenants were left with the unenviable task of explaining the 'official mind' to the Emir of Yola. They tried, but the Emir could not conceal his disgust and disappointment from the British officials. In order to sweeten the Emir's wounded pride, Lugard recommended that he should be given a personal gift of £250[86] as a token of appreciation by the imperial government. Whatever the Emir, who had spent some thousands of pounds in the cause of British war effort, was supposed to do with this paltry sum showed the confusion which the shock of the provisional partition caused in Nigeria. While Lugard was licking his wounds, the French moved in to set up their administration, which by all consideration appeared to be neither temporary nor open to change.

One fact that stands out in the Cameroons' provisional partition was that the British Foreign Office and, initially, Lewis Harcourt, Secretary of State for the Colonies, felt that the Cameroons was expendable, and even until the last moment Harcourt saw the Cameroons only as something which could be used to get concessions elsewhere. It was not until the French raised the question of sharing in the spoils in German East Africa, that the Foreign Office became more conciliatory towards the French.[87] This illustrates the importance of West Africa in imperial defence calculations *vis-à-vis* East Africa. The British obsession with keeping foreign powers out of the Indian Ocean made them more generous in West Africa, and the attempt to use the Cameroons to get the French out of their strategic foothold of Djibuti was part of the imperial policy of keeping the Indian Ocean route free of enemy or potential enemy bases.[88]

Another interesting point that emerged in the question of Adamawa and Borno was the relative ease with which the French disposed of the British claim to Adamawa, while they did not even contest the incorporation of Dikwa (German Borno) into the old Sultanate of Borno. They were unwilling to take the burden of administering Dikwa under Shehu (Sheikh) Umar Sanda, who before the war had been in the habit of arming rebels in French Chad.[89] Alienating the Shehu of Borno was not in French interests and since their acquisition of Dikwa would have resulted in that, French subjects in Chad (especially in the unstable Kanem, Borkou, Wadai and Ennendi) looked to the Shehu of Borno as their 'Sultan'. The French authorities were exploiting their friendship with the Shehu to counteract Senusi influence, which was undermining their authority not only in Chad but in their *territoire militaire du Niger*, where Islamic fanaticism led by Senusis had manifested itself since February 1914, was further accentuated by the war.[90]

In the case of Adamawa the French could ignore the feelings of the Lamido of Yola, whose influence over Adamawa was historical and at the time of the war of little political significance. Furthermore, Adamawa was not completely Islamised and the population was very heterogeneous, so there was no fear of pan-Islamism which was very present in French official thinking concerning Dikwa. The British Colonial Office was not even willing to support the Lamido of Yola's claim to Adamawa,[91] and the dynastic ties between the various Fulani states in Adamawa were not as close as in Borno. All these factors must be taken into consideration in unravelling the mystery surrounding the 'sell-out' of the 'Lamido of Adamawa'. But when all this has been said the overriding factor was British willingness to conciliate the French in areas where Britain was prepared to spare territories without undue danger to her world-wide interests.

In the struggle over the Cameroons Britain tried to champion the cause of African rulers and perhaps to get more sensible ethnic frontiers which earlier partition had ignored. She failed because the powers were less interested in such typical African issues. The repartition also brought back memories of the earlier partition[92]; this is borne out by the constant reference to the past by Lugard in particular, and his participation in both partitions made him much more aware of the shortcomings of the Nigerian–Cameroons boundary, which in spite of all his efforts he failed to alter.

Notes

1 Ronald Robinson and John Gallagher with Alice Denny, *Africa and the Victorians: The Official Mind of Imperialism*, Macmillan, London, 1965, chs x–xiii.

2 Paul Guinn, *British Strategy and Politics, 1914–1918*, London, 1965, pp. 22–3.

3 C.O. 583/18/43993, K. V. Elphinstone's report, enclosed in Dobell to Harcourt, 4 Oct. 1914.

4 *Ibid*. These firms were R. and W. King Ltd, John Holt & Co. Ltd, Hershells & Co. Ltd, and Hatton & Cookson Ltd.

5 C.O. 583/28/50778, Lugard to Colonial Office, 29 Nov. 1914.

6 C.O. 583/28/50778, Bayne's minute, 22 Dec. 1914.

7 C.O. 583/18/43993, K. V. Elphinstone's report enclosed in Dobell to Harcourt, 4 Oct. 1914.

8 C.O. 583/28/50778, Lugard to Colonial Office, 29 Nov. 1914.

9 C.O. 583/30/8634, Lugard to Colonial Office, 4 Feb. 1915.

10 C.O. 583/29/50748, Dobell to Lugard, 6 Nov. 1914.

11 C.O. 583/28/50778, Lugard to Colonial Office, 29 Nov. 1914.

12 C.O. 583/28/51643, H. J. Read to Foreign Office, 12 Dec. 1914. See also Gustave Regelsperger, 'L'œuvre française au Togo et au Cameroun conquis', *Revue de l'école libre des sciences politiques*, 40, 1918, pp. 77–92.

13 C.O. 583/28/41270, Harcourt to Lugard (private and personal), 29 Sept. 1914.

14 J. D. Hargreaves, *Prelude to the Partition of West Africa*, Macmillan, London, 1963, p. 348. See also chs 4, 6, 7.

15 C.O. 583/28/41270, Lugard to Harcourt (private and personal), 29 Oct. 1914. The point here was that when the height of the Benue bridge was being discussed before the war, Germany had rights under the Berlin Act to be consulted in order to satisfy them that the bridge would not constitute an impediment to German going to and coming from Garua.

16 See J. E. Flint, *Sir George Goldie and the Making of Nigeria*, Oxford University Press, London, 1960, ch. 8, pp. 158–86.

17 C.O. 583/28/41270, Lugard to Harcourt (private and personal), 29 Oct. 1914.

18 Flint, *op. cit.*, pp. 181–2.

19 C.O. 583/36/44714, Strachey's minute, 6 Oct. 1915.

20 C.O. 583/36/44714, Acting Resident G. W. Webster of Yola to Lugard, 9 July 1915. The Fulani chiefs in Adamawa came to receive their flags on appointment, and on the death of any of the emirs of Yola, came in again to receive confirmation of their appointments from his successor. The last time this occurred was at the accession of Lamido Zubir of Yola about 1890.

21 *Ibid.*

22 A. H. M. Kirk-Greene, *Adamawa Past and Present*, Oxford University Press, London, 1958, p. 68.

23 Lt-Col Jean Ferrandi, *La conquête du Cameroun-Nord, 1914–1916*, p. 191. *Ardo* in Fulani meant something like a Lieutenant, while *Lamido* was a General.

24 C.O. 583/31/19348, Lugard to Colonial Office, 30 March 1915.

25 *Lugard Papers*, ii, pp. 24–5. Report on the Dikwa Emirate, by G. L. Lethem, District Officer.

26 Of the 200,000 inhabitants of Dikwa about 175,000 were Muslims and the remaining 25,000 were pagans. Out of the Muslim population about 87,500 were Shuwa Arabs, 2,000 Fulanis and about 85,000 Kanuris (described as people with mixed Berber, Arab and Negro blood); whereas there were just about 10,000 Shuwa Arabs and about the same number of Fulani in British Borno. See *Lugard Papers*, ii, p. 12, and Ferrandi, *op. cit.*, p. 104.

27 Charles Lindsay Temple, 1871–1929. Acting Consul, Paraguay 1899; Vice-Consul Brazil (Manãos) 1901; Resident, Northern Nigeria 1901; Chief Secretary, Northern Nigeria 1901–13; Lieutenant-Governor Northern Nigeria 1914–17. He was the son of Sir Richard Temple, a very eminent member of the Indian Civil Service and later a Member of Parliament.

28 C.O. 537/123, Nigeria Secret, 126, Lugard to Colonial Office, 12 Oct. 1914.

29 C.O. 583/20/47256, Lugard to Colonial Office, 30 Nov. 1914.

30 *Ibid.* There was a dispute as to naval command. The Admiralty wanted the French to take over command because Captain Fuller was needed in another part of the world, but General Dobell and other officers of the British Navy said they could not work under a French naval officer, so Captain Fuller remained in the Cameroons until after the operation there.

31 C.O. 583/28/50778, Lugard to Colonial Office, 29 Nov. 1914.

32 *Ibid.*

33 *Ibid.*

34 C.O. 583/20/47256, Harding's minute, 1 Dec. 1914.

35 *Ibid.*, Sir George Fiddes's minute, Dec. 1914.

36 *Ibid.*, Sir John Anderson's minute, 7 Dec. 1914.

37 C.O. 583/28/51643, Sir Francis Bertie, H.M. Ambassador in Paris, had a discussion on these lines with M. Delcassé, French Foreign Minister, on 14 Dec. 1914.

38 C.O. 583/28/50778, Lugard's report on his visit to Duala, 29 Nov. 1914.

39 *Ibid.*

40 *Ibid.*

41 C.O. 583/29/48795, Dobell to Colonial Office, 15 Nov. 1914.

42 *Ibid.*

43 *Ibid.*

44 C.O. 583/28/49493, Captain Fuller to Admiralty, 14 Nov. 1914.

45 C.O. 583/28/48343, 'Confidential', Admiralty to Colonial Office, 4 Dec. 1914.

46 C.O. 583/28/49842, Secret and immediate, Admiralty to Colonial Office, 12 Dec. 1914.

47 *Ibid.*

48 *Ibid.*

49 C.O. 583/28/44755, Harcourt's minute, 21 Nov. 1914.

50 C.O. 583/28/51643, Sir Francis Bertie to Foreign Office, 14 Dec. 1914.

51 C.O. 583/28/51643, Eyre A. Crowe (Permanent Under-Secretary, Foreign Office), to Colonial Office, 23 Dec. 1914.

52 C.O. 583/28/51643, H. J. Read to Foreign Office, 25 Dec. 1914.

53 *Ibid.*

54 *Ibid.*

55 *Ibid.*

56 ADM 137/380/M.O. 1525/16, 19 Dec. 1916, Minute by Vice-Admiral D. A. Gamble.

57 *La presse coloniale*, 19 May 1915, p. 1.

58 C.O. 583/30/8634, Lugard to Colonial Office, 4 Feb. 1915.
59 C.O. 583/30/8634, Colonial Office to Lugard, 15 March 1915.
60 C.O. 583/31/15527, Colonial Office to Lugard, 13 March 1915.
61 C.O. 583/33/30183, Lugard to Colonial Office, 11 June 1915.
62 C.O. 583/33/30183, Bayne's minute, 1 July 1915.
63 *Ibid.*, Bayne's draft of the despatch to be sent to Lugard, 1 July 1915.
64 C.O. 583/31/19348, Lugard to Colonial Offide, 30 March 1915.
65 W.O. 106/644, 5 May 1915.
66 W.O. 258/542, (undated). Total Allied casualties numbered 4,672 killed and wounded; 2,774 were French troops and the British suffered casualties of 1,898. Belgian figures not given.
67 W.O. 106/644, Sir George Fiddes's minute, 5 May 1915.
68 C.O. 583/37/52666, Cunliffe to Boyle, 29 Sept. 1915.
69 C.O. 583/36/45313, Harding's minute, 4 Oct. 1915.
70 C.O. 583/39/8396, Lugard to Colonial Office, 30 Dec. 1915.
71 C.O. 583/44/8022, Lugard to Colonial Office, 24 Jan. 1916.
72 C.O. 583/45/13624, Colonial Office to Lugard, 23 March 1916. According to Article 43 of the Hague Convention dealing with laws of war on land, the occupying military power had no right to alter existing law in an occupied territory.
73 C.O. 583/44/8079, Lt-Col Webb-Bowen to Lugard, 22 Jan. 1916.
74 C.O. 583/44/9257, Lugard to Colonial Office, 24 Feb. 1916.
75 *Ibid.*
76 Memorandum by Lewis Harcourt, 'the spoils', secret, 25 March 1915; Harcourt papers. See William Roger Louis, *Great Britain and Germany's Lost Colonies 1914–1919*, Clarendon Press, Oxford, 1967, pp. 59–60.
77 See Hargreaves, *op. cit.*, ch. iv, pp. 145–95.
78 CAB 37/143/120, Confidential, 24 Feb. 1916.
79 *Ibid.*
80 General Aymerich, *La Conquête du Cameroun*, p. 157.
81 Harcourt to Asquith, secret (copy), 25 Feb. 1916; Harcourt papers. See W. R. Louis, *op. cit.*, p. 61.
82 *Lugard Papers*, ii, p. 39.
83 ADM 137/339, 1 April 1916.
84 Perham, *Lugard: the Years of Authority*, p. 544.
85 *Ibid.*, pp. 544–5.
86 C.O. 583/50/843, Lugard to Colonial Office, 2 Dec. 1916.
87 CAB 37/143/120, confidential, 24 Feb. 1916.
88 Ronald Robinson and John Gallagher with Alice Denny, *op. cit.*, make this point, and this no doubt was still true up to the period under consideration.
89 Lt-Col Jean Ferrandi, *op. cit.*, pp. 23–4.
90 L.A.O.F., XII/58, 8 Feb. 1914. See also L.A.E.F., Affaires politiques, Carton 907, Dossier 2, M. de Guise, Ministre des Colonies, 1 July 1924, on Islam in Chad; he said Chadian Muslims recognised the Shehu of Borno as their Sultan.
91 C.O. 583/36/44714, Strachey's minute of 6 Oct. 1915 on the Emir of Yola's claim: 'It seems clear that we shall have to ignore these claims

in any future arrangements with France. We know before that Adamawa extended right across the Cameroons, but not that the Emir of Yola claimed allegiance so far North and South. . . .'

92 See F. D. Lugard, *The Dual Mandate in British Tropical Africa*, 1922, reprinted by Frank Cass & Co. Ltd, 1965, p. 49: 'Some features of the era of aggressive acquisitiveness which the completion of the partition of Africa had brought to a close, have been recalled, by the allocation between the victorious Allies of the tropical colonies wrested from Germany.'

8 Nigerian soldiers to fight the Empire's war, 1916–18

As long as there was a disputed area in Africa between Germany and the Allies, it was almost inevitable that Nigeria, the most populous of British African dependencies, would be called upon to play a role in the military operation necessary to drive away the 'Huns' from Africa. The government decided to use 'native soldiers' in East Africa because of the high rate of mortality of white soldiers in German East Africa and the protracted nature of the campaign, in which the Germans had used with tremendous success some thousands of adaptable *askaris* to tie down thousands of imperial troops who might have rendered better account of themselves in more favourable climes. Tied up with this was the refusal of the South African Government for purely political considerations to allow the imperial government to recruit soldiers for the East African campaigns from the 'soldiering' races of South Africa such as the Zulus.[1]

Faced with this situation the British Government had no alternative but to make use of other African troops in what was considered strictly an African 'sphere', with the implication that Africans should share in the burden of ridding their continent of the 'undesirable' Germans. While the pursuit of this policy of militarisation of Africans served its immediate purpose, it nevertheless became clear that this was a policy fraught with danger of a possible revolt by a large and well-trained body of African troops full of 'swank' after having seen action in various theatres of military operations. This was particularly feared in Nigeria where the British hold on the country was so precarious and where that hold was dependent on these same African servicemen. Furthermore, there was the remote possibility that the African troops might start feeling that the Empire was so weak that it depended on them for the security of its parts, and since these troops were not immune from the various new ideas thrown up by the war, they might be more assertive in some of their demands. Their homecoming became something of a dread to an administration that imagined it might be losing control over the monster which it had created. Besides these possibilities, there was the problem of restlessness created by mass recruiting of Africans, coupled with the depletion of the administrative staff which invariably accompanied such an exercise, since the raw recruits had to be accompanied by men who knew them and their country well, so that the African soldiers could be effectively used. The Nigerian Government had to contend with many difficulties during this period, but surprisingly enough the War Office, which was responsible for the 'call-up' of Africans, remained passively unconcerned about the questions that arose, being more interested in winning the war and believing that the problems of victory could be faced afterwards.

With the provisional division of the Cameroons into distinct administrative spheres under the control of the Nigerian Government and French authorities in Equatorial Africa, the greater portion of the W.A.F.F. returned to their peace stations and were enjoying a brief but well-earned rest after the labour of eighteen months' campaign in the Cameroons. The question of whether the services of the W.A.F.F. should be utilised elsewhere was not at that time seriously considered. Many issues were involved before a decision on such an important point could be taken.

The greatest factor in this case was the number of officers the War Office was prepared to release for service in Africa. The War Office's attitude on this question had become clear even before the completion of the Cameroons operations. The Army Council, in spite of insistent prodding by the Colonial Office, had adamantly refused to send officers to replace the worn-out officers of the Nigeria Regiment, apparently believing that all the tropical 'skirmishes' were of very little importance to the outcome of the European War. The Army Council had decided in 1915 that they were not going to spare any senior officer for service with W.A.F.F. even if the officer concerned opted to serve in West Africa,[2] and under no circumstances were they prepared to ask officers to serve in West Africa against their will. This was a difficult problem, since many of the officers serving with the troops in West Africa were itching to leave for the more 'exciting' European front where chances of promotion and recognition were better than in the 'malarious jungle' of Africa. The irony of the whole situation was that while the Army Council wanted the colonial regiments to be effective as a fighting force, they were not ready to provide the officers badly needed to achieve this end. Rather than do this the Army Council advised the Government of Nigeria to make use of civil officers or other residents 'who hold or have held military rank, whose services might be available in time of emergency for military duty'.[3] This source had really been exhausted and to the man on the spot the Army Council seemed to have been misled into believing that once the Cameroons campaign was over the role of the Nigeria Regiment would be solely that of a civil police force which could be officered without the active assistance of military authorities in Britain.

To make the War Office aware of its responsibility it was pointed out to them that:

> it must not be forgotten that a West African native trained to the use of arms and filled with a new degree of self-confidence by successful encounters with forces armed and led by Europeans was not likely to be more amenable to discipline than in peace time.[4]

It was at this juncture that the War Office became more flexible in its attitude, and finally reluctantly promised to supply a few officers to replace the war-weary W.A.F.F. officers after the conclusion of the Cameroons campaign; but this promise fell short of the expectations of the Nigerian Government.[5] This was an intolerable situation and the Governor-General reacted by ordering something like a 'general European mobilisation and compulsory service' so that some civilians who were not 'reserve' officers could be compelled to serve with the W.A.F.F., after having undergone some weeks of training in Nigeria.[6] What really worried Lugard was the fear that so large an African force which was battle tested would constitute a dangerous element in Nigeria if they were to get out of hand without an adequate number of officers who knew and had influence over them. In the face of this shortage of military officers after the Cameroons campaign, the thought of sending the Nigeria Regiment to fight in East Africa never occurred to any right-thinking official on the spot. What changed the 'official mind' was the disastrous military situation in German East Africa.

The year 1916 saw the transformation of the fighting in East Africa from a shrewdly planned and boldly initiated offensive against the forces of General Paul von Lettow-Vorbeck,[7] of which great things had been hoped, to a war of attrition.[8] The imperial force in East Africa from 1914 to the middle of 1916 consisted of the King's African Rifles from Rhodesia, British East Africa (later Kenya) and Uganda, some West Indians as well as several battalions of Indian imperial service troops and white soldiers from British Rhodesia and the Union of South Africa. The white and Indian troops suffered so much from the generally unhealthy conditions of German East Africa that by the end of 1916 they had ceased to be an effective fighting force.[9] Describing the condition of the white troops, Captain W. D. Downes of the Nigeria Regiment later wrote:

> After a few weeks, thousands of these once healthy men returned to the Union [of South Africa] broken in health, not to know for months after leaving East Africa, what it was to be really healthy and free from pain. Many never will get over their experiences, whilst again many a strong and healthy man never returned to his native land, but fell a victim of malaria, dysentery ... contracted in German East Africa.[10]

The first white troops who arrived in East Africa early in 1916 suffered so much that within months eighty per cent of the regiments were no longer fit for active service.[11] As a result of this high rate of mortality of white soldiers and the effectiveness of German *askaris* the military authorities there realised that the use of European troops in that theatre was most wasteful; thus it was decided that African troops would have to take their place.

The idea of the use of W.A.F.F. in East Africa had apparently occurred to officials at the War Office as early as the beginning of April 1916, but not until May that year was this translated into action. The War Office then asked Lugard to find a battalion of about 40 Europeans and 740 Nigerians for service in East Africa.[12] The Governor-General received this order with much surprise, and wondered how people at the War Office could be so naïve as to ask him to organise a force for East Africa without prior warning. He informed the Colonial Office that any attempt at compulsory service for East Africa would be dangerous, but he saw no other way of obeying the War Office orders except by coercion. The Colonial Office refused to be persuaded, pointedly asking why the Gold Coast was prepared to send a battalion to East Africa and Nigeria was not, especially when sending such a battalion meant that the Gold Coast was losing fifty-five per cent of its total strength of troops.[13] The Colonial Office told Lugard that the military situation in East Africa demanded that Nigeria should contribute men since South Africa could not keep General Jan Smuts's force up to strength. It was pointed out to the Governor that India, the only other source of supply, was nearly exhausted and that fresh battalions of the King's African Rifles were at the stage of formation, and that the only force readily available and reliable was the Nigeria Regiment. Lugard found himself in a position in which the home government was making him appear an impediment to the Empire's war effort.

While recognising the urgency of the situation Lugard now pleaded for patience and caution to be exercised in handling the men of the Nigeria Regiment. After the difficult campaigns in the Cameroons, they naturally expected that they would rejoin their families. No indication was given them that their services would be required elsewhere. They had not even had time to get used to the new officers who had replaced those whom they knew and trusted. With his special knowledge of African soldiers Lugard commented:

> In these circumstances it would be unwise to force the men to embark for East Africa. It was precisely in similar circumstances that the Sudanese mutiny arose in 1896. . . . After a short period of rest with their women and when their sore feet had had time to heal, when their tattered rags had been replaced and their arms and accoutrements overhauled they would respond to any call if led by officers who were not strangers to them.[14]

He said, however, that only volunteers could be expected to go to East Africa and that if the matter were handled judiciously 'a fine body of men' might be secured who would be of greater value than a discontented lot who might feel that faith had been broken with them. He was ready to co-operate with the War Office but not at the expense of his administration's survival.

One battalion of the Gold Coast regiment which sailed for East Africa in June 1916, arriving in that country for the July–November operations,[15] was a challenge to Nigeria, and the performance of this battalion made the War Office more insistent in its demands on Nigeria. Much as the Governor-General would have liked to rush troops to East Africa in the wake of the Gold Coast example, there still remained many problems to contend with before embarking on such an adventure. Nigeria was not the Gold Coast, and the military establishments of the two countries differed. The Nigeria Regiment was a much larger force, consequently more preparation of provisioning arrangements and transports was needed. Furthermore, the Nigerian infantry companies had been reduced after the Cameroons campaign, and about 1,000 'time expired' men were allowed to take their discharge.[16] Since the Nigeria Regiment had borne the brunt of the fighting in the Cameroons, they had suffered more casualties than any other single unit of the W.A.F.F.

The Colonial Office therefore allowed Nigeria time to prepare for East Africa, with the proviso that rather than send a battalion Nigeria would have to furnish a full brigade of four battalions by August 1916.[17] It was later realised that the time given was too short and the date of the Brigade's departure was consequently postponed to October.[18]

Recruiting commenced in July with the recruits being promised a small bonus as an inducement. Members of the Nigeria Regiment were given the option of volunteering for service in East Africa or staying at home. Many actually volunteered to serve and the thousand 'time expired' men and 'unofficial' Europeans enlisted in the regiment.[19] By August 1916, when General Cunliffe returned to Lagos to take charge of affairs, sufficient volunteers had been got for the formation of a brigade of four infantry battalions and one battery. The Nigerian overseas contingent was initially planned to be 2,400 strong with a monthly reinforcement of 200 trained soldiers. Nigerian authorities made it clear to the War Office that this commitment would be met only if the War Office was prepared to replace officers who would be accompanying the troops to East Africa. This clarification of Nigeria's position was necessary because taking 2,400 troops from the country called for provision of an adequate body of officers by the War Office, to train recruits, both to fill the void that would be created and to provide regular reinforcements to replace wastage. It was necessary to maintain the Regiment at full strength, even after the despatch of troops to East Africa, since if trouble were to break out in Nigeria, it would be difficult to call the soldiers back, nor would the Gold Coast Regiment, the only other effective force in West Africa, be in a position to provide help. Nigeria was therefore asked to recruit up to sixty per cent[20] above normal establishment of 5,000 after filling the place of troops that were going to East Africa. General Cunliffe was instructed to give a bounty of £3 to ex-soldiers who re-enlisted for service in East Africa, if he should find it difficult getting the number of troops needed.

The War Office blamed Lugard for introducing the idea of 'voluntary' service in the Nigeria Regiment:

> this basis is one which the Army Council in any but exceptional circumstances deprecate in the case of regular troops already serving. Should there be any likelihood of delay or difficulty in raising the numbers required. ... These troops whose terms of engagement provide for general service outside their own territories should be placed under orders as required in the same manner as all other Imperial regular troops serving under approximately similar conditions of service.[21]

The War Office apparently thought Lugard was being too soft with his Nigerian soldiers, who were after all under oath to serve the Empire when ordered to do so. When Bonar Law learnt that adequate numbers of recruits to fill the place of departing soldiers as well as to provide recruits to be trained as reinforcements were not forthcoming he wrote, 'every effort must be made to induce native administration and political officers to give energetic and wholehearted support to the recruiting Campaign'.[22] The Nigerian Government was asked to consider sending all its troops to East Africa and replacing them with troops from Sierra Leone, who were disqualified from participation in the East African campaign because of their poor performance and indiscipline during the Cameroons campaign. The Sierra Leonians were said by Colonel Hastings, their Commandant, to be only effective against Africans armed with dane-guns and cutlasses and certainly not against seasoned German *askaris*. The Nigerian Government for the same reason of indiscipline complained about the Sierra Leone Regiment, and refused to accept them.[23]

The obvious way out then was to step up recruitment and create training depots in various parts of Nigeria. Preparations for sending the first batch of Nigerian troops to East Africa were completed by the middle of October 1916 and transports for East Africa finally arrived on 8 November 1916, which delayed their immediate departure. The Nigerian overseas contingent consisted of battalions one to four divided into sixteen companies. In addition there was a 4-gun mountain battery.[24] The entire Brigade was commanded by Brigadier-General Cunliffe. One of the difficulties the Brigade ran into was that the new shorter rifles with which the troops were to be armed arrived late with the transport vessels and the guns were not handed over to the men until they embarked. Thus the contingent found itself actually embarking for active service in possession of rifles which most of the men had never used, and they had to learn the use of an entirely new weapon during the voyage.[25] The troops left in four transport vessels between 15 and 27 November 1916.

The sailing for East Africa of the first batch of Nigerians marked the beginning of deeper involvement in the Empire's war effort. The War Office was now committed to using Africans on a wide scale to release 'as many white troops as possible from those employed in the minor theatres for service on the British main front. . . .'[26] It became imperative that novel plans for recruitment should be projected. Having failed to cajole the South African Government into allowing her to raise a considerable number of battalions from the 'fighting races of South Africa',[27] the imperial government turned its eyes on Nigeria as the next available human reservoir for black soldiers. It is rather difficult to believe that the British Government would have thought that the South African Government would allow Africans from the Union to be recruited to serve and to gain military knowledge which might have been used to unsettle the delicate internal situation in South Africa. In a way the refusal of the Union government to allow the recruitment of black soldiers in its territory as a result of the government's racial policies did more than anything to bring Nigeria into greater participation in the East African campaigns.

In order to fulfil her new role of supplier of Black troops, a more systematic approach to the question of recruiting in Nigeria had to be made. British public opinion was already in favour of the use of coloured troops, at least if not in Europe in some other parts of the world where the enemy was to be encountered. After visiting East Africa and seeing African soldiers in action Lieutenant-Commander Wedgwood, Liberal M.P. for Newcastle under Lyme, demanded that Britain should be able to raise a force of two and a half million troops from 'African soldiering peoples',[28] and he was backed by other members of parliament who wrote to *The Times* editor urging the public to demand that action to this effect be taken.[29] Responding to this public pressure Bonar Law informed Lugard of the appointment of Colonel Haywood as Assistant Director of Recruiting, but added:

I am particularly anxious (and the Army Council have expressed their entire concurrence in this view) that the inference should not be drawn from the creation of this new post that there is any want of confidence in the desire or ability of officers of W.A.F.F. to carry on as hitherto the work of raising and training recruits.[30]

Lugard took offence. He had received a series of despatches, 'urging' and 'ordering' him to pull his weight and he could not remain silent, for he felt the Colonial Office showed a singular lack of understanding of the complexity of the problems in Nigeria. Bonar Law had instructed Lugard to mount a 'special recruiting campaign', with a view to providing increased forces overseas. Lugard replied that 'the recruitment of a negro army must be either by coercion or by voluntary enlistment; for the former, we must have the means – which we have not – nor would the methods be such as could possibly be reconciled with British policy'.[31] Lugard believed that sending Colonel Haywood instead of sending training officers was a waste of time, and that since Haywood himself would not be accompanying the troops, his influence would be nil. The Governor-General argued that if Haywood's mission was to fix such 'special financial inducements' as might encourage men to enlist, it would have been cheaper for the War Office to entrust such into the Governor's hand 'as they had already done in the case of the Marine ratings sent to Mesopotamia at my suggestion relying on me to do the best I can for the Empire'.[32] Lugard did not succeed in stopping Haywood from coming to Nigeria. Colonel Haywood's appointment revealed a definite wish to overrule Lugard's tenderness for Nigerian susceptibilities. Haywood was to report directly to the War Office and he was to recruit in all four British West African colonies. The War Office gave specific instructions to Colonel Haywood; he was to consider:

(a) the possibility of raising battalions for service in Europe, Egypt and the Near East, Mesopotamia, East Africa and Somaliland;
(b) raising of native auxiliary or labour units for employment in the major theatres of operations in order to release white troops.

The War Office also introduced the idea of 'fresh combatant native units' being possibly formed into organisations separate from the W.A.F.F. and the employment of such units as well as of the W.A.F.F. in Europe. The Colonial Office, however, was determined not to allow a force under War Office management to compete with W.A.F.F. in West Africa because of the history of clashes between the War and Colonial Offices over the control of the imperial garrison in Sierra Leone – the West African

Regiment (W.A.R.). The most foolish of the War Office instructions was that Haywood should recruit German African troops returning to the Cameroons from Fernando Po as well as French subjects in territories adjoining British colonies.[33] First of all there were no German troops returning from Fernando Po, and as to French subjects, Strachey commented, 'we could have told them [the War Office] that we were engaged at the instance of the French in forcibly repatriating natives of French territories who had taken refuge in Nigeria to escape French conscription'.[34] On the question of recruiting in the British sphere of the Cameroons some officials at the Colonial Office justified it on the grounds that the Germans had tried to enlist Irish prisoners of war to fight against Britain; when doubts as to the legality of this action were expressed by the French,[35] A. J. Harding minuted:

> this is of course nothing more than the Germans are doing in Poland and so long as no form of compulsion is used . . . to make natives of British sphere of the Cameroons enlist I don't see that there is any real objection. Some of them may be glad to pay off some old scores against the Germans.[36]

Sir George Fiddes said that no matter what was done to ensure that the Cameroonians enlisted voluntarily, the Germans would allege that 'compulsion was used and give this as a justification for their treatment of the Belgians . . .'[37] As a result of this reservation, recruiting of soldiers in the Cameroons was dropped. With the increasing demand for West African troops General Dobell, who had earlier supported the use of African troops in Africa, wondered what these troops, if recruited in the numbers being urged by the War Office, would be used for. He commented:

> I personally cannot picture the 'million African black army' hastily trained troops, without a good proportion of old soldiers . . . they could not be relied on unless they belonged to the best of the fighting types . . . the Gold Coast was of course by no means a productive recruiting area before the war. . . . In Nigeria the individual goes for everything and Haywood is little known in the North. . . . I don't quite understand where the army, when raised and trained, is going to be employed. Is it only for East Africa? which we are always informed is just over.[38]

Colonel Haywood set out on his rather impossible mission by first visiting the Gold Coast, where he reported full co-operation from officials there, especially A. R. Slater, the Acting Governor.

Although this did not produce many recruits at least Haywood felt that he had recruited the 'maximum obtainable under voluntary conditions'. Haywood then went on to Lagos where his reception was an unhappy one: 'I could not but get the impression that my presence was resented by the Governor-General ... and regarded as interference'.[39] In spite of this hostility Nigeria was the only part of British West Africa where there could be hopes of recruiting large numbers of soldiers. Gambia was too small to be regarded seriously as a recruiting ground, and Sierra Leone was only good for carriers. The Gold Coast, except Asante and part of Eastern province and the Northern territories, did not offer much. To make matters worse the Ashanti were unwilling to serve in the army since they made more money from the mines and their cocoa farms. The Moshi, Wangara and Zaberma, who had hitherto supplied forty-eight per cent of the Gold Coast Regiment, could not be enlisted since they were in French territory and the French needed recruits too.[40] Nigeria then was thus the only territory where a sufficient number of recruits could be obtained. Making allowance for those needed for public works and other departments, and for the unfit, Haywood arrived at the conclusion that 8,000 troops including those already in training depots in Nigeria (and excluding over 6,000 soldiers and 4,000 carriers who had sailed for East Africa up to the end of May 1917) could be raised immediately by voluntary enlistment, but that over 70,000[41] soldiers could be conscripted by compulsion in Nigeria.

Haywood was apparently on the side of those who advocated compulsory military service, though most of the local officials in West Africa, except those in Gambia, were opposed to the idea. Haywood was told that Nigerians would resist any attempt to coerce them to join the army, and since available forces were too small it would have been difficult to enforce. Edward Cameron, the Governor of Gambia, who was in favour of compulsion, said 'a show of armed force and intention to use it if necessary to obtain what we want ... is the only practicable one', and he added that an alternative could be some 'form of short ordinance authorising the executive to obtain recruits for H.M.'s forces and giving the widest discretionary power as to means'.[42] It is not surprising that the Governor of a small colony like the Gambia with less than a quarter of a million inhabitants to control should advocate compulsion. Others like Sir Hugh Clifford and Sir Frederick Lugard had different ideas. Clifford was of the opinion that the government would have committed a 'fatal error of judgement' had it attempted to institute any system of compulsory service. He was convinced that such an attempt would have met with fierce resistance and would have produced few if any recruits for the army. Clifford commented: 'the recruiting campaign has spread the belief that government is weaker than it was thought to be . . . this has manifested itself . . . by a tendency on the part of one or two chiefs to take the law into their own hands instead of appealing to the government.'[43] Other officials even doubted the government's assertion that military service was voluntary. One of these men said: 'volunteers for military service are actually victims of compulsion, though the immediate instrument which compels them is the chief acting at the instance of the government itself.'

This official said that in his recruiting campaigns he had laid particular stress upon the fact that the men were required not to form first line troops but to guard lines of communication. He added: 'it is pretty certain that unless the war ends with unexpected abruptness and in a very short time, the government would be open to the very serious accusation of having obtained recruits by false representation'.[44] Some officials felt Africans owed it as a duty to serve anywhere during the war since the British presence had brought incalculable benefits to them, they 'have enjoyed under imperial protection during the present generation very great benefits, moral and spiritual far greater than those enjoyed or rather endured by slum dwellers of English cities . . . we are morally justified in asking for the aid of the natives in the prosecution of the war'.[45] Haywood, arguing from another angle, said that apart from producing thousands of combatants, compulsion would please the French, because the exodus of French subjects into havens in British territories would cease. Haywood felt that 'the number of natives who enlist from pure love of soldiering is very small', and that most Africans had prejudices of one kind or the other against military service overseas. This arose from the fear of the sea and for some 'it is against their customs to cross the water', and there was an 'instinctive dislike of food other than that to which they were accustomed'.[46] He also thought that the superior financial attractions of pay in the police or mines weakened recruiting efforts.

In order to make the army more attractive a bonus of £5 was given to every man who enlisted and the pay of one shilling a day plus rations was increased to one shilling and threepence plus rations to compete with that of a policeman or a miner. The number of African drill instructors was increased to cope with the problem of training 8,000 recruits annually in four centres in Nigeria (Zungeru, Lokoja, Ibadan and Okigwi). The lack of officers continued to be a problem and Lugard to his amazement was told by the Secretary of State, Walter Long, to provide these himself. Long, indeed, almost suggested a want of patriotism among the European officials in Nigeria: 'There are some colonies where conditions do not essentially differ from those in Nigeria in which the percentage of civil officers on military duties of all kinds has reached about forty whilst the proportion of Nigerian staff so employed does not appear to exceed half this figure.' Walter Long added that while recognising that political and police departments needed to be fully staffed to avoid serious risk of troubles, he concluded:

> I would ask you to consider whether some departments whose existence is not essential to the safety of the country; such for example as Forestry and Education departments cannot be reduced much below their present strength until after the present crisis and whether other more essential departments such as political, secretariat and public works have in fact reached the irreducible minimum.[47]

To placate the Colonial Office Lugard cancelled all leave for his officers and put them under military orders, but much as the Governor-General tried to please the home government, the Colonial Office continued to find fault.

After seeing the problems raised by the recruiting campaign, the Colonial Office began to realise that the idea of a 'Black army of millions' was a chimera, but Lugard was accused of exaggerating the problem of shortage of officers, even by senior Colonial Office officials like Fiddes, who quoted a 'shrewd' observer just back from West Africa as saying:

> there are I believe many eligible civil servicemen probably in each West African colony who could be spared. . . . There were few I saw who were working at any pressure. . . . I well know the necessity for able bodied men in West Africa, but to be quite honest, people there don't realise we are at war and no one speaking generally had been inconvenienced so far.[48]

This must have seemed a rather unfair attack on an administration whose civil establishment was down to sixty-two per cent of pre-war level, but the most shattering comment on Lugard's officials came from a frustrated junior officer who in a private letter to Charles Strachey declared:

> All branches of the service are very unhappy. Juniors because they are not allowed to go and fight and satisfy honours, seniors because they see their provinces often with staffs ... majority being young men. The result is that senior officers, many of whom have seen active service are galled by the thought that although doing extended tours they have not the satisfaction of knowing that thereby juniors are set free for military duties ... as a non-essential department my own [Education] if closed or run by two or three from headquarters, admittedly could only produce a score of men ... quite one hundred men could be spared from different departments in Nigeria ... the majority of whom are unmarried and usually with O.T.C. [Officers' Training Corps] training at least. ... At home there are those who consider we are hiding behind our official duties ... that we make profession of militant desires, knowing full well that there is no likelihood of our offer being accepted. I know of more than one instance where a man's family have become sceptical about his honest desire to take up the sword. They point to other colonial services ... and are apt to shake the head and say 'where there's the will & C.' Those of us who have older and married brothers fighting in France feel our position keenly, especially when we know that our work is not absolutely essential.[49]

Lugard's position was unenviable; there were rebellions all over the country, demands for troops in Nigeria and East Africa, officers who were bored or homesick wanting action on the Western Front, while transient visitors reported many young men lazing around at the same time as Lugard continued to complain of depletion of his staff. After sending over 5,000 soldiers and around the same number of carriers to East Africa up to August 1917 and with about 1,300 recruits still in training, Lugard maintained that only 895 British officials remained in Nigeria and these were mainly officials of the railway and marine departments. Thirty-eight per cent of his administrative staff was on military duties in East Africa, the Cameroons or in Nigeria. Toeing the Colonial Office line about releasing more men from his administration, Lugard asked 56 officers on leave in England to proceed to East Africa to join the Nigerian troops there, but on being told that the men might have to stay in England, he wrote angrily to the Colonial Office:

I am calling on my officers here to do double and treble work and I am accepting risks in detaching these officers from our already depleted staff; it is natural that while everyone here is more than willing to accept this burden if he hears that the officer whose work he is doing is employed in the fighting ranks, he should feel much disappointed should he later hear from his friend that they are merely employed in 'war work' in England or to lighten the strain in some office and impose it upon himself.[50]

The debate continued until the end of the war, with the War Office continuing to apply pressure *via* the Colonial Office on the Nigerian Government.

At the beginning of 1917 Nigeria was called upon not only to furnish combatants for the campaign in East Africa, but to provide carriers as well. This decision was taken following the Admiralty's opposition to further recruiting of carriers in Sierra Leone, opposition based on imperial defence grounds. It was stated that Freetown (Sierra Leone's port) was rapidly increasing:

as a port for transports and escorting men-of-war, and in order to coal these vessels, a considerable amount of labour is required which it is very difficult to get ... unless sufficient numbers are retained the movement of transports between Australia and England will be seriously interfered with.[51]

This led the War Office to try to find other areas for recruiting carriers outside West Africa. British East Africa had been almost exhausted because of over-recruiting, consequently Portuguese East Africa was tried but the numbers obtained were few. The French, when approached as to the possibility of recruiting carriers in Madagascar, refused on the grounds that the British had refused them permission to recruit labour in British Somaliland.[52] The French were also piqued at not being asked to participate in the fighting in East Africa, something which they expected since they had a force in Madagascar waiting for a call which never came. When the question of recruiting carriers in the Belgian Congo was mentioned, a Colonial Office clerk minuted, 'there are reasons of policy which render it undesirable to put ourselves under obligations to them [the Belgians] where German East Africa is concerned'.[53] Britain did not want Belgian Government involvement to be greater than it was then, in view of complications that might arise later as to the division of spoils of war in a strategically important place like East Africa.

The War Office therefore fell back on Nigeria for carriers and the Nigerian Government was asked to provide 4,000 every month, as well as the reinforcements for troops in East Africa.[54] Recruiting was maintained at a high rate in Nigeria until October 1917, when a fall-off in numbers was noticed, particularly in Kano province, the centre of recruiting in the North. The cause of this was the prosperity which 'high' producer price of groundnuts brought to the people who might have been attracted to the army or carrier corps. The mining companies in Bauchi also began to compete more vigorously as the price of tin rose on the world market. It became necessary to look outside the traditional areas for recruits, and it was in this way that the Tiv (Munshi) began to be recruited in substantial numbers into the Nigerian army.[55] To the surprise of the Nigerian authorities the Tiv[56] proved to be very efficient soldiers and quickly mastered Hausa, the language of command. For the first time in the military history of Nigeria, the Tiv were recognised (as they are today) as good fighting men and gradually they began to be recruited into the Nigeria Regiment, thus serving a double purpose of opening up their 'country' and helping to solve British manpower needs.

The recruiting of Ezzas (Ibo-speaking people of Okigwi division) who were being trained at Okigwi, was stopped because they proved bad military material. The training depot was therefore closed down and the remnants moved to Ibadan.

Recruiting of the Yoruba also fell away considerably as from March 1917 and recruits forcibly sent in by the Alafin deserted in large numbers. The Yoruba refused to serve because of the suffering which had followed the Okeogun rebellion of 1916 and because of the brutal suppression of the rebellion by the government. Secondly, like the Ashanti, the Yoruba were also becoming too prosperous as a result of enhanced prices of cocoa during the war, consequently they were not willing to leave the placid life of their cocoa farms for the hardship of army life in an unfamiliar environment.[57]

All the Residents were told to exert their influence, but most of them were unanimous in reporting a scarcity of willing recruits. These included Residents of most of the important provinces – Ilorin, Zaria, Borno, Nassarawa, Kontagora, Kano, Sokoto, Bida, Bassa, Oyo and Yola. The resident of Yola stated that 'men who served in the Cameroons are still talking of hardship they endured through having to serve under white men who did not speak their language'. The delay in settling soldiers' accounts after the Cameroons campaign did a lot of damage to the military enthusiasm of the 'fighting races of Nigeria'.[58] This unwillingness of the traditional source of supply to produce recruits made Lugard consider recruiting 'primitive pagans' such as Tiv, Mumuye, Mada, Angass, Bassa, Bashama, Montoil, Sura and Tangale. The acting Lieutenant-Governor of Northern Nigeria said he was opposed to recruiting the 'primitive pagans' and that with the exception of the Tiv, far from their homes 'they become depressed and morbid, unable to withstand hardship and the sick rate among them is high'.[59] Lugard visited the North to oversee things himself but not much success, in terms of recruits, came out of his visit.

Towards the end of 1917 the War Office wanted Nigerian recruits to be used to bring up to strength the much expanded King's African Rifles, but the difference in the languages of command militated against the possibility of a successful implementation of this scheme. The War Office was told this and the proposal was dropped. The Commandant of the Nigeria Regiment urged the War Office to allow some Nigerian soldiers to return home, because he felt their return in batches from time to time would stimulate recruiting and allay apprehension. This was not possible because of the military situation in East Africa. In spite of all the difficulties encountered in meeting the Empire's manpower call, another 2,000 recruits left Nigeria for East Africa in May 1917. From all the difficulties arising out of the recruitment drive, it dawned on the home government that some of the instructions given to Haywood to raise all types of battalions – labour, combatant, carriers – could not be complied with and that Nigeria was incapable of satisfying all the needs of the War Office; and since Haywood's idea of possible compulsory service was not acceptable to the local officials in West Africa, the War Office had to make do with what 'voluntary' effort could provide.

A novel but rather foolish idea to release Nigerian troops on garrison duties for service in East Africa was put forward by a War Office 'expert' by the name of Captain W. B. Hellard. From his experience in German East Africa he had arrived at the conclusion that an aeroplane fitted with bombs was equivalent to a battalion of African troops. He therefore suggested that Zungeru should be used as the headquarters of the new 'Air Force' to be set up. Since Zungeru had a race-course which could be converted into 'an excellent aerodrome', and furthermore since the town was within easy flying distance from Kano and Ibadan (the other two towns with race-courses that could be converted into aerodromes), Zungeru naturally recommended itself as the headquarters of the 'Air Force'. Hellard was of the opinion that the 'Air Force' could be used for scouting enemy forces, straffing and bombing or machine-gunning rebellious or enemy forces. To drive home his point about the effectiveness of an air force, he wrote that 'the point of the incalculable moral effect in the native mind' should be borne in mind. He added,

> this was the point which struck me most in German East Africa and in Egypt. There is no doubt that the mere presence of aircraft over the heads of natives inspires a terror in their minds which cannot . . . be understood unless seen by Europeans. I have seen the Askari German soldiers running about in quite aimless fashion on hearing the engine of an approaching aeroplane. Having this effect on trained native soldiers, one can easily understand the influence of aircrafts in the minds of a native civil population. The effect of the prestige attaching to the English if they are the first to introduce the aeroplane into West Africa should not be overlooked.[60]

This was of course nonsense. The illogicality of this proposal lay in the fact that no matter how efficient an air force at that time, or perhaps even at any time, might have been, the infantry still had to do the mopping-up operation after bombing raids; this scheme overlooked the possibility that the frail aircraft produced at that time might break down. What would have happened if after troops had been replaced by those aircraft, rebellion were to break out and the aircraft were to be out of order, was not considered. The scheme did not explain how pioneer aircraft could have been effectively used to suppress rebellions in the thick forests of Southern Nigeria. It is therefore not a surprise that the proposal was shelved after receiving only academic consideration. The last batch of 500 Nigerian soldiers left for East Africa on 17 December 1917,[61] but this did not mean the end of the idea of employing Nigerian troops elsewhere when fighting ceased in East Africa.

NIGERIANS AND THE EAST AFRICAN CAMPAIGN

Throughout their time in East Africa in 1916 Nigerian troops fought mostly in high and comparatively healthy localities, but the inevitable horrors of war came in 1917 when they were moved to the Rufiji Valley. The cause of their difficulties was the supply problem. It was first thought that the Rufiji river would be used, but this idea was soon given up because of wild fluctuations in the volume of water in the river and because of the unusually heavy flood of the first half of 1917.[62] As a result, lines of communication broke down and hunger caused more havoc among the troops than German bullets: 'The men driven by hunger were eating roots, leaves and berries, and in consequence a large number of cases of alkaloidal poisoning occurred through which several men lost their lives.'[63] This hardship lasted until the middle of 1917 and 'the men got terribly thin and wretched, till they became almost unfit to take the field in any active operations'.[64] Lugard was very much disturbed by the reports which reached him from East Africa. He regarded as nonsense the suggestion made earlier about death rates of Nigerians in Mesopotamia, that high mortality was inevitable among natives, and said he knew from reliable sources that the reason was 'culpable lack of foresight on the part of those responsible'. Lugard said he had learnt that the men had an average of about seventeen ounces of food per day; a letter written to him from East Africa described the Nigerian Brigade, which on landing was 'an exceptionally fine body of men', as reduced after some months to 'a collection of heart-broken skeletons – 30 per cent had become casualties from sickness and starvation and of the remainder, 50 per cent were attending hospital'.[65]

Lugard genuinely felt responsible for the welfare of the Nigerians sent to East Africa by him under War Office pressure, and his angry protest made the Colonial Office demand War Office intervention. Surgeon-General Pike was sent to East Africa to enquire into the conditions under which the African soldiers were serving, and he reported negligence on the part of the commanders.

In spite of all the privations, Nigerian troops still gave a good account of themselves after their ghastly experiences in the Rufiji Valley. They joined other imperial forces in the hot pursuit of General Lettow-Vorbeck across the Rovuma river until the latter left German East Africa on 25 November 1917[66] to continue his guerrilla campaign in Portuguese East Africa and later on in the Rhodesias and Nyasaland. This military development had been foreseen in 1916 by Captain R. Meinertzhagen, the British intelligence officer in German East Africa, who had summed up the military situation then in these prophetic words:

It is difficult to say what will be the last phase unless Smuts manœuvres Von-Lettow into Portuguese East Africa and rounds

him up somewhere near Pretoria. But Von-Lettow is slippery and is
not going to be caught by manœuvre. He knows the country better
than we do, his troops understand the last word in bush warfare and
can live on the country. I think we are in for an expensive hide and
seek and Von-Lettow will still be cuckooing somewhere in Africa
when the ceasefire goes.[67]

True to form von Lettow-Vorbeck surrendered in Northern
Rhodesia two days after the Armistice had been signed in Europe,
and this he did after much persuasion since by that time he had
rearmed his Askaris with new British weapons captured from the
feeble Portuguese in Mozambique and he was about to cross back
into German East Africa to continue the war.[68]

As far as the Nigerians were concerned their involvement in this
costly and destructive East African campaign[69] ended after von
Lettow-Vorbeck moved deeper into Portuguese Mozambique and
when the British felt he had ceased to be a serious menace to them.
The Nigerians left East Africa during the second week of February
1918, leaving behind their carriers, who returned after the conclusion of hostilities.[70] The Nigerians spent about fourteen
months in East Africa, only half of which could be said to have
been effectively spent on the battlefield.

In spite of the obvious handicaps which the Nigerians suffered
in East Africa, it was asserted that without them the story of the
war in East Africa might have been otherwise.[71] 'Nigeria had good
reasons to be proud of her sons', wrote a British official:

> they had made for themselves in East Africa a reputation second to
> none and had proved that African troops . . . were capable of fighting
> the Empire's battle in spheres however distant and under circum-
> stances however novel. Their losses had been heavy. But they . . .
> have the satisfaction of knowing that they have a prepondering share
> in a most essentially African concern – the elimination of the German
> flag throughout the continent.[72]

Whether this was an African concern is perhaps doubtful. Whether
Britain or Germany ruled any portion of Africa may not have been
a fundamental question for Africans. Nigerians fought because
they were ordered to do so and not because of any patriotic reason
or because of any African desire to escape from the 'Prussian
lash' in Africa. The role of Nigerian troops, though often exaggerated by their officers, was nevertheless commendable and
brought a lot of attention to them and their race, if not from

important politicians in England at least from British officers who fought with and were comrades-in-arms with the Nigerians. One of them wrote later:

> the Empire owes more recognition than has up to date been given to the negro soldier for all that he has had to endure and all the appalling hardships in East Africa and the Cameroons he had gone through for the sake of the Empire. Their deeds have not been done in the limelight and the public have heard very little of their doings. None of the battles fought by them will ever be really famous in the world's history ... but they have fought, conquered, suffered and died for the British Empire ... I sincerely hope that all the negro has done for the British race will not be forgotten and that the welfare of the African will be one of Britain's first considerations after the war ...[73]

PLANS FOR FURTHER OVERSEA SERVICE AFTER THE EAST AFRICAN CAMPAIGN

As the war in East Africa showed signs of nearing its end, the War Office began to consider sending about 10,000 combatants from Nigeria and an equal number of carriers to the Middle East. The difficulty in the implementation of this proposal was that a definite undertaking had been given to the original Nigerian Brigade (not the later reinforcements) who had been sent to East Africa that maximum service would be limited to the period of hostilities in East Africa.[74] Even the Colonial Office was not sure what the officers had promised the later reinforcements as to the duration of their service. Until this was found out the Colonial Office was non-committal on the point of sending troops to the Middle East. H. J. Read impressed it on the War Office that:

> the impression on the native mind of statements made by their white officers is a factor in the consideration of this question – which cannot be underestimated. The reliance placed by the West African soldier on the promise of his European officers is absolute and the Army Council will appreciate that this confidence should be maintained.[75]

The Army Council was again reminded that it was very difficult to raise the East African contingent in the first place, because the Nigerians had thought that they would not be called upon to fight after the Cameroons campaign. In all this one can see the

Colonial Office trying to discourage the Army Council, in their desire to turn Nigeria into a human reservoir.

The War Office up to the beginning of 1918 was committed to a policy of employing 'non-combatant West African native personnel in diluting the auxiliary services of British and Indian formations employed in Asiatic theatres'.[76] This is reflected in the employment of Nigerian and Sierra Leonian 'marines' in Mesopotamia; it seems they had refused seriously to contemplate employing West African troops outside Africa and the Middle East. The Army Council, in reply to persistent French demands following their decree introducing general military service in their West African possessions and their plea that the British should follow suit,[77] outlined the reasons for not employing West Africans as combatants in Europe as:

(a) their inherent limitations especially as regards mental aptitude and ability to withstand climatic conditions,

(b) the relatively large European cadres necessary; the difficulty of providing these and the length of time they must be withdrawn from other useful service,

(c) the long period of training necessary to prepare African troops for warfare outside Africa, and

(d) the difficulty in maintaining these troops in distant theatres.[78]

At the same time the Army Council had plans of utilising the West African contingents on their return from East Africa, in forming an African reserve force to be stationed in Nigeria and the Gold Coast, for emergency service anywhere in the British Empire in dealing with 'native rebellions'. The formation and maintenance of this reserve force was to be extra to the normal colonial garrisons in Nigeria and the Gold Coast.

This idea finally led to the decision to create a 'W.A.F.F. Service Brigade'. Brigadier-General Cunliffe warned that before the new force could be employed outside Africa, a wholly new system of drill must be introduced, including instructions in bombing and trench warfare and the use of Stokes and Lewis machine-guns. Cunliffe added: 'the employment of Nigerian troops in any of the larger theatres of war where highly trained and well armed enemy troops would be met with would be seeking disaster unless this was carried out'.[79] Lugard in the absence of Cunliffe, who was on leave in England, had since April 1918 introduced the new drill which the General had in mind.

Organisation of the brigade began in earnest in May 1918 and the brigade was code-named 'WASPS'. It was decided that it should consist of 7,000 instead of the 10,000 originally planned and the force was to be commanded by Colonel Haywood, who had long experience of service with the W.A.F.F. and was younger than Cunliffe, who had declined the post because of failing eyesight. The brigade was to have five battalions, four of which were to be in Nigeria while the remaining one was to be stationed in the Gold Coast. The general officer commanding was to have his headquarters in Nigeria.[80]

There were sufficient numbers of soldiers in Nigeria after their return from East Africa so that by July 1918 the first brigade composed entirely of Nigerians was ready. The Army Council, impressed by the speed with which the brigade was organised, decided to form a second 'WASPS' brigade, for which the Gold Coast battalions in West Africa and those returning from East Africa would form the nucleus, to be supplemented by drafts from Nigeria. These two brigades were to be sent to Palestine, with the Nigerian one going first, while the second was being organised.

Lugard was told that the War Office was forwarding ammunition, materials, guns or any military equipment the first brigade might be short of, to Egypt to meet the arrival of the brigade there. He was asked as a matter of urgency to say when the troops would be ready to leave for the Middle East.[81] The 'secret' despatch that followed must have jolted Lugard because the Army Council asked him when transports should be sent down to pick up the troops.[82] Lugard wanted the Nigerians to be given time to prepare, but he was informed that whatever preparations he had to make, he had better make them fast, since five ships to take the first brigade of 7,000 to the Middle East would be arriving in Lagos on 21 September, 4 October, 16 October, and 28 October respectively.[83] It is rather strange the way the War Office behaved throughout this war as regards military demands on Nigeria. They hardly made any allowance for the inconveniences of the men concerned nor did they show any sign that their hasty action could conceivably lead to an explosion.

Lugard had always feared that if too many demands for sacrifice were made on illiterate Nigerian soldiers, they might out of weariness refuse to obey orders. This was borne out by a 'mutiny' in September 1918 in Zaria, when soldiers there began to show signs of insubordination. The reason for this discontent did not become clear immediately, but the increase in the rate of desertion, as from the time of the proposed Middle East campaign, became alarming. The ostensible reason was the poor pay and complaints of the soldiers over their suffering in the Rufiji Valley in German East Africa.[84] Lugard reported urgently to the Colonial Office: 'I do not feel sure in the existing circumstances, and I again urge advisability of sending Cunliffe or if he is medically unable, sending Colonel Sargent and all officers known to the men'.[85] The Colonial Office quickly sent back all senior military officers on leave.

Lugard, on the advice of Colonel Jenkins, the acting Commandant of the Nigeria Regiment, went to Zaria to speak to the troops. He told the men that they were spoiling the good name they had earned for gallantry and loyalty in East Africa, adding that the government was making the last demand on them, by requiring their services 'in a country near Egypt' where food was plentiful and where the men would not be starved as they had been in East Africa. He told the men they would be allowed to see the beautiful places of the Near East and that General Cunliffe and officers known to them would be waiting for them in Egypt. Lugard reported: 'my speech was interrupted by loud murmurs from the ranks, which I understand to be to the effect that they had done their share and it was the turn of the garrison troops, and that they had grievances regarding their pay which have not been heard or adjusted'.[86]

Lugard in a conciliatory way called out the company sergeants-major and told each to select two men of his company to explain to him the discontent. He then assured the whole rank and file that he would satisfy whatever their representatives wanted. Lugard promised the men that the garrison troops would follow the Middle East Contingent as drafts. He so impressed the men that things became relatively calm. Sergeant Major Mama Zozo, who had won the D.S.M., spoke for the men, saying they were not afraid to fight, but that his men had been promised a bonus of £6 each after the Cameroons campaign which other battalions except his had received. Lugard said no such promise or payment was made or given. Mama Zozo complained that immediately on their return from East Africa they were put on Nigerian rates of pay, though recruits who had not fought in East Africa were getting oversea rates. Lugard rectified this anomaly and ordered continued oversea pay or a bonus of £2 a man.[87] Next, the soldiers complained that for five months they almost starved to death in the Rufiji Valley and had been consoled by their officer, who promised them that their accumulated ration money would be paid. Lugard immediately ordered that the men be paid three pence per day each for five months in lieu of the food they had missed in East Africa.

Lugard's appeasement annoyed the British officers of the brigade, who were unanimous in dismissing the complaints regarding pay as 'frivolous', arguing that they were put forward to cover the soldiers' unwillingness to go to the Middle East for military service. Colonel Jenkins, the acting Commandant of the Nigeria Regiment, who like Lugard had profound understanding of African soldiers, sympathised with the soldiers. For him the discontent arose from the paucity of officers and British N.C.O.s who knew the men, and he argued that 'just claims' for arrears of pay had not been settled. He disclosed that when the brigade which was to go to Palestine held their farewell parade, he could see that a large number 'who were utterly unfitted through age, wounds or other disability' were included.[88] The British N.C.O.s were wholly unsuited to handle the men because of their lack of experience; Colonel Jenkins said these N.C.O.s had in some cases treated the Nigerian soldiers as 'Niggers' and that in one case one N.C.O. had struck a man on parade. He concluded: 'Such a state of things would make the best native troops in Africa unwilling to go on service with such officers and N.C.O.s'.[89] The whole affair was unprecedented in the history of the W.A.F.F. and showed the awareness of the men of their rights as well as the danger inherent in having a 'large' body of trained Nigerian soldiers who knew their rights.

As if by divine intervention, the situation was saved when an influenza epidemic broke out towards the end of September 1918,[90] thus leading to the postponement of the departure of the brigade. The two ships sent to Lagos had to leave without the brigade and proceeded to South Africa to collect reinforcements there. The Army Council finally put paid to the whole project when authorities in Nigeria were informed on 8 November 1918 that the troops would not be needed because of the sudden collapse of Turkey and the changed situation in the Middle East.[91] The 'WASPS' brigades however, continued to exist until the first day of January 1919, when the force was disbanded.[92]

DEMOBILISATION AND THE FUTURE OF THE
NIGERIA REGIMENT

The problem of demobilising the expanded Nigerian force was a difficult one, and the government deliberately set out to make the transition from military to civilian life as easy as possible. Nigeria was fortunate in having Lugard, who was attached to and sympathetic towards the African servicemen. General Cunliffe and Colonel Jenkins could also be relied on to be sympathetic towards the men in the Regiment. Convinced that the old pensions granted to soldiers were grossly inadequate and that the government must increase them, Colonel Jenkins asked for the minimum for a 'totally permanently' disabled soldier to be increased from 12s. a month to 15s, and for a 'partially disabled' soldier to receive a gratuity plus a small pension.[93] Walter Long wanted a 'permanently partially' disabled soldier to be offered the means of supporting himself by being taken into government employment and only when such employment could not be found or was not accepted by a man, should he be given a pension. Thus the pension awarded to such a man would cease if and when he entered government employment. The officers on the spot pointed out that since this rule could not be applied to disabled soldiers in receipt of pensions who obtained employment with commercial firms, this was bound to lead to some dangerous agitation by ex-soldiers working for the government, who would consider the government they fought for was the more niggardly employer. Cunliffe urged that 'no abatement should be made from the pension of a man permanently partially disabled on account of any employment subsequently found for him in the government service'.[94] Before a decision was reached a scheme formulated by the Governor-General of French West Africa for dealing with all soldiers disabled in the war reached Lugard. The scheme recommended that all African soldiers who had fought and had been disabled were to be given:

(a) a pension or gratuity based on their disability,
(b) surgical or medical assistance as may be necessary,
(c) subsistence allowance on a sliding scale based on cost of living in their districts.

Lugard argued that the provision for disabled soldiers made by Nigeria should not be on less generous scale than that awarded by the French. The Colonial Office approved the 'French' scheme put forward by Lugard, and communicated this to all Governors in British West Africa in order to achieve uniformity.[95] The terms for demobilisation and compensation for wounded soldiers, although not generous, were adequate. Those of them who needed it were given surgical equipment, and they were favoured by employment agencies, private or public. They continued to meet as a 'Veterans Association', but not to protest any grievances, for after all there were very few Nigerians at the time who had security of employment or regular pension as a source of income.

What could have helped the Nigerian soldier better was a proposal by Colonel Haywood, the new Inspector of the West African Frontier Force, to employ Nigerians permanently in Sierra Leone as the colonial garrison there because of the reputedly poor military quality of Sierra Leonians. While this seemed theoretically sound, Sir Hugh Clifford, the new Governor of Nigeria, had reservations. He pointed out that it would have been necessary to offer special rates of pay to Nigerians who would be permanently based in Sierra Leone, and this higher pay, Clifford felt, could result in disaffection among Nigerians who were based in Nigeria.[96] This was a lame excuse, but Clifford added:

> it would almost inevitably be argued that the Great War had so seriously depleted the forces of the Empire that the British government was ... compelled to recruit Nigerian soldiers in order to enable it to maintain its hold over its other African possessions. The impression of the weakness of the government and of its dependence upon local assistance which would thereby be conveyed, might very easily be attended by embarrassing consequences for this administration.[97]

In an uncharacteristic way Clifford used the bogey of contact with educated natives against the scheme:

> Freetown, its past and very recent history and the whole traditions of its Creole population which dates from the period of emancipation controversy when Zachary Macaulay was its well meaning but sentimental Governor, has on the West Coast a peculiar atmosphere of its own with which it is not at all desirable that considerable numbers of the virile population from whose ranks the bulk of the Nigeria Regiment is recruited should be allowed to become unnecessarily familiar.[98]

The Governor felt that Nigeria had borne her share of the burden[99] of the war and that her men should stay at home and help in the economic and material development of the country which was foremost in Clifford's mind. The proposal was therefore dropped and Sierra Leone was asked to make do with its supposedly poor soldiers.

In the war–time effort of Nigeria one can see that 'overseas' contribution was very largely inspired and pushed on a reluctant but realistic Lugard. His administration and the West African Frontier Force's officers realised the limitations of Nigerians, and generally shared Lugard's view in this respect. Lugard, in his cautious approach to war–time problems, tended to see Nigerian interests before imperial interests. He even courted insinuations of lack of fervour and patriotism for this (which must have been hard for him to take!). On the whole Lugard emerges as a more sympathetic character than the others, more humane and less aloof. The settling of the soldiers' grievances was most un-characteristic of Lugard; his 'softness' towards the soldiers illustrated the utter dependence of his administration on the loyalty of these men and also showed a sound understanding of the problems faced by a man who could be described as one of them.

Notes

1 C.O. 537/604, Memo submitted by Secretary of State for the Colonies, Andrew Bonar Law to the Cabinet, 18 Oct. 1915. Bonar Law stated that in spite of the 'large number of warlike natives ... Zulus, Matabeles, Basutos & Co. South of the Zambesi', the Union govern-ment said 'training of a large native force is unacceptable to the Dutch and English elements in South Africa.' The Governor-General of South Africa in August 1915 reported that the Union government was prepared to allow the formation of *one* battalion of Cape Coloureds to fight in East Africa and to raise *not* a fighting force, but a 'general transport and remounts service corps ... consisting of say 1,000 natives'. The Colonial Office rejected this proposal.

2 C.O. 445/35/57737, Bonar Law to Lugard, 14 Dec. 1915.

3 *Ibid.*

4 C.O. 445/35/57737, H. J. Read to War Office, 24 Dec. 1915.

5 C.O. 445/36/19325, Lugard to Colonial Office, 4 April 1916. When in April 1916 Lugard asked the War Office to supply him with 42 senior army officers to replace officers of the Nigeria Regiment invalided as a result of the Cameroons Campaign, the War Office replied that only 15 junior officers could be supplied.

6 *Ibid.*

7 Major-General Paul von Lettow-Vorbeck was born in Saarlouis, Germany, in 1870 to a father who was an Army General. Lettow-

Vorbeck joined the army at a young age like his father; he served with
the Imperial Army in China and in South West Africa during the
Herero rising, during which he lost an eye. He was appointed com-
mandant of German East African garrison in January 1914 when a
Colonel and was promoted Major-General during the First World
War. He became famous as the last German General to surrender.

8 Lt-Col Charles Hordern, *History of the Great War*: based on official
Documents. *Military Operations: East Africa*, i, *August 1914–
September 1916*, H.M.S.O., London, 1941, p. 519.

9 *Ibid.*, pp. 520–2.

10 Captain W. D. Downes, *With the Nigerians in German East Africa*,
Methuen, London, 1919, p. 31.

11 *Ibid.*, p. 32.

12 C.O. 583/46/23409, Colonial Office to Lugard (undated), May 1916.

13 *Ibid.*, General Charles Dobell's minute, 18 May 1916. To compare the
Nigeria Regiment with that of the Gold Coast was a bit unfair
because the Gold Coast had a considerable proportion of men who
had not been engaged in active operations since the two-weeks'
operation in Togoland in 1914; whereas the Nigerians almost to a
man were involved in the Cameroons Campaign. Secondly, the Gold
Coast Regiment had some inkling of their imminent departure to
East Africa and the Gold Coast Regiment still had most of its officer
rank intact. Only half the number of the Gold Coast Regiment
served in the Cameroons.

14 C.O. 583/46/26633, Lugard to Colonial Office, 17 May 1916.

15 C.O. 445/47/28875, E. Saint Christopher Stobart's (intelligence
officer, Nigeria Brigade to East Africa) report, enclosed in Boyle to
Milner, 12 April 1919.

16 C.O. 445/36/34694, Temple to Colonial Office, 22 July 1916.

17 C.O. 583/52/32665, Colonial Office to Lugard, 14 July 1916.

18 C.O. 445/36/34694, Temple to Colonial Office, 22 July 1916.

19 *Ibid.*

20 C.O. 445/37/42406, War Office to Colonial Office, 4 Sept. 1916.

21 C.O. 445/37/48999, War Office to Colonial Office, 13 Oct. 1916. The
relevant section of the W.A.F.F. ordinance that could be invoked
was Section 5a which states: 'It shall be lawful for the Governor to
order that the regiment or any part thereof shall be employed out of
and beyond the colony.'

22 C.O. 445/36/53161, Bonar Law to A. G. Boyle, 7 Nov. 1916.

23 C.O. 445/36/60721, Lugard to Bonar Law, 22 Nov. 1916.

24 C.O. 445/36/853, Lugard to Colonial Office, 14 Dec. 1916. Details of
the force that left for East Africa were as follows: 123 British officers,
5 medical officers, 70 British N.C.O.s, 7 Royal Army Medical Corps
N.C.O.s, 2,467 rank and file, 790 carriers, 2 African clerks, 5 dressers,
15 African telegraphists, 184 domestic servants; total 3,668.

25 Downes, *op. cit.*, p. 46.

26 C.O. 445/37/55218, War Office to Colonial Office, 10 Nov. 1916.

27 CAB 1/23/2, memo on steps taken to increase the supply of coloured
labour, Jan. 1917.

28 *The Times*, 26 July 1916.

29 *The Times*, 1 July 1916. A few M.P.s and others wrote to *The Times* editor urging the government to imitate the French.

30 C.O. 445/37/56748, Bonar Law to Lugard, 28 Nov. 1916.

31 C.O. 445/36/3520, Lugard to Walter Long, 27 Dec. 1916.

32 The Admiralty in conjunction with the War Office sent two officers to Nigeria in October 1916 to recruit 1,500 African ratings for Marine service in Mesopotamia. Recruiting was relatively easy since many mates had become jobless following the sale of government river boats and retrenchment in the Nigerian Marine department. The War Office bought the Governor's yacht *Ivy* and the India Office purchased the dredger *Quora* formerly used in Forcados by the Nigerian Marine, and with these two vessels in hand 500 'native marines' were sent to Mesopotamia in December 1916. See C.O. 583/50/844, Lugard to Colonial Office, 1 Dec. 1916.

33 C.O. 445/41/3895, B. B. Cubitt (Secretary, War Office) to Colonial Office, 20 Jan. 1917.

34 C.O. 445/37/59718, Strachey's minute, 23 Dec. 1916.

35 C.O. 445/41/3895, War Office to Colonial Office, 20 Jan. 1917. The Foreign Office received a note from the French Government challenging the legality of British planned recruiting in the Cameroons, and the French pointed out that they had protested on this ground against German recruitment of Poles, Serbs, etc., in areas occupied by the German army.

36 C.O. 445/38/2032, Harding's minute, 11 Jan. 1917.

37 *Ibid.*, Sir George Fiddes's minute, 12 Jan. 1917.

38 C.O. 445/42/3075, Dobell to Major Beattie, 4 Jan. 1917.

39 C.O. 445/42/27100, Haywood's report, enclosed in War Office to Colonial Office, 24 May 1917.

40 *Ibid.*

41 *Ibid.* Col. Haywood gave the figures of 'soldiering tribes' in Nigeria as follows:

Tribes	Population	Total No. of Males	Total No. of Males Fit and Available
Hausa	3,489,000	1,744,500	28,958
Yoruba	2,550,000	1,275,000	21,165
Fulani	1,000,000	500,000	8,300
Nupe	700,000	350,000	5,810
Kanuri	600,000	300,000	4,980
Ezza (Ibo-speaking people in Okigwe	130,000	65,000	1,079
TOTAL	8,469,000	4,234,500	70,292

The figures of 'non-fighting tribes' who could be used as carriers were as follows:

Tribes	Population	Total No. of Males	Fit and Available
Ibo	3,280,000	1,640,000	27,224
Ibibio	479,000	239,500	3,975
TOTAL	3,759,000	1,879,500	31,199

42 C.O. 445/38/36411, Edward J. Cameron to W. Long, 10 June 1917.

43 C.O. 445/39/31551, Clifford's minute, 29 March 1917.

44 *Ibid.*, Major Montray Read of W.A.F.F. minuted on 29 May 1917 that a bonus of ten shillings and five shillings was given to recruiting chiefs in the Gold Coast and Nigeria respectively for every recruit brought in; he wrote that the chiefs forced many men to present themselves as volunteers.

45 *Ibid.*, minute by C. H. Harper (Assistant Colonial Secretary, Gold Coast), 31 May 1917.

46 C.O. 445/42/27100, Haywood's Report, 2 May 1917.

47 C.O. 445/40/3060, Long to Lugard, 26 Jan. 1917.

48 C.O. 445/42/27100, Sir George Fiddes's minute, 14 June 1917.

49 *Ibid.*, C. B. Smith (Katsina), undated private letter to Charles Strachey, June 1917.

50 C.O. 445/40/44199, Lugard to Colonial Office, 9 Aug. 1917.

51 C.O. 445/41/2737, Admiralty to Colonial Office, 13 Jan. 1917.

52 C.O. 445/41/9123, Walter Ellis minute, 19 Feb. 1917.

53 *Ibid.*

54 C.O. 445/41/10273, War Office to Colonial Office, 2 April 1917. At this time General Hoskin's (the G.O.C.) Carrier Corps alone numbered the staggering figure of 70,000.

55 C.O. 445/44/18468, Major G. W. Moran (Training Officer, Nigerian Regiment) Report for 1917 published in Kaduna, 1 Jan. 1918.

56 The Tiv lived (and still live) in the Valley of the Benue river. They are a virile people of 'Bantu' stock. British administrators used to see them as a primitive, disorganised group of people with no centralised forms of government. The Tiv during this period went about their farms virtually naked and because of all these unsavoury attributes compared with the Hausa-Fulani with whom they were grouped in the Northern provinces, the Tiv presented a bad picture and their sudden discovery as good fighters during the war surprised the administrators, since Tiv society in spite of about 17 years (i.e., 1900–1917) of official British administration in Northern Nigeria remained virtually untouched.

57 C.O. 445/44/18468, Major Moran's Report, 1 Jan. 1918.

58 C.O. 445/40/17933, Resident of Yola enclosed in Lugard to Long, 13 March 1917.

59 C.O. 445/40/22602, Lugard to Long, 9 April 1917.

60 C.O. 583/81/1273, Captain W. B. Hellard of the War Office to Charles Strachey, 1 Dec. 1917.

61 C.O. 445/42/61983, War Office to Colonial Office, 17 Dec. 1917.

62 General Paul von Lettow-Vorbeck, *East African Campaigns*, New York, 1957, p. 164.

63 C.O. 445/44/24800, Cunliffe, Lagos, 3 March 1918.

64 W. D. Downes, *op. cit.*, p. 90.

65 C.O. 445/40/56471, Lugard to Long, 12 Oct. 1917.

66 Edwin P. Hoyt Jr, *The Germans Who Never Lost: the Story of the Könisberg*, New York, 1968, p. 229.

67 Leonard Mosley, *Duel for Kilimanjaro: an account of the East African Campaign 1914–1918*, Weidenfeld & Nicolson, London, 1963, pp. 145–6.

68 Hoyt, *op. cit.*, p. 234. Von Lettow-Vorbeck had just captured one Portuguese gun, 37 machine-guns, 1,070 rifles, 280,000 rounds of ammunition and 40 rounds of artillery ammunition.

69 Brian Gardner, *On the Kilimanjaro: the Bizarre Story of the First World War in East Africa*, Macrae Smith & Co., Philadelphia, 1963, p. 265. Von Lettow-Vorbeck had fought against or tied down an army of at least 200,000 in East Africa (see CAB/24/4 'C' 182, Lord Curzon, 5 Dec. 1917, circulated to War Cabinet). Von Lettow-Vorbeck had caused an expenditure of £72,000,000 by the British alone to say nothing of that incurred by Portugal and Belgium. As for the British and their colonial troops they had fought one of the most depressing of campaigns, following an elusive enemy. The official British casualty figures were 62,220 (not including those admitted to hospitals through diseases) of whom 48,328 died. These do not include the thousands of deaths among carriers. The largest British force was the King's African Rifles – having 22 battalions and a total strength of 35,424 on 1 Nov. 1918.

70 C.O. 445/47/28875, E. S. C. Stobart to Milner, 12 April 1919.

71 Sir Charles Lucas (ed.), *The Empire at War*, iv, *Africa*, first published by Royal Colonial Institute, London, 1921, reprinted by Oxford University Press, London, 1924, pp. 137–48. See also Commandant J. Buhrer, *L'Afrique Orientale Allemande et la Guerre de 1914–1918*, Paris, 1922, p. 360.

72 C.O. 445/47/28875, Stobart, enclosed in Boyle to Milner, 12 April 1919. The number of Nigerians that returned in March 1918 was 5,760 rank and file, 113 officers and 128 British N.C.O.s. 37 British officers were killed, about 1,000 Nigerians lost their lives. No statistics exist on the number of carriers who died out of about 6,000 recruited and sent to East Africa. See C.O. 445/44/31456, Lugard to Long, 5 April 1918.

73 Downes, *op. cit.*, pp. 288–9. For a German account of the East African Campaign, see Kontreadmiral von C. Raeder, *Der Krieg zur See 1914–1918*. Kreuzerkrieg, Bd. 2. Berlin, Verlag von E. S. Mittler & Sohn, 1923.

74 C.O. 445/41/60110, H. J. Read to Secretary, War Office, 6 Dec. 1917.

75 *Ibid.*

76 C.O. 445/45/7738, B. B. Cubitt (Permanent Under-Secretary of State) War Office to Colonial Office, 10 Feb. 1918.

77 C.O. 445/44/26065, M. Fourn, Lt-Governor, Dahomey, to Lugard,

2 March 1918, a French Government decree of 14 Jan. 1918 made military service compulsory for all males between the ages of 18 and and 35 in French Africa. M. Fourn asked Lugard to co-operate by recruiting in Nigeria simultaneously when recruiting was on in Dahomey.

78 C.O. 445/45/7738, Cubitt to Colonial Office, 10 Feb. 1918.
79 C.O. 445/44/21458, Cunliffe to War Office, 8 Aug. 1918.
80 C.O. 445/44/23299, Major Beattie's minute, 24 March 1918.
81 C.O. 445/45/37091, Cubitt, War Office to Colonial Office, 31 July 1918.
82 *Ibid.*
83 C.O. 445/45/40594, Long to Lugard, 22 Aug. 1918.
84 C.O. 445/45/44474, Lugard to Long, 11 Sept. 1918.
85 *Ibid.*
86 *Ibid.*
87 C.O. 445/45/44474, Lugard to Long, 11 Sept. 1918.
88 C.O. 445/44/53314, Col. Jenkins, enclosed in Lugard to Long, 8 Oct. 1918.
89 *Ibid.*
90 C.O. 445/47/13359, Lugard to Long, 1 Oct. 1918.
91 C.O. 445/44/5604, Long to Boyle, 22 Nov. 1918.
92 *Ibid.*
93 C.O. 445/44/56760, Lugard to Long, 5 Nov. 1918 enclosing Major Beattie's and Colonel Jenkins's recommendation.
94 *Ibid.*, General Cunliffe's minute, 31 Oct. 1918.
95 C.O. 445/44/56760, Colonial Office to Governors of all British West African possessions, 8 Nov. 1918.
96 C.O. 445/51/29802, Sir Hugh Clifford to Lord Milner, 13 May 1920.
97 *Ibid.*
98 *Ibid.*
99 Altogether, Nigeria during the war provided 17,000 combatants, 1,800 gun carriers, 35,000 transport carriers, 350 motor drivers, 800 inland water transport men, 500 railway men, postmen, policemen and artisans; see Sir Charles Lucas, *op. cit.*, p. 130.

9 The final partition of the Cameroons

The Allies had no intention of returning to Germany any of her conquered colonies unless forced to do so as a result of an inconclusive war. This was a natural attitude in the climate of the time. Germany was seen as being responsible for the war which had cost the Allies so much in the expenditure of blood and money. The fear of Germany using her colonies as bases for offensive operations in a future war was entertained by many Allied leaders. The potentialities of African territories, in terms of both human and material resources, which Germany might exploit in her pursuit of world hegemony also made the Allies very adamant in their determination to deprive Germany of any advantage in the event of a future confrontation. The British also felt that a return of the Cameroons to Germany would affect the British image in Nigeria, while the French demanded the retention of the Cameroons on the grounds that her overseas possessions had proved to be such great assets in human and material terms during the world crisis.

Since the provisional partition of the Cameroons, Britain and France had gradually come to accept the fact that each power would keep its occupied territory after the war. Historically, Britain in a victorious war had always satisfied her territorial ambitions by annexing the colonies of her enemies. In the Cameroons, this position was rationalised by various arguments. The British argued that the campaign in the Cameroons concerned Nigeria more than any other West African colony and that its successful conclusion was naturally regarded by Nigerian soldiers, chiefs and emirs as due to their valour, and that to return the Cameroons was to undermine British prestige in Nigeria. It was stated: 'the chiefs are accustomed to seeing the conqueror take over the land of the conquered and the general opinion would no doubt be that whatever we might say we had not beaten the Germans',[1] if this were not done. It was pointed out that from the German point of view 'the operations in Africa can only be regarded as a military diversion of the most successful character in which very limited German forces, cut off from all hope of support have detained far larger Allied forces'.[2]

Final repartition of the Cameroons

Furthermore, the British Government assumed Germany would strive at world hegemony again. Fighting in the German colonies had cost the British Empire such appreciable sacrifices and involved it in so prolonged a diversion of effort from the main theatre of war, that it was clearly an undesirable risk to incur similar sacrifices and difficulties in the conceivable event of a future war. Duala, the British were convinced, would be converted to a strong naval base to threaten the trade routes to South America and South Africa.[3] It was argued that the development of the resources of British tropical possessions would be the most important factor in that general increase of productive power after the war, and that this object would be frustrated if the military drain upon these colonies both arrested the development and swallowed up its resources. To guard against military expenditure in the colonies the Germans had to be removed from their colonial sanctuaries.

The British Government maintained that the German colonies could not be returned to Germany, on humanitarian grounds. Lord Curzon recalled the savagery and bloodshed connected with the name of Karl Peters and the treatment of the Hereros by von Trotha 'who massacred that unhappy people by thousands'. Such cruelties, it was alleged, had been repeated by the Germans during the war, so that to return to Germany her former colonies, 'with the added certainty of fearful vengeance that would be wreaked upon the wretched natives who have aided or abetted our cause', would result in 'a carnival of blood which would be inaugurated in every territory so restored'.[4]

The British Colonial Office was still hoping that the provisional partition of 1916 would be subject to revision. In 1917 the Colonial Office laid claim to Duala on the grounds that,

> the capture of Duala was effected by British forces and it was occupied by British forces for 17 months ... our prestige must have suffered by our withdrawal, but if as a result of the provisional partition and arrangements in other parts of the world the British government could not obtain Duala and the surrounding districts, then minor adjustments of the Anglo-French boundary in the Cameroons are desirable.[5]

It was considered necessary that Britain should obtain the Mandara emirate because of its historical connection with Borno and so that the Mandara mountains could serve for a considerable distance as a natural barrier between British and French territories. Officials at the Colonial Office intended to put claims for the western valleys of the Mandara mountains, the country around Garua, and the rest of the emirate of Kontscha, Lere and Dodo, all of which were formerly under the Emir of Yola and were detached from his dominion by the Anglo-German treaty of 1893. Britain was also to demand from the French the retrocession of the remainder of the old Dschang district so that tribes would not be split unnecessarily by the provisional line drawn straight across this district.[6]

The British however conceded the fact that from the point of view of political and strategical geography, the retention of the Cameroons was much less important to themselves than to the French, for whom it would mean a great improvement in the configuration of their territories to the north of the Congo. It was recognised that Duala 'is the natural port for the future development not only of the Cameroons but of the French territory further East, viz: Ubangi and Wadai', and that the French regarded the possession of Duala 'as essential and as a matter on which there could be no compromise'.[7] The British noted that nothing had happened to change the French attitude to the port. The sub-committee on territorial changes arrived at the conclusion that Britain could not lay claim to Duala unless she was prepared to extend her claim to the 'back country for which it is the natural entry'. It was clear that the French meant to retain a large part of the Cameroons 'as an offset' to what Britain had secured in East Africa and South-West Africa. The sub-committee added:

> while we may be prepared to acquiesce in the French intention to retain the whole of the area which they now occupy ... the pro-visional nature of the partition should be postulated in order if possible to secure some *quid pro quo* elsewhere in return for our eventual acquiescence in its becoming permanent.[8]

To show what premium Britain placed on the Cameroons, it was recommended that in the event of an unsatisfactory peace, Togoland should be surrendered first to the Germans, then the Cameroons and perhaps part of East Africa, but that Britain should retain 'a strip of continuous territory between the present Belgian frontier and a line drawn between Lake Victoria and the head of Lake Nyasa'.[9] Apparently the dream of Cape to Cairo was not dead! It is interesting to note that the three big powers in Africa – Germany, Britain and France – always thought in terms of contiguity of colonial territories in their territorial aims during the war, though each power criticised the other for so thinking, only to use the arguments of its adversary to advance reasons why some territories should be in her sphere and not in the others!

It was believed in official British circles that Germany could easily be persuaded to relinquish her rights to her colonies in the interests of peace. The arguments were usually that:

> the German colonies represent no great historical tradition ... the

loss of the whole of them would leave less permanent resentment in the mind of the German people than the loss of either Alsace or Posen ... it would also be the death blow to a policy with which the present emperor's name is associated but no serious or lasting wound to the national life of Germany.[10]

This was of course not entirely true, the age-long *Drang nach Osten* represented a sort of colonial tradition and experience, though of a different type. This argument also failed to take into account that it was not only Kaiser Wilhelm II who was interested in colonies; quite a large section of the thinking public recognised the importance of colonies as sources of essential tropical materials that industrialised Germany could not do without. However, British policy-makers were aware of the enormous propaganda for German imperial ambitions in Africa which was being circulated in Germany at this time. One, which seems to have been the most comprehensive (Emil Zimmermann's *Das deutsche Kaiserreich Mittelafrika als Grundlage einer neuen deutschen Weltpolitik*) was discussed by the war cabinet.[11] This book gave the British Government an idea of current colonial ambitions in Germany. What shocked the cabinet more than any other thing was that Emil Zimmermann argued that a central African empire was needed by Germany to destroy British hegemony in the world. Curzon noted that Professor Hans Delbruck, one of Germany's leading historians and publicists and the successor of von Treitschke in the editorial chair of the great monthly periodical the *Preussische Jahrbucher*, was quoted as saying that Germany would demand and receive from the Allies:

> the whole of Central Africa, Senegambia, Sierra Leone, the Gold Coast and Dahomey, Nigeria ... the Cameroons, San Thome and Principe, the French and Belgian Congo, Katanga and Northern Rhodesia, Nyasaland, Mozambique and Delagoa Bay, Madagascar, Zanzibar, British East Africa, Uganda, Ponte Delgrado (Azores) and Porto Grande (Cape Verde Islands).

Lord Curzon added:

> it is difficult to find in the above catalogue what is left to anyone else, apart from North Africa which would be reserved for the next war except the Transvaal and the Cape which are no doubt to be handed over to a reconstituted and friendly Boer Republic.[12]

Lord Curzon pointed out to the War Cabinet that the objects of the Germans from all available sources were:

(a)   recovery of the whole of their colonial possessions,
(b)   destruction of rival powers especially Britain,
(c)   annexation of British, French, Portuguese and Belgian colonies, and
(d)   the creation out of these spoils of a great 'central African German Dominion – an India in Africa',
(e)   the creation of a huge black army, 'an army of offense and aggression against the rest of Africa'.

Curzon was of the opinion that this 'black army' would be a threat to civilisation itself. He warned that for Britain to acquiesce in the return of German colonies would amount to 'committing voluntary suicide'. The future of world peace, he felt, demanded the exclusion of Germany from Africa, but to those who wanted internationalisation of Africa he said 'international administration would only be a nursery of international quarrel and the prelude to greater disaster'.[13]

The Germans themselves were against internationalisation of the colonies. The writings of the *Mittelafrika* supporters undermined such an attempt at compromise, and Dr Solf, the German Secretary of State for the Colonies, was quoted as saying in Leipzig in 1918:

> the idea of internationalisation ... with a joint administration by European Protecting States is propagated by a certain philanthropic circle in England. The most emphatic opponents of such internationalisation are likely to arise in England itself. But quite apart from that, an organization of this kind would be feasible only if it were supported by a feeling of solidarity in the European states. Such a feeling of solidarity will no doubt arise in the form of an aspiration out of the ruins of this war ... before one lays such a stupendous task as that of ruling overseas territories in harmonious cooperation upon belligerents of today ... the international consciousness would have to have been developed and confirmed in Europe by the actual practice of international dealings. We must therefore hold fast to the principle which has hitherto prevailed in colonization – a partition of the tropical countries amongst the civilized European states, in the Treaty of Peace there can only be the question of a fresh partition.[14]

Since the publication by *Pravda* of the 'secret treaties after the 1917 Bolshevik revolution', documents selected so as to show the war as a struggle between various capitalist powers for the repartition of the world and its markets, the socialists of Western Europe began to agitate for a peace without annexation. The British

Labour Party issued a series of press releases, one of which announced:

> We believe that the formula of no annexation applies more absolutely to Tropical Africa than to other parts of the world, because there is less scope here for the principle of self-determination. . . .
>
> We see no evidence that German administration in Tropical Africa has been so much worse than that of other European Governments that the Peace Conference would be justified in singling it out for special treatment. But since a comparison of the merits of the various European administrations is highly invidious, and cannot in the nature of the case be made with the precision which the gravity of such an inquiry demands, we believe that the Peace Conference will be better advised to place all Tropical Africa under a uniform international control.[15]

Arthur Henderson, representing Labour in the War Cabinet, wasted no time in telling his colleagues in the cabinet that his party would not tolerate an annexationist policy, but according to Lloyd George no one paid any attention to his views.[16] The day of 'democratic control' of British foreign policy was yet to come.

The government had of course anticipated this change of trend in opinion. In a memorandum presented to the War Cabinet on 2 January 1918, Sir George Fiddes of the Colonial Office pointed out that it would be seen that as the war drew to an end, there would be a 'mobilization of all forces' in England and abroad which favoured the return of German colonies. This force he said would be made up of 'German agents, pro-Germans, pacifists and partisans of peace without annexation, sentimentalists who call for magnanimity in the hour of victory, moderates who in all circumstances favour compromise, who will invite us to beware of humiliating Germany by stripping her of her cherished possessions'.[17] Sir George felt that 'all these will form a combination whose strength it would be unwise to ignore'. Since the 'Southern dominions' would not give up German colonies which they had conquered, and since South Africa was interested in the future of German East Africa, which she helped to conquer and which might threaten her security if given back to Germany, Fiddes felt that the 'battle of compromise' would centre upon Togoland and the Cameroons. He added that the experience of the war had led everybody to revise estimates of the value of the 'coloured soldier' and consequently handing over the Cameroons and Togoland to Germany was an unnecessary risk. He commented:

Formerly we regarded the coloured soldier as a negligible quantity in European warfare or against European troops armed with all the resources of civilization. ... Likewise we held to the comfortable belief that only British officers were capable of getting full value out of native troops ... we can now discard both beliefs ... our Nigerian troops in assaulting difficult positions in the Cameroons border behaved in a way that would have been commendable in the case of British infantry ... coloured German troops have put up 3 years fight which compels our admiration, against all forces that we could bring against them and have shown in depressing circumstances a staunchness and loyalty to their leaders that should give us food for thought.

When the Germans were leaving the Cameroons they told the Africans there:

we are leaving now, but we shall return soon ... no amount of explanation would make a native understand the lofty motives that had inspired our action, with them it is the vanquished and not the victor that disgorges ... the Cameroons ... are a proved menace to Nigeria ... the strategic importance of the colony is that it is posted on the flank of our Cape and within striking distance of our West African trade route.[18]

The debate on what should be done with the colonies of 'un-regenerate Germany' continued both in and outside government circles during 1918. When German leaders began to realise that the war could not be won, in October 1918, they began echoing Woodrow Wilson's 'peace without annexation' and the fifth of the Fourteen Points which provided for 'a free, open minded and absolutely impartial adjustment of all colonial claims' based on the principle that the 'interests of the populations concerned must have equal weight with the equitable claims of the government whose title is to be determined'.[19] This was an elastic principle which could be stretched to cover the ambitions of opposing nations. The British prime minister had also repeatedly said that the German colonies were held at the disposal 'of a conference whose decision must have primary regard to the interests of the Native inhabitants of such colonies'.[20] In view of this statement both Britain and Germany saw in Wilson's declaration what suited them. The Germans contended that the stiff resistance of their African soldiers both in Cameroons and particularly in East Africa was sufficient evidence to show that the colonies would choose to remain under Germany. Jan Smuts argued that since

Africans lived in tribal groups, their chiefs and councils were competent to speak on behalf of the African population, and therefore added: 'the general principle of self-determination is therefore as applicable in their cases as in those of occupied European populations'.[21] Smuts was saying this because like Walter Long[22] he believed that given a chance to choose whom their masters should be, the Africans would most surely prefer British tutelage to German.

The only senior minister who was more conciliatory to Germany during this time was A. J. Balfour, since he was opposed to Britain retaining any colony for 'territorial reasons'. He suggested that all German soldiers should be 'surrendered to the Allies or placed under some form of condominium from which Germany may be, but need not be excluded'.[23] Balfour was immediately attacked for his 'soft' approach to Germany by Walter Long and Lord Curzon. Lord Curzon did not believe in satisfying the scruples or placating the jealousies of Britain's enemies as he alleged Balfour was doing. As to the internationalisation implied in Balfour's proposal, Lord Curzon said:

> International government has never been known to develop an international conscience, the Congo, the Sudan and other classical illustrations are a testimony to that melancholy truism.[24]

Lord Curzon wondered how this idea of international control could be reconciled with the British policy of imperial preference which by then had just been proclaimed. Walter Long was emphatic in his stand against any concession to Germany:

> I regard the refusal to allow the German colonies to return to Germany as absolutely vital to the retention of our African Empire. . . . I believe this war with all its glorious sacrifices will have been fought in vain and that future generations will never forgive us, if we allow the pen to lose what the sword has won.[25]

Long favoured American administration of East Africa, if possible, in order to please those who were against British annexation and those like Edwin Montagu and Winston Churchill who felt British territorial claims should not be pressed to such a point as to alienate the sympathies of the United States.[26] Long was however still insistent on retaining part of the Cameroons under British administration in the interest of British prestige in Nigeria.[27] Edwin Montagu advised the War Cabinet that British opposition to the return of German colonies should be based on 'the gross mismanagement of these colonies by Germans in the past', and he hoped President Wilson would be persuaded to see the question from the British point of view once it was based on this idealistic basis, which could provide 'an effective reply to charges of capitalism ... monopolism and imperialism' which were current and widely believed slogans of the time.[28]

The 'evidence' of the moral incapacity of the Germans to rule over non-European peoples was provided by official as well as non-official publications such as Evans Lewin's *Germans and Africa*, in which Germans were said to be singularly unfit to guide 'weaker races' towards higher civilisation. Lewin denounced German policy in Africa as:

> the mailed fist methods and sledge-hammer proceedings of the military. The unimaginative operations of the bureaucratic officials ... the dry scientific investigations of learned professors who have wandered over the German colonies in search of anthropological measurements ... and above all the entire disregard of native manners and rights have produced a deep resentment amongst the native races that has too often resulted in revolt and has sometimes led to their almost complete annihilation.

He charged the Germans for having raised their 'colonial system upon a foundation of blood'.[29] Other writers like John H. Harris of the Anti-Slavery and Aborigines' Protection Society, author of *Germany's Lost Colonial Empire* published in 1917, attacked the Germans for their wickedness to Africans; Sir Harry Johnston, the veteran African explorer and administrator, wrote several articles of the same nature. All these, reflecting official propaganda,[30] had a profound effect on the British public, which was not even in a mood to be sceptical of official propaganda.

This propaganda barrage also had its effect on neutrals and the 'impartial', 'associated' United States. Wilson, in spite of himself, became caught in the web of Allied propaganda, declaring in a speech in Paris on 14 February 1919:

> it has been one of the many distressing revelations of recent years that the great power which has just been happily defeated placed intolerable burdens and injustices upon the helpless people of some of the colonies which it annexed to itself, that its interest was rather to possess their land for European purposes and not to enjoy their confidence that mankind might be lifted to the next level in those places. Now the world expressing its conscience in law says there is

an end to that, our conscience will be applied to this thing, states will be selected which have already shown that they have a conscience in this matter and under their tutelage the helpless peoples of the world will come into a new light and into a new hope.[31]

By such declarations Germany's moral incapacity for colonial administration was accepted, and the Allies, especially Britain, manipulated American public opinion into believing that this was the major reason why Germany was being deprived of her colonies.[32]

The case for outright annexation had been weakened by Wilson's self-determination manifesto and the Bolshevik propaganda which became strident in 1918. In the midst of all the conflicting proposals General Smuts's idea of a mandate became useful, and the '*pro forma* internationalisation envisaged in the mandate system appeared a satisfactory answer'.[33] The mandate idea almost succeeded in reconciling two irreconcilable proposals – annexation and internationalisation. In spite of the resolution of the problem of what system of rule to adopt in the conquered colonies, the problem of who the mandatories should be remained undecided.

President Wilson's idea was that the German colonies should be held as 'sacred trusts of civilization' by the small and neutral countries of Europe, but his idealism was checkmated by the imperialistic ambitions of people like Lord Milner and Henri Simon, who continued to negotiate for the partition of German colonies in West Africa behind the back of the American President. The British, according to Milner and Smuts, were prepared to share the white man's burden with the United States by asking her to take over one of the German colonies;[34] preferably it should be either the Cameroons or Togoland, hotly disputed between the French and the British, but certainly not East Africa.[35] The British found a sympathetic listener in George Louis Beer, the colonial historian and adviser to Wilson on colonial questions. After sounding out French opinions, Beer advised Wilson to accept in theory, American willingness to undertake a mandate for the Cameroons.[36] But this effort was immediately frustrated by Henri Simon, who resisted the idea that the future of the Cameroons could be settled by Franco–American bargaining.

The officials on the local scene were not inactive. According to the British Consul in Dakar the Governor of French West Africa was pushing the idea of a radical repartition of West Africa, which would give the Gambia and Sierra Leone to France in exchange

for Dahomey, and Togoland to the British for a French acquisition
of Portuguese Guinea and Liberia; in this way British territory
would stretch uninterrupted from the Gold Coast to Nigeria,
while of course France would annex the whole of the Cameroons.[37]
This was an interesting proposition though not a new one. This
idea had been put forward by the British Colonial Office before
the provisional partition, and the Gambia had been the subject
of bargaining since the early nineteenth century. The only new
thing in this French proposal was the inclusion of French annexation of Liberia and Portuguese Guinea. The French Colonial
Minister apparently was not aware of this plan, for it was never
discussed with the British. Sir Hugh Clifford, the new Governor
of Nigeria, wrote home to say 'French rule in West Africa is in
even worse odour among the natives than was that of the Germans
before 1914'. Sir Hugh complained that the French were using
force to silence opposition in conquered German colonies and
that French officials in the Cameroons were calling on chiefs
there to sign declarations of loyalty.[38] The British Consul in
Duala also reported that the chiefs were refusing to comply,
saying they would rather have German rule than French. The
Consul even went further and accused the French of locking up
King Akua of Duala and his brother until they died in jail because
they refused to co-operate. When the chiefs called on the Consul
he told them not to sign anything and that 'everything would
have to be settled at home'.[39] This brought sharp comments from
the officials at home, who could not understand the 'clumsiness'
of their men on the spot. Charles Strachey minuted:

> I am afraid it is impossible for us to depart from the agreement with
> the French on our own initiative, nor can we put forward claims
> based on grounds of this kind ... we have no *locus standi* at Duala
> and unless Mr. Holden is very careful he will get himself into
> trouble with the French. ... I should not be surprised if we get a
> complaint from the French to the effect that the loyal ardour of the
> Duala chiefs is being checked by a British agent who is dissuading
> them from signing addresses and testifying their devotion to
> France. ...[40]

Another official minuted: 'I fear we cannot hope to take into the
British sphere all the peoples in the world who would doubtless
like to enter it.'[41]

The business interests joined in the opposition to British policies
on the partition of Togoland and the Cameroons. In January 1919

the Association of West African Merchants wrote to the Foreign Office drawing its attention to a press conference given in Paris on 28 January 1919 by M. Simon, during which he said France was going to claim complete sovereignty over Togoland and the Cameroons.[42] The French minister based his claim on the grounds that the Cameroons had been captured from the Germans almost exclusively by French troops. The Association was furious that no member of the British Government had protested against or contested this palpably false statement. They went on to say that it would be a betrayal of trust if the African population was not given the chance of choosing who should be their masters. They said, 'if left to them [the Cameroons] the major portion of the colony would fall under British administration'.[43] What the merchants failed to realise was that in spite of their interests (which were considerable in the Cameroons, where the French had no trading concerns before the war), the home government had become so saturated with captured Turkish and German possessions that the Cameroons was merely a convenient area where the French could be accommodated.

The French also had in Henri Simon an ambitious minister of the colonies, and he was no doubt following the wave of anglophobia which began to sweep through the French press from 1919 onwards, because of the conflicting colonial or territorial interests all over the world. Some of the newspapers called for the retrocession of Mauritius to France and another published an article on 'L'Angleterre contre les droits des peuples' and accused Britain of indifference to the rights of millions of Egyptians, Indians, Persians and Irishmen.[44] They went to the extent of saying that it was only France that was interested in the League of Nations while Britain pursued a new policy of imperialism which was designed to destroy the League of Nations and the treaty of peace, which they accused Britain of treating as a *chiffon de papier*.[45] Others were less subdued, and asked for unilateral annexation of the Cameroons following what they called the example of Britain in East Africa; they lamented that France had bled to death on the Western Front just to replace German hegemony with *l'imperialisme britannique*.[46] Although the press might not have reflected French official views, yet ministers could not ignore such comments coming from *La Presse Coloniale*, which regarded itself as 'organe de défense des intérêts coloniaux et du commerce extérieur et colonial de la France'.

When Lord Milner met M. Henri Simon and M. Duchene (Director of the French Colonial Office) on 6 March 1919 to discuss the eventual partition of the Cameroons and Togoland, M. Simon said his government would be found very accommodating in the Cameroons since France in any case had nine-tenths of the territory, but that he could not adopt quite the same policy on Togoland.[47]

M. Simon desired, generally speaking, the acceptance of the 1916 provisional partition in the Cameroons as final except that he still wanted Britain to cede a piece of territory near Dschang to them because it would be needed in the future extension to Garua of the railway running northwards to Bare, and the French said Dschang would be on this route. The British *desiderata* were stated to be readjustment of the boundary in the extreme south so as to allow the frontier to coincide with the mouth of the Mungo river and then to run from there across to the Bimbia flats. As regards the provisional boundary, it was pointed out that since the line had been hurriedly drawn it would be necessary to make a good many adjustments, for which a boundary commission would be required.

The experts on both sides then set out to work out in detail where the boundary should be. The British said they wanted the entire German Borno, a strip of which was left in the French sphere by the 1916 line, as well as the Emirate of Mandara. The British laid claim to the remainder of the Emirates of Kontscha, Lere and Dodo which the provisional partition cut off from the rest of the districts and left in the French sphere. In exchange for these areas the British authorities were willing to agree that the whole of the Emirate of Banyo, part of which was assigned to the British in 1916, should go to France. The French agreed that the entire German Borno (Dikwa) should go to Britain, but refused the British request for Mandara Emirate, because they said the road from the south to Mora passed through Mandara Emirate cutting it into two parts; the British could have a third of the Emirate which was west of this road.[48] This road, in its southern section, cut through Meiha and Holma, and left small pieces of Zumu and Malau to Britain; which were provisionally united with Yola in 1916. The French turned down completely any idea of Britain's securing the former Adamawa possessions of the Lamido of Yola. In the south the French after much persuasion gave Britain the Mungo river, which formed a most valuable means of transport between the coast and the up-country plantations in the British sphere; the French, however, secured most of Kontscha Emirate and Dschang District.[49]

Lloyd George had in May 1919 proposed that France should become the Mandatory for the Cameroons subject to an arrangement between France and Great Britain for a readjustment between the Cameroons and Nigeria.[50] This arrangement was rejected then because M. Simon felt it would cause the French some inconvenience owing to the fact that a part of the Cameroons would pass under the direct and unrestricted sovereignty of the British Empire.[51] There was sense in this argument; the British wanted cleverly to annex the 'little bit of the Cameroons' (some 35,000 square miles or about one-ninth of the whole colony, containing about one-sixth of the population) – while the French were to be 'saddled' with administration of the remaining part of the territory as a Mandate. A compromise was reached by a declaration that in Togoland and the Cameroons, 'France and Great Britain shall make a joint recommendation to the League of Nations as to their future', which meant that even as late as May 1919 it remained unclear whether these two colonies would be put under the mandate system. However, Lord Milner and Henri Simon signed in London on 10 July 1919[52] a declaration that recommended the adoption of the boundary worked out by the experts of the two Colonial Offices. Local delimitation by officials from Nigeria and the French sphere of the Cameroons was carried out and finished by the end of January 1921.[53] The Cameroons was not put under the mandate system until 20 July 1922,[54] when the British and French spheres were assigned to their respective administering powers as mandates in the 'B' category. In this way the partition of the Cameroons was given the sanction of international law, whereas in actual fact the mandates were nothing more than concealed annexation. Article 9 of the terms of the Mandate, practically said as much:

> the Mandatory shall ... be at liberty to apply his Laws to the territory under the Mandate subject to the modifications required by local conditions and to constitute the territory into a customs, fiscal or administrative Union or Federation with the adjacent territories under his sovereignty or control provided always that the measures adopted to that end do not infringe the provisions of the Mandate.[55]

That the mandate idea was moralistic rationalisation for the traditional concept of imperial expansion is revealed by L. S. Amery's words:

> the great thing to my mind is to make Mandatory occupation as near as possible to the ordinary occupation of territories in Africa which has taken place by arrangement between powers. We ought in fact to treat the Mandate principle simply as an extension of occupation by agreement, and not really as setting up a new type of sovereignty or anything implying even the shadow of an international government.[56]

This was precisely what happened in both the British and French spheres; the two pieces of the Cameroons, north and south of the Benue river were administered as part of the neighbouring Nigerian group of provinces, whilst the French sphere gradually became part of their Equatorial African possessions.

The partition of the Cameroons brought to an end the process which began in the 1880s, and demonstrated in no small way the extent to which Africa had been used in European diplomacy before and during the war. Britain conceded most of France's requests in the Cameroons because of her desire to have a preponderant position in East and South Africa as well as the Middle East – a policy dictated by her world-wide security arrangements which necessitated keeping the trade routes to the East open at all times. In accommodating France on generous terms in the Cameroons, Britain did not have much to fear from France, which was not an aspiring naval power, as Germany had been.

The Cameroons partition did not got down well with the Nigerians and the British officials on the spot. Lugard felt the Mandatory power should have been made to accept that 'in all former territories where any arbitrary boundary has been fixed since the year 1885, intersecting tribal units as well as defined and fairly homologous territory under the rule of a recognised chief, the original boundaries shall be restored'.[57] He was no doubt thinking of Yola when he suggested this modification in the terms of the mandate. The National Congress of British West Africa meeting in Accra in 1920 condemned 'the partitioning of Togoland between the English and the French, and the handing over of the Cameroons to the French government without consulting . . . the people in the matter'.[58] The Emir of Yola could not conceal his resentment when he met Sir Hugh Clifford in October 1919. When the Emir challenged him on the partition of Cameroons, Clifford told him that owing to the invasion of France by the

Germans, the French had suffered much material damage and that the King of England had recommended that the French should be compensated in the Cameroons. The Emir asked why the French were not compensated in another part of the world but were given the territories of his forefathers, which had been promised him by British officials during the war. Clifford had to break off the discussion by presenting the Emir with the insignia of the C.B.E. conferred upon him by His Majesty in recognition of his loyalty and good services during the war![59]

What eventually decided the fate of the Cameroons, among other things, was that the Colonial Office had by 1919 recognised that France was too strongly entrenched in the Cameroons, and the delegates to the Paris Peace Conference were presented with a *fait accompli*. Apart from this the Colonial Office by the end of the war had become so absorbed in foreign policy that colonial problems became of secondary importance to men who were determined to see that the Great War would be in reality 'a war to end all wars'.

Notes

1 CAB 24/3 'G', 118[A]. Memo on military and political objections to the restoration of the colonies to Germany submitted to the War Cabinet by sub-committee on territorial changes, 22 March 1917.

2 *Ibid.*

3 CAB 24/10 'GT' 448, L. S. Amery, 'notes on possible terms of peace', 11 April 1917. The same point was made by Lord Curzon: see CAB 24/4 'G' 182, 5 Dec. 1917. William Roger Louis, *Great Britain and Germany's Lost Colonies 1914–1919*, has dealt with this question of repartition extensively. What I hope I have added is the emphasis on 'local' considerations in the British attitude to the Cameroons partition, among other things.

4 CAB 24/4 'G' 182, Lord Curzon, 5 Dec. 1917.

5 CAB 24/11 'GT' 592, Colonial Office memo on British desire for readjustments of the Cameroons boundary, 18 April 1917.

6 *Ibid.*

7 CAB 24/3 'G' 118[A]. Memo on military and political objections to the restoration of the colonies to Germany, by the sub-committee on territorial changes, 22 March 1917.

8 *Ibid.*

9 CAB 24/10 'GT' 448, L. S. Amery 'notes on possible terms of peace', circulated to War Cabinet, 11 April 1917.

10 *Ibid.*

11 CAB 24/10 'GT' (undated), 1918. Circulated to the War Cabinet.
12 CAB 24/4 'G' 182, Lord Curzon, 5 Dec. 1917. Note circulated to War Cabinet. German colonial aims are well treated in recent books, contemporary writings of the time and dissertations, such as
   (a) Fritz Fischer, *Germany's Aims in the First World War*, chs 5–8.
   (b) Dietrich Kersten, 'Die Kriegsziele der Hamburger Kaufmann-schaft im Ersten Weltkrieg: Ein Beitrag zur Frage der Kriegziel-politik im Kaiserlichen Deutschland, 1914–1918.' Doctoral dissertation, Hamburg University, 1963.
   (c) *The Times*, 12 April 1917, 'Central Africa: the last stage of world power.'
   (d) Dr Oskar Karstedt, *Koloniale Friedensziele*.
   (e) *Deutsche Weltpolitik und kein Krieg*, London, 1913, author not known, but believed to have been written by von Kuhlmann (who worked in the German embassy in London up till the out-break of the War and later became secretary of state for foreign affairs in 1917).
   (f) Edwyn Bevan: Introduction to Emil Zimmermann's *The German Empire of Central Africa* (translation of *Das deutsche Kaiserreich Mittelafrika als Grundlage einer neuen deutschen Weltpolitik*, pp. viii–lxiv.
13 CAB 24/4 'G' 182, Lord Curzon, 5 Dec. 1917.
14 CAB 24/41 'GT' 3592, German scheme of an African Empire Intelligence Bureau, department of information's memo circulated to War Cabinet early in 1918.
15 *The Times*, 16 Jan. 1918.
16 Lloyd George, *War Memoirs*, i, Ivor Nicholson and Watson, London, 1936, p. 1037.
17 CAB 2437/ 'GT' 3174, Sir George Fiddes's memo on German Colonies circulated to the War Cabinet, 2 Jan. 1918.
18 *Ibid.*
19 T. Bailey, *Woodrow Wilson and the lost peace*, Macmillan & Co., New York, 1944, p. 171; see also Fritz Fischer, *op. cit.*, p. 635.
20 CAB 24/37 'GT' 3180, Jan Smuts to War Cabinet, 3 Jan. 1918, quoting Lloyd George's earlier declaration on the subject in Scotland in July 1917 in which he had said in connection with the German colonies: 'the wishes, the desires and the interests of the people ... must be the dominant factor in settling their future government. ...'
21 *Ibid.*
22 CAB 24/54 'GT' 2816, Walter Long to War Cabinet, 11 June 1918.
23 CAB 24/53 'GT' 4774, A. J. Balfour to War Cabinet, Feb. 1918.
24 CAB 24/5 'G' 128, Lord Curzon to War Cabinet, 12 Jan. 1918.
25 CAB 24/62 'GT' 5515, Walter Long's memo, 24 Aug. 1918.
26 CAB 1/23/23, Winston S. Churchill, 7 July 1918.
27 CAB 24/66 'GT' 5994, Walter Long to War Cabinet, 15 Oct. 1918.
28 CAB 24/67 'GT' 6028, memo by Edwin Montagu, 18 Oct. 1918.
29 Evans Lewin, *The Germans and Africa*, Cassell and Company Ltd, London, 1915, p. 270.

30 Cd. 8306, 1916, xx, 1: German Atrocities and Breaches of the Rules of War in Africa: accounts and papers, xx.
31 Mary E. Townsend, *The Rise and Fall of Germany's Colonial Empire 1854–1918*, Howard Fertig, N.Y., 1966 (reprint), p. 376.
32 CAB 24/67 'GT' 6028, memo by Edwin Montagu, 18 Oct. 1918.
33 Ernst B. Haas, 'The reconciliation of the conflicting colonial policy aims: acceptance of the League of Nations Mandate System,' *International Organisation*, p. 524.
34 John Evelyn Wrench, *Alfred Milner*, Eyre and Spottiswood Ltd, London, 1958, pp. 330–1.
35 L. S. Amery to Smuts, 1 Nov. 1918. *Smuts Papers*, iv, p. 683.
36 W. R. Louis, 'The United States and African peace settlement of 1919: the pilgrimage of George Louis Beer', *Journal of African History*, pp. 413–33.
37 C.O. 554/42/5567, R. E. F. Maughan, British Consul in Dakar, Senegal, to Foreign Office, 9 Dec. 1918.
38 F.O. 608/216/2230, Clifford to Long, 17 Dec. 1918.
39 F.O. 608/215/2050, Edward C. Holden, British Consul in Duala, to Foreign Office, 22 Dec. 1918.
40 *Ibid.*, Strachey's minute, 15 Feb. 1919.
41 F.O. 608/215/290, A. Spicer's minute, 29 Jan. 1919.
42 F.O. 608/215/2910, Association of West African Merchants to the Foreign Office, 30 Jan. 1919.
43 F.O. 608/215/1207, John Holt & Co. to Lord Curzon, 25 Jan. 1919.
44 *La Presse Coloniale*, 2 June 1920, p. 4.
45 *La Presse Coloniale*, 16 June 1920.
46 *La Presse Coloniale*, 21 July 1920.
47 F.O. 608/215/4059, Strachey's minute of meeting of Lord Milner and M. Simon, 7 March 1919.
48 F.O. 608/215/11233, Strachey's minute, 22 July 1919.
49 *Ibid.*
50 CAB 29/37/ 'I.C.' 181^d, 6 May 1919. Meeting held at Quai d'Orsay with Woodrow Wilson, Lloyd George and Clemenceau present, 6 May 1919.
51 CAB 2937 'I.C.' 181^g, 7 May 1919, Sir Maurice Hankey's minutes.
52 F.O. 608/215/11233, Strachey's minute, 22 July 1919.
53 Raoul Nicholas, *Le Cameroun depuis le Traité de Versailles, 29 Juin, 1919*, Saint-Amand, 1922, p. 9.
54 Cmd. 1794, 1923, xxiv, 475. Cameroons Mandate.
55 Cmd. 1794, 1923, xxiv, 475. Terms of the Cameroons Mandate, London, 20 July 1923.
56 L. S. Amery to Smuts, 20 March 1919. *Smuts Papers*, iv, p. 78.
57 *Lugard Papers*, i, Lugard to John H. Harris, of the Anti-Slavery and Aborigines Protection Society, 3 June 1919, p. 150.
58 C.O. 554/49/46935, Resolution (36) of the Conference of the National Congress of British West Africa, 11–29 March 1920.
59 C.O. 583/78/66560, Clifford to Milner, 26 Oct. 1919.

PART III

10 The war and its aftermath

The war had far-reaching effects on every aspect of Nigeria's development. Economically it was almost ruinous, politically it was upsetting; to some extent it was socially destructive, and in terms of the morale and discipline of the administrative staff, it was a disaster. But there was also a bright side to the aftermath of the war in Nigeria. It ushered in an era of political liberalisation in the country. This change of policy was the result of a change of Governor as much as a response to the social and political ideas and aspirations which had spread to all peoples during the war. The mandate system, which laid down some principles which were to guide the actions of mandatories in areas put under their control indirectly was to influence the attitude of colonial powers in post-war administration of their colonies, since in criticising Germany for maladministration in her colonies, different and enlightened standards were unwittingly set by which any colonial power laid itself open to criticism or praise in the changed world situation.

With the involvement in the war of the staff of the Marines, Railways and Public Works departments, the economic development of Nigeria was arrested. Work was suspended for a time on the Lagos Harbour and Wharfage Scheme and the development of Port Harcourt as a full-fledged railway terminus and port had to wait until the end of the war for work on the whole eastern line to be continued to link up with the western line at Kakuri. Moreover, maintenance of the existing lines was not effectively and constantly carried out during the war. Rolling stock could not be replaced since most railway workshops in England had had to be converted to munitions factories and the financial stringency necessitated by the war in some cases made the Nigerian Government cancel orders even for most vital materials for repairs. The most noticeable effect of the war on the railways was the utter lack of modern and up-to-date workshops. The Nigerian railways system exceeded 1,100 miles by 1919 and throughout the whole distance there was not a single point at which adequate facilities existed for lifting the smallest locomotives or carrying out repairs promptly.[1] Building of workshops, especially at Ebutte Metta, did not start until the end of the war and the workshops that were started in Kaduna by Lugard during the war had to be abandoned because of the lack of skilled artisans in the area and because those in the south were unwilling to go to the north for fear of the Emir's *Dogorai*.

Owing to the war-time shortage of staff, construction of roads in a thoroughly efficient and satisfactory manner became impossible. No proper surveys were made and the routes were not thoroughly reconnoitred before road construction was commenced. In consequence the routes chosen in some cases were not the best. Since an extensive road programme was necessary for the economic development of Nigeria, a rejuvenated surveys department became a top priority in the post-war 'Cliffordian' era.

Nigerian merchants went bankrupt because of lack of shipping space for the exportation of their produce during the war. These Nigerians were further squeezed out of business by the 'combines' of British firms which came into being during the period under consideration. The average Nigerian producer did not benefit from the rising prices for primary products during the last two years of the war, because the prices were kept low by British firms who did the bulk buying for the imperial government. Where prices went up as a result of war-time demands for vegetable oils, the fall in the value of money neutralised the effect of these higher prices.

There was also the very difficult problem of the shortage of silver currency in Nigeria after the war, for which the government was forced to substitute paper money. The immediate result of this was the hoarding of silver coins by trading companies and the people, and this drove silver coins out of circulation. This led to increases in the prices of local foodstuffs and imported articles and to a depreciation of the face value of the currency notes in circulation. This inflation was of course a world-wide experience and it led, as in England, to demands for higher wages by government workers, both Nigerian and British.

The demand for higher remuneration first centred upon war bonus, to which the Colonial Office responded in September 1918 by sending a commissioner to Nigeria and the Gold Coast to determine how much should be given to the officials, who had complained that the cost of living had risen by between thirty and seventy-five per cent of pre-war level.[2] When the Commissioner, Sir Wood Renton (former Chief Justice of Ceylon) submitted his report recommending a liberal scale of war bonus to officials in Nigeria, the home government was rather hesitant to sanction the recommendations, until workers in the Nigerian railways threatened to strike.[3] This was an unusual thing in the history of the colonial civil service. But having submitted to the threat of strike before making necessary concessions, the Colonial Office opened the flood gates to greater demands for their employees. Apart from receiving war bonus ranging from £120 a year for junior officers to £60 a year for senior officers, the Nigerian administrative personnel decided that the time was ripe for them to press for an all-round revision of salaries instead of being satisfied with a temporary war bonus.

The agitation was spearheaded by Europeans in the railway departments who, having seen the efficacy of the striking power as a way of negotiation, decided they would stop work if the government did not agree to their demands. The men made it clear that if further concessions were not made a strike was not only possible but inevitable. They pointed out that the African artisans were watching what was going on and that if Europeans went out on strike, the Africans would follow them. It was pointed out to A. G. Boyle, the Governor's Deputy, that even if the Africans could be coerced to work, the cessation of work by supervisory staff would naturally lead to a shut-down of the works and railway departments. The men pointed out that bonuses were being granted to railway artisans in England and argued that their lot was worse than that of those in England.[4]

The movement finally resulted in the formation of the 'Association of European Civil Servants in Nigeria' early in 1919 and the Postmaster-General, Somerville, was made President.[5] The association included most of the heads of departments in the Civil Service, who claimed they were involved because they wanted to prevent the militant junior officials from taking over the control of the movement. The association demanded representation upon any committee that might be set up to enquire into and report on the subject of salary revision in Nigeria. This was an open rebellion and the Colonial Office had no choice but to recognise that fact.

This association constituted an abrupt departure from the traditions and procedure which had hitherto prevailed in the public service of the tropical colonies and protectorates. Sir Hugh Clifford, who was always sympathetic to civil servants because he came up through their ranks, felt the movement had gone too far. He commented:

> I regard them as a menace to the reputation, to the efficiency and to the discipline of [the] service. I am however convinced that any attempt at summary suppression would only make the position worse than it at present is. Many members of the public service ... are apparently in a very discontented frame of mind, believe themselves to have suffered neglect in the past and are suffering from various grievances real or imaginary which they at present have no means of ventilating effectively.[6]

Many of these officials wanted not only a revision of salaries but also a radical change in the rules and regulations governing appointment to the Colonial Civil Service.

The association claimed, however, that they had a precedent for what they were doing. They said the formation of their union was based on the Whitley Report on the Administrative Departments of the British Civil Service. The relevant section on which they founded their association said,

> we conceive that the main objects of establishing a system of Whitley councils for the administrative departments are to secure a greater measure of cooperation between the state, in its capacity as employer, and the general body of civil servants in matters affecting the Civil Service with a view to increased efficiency in the public service, combined with the well-being of those employed: to provide a machinery for the ventilation of grievances and generally to bring together with a view to the free discussion of the many diverse and complex different points of view of representatives of the many grades and classes constituting the Administrative, clerical and manipulative civil service of the country [Britain].[7]

The association levied a fee of £1 on each of its members, and in its Constitution a general committee, which was to be in London, was provided for. This committee was to consist of certain ex-officials of the West African Civil Service as permanent members. The management of the Nigerian section was vested in three committees, one based in Ebutte Metta (representing officials in Lagos and all others west of the Niger); the second committee was based in Kaduna to represent the Northern officials, while the third had its headquarters in Port Harcourt and was to represent members east of the Niger.

The association demanded the grant of a war bonus to all their members on a scale similar to that given to civil servants in England, i.e., a minimum of £150 a year (which was an unreasonable demand since the home-based civil servants paid heavy income tax). The association also wanted officers retiring on pension, prior to the revision of salaries, to receive the same treatment as officers retiring from the home service and wanted existing pensions increased by twenty per cent. They also demanded that pensions under the West African widows and orphans pension scheme be increased by twenty per cent.

The Secretary of State for the Colonies was shocked by these extravagant demands, but the conditions were such that concessions had to be made or else the whole administration of Nigeria might collapse. Lord Milner asked Sir Hugh Clifford to accord recognition to the association and to acknowledge that their demands would be studied and necessary reforms would be made as well as a general salary review.[8]

The effect of the movement was not lost on the Nigerians employed in the civil service, who responded by forming their own union called the 'Nigeria Civil Service Union'. They had a better case than their European counterpart. They complained about the fact that the civil service in Nigeria was not thrown open to talent. They petitioned Lord Milner, saying 'this singular policy of restrictive appointments in the service of our country represses our natural and legitimate aspirations and tends to paralyze all initiative and energy'.[9]

They protested against the practice in Nigeria which made it impossible for Nigerians to earn more than £300 per annum as discriminatory. There was no law stipulating the scale of salary of 'native' officials but it was understood that Africans should not earn more than £300. They yearned for the good old days of the colony of Lagos and the old Protectorate of Southern Nigeria when Africans served 'under liberal policy then obtaining', when Africans were appointed to fill such posts as Colonial Treasurer, Assistant Secretary for Native Affairs, Colonial Postmaster, Inspector of Schools and Superintendent of Police. In order to forestall the government from holding up Henry Carr to them as an African who was in a 'European' position, the Union wrote:

we are not unminded of the fact that an African at present fills with distinction the high office of provincial commissioner of the colony but we would respectfully point out that the gentleman is a survival of the liberal policy of the past which unfortunately no longer exists; this affords a strong proof if any were needed of what a valuable asset the African given equal opportunities and proper encouragement is and could be in the government of his country.[10]

The Nigerians explained that they had not received any increment since 1906 in spite of the phenomenal progress which the country had made since then, with its corresponding rise in the cost of living. They pointed out the almost complete lack of vacation which they had to endure because the government expected them not to be tired in an environment where they were born. On pensions for Africans, they said that according to the regulations, Africans did not qualify until they had served thirty-seven years. They claimed that since many Africans entered the service after twenty years of age, the very few who attained to pensionable age after a long service did so only to die a short time after, and since gratuities were not paid to the dependants of those who died in service, many of the Africans felt unfairly treated. The African civil servants' complaints were not extravagant and Sir Hugh Clifford felt them worth consideration.[11]

Revision of salaries was embarked upon by March 1920, a comprehensive report was drawn up, and salary increments from fifty per cent in the lower ranks of officials, twenty per cent in the intermediate to twelve and a half per cent in the higher grades were awarded to Europeans. A better pension scheme was also sanctioned by the Colonial Office. The Africans also received increments ranging from twenty to thirty per cent depending on their grades. Sir Hugh Clifford also said he was in favour of giving Africans with superior qualifications higher positions of responsibility than had hitherto been the case.[12] Clifford ruled against the prefix 'native' while referring to African medical officers, because the latter objected to it as derogatory. The Governor also raised their salaries, but not to the same level as that of their European counterparts.

If for Nigeria the war did not end with a bang, it certainly ended with much whimpering in official circles! The outgoing Governor, worn out and full of resentment against the Colonial Office, complained of bad treatment especially in the cancellation in 1917, by Walter Long, of his proposal for 'continuous administration'.

When Lugard raised the issue after the war, Long made it clear that 'the objections which ... in my judgement are fatal to the efficient administration of the colony from England are in no way personal to yourself. I am convinced that such an arrangement by whomsoever carried out could not exist without prejudice to the public service'.[13] The Governor's Deputy, A. G. Boyle, who was also Acting Governor for nine months before Clifford finally took office in Nigeria, bemoaned his lot over the appointment of General Guggisberg as the new Governor of the Gold Coast. In a rather pathetic note to the Colonial Office, he lamented:

> Now at the turning point of my career, I see an officer who served in this colony as Director of Surveys in 1911 while I was acting Governor and who has no training in colonial administration appointed Governor of a progressive colony ... In spite of the eulogia of Mr. Secretary, Walter Long, on the self-denying service of the colonial civil servants during the war, we now see the possible rewards of our work taken from us and distributed to military officers without any training in colonial administration.[14]

In support of this protest (from a man for whom Clifford had little affection and who was retired compulsorily by the Governor some months later!) the new Governor wrote:

> As a colonial civil servant of nearly six and thirty years standing, I have no hesitation in recording the opinion – an opinion based upon intimate knowledge of that service – that the action referred to has had and is having a profoundly discouraging effect in every part of the tropics with which I am familiar, upon the members of the colonial civil service and tends to depress their energies and to extinguish their enthusiasm to an extent which it is perhaps only possible for one of themselves fully to realize and appreciate.[15]

This protest met with a cold reception in the Colonial Office and Lord Milner passed the word to Boyle that 'the office of Governor is not a post to which officials in the public service of a colony or protectorate have any claim as of right to be appointed'.[16] The colonial civil service was in a rebellious mood and even the military establishment felt let down because representatives from the Nigeria Regiment were not invited to participate in the Peace Parade in London.[17] The Colonial Office had, however, decided it would be absurd and 'impolitic to bring to this country coloured detachments to participate in peace processions'.[18] This petty and penny-pinching piece of trivial racism was poor recognition for the

sacrifices of those Nigerian soldiers who died, often unrecognised
and unidentified, in the battles of the Cameroons or East Africa.

Clifford, with his experience in Ceylon and Malaya, where implementation of government policies was directed from a central
secretariat, was unimpressed by Nigeria's lack of a proper central
secretariat. Clifford was not completely unfamiliar with the idea of
indirect rule. He had come in contact with this in Malaya with its
princely system and he had himself adopted the system in the
Gold Coast in his government's relation with the *Asantehene*. In
all these places attempts had been made to curtail the power and
privileges of these rulers and not to perpetuate them indefinitely.

On coming to Nigeria, Clifford had nothing to commend in his
predecessor's administration. Clifford rather unfairly blamed
Lugard for allowing the political staff of the country to be so
dangerously depleted. At the end of 1918 there were 134 British
political officers in charge of about nine million people in Northern
Nigeria.[19] Kano Province, for example, with a population of
2,826,897 – more numerous than the Gold Coast which at that
time was under two million – was being administered by only
nineteen officials.[20] This lack of supervision and control in the
North had led to much corruption, oppression and injustice on the
part of the ruling class; as Clifford pointed out:

> the native administrations . . . have in some cases and in some degree
> become emancipated from control . . . they stand more in need of
> very close supervision by a strong staff, than has been the case during
> any period of their recent history . . . one of the effects of the Great
> War has been to occasion a recrudescence of former evil practices
> and to prevent us from discharging efficiently our obligations to the
> rank and file of the indigenous population.[21]

Sir Hugh went on to strike a critical note on the system of
administration which Colonial Office clerks had held up roman-
tically for so long as the model of imperial rule in areas of the
Empire inhabited by non-whites:

> the maintenance of the *status quo*, the perpetuation of more or less
> medieval conditions by the aid of every natural and artificial expedient,
> the staving off of innovations and a successful effort to preserve
> untouched and unimproved the intellectual and material standards of
> culture to which a primitive people had already attained when first
> they came under alien influence . . . are not ordinarily regarded in any
> of Great Britain's tropical possessions as the legitimate aims of the
> efficient administrator.[22]

His opinion was not shared by the Residents in Northern Nigeria! Some even felt that the social effect of the war in Northern Nigeria had convinced even the apostles of direct administration that it would be 'prudent to take time by the forelock and foster a tribal and racial patriotism as a prophylactic to the disease of anti-Europeanism',[23] which was sweeping across the whole Sudan belt of West Africa. The effect of the campaign in East Africa on the good citizenship of members of the carriers corps and disbanded soldiers, especially those recruited from the rural districts, was not encouraging. It was alleged that they returned to their villages unamenable to discipline and inclined to demand to be maintained in luxury as having taken part in a 'Jihad'. Some even went round demanding tolls as government men and some of them were so mentally 'unsettled' that they joined the 'worst riff-raff of the large towns'.[24]

Sir Hugh knew that most of his reforms would be resisted in the North, but he was convinced that it was only by the provision of a numerically adequate political staff that 'the necessity for the frequent punitive patrols which are today so distressing a feature of administrative work can be obviated'.[25]

With Clifford in control of Nigeria, there was a shift of emphasis from administration *per se* to a more enlightened and liberal economic policy. Before Clifford, the task of administration was regarded not only as the most important but practically as the sole *raison d'être* of the government

> while the work of development such as results from immigration and from the stimulation of commerce and enterprise has been looked upon with apprehension and suspicion as tending to disturb native institutions, to weaken the authority of government by lowering the prestige of its officers and by infecting the local population with more emancipated notions to render the task of administration more difficult.[26]

While recognising the problems of Lugard and his wartime administration, and the limitations placed on him by the paucity of administrative staff, Clifford felt that the material limitation of the power of the chiefs, especially the Northern Emirs, which ought to have been done, was never attempted. Indeed their personal power and influence over their subjects were supported by the government, occasionally by force:

> In a word the efforts of the Nigerian government have of late years

been directed to an organised effort to preserve the *status quo* in-definitely ... to restrict and discourage the intrusion of both Europeans and natives who are out to make money and who are not animated by a similar desire to perpetuate the medieval conditions which at present prevail.[27]

Clifford was not against preserving indigenous political institutions and customs, but deplored carrying their preservation to such an extent that they hampered and retarded development. 'I cannot however regard their maintenance as the most important, far less the final object of the British government in Nigeria.'[28] He would have preferred to adapt them to the changed situation so that they would be able to withstand the strain to which opening up the country would subject them.

He was against the special powers conferred on emirs and Residents in the North to forbid 'alien natives' to set up trade or reside among their fellow countrymen. This policy had led to a state of affairs in which ghettos of 'alien natives' sprang up all over Northern Nigeria. He was of the opinion that this was a case in which work of development was considered opposed to adminis-tration.

On the future economic development of the country, the new administration wished to relax some of the laws passed under Lugard making private investment difficult. Clifford hoped for laws which would make it possible for generous 'land and mineral concessions' to be given to developers while still preserving 'native rights'.

In order to begin his programme, Clifford felt there was the need for a clean break with the past. He decided he would overhaul the whole of the Lugardian administrative system. He proposed abolishing the posts of Lieutenant-Governor and substituting the title of Chief Commissioner in the north and abolishing the office in the south, since the Governor himself was stationed in Lagos and could look after affairs in his immediate neighbourhood. He intended to create a new post of Chief Secretary to the Govern-ment, who would rank next to the Governor. He was of the opinion that this would bring Nigeria's civil service up to a standard comparable with that of a typical colony like Ceylon. He also intended abolishing all the former Southern and Northern secretariats and replacing them with a Nigerian secretariat so that amalgamation would be actual rather than nominal.[29]

The home government, however, stood in the way of these

radical changes. While not challenging the basis of Clifford's criticism of the Lugardian system, A. J. Harding minuted:

> either as a result of the environment or more likely because of pre-conceived opinions formed in very different circumstances, Sir H. Clifford has contracted a most violent attack of anti-Lugardism. . . . In spite of Sir F. Lugard seeing a good secretariat work in Hong Kong he never really got used to it. He would not let anyone but himself do the work though he managed fairly well during his first administration in Northern Nigeria, as the service was then small, his system practically broke down when he was put, in 1912, in charge of Southern Nigeria as well as a much more developed Northern Nigeria. . . . Accordingly we had three secretariats working almost independently – the only connecting link being Sir F. Lugard with his rather defective memory and his so-called 'political secretary' who was not as his name might be thought to imply . . . a sort of secretary for native affairs, but was merely Sir F. Lugard's brother, Major Lugard – a sort of glorified highly paid inefficient private secretary or confidential clerk who might more appropriately have been called the 'fraternal secretary'.[30]

The Colonial Office was of the opinion that it would be unwise to run Nigeria on 'centralised lines' which worked well enough in colonies with a few hundred or thousands of square miles and a few hundred thousand inhabitants, but might not work well in Nigeria with its 337,000 square miles and about twenty million people – 'an area one third of that of British India and . . . a population greater than that of Ceylon, British Malaya, Australia, New Zealand and British West Indies all added together'.[31]

Lord Milner, while favouring the idea of rapid economic development as put forward by Clifford, commented: 'I greatly dislike the idea of getting rid of Lt. Governors and putting the whole country under a single *Poo-Bah* with only superior clerks to help him.'[32] Lord Milner, however, favoured the idea of Chief Secretary to co-ordinate national policies. Clifford went ahead and appointed the former Central Secretary, D. C. Cameron, to the new position.[33]

Clifford, shocked by the 'comfortless' accommodation that existed in Nigeria, embarked with all speed in developing Ikoyi as a European reservation, believing that if good accommodation was provided officials would have to stay longer on their jobs rather than serve the previous short terms followed by annual holidays in England. He decided that Lagos was going to remain the capital of Nigeria and not Kaduna as previously planned. Kaduna to him was too far removed from the commercial centre of Nigeria and from any large Nigerian town. He was not going to allow his officials to reside in 'dignified seclusion in a specially prepared isolation camp'.[34] Clifford's criticisms of the Lugardian system tallied well with the reputation of the new Governor. He was a man strongly influenced by the war and the ideologies it threw up. He brought a 'modernism' to Nigeria to replace Lugard and his followers. Besides this fact, Clifford's criticisms are simply the reflections of a man with a different cast of mind and attitude to subject people. This difference had come to the surface in the attitudes of the two Governors to colonial subjects during the war. A typical example was the refusal of Clifford to follow Lugard in introducing the £2 export duty on vegetable oils in 1916, because he felt this was not in the interests of producers.

In order to raise revenue for all the works of reconstruction which he planned, Clifford was in full agreement with the proposals for post-war control of Nigeria's primary agricultural exports, such as palm oil, palm kernels and groundnuts. Clifford even raised the export duties on these articles from the war-time level of £1 2s. 6d. per ton on palm kernels to £2 per ton, and from £2 per ton on palm oil to £3, and on groundnuts from ten shillings to £1.[35] This decision, which was in compliance with the Ministry of Food's decision to channel the Empire's resources into British markets,[36] was opposed by many influential groups and politicians in Britain on the grounds that since the Treaty of Peace with Germany was signed there was no longer any question of the colonies being called upon to sacrifice their own interests in order to help win the war. It was argued that forcing Nigerian produce into Britain by means of export prohibitions and fixing a maximum price as the Ministry of Food had done, instead of allowing natural prices which would otherwise have prevailed as a result of ordinary competition in the world markets, was an unfair policy, especially in view of the inadequate prices which the producer had received during the war.[37] Since these duties applied only to goods exported to foreign countries and not to Britain, the Liberals, who were against any form of protectionism, came out strongly against it. Lord Beauchamp speaking in the House of Lords on 17 December 1919 described the export duties as 'a curious result of an attempt at Imperial preference . . .'[38] The government agreed that the measure was a form of Imperial preference, designed to protect the vital margarine and soap industry which had been established in England during the war, against competition from the foreign manufactures, but this lame defence did not satisfy many of the critics of this new mercantilism. Since the Colonial Secretary was in the Lords, most of the debate over the export duty was held there.

Lord Emmott, who was once Parliamentary Under Secretary in the Colonial Office and then Head of the War Trade Department during the war, was most virulent in his attack on the export duty. For him all empires fell when exploitation of their subject races became their governing note. Britain had not yet learnt her lesson from the American Revolution! He added:

> is the war to start a new era of selfish exploitation of the native races for the benefit of the people here at home? If so I am sadly afraid that the Empire, already dangerously large, will soon fall to pieces owing to the trouble and difficulties that will be created. To me the new principle involves the exploitation of the native races for our own interests to which I object. It is an absolute reversal of the policy of the last 60 or 70 years. If continued it will prove to be policy of ill omen to all of us.[39]

Lord Emmott brought out the potential importance of the mandate system:

> this duty whilst it could be imposed in Nigeria would be illegal in the British sphere of the Cameroons ... therefore the natives of those former German colonies are now able to sell at the best price they can obtain in the open markets of the world, while the natives of our own colonies who stood by us so loyally during the war are unable to do so. How can we expect contentment in our old colonies when an unfairness so grave and palpable as that is being perpetrated.[40]

The export duty, he said, was for the benefit of manufacturers and not consumers and it was not needed against Germany, since Germany could get substitutes elswhere, and England should not set an example of export duty which other powers might follow; the trade in Britain was quite profitable and there was no need of protection. He concluded 'if protection is necessary, in heaven's name let it be protected by subsidy or some other rational measure and not by the mean and un-English policy of exploiting the native races for the benefit of the traders at home'.[41]

Lord Bryce also used the mandate principle when he said:

> Nigeria is not subject to a Mandate, these territories were already

ours and they will not come under the Mandate. But there is the principle. Is it right for us having recently affirmed that principle, to deviate from it in this particular case and to refrain from giving equal opportunities simply because we happened to have Nigeria already. I think it is inconsistent with the line of policy we have taken. It would not be fair and would be very likely to give rise to attempts at evasion on the part of other countries.[42]

Lugard too joined the noble Lords in protesting against the policy of post-war control and in a letter to *The Times* of 31 December 1919, he wrote:

These proposals were the outcome of war conditions. No one is more wholly in agreement with Lord Emmott's attitude as regards the native producer than myself, or holds more insistently to the great principle that the Power in control in dealing with subject races should in no remote way seek her own advantage at their expense – that any sacrifice asked from them in return for however great sacrifices by the Suzerain Power, must be wholly voluntary, and that imperial Preference as applied to Crown Colonies and Protectorates is a policy of selfish advantage unless it is reciprocal.[43]

The government however maintained that the measure was to secure the home market for colonial goods and that it was based on the policy of imperial preference. Clifford got caught in this web of arguments. He had agreed to the export duty only as a means of raising revenue and not because of imperial preference, but the home government was more doctrinaire in their approach to the question, and Clifford found himself being lumped with those who were said to be against the welfare of Nigerians. One concession was made to Nigerian producers at the intervention of Clifford. The Ministry of Food removed the pegging of the price of vegetable oils at a fixed maximum, but export duty continued until 1921.[44]

Another attempt at imperial preference was quietly refused, when the Canadian Minister of Trade asked whether preference could be granted to Canadian imports and exports from and to Nigeria.[45] He was told that the introduction of preference would mean a reversal of British policy pursued with marked success in directing the affairs of subject races so as to allow equal opportunities for trade and commerce to all. The Canadians were told that it was not in the interest of Nigeria to allow all Canadian goods into Nigeria free of import duties, as well as to allow

Canada to take Nigerian exports of vegetable oils without paying duties on them.

The crux of the whole thing about the export duty was that it was feared that soap and margarine manufacturers would benefit at the expense of the 'native' producers. By prohibiting export to foreign countries unless duties varying from £1 to £3 depending on the article being exported were paid meant that British buyers would be paying exactly those amounts below world-market value of the products. On the other hand, it is possible that Nigeria would have benefited, because price in a competitive market is not all it was claimed to be by the free-traders. A guaranteed market for planned quantities of production with guaranteed prices somewhat below current market prices is definitely preferable for developing countries; then they can plan production, set up marketing boards to take a levy on prices which can be used for research and planning, and use the stability of the staple crop to diversify the economy and reduce their reliance on one crop, as was done in many colonies during and after the Second World War.

The opposition to export duty, or 'imperial preference' as they called it, is compounded of several attitudes and ideas, some new, some old, in a very interesting mixture. There is first of all the traditional free-trade nineteenth-century orthodoxy: colonies must not be forced to trade with the mother country by mercantilist controls or their produce will in the end be dearer to Great Britain and their economies become inefficient. The arguments are reminiscent of the Liberal attack on the Conservatives in the 1905 and 1906 elections, and of the split in the Conservative ranks following Joseph Chamberlain's opting for imperial preference. The whole issue is connected with the still strong feelings that 'peace and normalcy' must mean a return to secure raw material supplies at whatever cost. The second argument is the one which links tariffs with the issue of African ownership and control of natural resources and production. The third is the new element of the introduction of the mandate principle and the ease with which it is applied to colonies and protectorates where there is no mandate – this anticipated the publication of Lugard's *Dual Mandate*, where he assumed that colonies *have to be* justified on the mandatory idea.

The duty levied on certain Nigerian exports going to ports outside the Empire was certainly a measure of imperial preference, but when Canada tried to exploit this preference in the interest of her trade with Nigeria and was refused, then the imperial preference breaks down to simple mercantilism. Clifford meant to use the measure to raise revenue, but since exports to Britain were not liable to this levy, the revenue raised must have been insignificant, because Nigerian trade was heavily dominated by the British. The 'export prohibitions' continued to operate until 1921, when they were finally abandoned.

Nigeria had played a major role in the supply of human labour during the campaigns in Africa, and attempts were made to tap this source again after the war had ended. First there was the suggestion that the Sierra Leone garrison should be replaced by recruits from Nigeria, which Clifford turned down on security grounds. Then came another request for labour in the Sudan, for the purpose of building the Makawr dam.[46] Viscount Allenby, the Governor-General of the Sudan, wanted 10,000 young *fellata* (as he called them!) recruited from Nigeria. He said that recruiting could be carried out with the assistance of a 'local senaar fellata chief', which suggested to Nigerian officials that he intended using agents of Mai Wurno – a son of the late Sarkin Musulmin Attahiru I who apparently intended to try to come back to Sokoto as Sultan. They felt this would be resisted by northern emirs, who were scared of Mai Wurno. The Sudan Government promised a free pilgrimage to Mecca after five years' work to each labourer, but the Nigerian authorities feared that if the 10,000 men were recruited, they would probably not return to Nigeria again and that even if they wanted to return Mai Wurno would not let them, and that it would not be wise to 'depopulate' Nigeria to save the Anglo-Egyptian Sudan.[47]

Others in Nigeria felt that the scheme was not desirable since the able-bodied men who would be taken were just the people who should remain in Nigeria. The floating labour supply of Nigeria had suffered a serious diminution as a result of deaths and disablement of soldiers and carriers in the Cameroons and East Africa, and the influenza epidemic of 1918 killed off a considerable number of labourers. Nigerians being devoted to agriculture, the floating labour was hardly adequate for work in the mines and for development projects which the government was initiating.

The Resident of Sokoto, G. W. Webster, was of the opinion that the required number could be got by compulsion. But he feared that if these recruits were to return to Nigeria as *Al-hajjis* 'they would be a privileged class entitled to support by the community. They would be denationalised, crammed with all the least desirable tenets of modern Egypt but half digested and therefore all the more readily cast abroad in perverted form.' They would constitute a dangerous and undesirable element in an un-developed but rapidly progressing community.[48] Nigeria's allotted role under the new dispensation of imperial unity was found to be impossible of fulfilment and gradually all the hopes raised during the war in this connection faded into thin air.

The post-war era ushered in a period of *rapprochement* between the administration and the educated elite. Clifford stopped all degrading practices of the past, especially the prostrating before colonial officials which had been maintained in the name of preserving 'native culture'. The Governor was also to rectify the anomaly in which government was divorced from contact with 'unofficial and progressive sections of the local public'. Clifford, as much as the educated Nigerians, detested the 'prostrating crowds of Oyo' and their types. He was repelled by the servile attitude of some emirs who were said by his predecessor to be the pillars of the 'native administrations'. Describing his visit to Ilorin, Sir Clifford wrote: 'a heavy shower had recently fallen, but this did not impede the Emir and his chiefs from subsiding into the mud and puddles at my approach, though I instinctively sought to prevent them from thus wantonly soiling their hand-some garments'.[49] He was of the opinion that it was not possible to

> 'withstand the tide of new ideas, hopes and aspirations with which the native populations of the tropics are rapidly becoming permeated ... to endeavour to delay by artificial means this process appears to me to be merely to postpone the inevitable instead of attempting to grapple from the outset with a problem which sooner or later must be faced'.[50]

Clifford opened the civil service to qualified Africans, and al-though he considered the resolutions of the Accra Conference of the National Congress of British West Africa, which called for elected representatives of the people with power over financial matters, unrealistic, he was nevertheless sympathetic with some of their ideas. Clifford carried out Lugard's April 1918 decision to introduce two elected members to the Lagos town council instead of nominating them.[51] This he did very early in 1920. He followed up this principle by introducing a new constitution in 1922 which provided for a new Legislative Council for forty-six members, twenty-seven of which were officials and nineteen unofficials. Three of these unofficial members were to be elected by all adult males in Lagos with a residential qualification of twelve months and a gross income of £100 per annum and one was also to be elected in Calabar.[52] The old Nigerian Council set up by Lugard was abolished. Clifford apparently introduced his reforms in 1922 because of the pressure of the educated Nigerians and European members of his own staff. Since December 1919 the European members of the Nigerian Council had consistently urged him to abolish the Nigerian Council, which they said served no useful purpose, and to replace it with a Legislative Council for the whole country.[53] This would have been introduced earlier than 1922 but for the prevarication of the Colonial Office.

When the Legislative Council was finally introduced in 1922 Clifford even went so far as to say it was but the first step towards eventual self-government for Nigeria.[54] He argued that his scheme was:

> . . . no more than a step in the direction of securing a fuller representation of local interest and of giving a larger share in the discussion and management of public affairs to articulate members of the various Nigerian communities than are provided by existing institutions . . . it is inevitably imperfect . . . but it at any rate represents a recognition of the principle that the local public has a right to obtain full information on questions affecting its interest and that the actions of the government are a legitimate object of scrutiny and criticism . . .'[55]

With the introduction of the elective principle of representation a constructive way opened up for those critics who before and during the war had no other option but to criticise, sometimes blindly, all actions of the government. In this way, the development of party politics as a focus for constructive nationalism began; and in the schemes and aspirations embodied in all the subsequent nationalist programmes, could be seen the ideas and ideologies which the war itself gave rise to.

Notes

1 C.O. 583/74/23397, C. M. Bland to D. C. Cameron, 26 Feb. 1919.
2 C.O. 583/71/39718, Lugard to Long, 5 Sept. 1918.

3 C.O. 583/72/2857, Harding's minute, 12 Jan. 1919.

4 C.O. 583/72/10095, Boyle to Walter Long, 12 Jan. 1919.

5 C.O. 583/77/55482, Clifford to Milner, 28 Aug. 1919.

6 *Ibid.*

7 *Ibid.*, Somerville to Boyle, 1 May 1919, quoting the Whitley Report published in London on 7 March 1919.

8 *Ibid.*, Milner to Clifford, 10 Oct. 1919.

9 C.O. 583/74/23312, Nigeria Civil Service Union to Lord Milner, 4 March 1919.

10 *Ibid.*

11 C.O. 583/84/15646, Clifford to Milner, 3 March 1920.

12 C.O. 583/85/20545, Clifford to Milner, 25 March 1920.

13 *Lugard Papers*, ii, Walter Long to Lugard, 13 Dec. 1918.

14 C.O. 583/76/51425, Clifford to Milner, 12 Aug. 1919, enclosure (1).

15 *Ibid.*

16 *Ibid.*, Lord Milner's despatch, 30 Sept. 1919.

17 C.O. 583/76/51430, Col Cole's protest note, enclosed in Clifford to Milner, 16 Aug. 1919.

18 C.O. 583/76/51430, Col Jenkins's minute at the Colonial Office, 15 Oct. 1919.

19 C.O. 583/84/7580, Clifford to Milner, 29 Dec. 1919.

20 C.O. 583/89/34687, Clifford to Milner, 25 June 1920.

21 *Ibid.*

22 *Ibid.*

23 C.O. 583/83/3057, H. R. Palmer, undated, August 1919.

24 C.O. 583/91/49541, G. W. Webster, Resident of Sokoto, to Clifford, 26 July 1920.

25 C.O. 583/80/71954, Clifford to Milner, 26 Nov. 1919.

26 C.O. 583/78/66560, Clifford to Milner, 28 Oct. 1919.

27 *Ibid.*

28 *Ibid.*

29 C.O. 583/80/73600, Clifford to Milner, 3 Dec. 1919.

30 *Ibid.*, Harding's minute, 27 Jan. 1920.

31 *Ibid.*, Harding's minutes, 1 Jan. 1920.

32 *Ibid.*, Milner's minute, 5 July 1920.

33 C.O. 583/80/73606, Clifford to Milner, 31 Dec. 1919.

34 C.O. 583/78/66560, Clifford to Milner, 28 Oct. 1919. It is to be noted that this highly critical view of Lugard's successor is not mentioned or dealt with by Margery Perham in her biography of Lugard.

35 C.O. 583/78/66568, Clifford to Milner, 31 Oct. 1919.

36 C.O. 554/44/48903, Ministry of Food to Colonial Office, 21 Aug. 1919.

37 C.O. 554/49/23293, Travers Buxton of the Anti-Slavery and Aborigines Protection Society to Milner, 7 May 1920.

38 *Hansard*, House of Lords, 5th series, 38, 1919, col. 226–7.

39 *Ibid.*, col. 231.

40 *Ibid.*

41 *Ibid.*

42 *Ibid.*

43 *The Times*, 31 Dec. 1919. Reprinted in *West Africa*, 27 Dec. 1919, p. 1283.

44 C.O. 554/44/66739, Ministry of Food to Colonial Office, 20 Nov. 1919.

45 C.O. 583/89/39689, Clifford to Milner, enclosing T. F. Burrowes's memo, 17 July 1919.

46 C.O. 583/91/49541, Clifford to Milner, 18 Dec. 1920.

47 C.O. 583/91/495, H. R. Palmer's enclosure in Clifford to Milner, 18 Dec. 1920.

48 *Ibid.*, G. W. Webster, enclosure in Clifford to Milner, 18 Dec. 1920.

49 C.O. 583/78/66560, Clifford to Milner, 28 Oct. 1919.

50 *Ibid.*

51 C.O. 583/66/21135, Lugard to Colonial Office, 30 April 1918.

52 Michael Crowder, *The Story of Nigeria*, p. 228.

53 C.O. 583/84/7580, Proceedings of the Sixth Meeting of the Nigerian Council, 2 Dec. 1919.

54 Michael Crowder, *op. cit.*, p. 228.

55 C.O. 583/100, Sir Hugh Clifford to Winston S. Churchill, Secretary of State for the Colonies, 26 March 1921.

Conclusion

A depleted British administration in Nigeria faced serious problems of resistance to its rule, economic dislocation, difficulties and demands of military recruitment. The issues raised by the war have influenced Nigeria's overall historical development. Thus events arising from the war make possible the re-evaluation of the pre-war administrative policies, which war-time administration continued to follow.

The economic consequences of the war on Nigeria were the general economic dislocation and disruption of normal trade relations both external and internal, and government's attempt to grapple with problems associated with such developments. In Nigeria, this dislocation was accompanied by the inevitable unemployment caused by the 'shut-downs' of enemy commercial enterprises, while the scarcity of essential materials even for government capital projects led to closing down of some development projects. The economic slow-down was complicated by the unmarketability of Nigeria's oil-producing nuts and seeds that had formerly been absorbed by German markets. This created a slump with consequent economic ruin for primary producers or 'collectors'. Combined with the economic chaos was the unscrupulous attempt at monopoly by big European firms, which tried to squeeze out of existence Nigerian merchants and small European merchants by a resort to combination and fixing of prices and monopoly of available ocean freight. This further depressed the market and made farming a losing venture. This in a way led to lowering of British prestige in the eyes of the Nigerian merchants and their educated counterparts, who were always quick to seize on popular causes to denigrate the administration and to bring into question the loyalty of the 'thinking' part of Nigerian public.

Another crisis of the period was that of ideas of administrative policy, notably the introduction by a stubborn Governor-General of a new administrative system of indirect rule to the Southern Provinces, particularly the south-western part, during a period when the depletion of administrative staff and the general malaise accompanying the outbreak of war made such a move an inevitable failure. Resistance to the measures manifested itself in numerous wildcat and at times widespread revolts and rebellions in many parts of the South Provinces, leading to a great loss of lives and eventually to the questioning of the basis of a policy which was so destructive in its application.

The country's security problems were further complicated by Turkey's entry into the war on the side of the Central Powers, and for a time the administrators lived in the fear of a Jihad. This apprehension was not baseless, in view of the supreme position of the Ottoman Caliph in the Islamic world. The policy of indirect rule in the Northern Muslim emirates had succeeded in making the indigenous aristocracy a part of the colonial establishment, with an identity of interests with the British. This made the Northern traditional elite as much a target for insurrectional upheaval as the British, and consequently the Muslim rulers were as concerned as the British were in maintaining the *status quo*, which depended so much on British backing and a demonstration of force and the readiness to use it when necessary. This is not to say that the Northern Provinces did not have their own share of revolts and uprisings, but those who could have been leaders of an effective anti-British, 'anti-infidel' Islamic revolt had been politically castrated and bought over by the princely salaries paid to them.

The general feeling of insecurity in the country was further exacerbated by the Senusi rising of 1916–17 in the immediate north and north-eastern part of Nigeria. The fear that this pan-Islamic revolt might spread to Northern Nigeria made the British administration in Nigeria willing to co-operate with France – a rather difficult ally – in suppressing the revolt.

This immense security problem was further complicated by the vulnerability of Nigeria's Atlantic coast to German attack, and the possibility of a landing by German marine commando units became the more real since it was feared that the hostile and pro-German administration in the Spanish Island of Fernando Po off the mainland of Nigeria might aid the enemy.

Another entirely different problem was the recruiting of large numbers of Nigerian servicemen to fight in the Cameroons and

East Africa and also the formation of well-trained brigades for the purpose of employing them in the Middle East. The fear of what might happen if this large body of armed men turned on their masters haunted the British throughout the period of the war. The 'discovery' of the African as a soldier shaped to a certain extent the decision by the Allied powers not to return the conquered German colonies to Germany after the war, for fear that Germany might pursue a policy of 'militarization' of Africa (which in fact the Allies had practised more than Germany).

The partition of the Cameroons was of special importance to the future of Nigeria's security and British prestige in Nigeria, for it was, after all, the reduction of the Cameroons that brought Nigeria into the war in the first instance. The partition and the subsequent placing of each section under the rule of the mandate system form important aspects of this book, especially in the reconciliation of British and specifically Nigerian war aims – the Shehu of Borno and the Lamido of Yola's expansionist or irredentist aspirations partly coincided with British strategic and political interests. The Partition of the Cameroons was inextricably tied up with the whole question of the divergent and often conflicting ambitions of Britian and France in the world, a situation which almost turned war-time allies into post-war enemies.

The effect on Nigeria of the economic stringency of the government made necessary by the war and its consequences on the administration and the transportation grid of the country were almost disastrous. The economic effects resulted among other things in widespread discontent among the colonial officials, and the insensitive approach to these grievances by the home government led to 'trade unionism' among them. This movement, which was devoted to fighting for better working conditions and better pay for European officials, reacted on the African civil servants, who also seized on the opportunity to press for better conditions of service, so that a movement which started primarily among British officials catalysed a racial struggle among British and African civil servants, a development which was unprecedented in the annals of the colonial service. The frustration in the service, for different and often personal reasons, spread from the autocratic Governor-General to the humble Nigerian clerk. The war ended for quite a large number of British officials on a very sad note. Disappointed and war-wearied civil officials complained of higher colonial appointments going to military officers with no experience in colonial administration. The Governor-General complained of being humiliated by the home government he had served so well in the hour of need. The Lamido of Yola lamented the loss of Adamawa for ever, in spite of the fact that he had thought and had been promised that he would recover all that belonged to his forefathers before the advent of the white man.

The changed international situation with the spread of ideas such as 'mandates', 'trusteeship', 'native paramountcy' was to lead among other things to the emergence of agitational politics which for a moment brought into focus all the shortcomings educated Nigerians had always criticised the British administration for. The granting of the right to Lagosians to vote for their representatives in the municipal council, constitutionally speaking, was the most important event associated with the war, since it placed Nigeria on the well-trodden path of constitutional evolution followed earlier by Canada and the 'white' dominions.

Bibliography

A. PRIMARY SOURCES

I. MANUSCRIPT

(a) *Official British Series*
Colonial Office Records at the Public Record Office, London, England

C.O. 583, vols 1–97. These are original correspondence and minutes 1912–20 (i.e. Administrative files) and provided the most important documentary sources for the book.

C.O. 445, vols 30–51. These are files of the West African Frontier Force and contain original correspondence and minutes. This selection deals with the period 1912–20, and was invaluable for the purpose of this work.

C.O. 554, vols 4–49, 1912–20. These contain West African original correspondence and Administrative files. They are very useful documents, especially in that they deal with the four British possessions in West Africa and throw light on the reasons for the application of different policies in these colonies and protectorates. These files also supplement those on Nigeria.

C.O. 657, vols 1–11, 1912–20. These files are Nigeria's Sessional Papers. They are relevant, but not of central importance.

C.O. 659, vols 1–3. These are Nigeria's Customs and Trade Journals from 1911 to 1916, very useful for the statistics on Nigeria's trade they provide, but the government discontinued publication during the war.

C.O. 660, 1913–20. West Africa: Miscellanea. This file contains useful and important material which could easily escape attention.

C.O. 537/135 Series. These files deal with the war years, classified under 'Africa – General'. This apparently very general classification contained much important material.

War Office Papers in the Public Record Office, London

W.O. 95. Nigerian Brigade War Diaries. Not particularly useful.

W.O. 106/532 – W.O. 106/645 and *W.O. 158/516 – W.O. 158/542.* These files deal with the military operations in the Cameroons and contain much material on Anglo-French rivalry in that theatre of military operation.

Admiralty Records in the Public Record Office, London

ADM/137, vols 27–339. These files give the naval as well as the military accounts of the Cameroons Campaign and reveal the Admiralty's ambitions in that region.

Foreign Office Papers in the Public Record Office, London

F.O. 438/11–12 and *F.O. 608/215–219.* These are important collections that reveal the nature of Anglo-French rivalry and the inter-departmental struggles between the Colonial Office, the Admiralty and the Foreign Office over Britain's colonial war aims.

Cabinet Papers in the Public Record Office, London

CAB '21' series. This series contains useful material on imperial defence and strategy before, during and after the war.

CAB 39/2–114. These files contain the decisions of the War Trade Advisory Committee with information on problems associated with trade embargo and what articles or foodstuffs should be exported to suspected neutral countries.

CAB 1/28. This series contains memoranda circulated to the Cabinet on colonial questions such as raising of coloured troops, etc.

CAB '37' Series. These also are memoranda circulated to the War Cabinet and are useful on overall government policies and those who initiated them.

CAB '24' 'G' 'GT' Series. These also are memoranda and other papers circulated to the War Cabinet (especially the 'GT' 1–8412 from 1915 to 1918).

CAB 23/37 – CAB 23/39. These are conclusions of Cabinet meetings relevant to the period of the war.

CAB '25' Series. These contain information on the Versailles Peace Conference. They also contain minutes and papers of the military representatives and other subordinate bodies set up by the Supreme War Council.

CAB 29 W.C.P. Series. These files contain memoranda submitted to the War Cabinet at the Paris Conference.

CAB 29 'HD' Series. This series contains minutes of the Supreme Allied Council and meetings of heads of delegations, 1919–20.

CAB 29 'C.F.' Series. These files contain minutes of the 'Council of Four'. They are important for they deal with the face-to-face negotiations of the heads of states or governments of the United States, Britain, France and Italy.

(b) *French Documentary Sources*

These were used to supplement the British documents, especially to give balance to the treatment of Anglo-French rivalry, and to give more evidence on Muslim attitudes to the war.

Les Archives Nationales, Quai d'Orsay, Paris

L.A.O.F. vol. XII/58. This is the only volume of documents opened to the public having any relevance to the war period at the French Foreign Office Archives. It deals mainly with the Senussis from 1912 to 1914 in French Chad.

Les Archives Nationales, Section d'Outre-Mer, rue Oudinot, Paris

The documents listed below deal mainly with military, political and religious situations in the much disturbed French territories in West and Equatorial Africa from 1914 to 1920.

L.A.O.F. Carton 170, Dossier 8
    ,,   ,,   907, Dossiers 1–10
    ,,   ,,   566, Dossier 2
    ,,   ,,   575, Dossiers 1–4
    ,,   ,,   574, Dossiers 1–4
    ,,   ,,   625, Dossier 2
    ,,   ,,   525, Dossier 4
    ,,   ,,   159, Dossier 1
    ,,   ,,   2801, Dossiers 5 and 6
    ,,   ,,   191, Dossiers 1 and 3
    ,,   ,,   907, Dossiers 1–3
    ,,   ,,   518, Dossiers 2, 17, 20
    ,,   ,,   582, Dossier 1
    ,,   ,,   534, Dossiers 1, 3, 10
    ,,   ,,   612, Dossier 3
    ,,   ,,   189, Dossiers 6 and 7

Cameroun et Togo, Carton 612, Dossiers 1–3

L.A.E.F. (1914–11) Carton 338, Dossiers 1–8.

(c) *German Documentary Sources*

The German sources do not throw much light on Nigeria's internal history during the war. They were thus used in a general way to balance British and French sources which related to the Cameroons or policy towards Germany or German interests. As they do not figure largely in this work, I have listed these sources below in some detail.

Hamburgisches Weltwirtschaftsarchiv, Firmenarchiv, Hamburg
Die Woermann Linie A.G. 1914–20 film No. 471, contains information on losses of ships by the company in the Cameroons and Nigeria as a result of British seizure.

Archiv der Handelskammer, Hamburg
Kolonial Politische Friedensforderungen: 6: Agu. 1915: 84. A. 3. 8. This film contains the 'peace' programme of Hamburg commercial interests in 1915.
Die Friedenswunsche des Hansabundes, 7 Jan. 1919: Film 44B No. 4. Another peace proposal of the same group. These proposals contain ambitious expansionist aims of the German colonial lobby in Hamburg, Lubeck and Bremen.
Erwerb von Fernando Po, 1909, Film 85B. This document is useful in that it corroborates the document seized in Duala by General Charles Dobell in 1914, which made it clear that the Germans wanted Fernando Po to remain in Spanish hands or be acquired by Germany.

Staatsarchiv, Hamburg
Die Deputation für Handel, Schiffahrt und Gewerb, 19 Feb. 1923. – XXII 5A, No. 37.
This was a delegation sent to Berlin by Hamburg's commercial shipping and industrial interests to put their case for compensation for losses suffered during the war.
Senate Kommission für die Reichs und Auswartigen Angelegenheiten, 23 Dec. 1921, XXX D.I. No. 6. This contains a list of financial losses suffered by Germans in ex-German colonies, prepared for the German Government by the State Government in Hamburg.
1921–24, XXI D.I. No. 16. This film contains the various correspondence with British and French government officials on German properties in mandated territories.

(d) *Private Papers*
The papers of the Anti-Slavery and Aborigines Protection Society, at Rhodes House Library, Oxford, England. These papers are useful for the series of protests and petitions over 'native' rights. *Lugard Papers*, vols I and II, deposited at Rhodes House Library, Oxford. They deal with the period of Lugard's appointment as Governor-General of the two Nigerias in 1912 down to his official retirement in 1919. They are collections of letters, some official, some private, written by either Lugard or his brother, Major Lugard. These collections also contain what Major Lugard called 'rough journal jottings' meant for the amusement of his wife. This last group form interesting reading and gives one insight into what Major Lugard felt about Africans and what he wanted his wife to know about them.

2 PRINTED

(a) *Parliamentary Debates*
Official reports (*Hansard*), House of Commons, 5th Series, vols lxxix–cxxxvi, 1915–20. House of Lords, 5th Series, vols xxvii–xliii, 1918–20.

(b) *Parliamentary Papers*
Cd. 6771, 1913, lxviii, 361: Reports on British trade in British West Africa.

Cd. 7791, 1914–16, xlv, 767: Report on the West African Currency Board.

Cd. 8247, 1916, iv, 15: Report of Committee on Edible and Oil-producing Nuts and Seeds.

Cd. 8248, 1916, iv, 63: Evidence before the Committee on Edible and Oil Producing Nuts and Seeds.

Cd. 8181, 1916, xv, 591: British trade after the war: commercial intelligence with respect to measures for securing the position after the war of certain branches of British industries.

Cd. 8306, 1916, xx, 1: German Atrocities and Breaches of the Rules of War in Africa.

Cd. 8482, 1917–18, xiii, 315: Commercial and industrial policy: Imperial preference.

Cd. 9034, 1918, xiii, 239: Final Report of the Committee on commercial and industrial policy after the war.

Cd. 9210, 1918, xvii, 379: Correspondence relating to the wishes

of the Natives of German Colonies as to their future government.

Cmd. 468, 1919, xxxiv, 609: Report by Sir F. D. Lugard on the
amalgamation of Northern and Southern Nigeria and Administration, 1912–19.

Cmd. 982, 1920, xxiii, 583: Trusts and Profiteering: Oils, Fats
and Margarine trades.

Cmd. 1350, 1921, xliii, 765: Draft mandates for Togoland (British)
and the Cameroons (British).

Cmd. 1600, 1922, xv, 19: Report of the Committee on trade and
taxation for British West Africa.

Cmd. 1794, 1923, xxiv, 475: Cameroons partition and terms of
League of Nations Mandate.

(c) *Printed Books and Collections of Printed Documents*

ANNET, ARMAND LEON, *En colonne dans le Cameroun: Notes
d'un Commandant de Compagnie, 1914–1916*, R. Debresse, Paris,
1949.

AYMERICH, GENERAL DE DIVISION, *La conquête du Cameroun:
ler Août 1914–20 Février 1916* in Collection de mémoires,
études et documents pour servir a l'histoire de la guerre
mondiale, Bibliothèque Nationale, Paris.

BEER, GEORGE LOUIS, *African Questions at the Paris Peace
Conference*, Macmillan, and Co. Ltd, New York, 1923; reprinted
1968.

CORBETT, SIR JULIAN STAFFORD, *Naval Operations* (4 vols).
History of the Great War, based on official documents, II.
Longmans, Green and Co. Ltd, London, 1920.

DOWNES, CAPTAIN W. D., *With the Nigerians in German East
Africa*, Methuen and Co. Ltd, London, 1919.

FERRANDI, LT-COL. JEAN, *La Conquête du Nord-Cameroun,
1914–1916*, Charles-Lavauzelle et Cie, Paris, 1928.

GEORGE, DAVID LLOYD, *War Memoirs*, vol. I, Nicolson and
Watson, London, 1936.

HANCOCK, SIR WILLIAM KEITH, and VAN DER POEL (eds),
Smuts Papers, iv, Cambridge University Press, London, 1956.

KIRK-GREENE, A. H. M., *Lugard and the Amalgamation of
Nigeria: Documentary Record*, Frank Cass and Co. Ltd, London,
1968.

LETTOW-VORBECK, GENERAL PAUL VON, *East African Campaigns*, Robert Speller and Sons, New York, 1957.

LEWIN, EVANS, *The Germans and Africa*, Cassell, London, 1915.

LUCAS, SIR CHARLES (ed.), *The Empire at War*, iv, *Africa*, Royal Colonial Institute, London, 1921.

LUGARD, F. D., *The Dual Mandate in British Tropical Africa*, London, Frank Cass and Co., reprinted 1965.

MOREL, E. D., *Africa and the Peace of Europe*, London, National Labour Press Ltd, London, 1917.

—, *The Blackman's Burden*, National Labour Press, London, 1920.

—, *Nigeria, its Peoples and its Problems*, Smith, Elder and Co. Ltd, London, 1911.

TEMPLE, CHARLES LINDSAY, *Native Races and Their Rulers*, London, Argus Printing Co., 1918.

VANDELEUR, LT SEYMOUR, *Campaigning on the Upper Nile and Niger*, with introduction by Sir George Goldie, Methuen and Co., London, 1898.

ZIMMERMANN, EMIL, *Das deutsche Kaiserreich Mittelfrika als Grundlage einer neuen deutschen Weltpolitik*, Berlin, 1917; Edwyn Bevan's translation, London, 1918.

(d) *Newspapers and Magazines*

African Mail (Liverpool), 1914–16. This newspaper was edited by E. D. Morel. It stopped publication early in 1916. British Museum Newspaper Library, Colindale, London.

African Times and Orient Review (London). This paper stopped publication in 1914 as a result of bankruptcy but restarted during the war. Its owner – Duse Mohammed – was a Sudanese resident in Britain who preached the doctrine of 'Africa for the Africans'. His paper, however, toned down this 'subversive' note during the war. British Museum Newspaper Library, Colindale, London.

African World (London), 1914–16. Journal devoted to African studies. British Museum Newspaper Library, Colindale, London.

L'Afrique Française. Bulletin mensuel du comité de l'Afrique et du Maroc (Paris), 1914–20. This is a semi-official organ of French colonial interests. Bibliothèque Nationale, Paris.

Les Annales Coloniales, 1914–20. Bibliothèque Nationale, Paris.

The Christian Commonwealth (London). Paper devoted to upholding the Empire. British Museum Newspaper Library, Colindale, London.

La Dépêche Coloniale (Paris), 1914–20. Bibliothèque Nationale, Paris.

La Dépêche Coloniale Illustrée (Paris), 1914–16. Bibliothèque Nationale, Paris.

Je Sais Tout (Paris), 1914–20. Bibliothèque Nationale, Paris.

Lagos Daily News (Lagos), 1922–3. London Museum Newspaper Library, Colindale, London.

Lagos Standard (Lagos), 1914–19. British Museum Newspaper Library, Colindale, London.

Manchester Guardian, 1916–17. Institute of Historical Research, London.

Nigerian Chronicle (Lagos), 1914–20. British Museum Newspaper Library, Colindale, London.

Nigerian Pioneer (Lagos), 1914–20. British Museum Newspaper Library, Colindale, London.

The Nineteenth Century and After, October 1917.

La Presse Coloniale (Paris), 1914–20. Bibliothèque Nationale, Paris.

The Times (London), 1914–19. Institute of Historical Research, London.

Times of Nigeria (Lagos), 1913–20. British Museum Newspaper Library, Colindale, London.

United Empire, January 1918.

West Africa, 1916–20. British Museum Newspaper Library, Colindale, London.

B. SECONDARY SOURCES

I. BOOKS

Authors' names as on title pages of works.

AJAYI, J. F. ADE, *Christian Missions in Nigeria 1841–1891: The Making of a New Elite*, Longman, London, and Northwestern University Press, Evanston, 1965.

ANTONELLI, ETIENNE, *L'Afrique et la Paix de Versailles*, Sirey et Cie, Paris, 1921.

AYANDELE, E. A., *The Missionary Impact on Modern Nigeria 1842–1914: A Political and Social Analysis*, Longman, London, 1966.

BAKER, R. S., *Woodrow Wilson and the World Settlement*, Garden City, New York, 1922.

BASDEN, G. T., *Among the Ibos of Nigeria*, etc. Frank Cass and Co. Ltd, London, 1921.

BIOBAKU, S. O., *The Egba and their Neighbours 1842–1872*, Oxford, Clarendon Press, London, 1957.

BOBNER, THEODOR, *Die Woermanns*, Verlag Die Boude zur Heimat, Berlin, 1935.

BRACKMANN, KARL, *Funfzig Jahre deutscher Afrika-Schiffahrt: Die Geschichte der Woermann Linie und der Deutschen Ost-Afrika Linie*, Andrews & Steiner Verlag, Berlin, 1935.

BUHRER, J., Commandant, *L'Afrique Orientale Allemande et la Guerre de 1914–1918*, L. Fournier, Paris, 1922.

BURNS, SIR ALAN, *History of Nigeria*, George Allen and Unwin Ltd, London, 1929; reprinted 1963.

CAMILLE, FIDEL, *L'Allemagne d'Outre-Mer: Grandeur et Decadance*. Boivin et Cie, Paris, 1915.

—, *Publicie et vulgarisation coloniales: Emigration, Expansion au dehors: Enquêtes en Grande-Bretagne et en Allemagne*. Société des Études Coloniales et Maritimes, Paris, 1925.

—, *La Paix Coloniale Française*, Sirey et Cie, Paris, 1918.

—, *La Nouvelle Allemagne et la Question Coloniale*, Sirey et Cie, Paris, 1920.

COLEMAN, JAMES, *Nigeria: Background to Nationalism*, University of California Press, Berkeley and Los Angeles, 1958.

CROWDER, MICHAEL, *The Story of Nigeria*, Faber & Faber, London, 1962.

DIKE, KENNETH ONWUKA, *Trade and Politics in the Niger Delta 1830–1885*, Oxford, Clarendon Press, London, 1956.

EGHAREVBA, JACOB, *A Short History of Benin*, Ibadan University Press, 1960.

EVANS-PRITCHARD, E. E., *The Senusiya of Cyrenaica*, Oxford University Press, London, 1965.

FISCHER, FRITZ, *Germany's Aims in the First World War*, New York, Norton Co., 1967. (A translation of the German version: *Griff nach der Weltmacht*, Dusseldorf, 1964.)

FLINT, J. E., *Sir George Goldie and the Making of Nigeria*, Oxford University Press, London, 1960.

FORDE, DARYLL, and JONES, G. L., *The Ibo and Ibibio Speaking Peoples of South-eastern Nigeria*, Oxford University Press, London, 1950.

GANN, L. H. and DUIGNAN, PETER (eds), *Colonialism in Africa 1870–1960*, I, *The History and Politics of Colonialism*, Cambridge University Press, London, 1969.

GARDNER, BRIAN, *On the Kilimanjaro: The Bizarre Story of the*

First World War in East Africa. Macrae Smith and Co., Philadelphia, 1963.

GEARY, SIR WILLIAM NEVILLE, *Nigeria Under British Rule*, Methuen and Co., London, 1927.

GEORGES, E. H., *The Great War in West Africa*, Methuen and Co., London, 1930.

GIFFORD, PROSSER, and LOUIS, WILLIAM ROGER (eds), *Britain and Germany in Africa*, Yale University Press, New Heaven and London, 1967.

GUINN, PAUL, *British Strategy and Politics, 1914–1918*, Oxford University Press, London, 1965.

HANCOCK, W. K., *Survey of British Commonwealth Affairs*, II, *Problems of Economic Policy, 1918–1939*. Oxford University Press, London, 1940.

HARGREAVES, J. D., *Prelude to the Partition of West Africa*, Macmillan and Co. Ltd, London, 1963.

HAUSER, HENRI, *La Guerre Europeane et le Probléme Coloniale*, Chapelot, Paris, 1915.

HIEKE, ERNST, *G. L. Gaiser: Hamburg–Westafrika: 100 Jahre Handel mit Nigeria*, Hoffmann and Campe Verlag, Hamburg, 1949.

HOGBEN and KIRK-GREENE, A. H. M., *The Emirates of Northern Nigeria*, Oxford University Press, London, 1966.

HORDERN, LT-COL CHARLES, *History of the Great War*: based on official documents. *Military Operations: East Africa*, I, August 1914–September 1916, His Majesty's Stationery Office, London, 1941.

HOYT, EDWIN P. JNR, *The Germans Who Never Lost: the Story of the Konigsberg*, Funk and Wagnells, New York, 1968.

HULOT, JOSEPH GABRIEL ETIENNE, Baron, *L'Allemagne en Afrique et la Guerre*, F. Alcan, Paris, 1918.

JOHNSON, the REV. SAMUEL, *The History of the Yorubas*, Routledge & Kegan Paul Ltd, London, 1969. First published London, 1921.

KARSTEDT, OSKAR, *Koloniale Friedensziele*, Duncker Verlag, Weimar, 1917.

KIRK-GREENE, A. H. M., *Adamawa Past and Present*, Oxford University Press, London, 1958.

LOUIS, WILLIAM ROGER, *Great Britain and Germany's Lost Colonies 1914–1919*, Clarendon Press, Oxford, 1967.

LUGARD, LADY, *A Tropical Dependency*, James Nisbet and Co. Ltd, London, reprinted 1964.

MOBERLY, F. J. (ed.), *History of the Great War*: based on official documents. *Military Operations: Togoland and the Cameroons 1914–1916*, His Majesty's Stationery Office, London, 1931.

MOSLEY, LEONARD, *Duel for Kilimanjaro: an account of the East African Campaign 1914–1918*, Weidenfeld and Nicolson, London, 1963.

NICHOLAS, RAOUL, *Le Cameroun depuis le Traité de Versailles 29 Juin, 1919*, Saint-Amand, 1922.

NICOLSON, HAROLD, *Peace Making 1919*, Methuen and Co. Ltd, London, 1964.

ORR, SIR CHARLES, *The Making of Northern Nigeria*, Macmillan and Co., London, 1911.

PERHAM, MARGERY, *Native Administration in Nigeria*, Oxford University Press, London, 1937.

—, *Lugard: the Years of Authority 1898–1945: The Maker of Modern Nigeria*, Collins, London, 1960.

ROBINSON, KENNETH, and MADDEN, FREDERICK (eds), *Essays in Imperial Government: Presented to Margery Perham*, Blackwell Press, Oxford, 1963.

ROBINSON, RONALD, and GALLAGHER, JOHN, with DENNY, ALICE, *Africa and the Victorians: The Official Mind of Imperialism*, Macmillan and Co., London, 1965.

ROTBERG, ROBERT I., and MAZRUI, ALI (eds), *Protest and Power in Black Africa*, Oxford University Press, New York, 1970.

RUDIN, H.R., *The Germans in the Cameroons 1884–1914: A Case Study in Modern Imperialism*, Yale University Press, New Haven, 1938; reprinted 1968.

SCHMOKEL, WOLFE W., *Dream of Empire: German Colonialism 1914–1945*, Yale University Press, New Heaven, 1964.

SCHULTZE, A., *The Sultanate of Bornu*, Translated from the German by P. A. Benton. Frank Cass & Co., London, 1913. New impression London, 1968.

STUDENT, ERICH, *Kameruns Kampf 1914–1916*, Verlag Bernard und Graefe, Berlin, 1937.

TALBOT, P. AMAURY, *Tribes of the Niger Delta*, Oxford Clarendon Press, London, 1956.

TOWNSEND, MARY E., *The Rise and Fall of Germany's Colonial Empire 1884–1918*, Howard Fertig, New York, reprinted 1966.

TRIMINGHAM, J. SPENCER, *A History of Islam in West Africa*, Oxford University Press, London, 1963.

WELLESLEY, DOROTHY, *Sir George Goldie: Founder of Nigeria*, Macmillan and Co., London, 1934.

WILSON, CHARLES, *The History of Unilever: A Study in Economic Growth and Social Change*, I, Cassell and Co. Ltd, London, 1954.

WRENCH, JOHN EVELYN, *Alfred Milner*, Eyre and Spottiswood Ltd, London, 1958.

2. ARTICLES

ALBRECHT-CARRIÉ, RENE, 'Italian Colonial Policy, 1914–1918', *Journal of Modern History*, xviii, 1946, pp. 123–47.

BERNARD, AUGUSTIN, 'Le Sahara français pendant la guerre', *Renseignements Coloniaux*, Jan. 1920, pp. 3–9.

BESSON, MAURICE, 'La question coloniale devient une question nationale', *L'Afrique Française*, Jan. 1920, pp. 23–6.

CURRY, GEORGE, 'Woodrow Wilson, Jan Smuts and the Versailles Settlement'. *American Historical Review*, lxvi, 1961, pp. 968–86.

FAURE, CLAUDE, 'Au Cameroun avec le corps expeditionnaire Franco-Anglais', *Renseignements Coloniaux*, Jan. 1920, pp. 9–21; Feb. 1920, pp. 41–7; March 1920, pp. 62–6; April 1920, pp. 96–103.

FERRANDI, LT-COL. JEAN, 'La conquête du Cameroun, La Colonne du Nord', *L'Afrique Française*, April 1916, pp. 109–23.

HAAS, ERNST B., 'The reconciliation of the conflicting colonial policy aims: acceptance of the League of Nations Mandate System', *International Organisation*, iv, 1952, pp. 521–36.

HATTON, P. H. S., 'The Gambia, the Colonial Office and the opening months of the First World War', *Journal of African History*, vii, 1, 1966, pp. 123–31.

HESS, ROBERT L., 'Italy and Africa: Colonial Ambitions in the First World War', *Journal of African History*, iv, 1, 1963, pp. 105–26.

LOCKWOOD, P. A., 'Milner's entry into the War Cabinet: December 1916', *The Historical Journal*, vii, 1, 1964, pp. 120–34.

LOUIS, WILLIAM ROGER, 'African Origins of the Mandates Idea', *International Organisation*, xix, Winter 1965, pp. 20–36.

—, 'Great Britain and the African Peace Settlement of 1919', *American Historical Review*, lxxi, 3, April 1966, pp. 875–92.

—, 'The United States and the African peace settlement of 1919:

the pilgrimage of George Louis Beer'. *Journal of African History*, iv, 3, 1963, pp. 413–33.

MCGILL, BARRY, 'Asquith's predicament 1914–1918', *Journal of Modern History*, xxxix, 3, 1967, pp. 283–303.

MAILER, HENRI, 'Le role des Colonnes françaises dan la campagne du Cameroun 1914–1916', *L'Afrique Française*, June 1966, pp. 187–224.

MILLER, DAVID HUNTER, 'The Origin of the Mandate system', *Foreign Affairs*, vi, January 1928, pp. 277–89.

OMU, FRED. I. A., 'The Dilemma of Press Freedom in Colonial Africa: The West African Example', *Journal of African History*, ix, 2, 1968, pp. 279–98.

POTTER, B. PITMAN, 'Origins of the System of Mandates under the League of Nations', *The American Political Science Review*, xvi, 4, 1922, pp. 563–83.

REGELSPERGER, GUSTAVE, 'L'œuvre française au Togo et au Cameroun conquis', *Révue de l'école libre et des sciences politiques*, xl, 1918, pp. 76–92.

TILHO, COMMANDANT JENA, 'Sur le Front du desert Libyqye', *Je Sais Tout*, 15 June 1918, pp. 642–53.

WOLPE, HOWARD, 'Port Harcourt: Ibo Politics in Microcosm', *The Journal of Modern African Studies*, vii, 3, pp. 469–93.

3. UNPUBLISHED THESES

COUGET, BERTRAND, 'Les colonies allemandes avant et pendant la guerre 1914–1917', thèse pour le doctorat de l'Université de Toulouse, Faculté de Droit, 1917.

ELUWA, G., 'National Congress of British West Africa and the Colonial Office Reforms of 1922/1923', Ph.D. thesis, Michigan State University, 1967.

HOPKINS, ANTHONY, 'Economic History of Lagos 1880–1914', Ph.D. thesis, London University, 1964.

KERSTEN, D., 'Die Kriegsziele der Hamburger Kaufmannschaft im Ersten Weltkrieg: Ein Beitrag zur Frage der Kriegszielpolitik im Kaiserlichen Deutschland, 1914–1918', Der Universität Hamburg, doctoral dissertation, 1963.

Index

Index

French Sahara, 155, 158–9
Fulani emirates, 5–6; *see also* Islam
Fuller, *Captain* Cyril, 184–5, 217–18, 230

Gambia, the, 211, 228–9, 281
Gani, Kitoro, 145
Garvey, Marcus, 88
Gazette Extraordinary, 140
Geary, *Sir* William, 9, 65
German East Africa, 239–44, 253–7, 276
Germany: attitude to war in Africa, 173–4; cancellation of trade, 25–6, 81; future of colonies, 270–82; 'moral incapacity', 279–80; press attitudes, 69–72, 77; prisoners of war, 181, 194–7; propaganda within emirates, 143, 149–50; resumption of trade, 111; revolts in Cameroons, 177–8, 187; trade with Nigeria, *viii–ix*, 16–17, 21–5, 72, 110; traders accused of incitement, 112–15; wish to retain Cameroons, 276–7
Gold Coast Regiment, 240–1, 259
Goldie, George, 7, 211–12
Grand Sharif of Mecca, 150
Green, Anthony, 108–9
Grey, Edward, Viscount, 206, 211, 220, 229
Griffin, *Rev.* Oliver, 130
groundnut trade, *see* oil and fat control
Guggisberg, General, 297
Gulfei, Sultan of, 187, 214
Gwanki, Maina, 146

Haldane, Viscount, 206
Harcourt, Lewis, 29, 68, 86, 90, 195, 210–12, 216, 219, 228–31
Harding, A. J., 40, 92, 130, 246, 301
Hardinge, *Sir* Arthur, 193
Harris, John H., 279
Hastings, Colonel, 243
Hausaland: Muslims, 34; education, 78; Hausa in Yorubaland, 119, 124
Haywood, Colonel, 192, 244–8, 253, 259, 263
Hellard, *Captain* W. B., 253–4
Henderson, Arthur, 276
Holland, trade with Nigeria, 21, 23, 30
House-rule system, 6, 34

Ibadan, 125; Egba Citizens' League, 101

Ijemo rising and massacre, 71, 103–8, 130; aftermath, 108–10
India, as comparison, 78, 80
Indian soldiers, 240–1
indirect rule, *ix*, 298; Egbaland, 108; elite and, 64; and Islam, 139; judicial system and, 9; Northern Protectorate, 5–6, 90; Southern Protectorate, 6; Yorubaland, 119, 126
Ireland, as comparison, 68, 70
Irving, lawyer and newspaper owner, 66, 82
Iseyin, 121–4; Aseyin, 121–3, 125
Islam: Egbaland, 102; emirates and wider Muslim world, 151–2; exile of emirs, 148–9; German propaganda, 143, 149–50; Hausa-Fulani rulers support Britain, 139–44, 148, 162; Hausaland, 34; and indirect rule, 139; Lugard and, 140–2; popular revolts, 144–50; and racial equality, 77; resistance movements, 139; Sudan, 139; and taxation, 34; as threat to government, 16, 133, 139–62; Yorubaland, 34, 77
Italy: evacuation of Tripoli, 151; in Libya, 16
Iyalode (women's leader), 102

Jackson, Horatio, 66
Jackson, J. P., 66
James, F. S., 68, 110–12, 114, 180
Japan, as comparison, 76, 87, 91
Jenkins, Lieutenant-Colonel, 154, 156–7, 260–2
Jesson, Mr, 54
Johnson, Chris, 66
Johnson, Bishop Oluwole, 117
Johnston, *Sir* Harry, 279
Joja, King of Fumban (Bafum), 187, 213
judicial system, 9–11, 65; Egba, 103

Kaduna, proposed as Nigerian capital, 82, 302
Kamina, radio station, 178–9
Kano, 5, 16, 151, 154–5; Emir of, 141–142, revolts, 146–7
Karfi, Mairigan, 148
Kariyesimu, Hauptmann, 149
Karsina, 151
Kwale uprising, 110

labour, as resource, 306–7

Index

Index

transport, 56; Road Construction Ordinance, 105; road programme, 292; *see also* railways; shipping
Tripolitans, 15–16, 139, 151
Turkey: enters war, 139–40; propaganda, 150

Umaisha, Sarkin, 144
Umar Sanda, Shehu of Borno, 142–3, 187, 206, 213–14, 224, 231
United Kingdom Oil Seed Products Association Ltd, 50–1
United States: and future of German colonies, 277–80; trade, 43
Usman dan Fodio, 148

Versailles Peace Conference, 88
Vischer, Hans, 77
von Crailsheim, Hauptmann, 179
von Lettow-Vorbeck, *General* Paul, 239, 255–6
von Raben, Captain, 192
von Trotha, 272

Wadai, 152–4
war bonus, 292–3, 295
warrant chiefs, 111, 115
Warri province, rebellion, 110–12
Webster, G. W., 306–7

Wedgwood, Lieutenant-Colonel, 244
West Africa, 88, 132
West African Frontier Force, *see* Nigeria Regiment
West African Regiment, *see* Regiment *under* Sierra Leone
Wiemann, Walter, 145
Wilhelm II, Kaiser, 274
Williams, George, 66
Wilson, D. E., 107–8
Wilson, Woodrow, 277, 279–80
Wurno, Mai, 153, 306

Yola, 150, 227; Lamido, 143, 149, 206, 211–13, 231–2, 272, 283, 285–6
Yorubaland: German popularity, 72; Hausa in, 119, 124; indirect rule, 119, 126; influence of press, 93; Lugard and, 119, 125–6; military recruitment, 252; Morel on, 85; Muslims, 34, 77; Okeogun rebellion, 118–26; taxation, 123–5, 132
Young, P. V., 104–8

Zanzibar, Sultan of, 140
Zimmermann, Emil, 274
Zimmermann, Lieutenant-Colonel, 184, 196
Zozo, Mama, 260